PRIMITIVE MENTALITY

AMS PRESS

NEW YORK

Primitive Mentality

By
Lucien Lévy-Bruhl
Professor at the Sorbonne

Authorized Translation
by
Lilian A. Clare

NEW YORK: THE MACMILLAN COMPANY
LONDON: GEORGE ALLEN & UNWIN LTD.

Library of Congress Cataloging in Publication Data

Lévy-Bruhl, Lucien, 1857-1939.
　　Primitive mentality.

　　　Translation of La mentalité primitive.
　　　Reprint of the 1923 ed. published by Macmillan,
New York.
　　　Includes index.
　　　1. Philosophy, Primitive. 2. Religion, Primitive.
3. Ethnopsychology. I. Title.
GN451.L5613　1978　　155.8'1　　75-41174
ISBN 0-404-14568-X

Reprinted from an original in the collections
of the Ohio State University Libraries

From the edition of 1923, New York
First AMS edition published in 1978
Manufactured in the United States of America

AMS PRESS INC.
NEW YORK, N.Y.

TRANSLATOR'S NOTE

ALTHOUGH, as the Author clearly states in his preface, this book is to be considered as a sequel to his earlier work on the mental functioning of primitive peoples, that fact need not deter anyone who has not seen the other (which was published in 1910 and is now in its third edition) from reading this one. The subject is treated from another point of view, of equal value to the scientist and the psychological expert, while the theories postulated by Professor Lévy-Bruhl, and the wealth of illustrative matter brought forward in support of them, will interest the veriest tyro in the study of mentality. In a colonizing country such as ours there are many who, like myself, while not possessed of any scientific knowledge of ethnological or anthropological matters, have yet had first-hand and varied experience of natives in some cases but slightly removed from the " primitive." To such, this book will prove a fascinating study, and its careful perusal will enable them to understand better, much that has puzzled them hitherto.

The very real sense in which the primitive " participates " in the mystic nature of all that surrounds him, the way in which he lives in the seen and the unseen worlds simultaneously, and his indifference to the law of contradiction, formed the main theme of *Les Fonctions Mentales dans les Sociétés Inférieures*. In the present volume the author examines more fully the content of the primitive's experience, lays stress upon his determinism, and emphasizes the consistent quality of his mental functioning, when regarded from his own standpoint, and interpreted in terms of his own orientation.

In case the term " collective representations," in constant use here, should not convey a very clear idea to those who have not read the earlier book, I am quoting from that work some passages where it occurs. Professor Lévy-Bruhl, speaking of the difficulty of applying the terminology of ordinary psychology to the consideration of a type of mental functioning which differs widely from our own, thinks it necessary " at any rate to specify the new meaning which an already existing expression should assume when applied to an object other than that it has hitherto betokened." In defining the term roughly, he says : " Collective representations may be recognized by the following signs. They are common to the members of a given social group ; they are transmitted from one generation to another within it ; they impress themselves upon its individual members and awaken in them sentiments of respect, fear, adoration, and so on, according to the circumstances of the case. Their existence does not depend upon the individual. This is not because they imply a collective entity apart from the individuals composing the social group, but because they present themselves in aspects which cannot be accounted for by considering individuals merely as such.[1] . . . Collective representations have their own laws, which—at any rate where ' primitives ' are concerned—cannot be discovered by studying the ' white, adult, and civilized ' individual." [2]

Although " representation is, par excellence, an intellectual and cognitive phenomenon . . . we cannot consider the collective representations of primitives thus. Their mental activity is too little differentiated for it to be able to regard the ideas or images of objects by themselves, apart from the sentiments, emotions, and passions which evoke them, or are evoked by them. Just because our mental activity is more differentiated, and we are more used to analysing its functions, it is difficult for us to realize, by any effort of imagination, more complex states in which the emotional or the motivating elements are integral parts of the representation. It seems to us that these are not really representations, and in fact if we are to retain the term we must modify its meaning in some way. By this state of mental activity in primitives we must understand

[1] *Les Fonctions Mentales dans les Sociétés Inférieures.* Introd., p. 1.
[2] Ibid., p. 2.

something which is not a purely or even partially intellectual
or cognitive phenomenon, but a more complex one, in which
what is really 'representation' to us is found blended
with other elements of an emotional or motivating character,
coloured and imbued by them, and therefore implying a
different attitude with regard to the objects they represent.[1]
. . . The collective representations of the primitive, therefore, differ profoundly from our ideas or concepts ; nor
are they the equivalent of them. On the one hand . . .
they have not the logical character of our ideas. On the
other hand, not being purely representations, in the strict
sense of the term, they express or rather they imply, not
only that the primitive actually has an image of the object
and believes it is real, but also that he hopes or fears something from it ; that some definite action emanates from it
or is exercised upon it. This action is an influence, a virtue,
an occult power, varying according to its objects and circumstances, but always real to the primitive, and forming
an integral part of his representation. If I were to express
in one word this general property of the collective representations holding so important a place in the mental activity
of undeveloped peoples, I should say that their mental
activity was a *mystic* one. I shall use this term in default
of a better, not referring thereby to the religious mysticism
of our communities, which is something quite different,
but employing it in the strictly definite sense in which
'mystic' implies belief in forces and influences and actions
which, though imperceptible to sense, are nevertheless real.

" In other words, the reality in which primitives live
is itself mystical. Not a single being or object or natural
phenomenon in their collective representations is what it
appears to be to our minds. Almost everything we perceive
in it escapes their attention or is a matter of indifference
to them. On the other hand, they see many things of
which we are unconscious. For instance, to the ' primitive '
who belongs to a totemistic community, every animal,
every plant, every object indeed, such as the sun, moon,
and stars, forms part of a totem, and has its own class
and sub-class. Consequently, everyone among them has

[1] *Les Fonctions Mentales dans les Sociétés Inférieures,* i. p. 29.

his special affinities and possesses powers over the members
of his totem, class, and sub-class ; he has obligations towards
them, mystical relations with other totems, and so forth.
Even in communities where this form does not exist, the
collective representation of certain animals (possibly of all,
if our records were complete) is mystic in character.[1] . . .
The same is true of plants . . . and each organ in the
human body has its mystic significance. . . . Certain parts
of animals and plants are believed to possess particular
virtues. In some cases, a noxious mystic power is said
to belong to all living things. . . . Regions in space, and
the cardinal points have their mystic significance.[2] . . .
Even objects made, and constantly used, by man have their
mystic properties and can become beneficent or terrible,
according to circumstances." . . . The spirit of conservatism, said to be peculiar to primitive peoples, " is the direct
result of an active belief in the mystic qualities belonging
to objects and connected with their form, through which
they may be controlled, though the slightest deviation
therefrom would enable them to defy human intervention.
An apparently quite insignificant innovation may . . .
release hostile forces and finally prove the ruin of its in-
stigator and of all connected with him." [3]

" . . . The profound difference existing between primitive mentality and our own is seen even in the ordinary
perception, or mere apprehension of the very simplest things.
Primitive perception is fundamentally mystic on account
of the mystic nature of the collective representations which
form an integral part of every perception. . . . It is not
correct to maintain, as is frequently done, that primitives
associate occult powers, magic properties, a kind of soul
or vital principle with all the objects which affect their senses
or impress their imagination, and that their perceptions are
surcharged with animistic beliefs. It is not a question
of association. To the primitive mind the mystic properties
of things and beings form an integral part of their representation, which is at that moment a synthetic whole. It
is at a later stage of social evolution that what we call a

[1] *Les Fonctions Mentales dans les Sociétés Inférieures*, i. pp. 30–1.
[2] Ibid., pp. 32–3. [3] Ibid., p. 35.

natural phenomenon tends to become the sole content of perception to the exclusion of the other elements, which at first will assume the aspect of beliefs, and later become superstitions." [1]

Though one is tempted to make more quotations from Professor Lévy-Bruhl's earlier volume, the excerpts given will probably serve to pave the way for the present work, throughout which the comparative method is applied to the study of primitive mentality, and the author shows how the undeveloped native acquires and deals with the data which his experience affords, his idea of causality, and the influence of that idea upon his thought and actions.

LILIAN A. CLARE.

November 1922.

Les Fonctions Mentales dans les Sociétés Inférieures, p. 38–9.

PREFACE

WHEN my work dealing with the mental functions of un-civilized peoples [1] appeared about twelve years ago, the book was to have been called " Primitive Mentality." But at that time the expressions " mentality," and even " primi-tive," were not current terms as they are to-day, and I therefore abandoned that title. I am making use of it for the present volume, which is enough to show that this is a sequel to the former one. Both treat of the same subject, although from rather different points of view. *Mental Functions* laid special stress upon the law of participation, considered in relation to the principle of identity, and also upon the fact that the primitive has but slight perception of the law of contradiction. The object of *Primitive Mentality* rather is to show what causation means to primi-tives, and the inferences derived from their idea of it.

This book does not pretend, any more than the other did, to treat exhaustively of primitive mentality under all its aspects and in its manifold forms of expression. Here, again, it affords but a simple introduction. I have merely aimed at determining, as exactly as it can be done, the orientation peculiar to this type of mind, what data it has at command, how it acquires them, and what use it makes of them—in short, what the limits and the content of its experience are. In doing this, I have been led to try and differentiate and describe certain mental practices

---

[1] *Les Fonctions Mentales dans les Sociétés Inférieures.* Paris, 1910.

characteristic of primitives and to show how and why they differ from our own.

In order to get hold, as it were, of the main point—the processes essential to primitive mentality—I have purposely chosen for my analyses the simplest and least ambiguous of facts. In this way I hoped to lessen the chances of error which in so complex a subject are very numerous, and to demonstrate more clearly the actual functioning of the constituent principles of this mentality. I have consequently adhered to the study of what, to primitives, are the unseen powers by which they feel themselves surrounded on all sides—their dreams, the omens they observe or incite, ordeals, "bad death," the extraordinary things brought by white people, their remedies, etc. The reader, therefore, must not expect to find here a study of primitive mentality as it relates to the technique of uncivilized communities (the inventing and perfecting of tools and weapons, the care of animals, construction of buildings, cultivation of the soil, and so on), or to their oft-times complex institutions, such as the organization of family life, or totemism.

If the general introduction given by the present volume, taken in conjunction with the previous one, has attained its end, it will allow us to define more precisely some of the vast problems raised by the institutions, technique, arts, and languages of primitives. An acquaintance with their mental habits, in so far as they differ from our own, will help us to present these problems in terms that render a solution possible, and furnish us with some sort of guiding line. It will become easier (at least in a certain number of cases) to discover the aims pursued, more or less consciously, by primitives. We shall better understand the methods, so often childish and absurd in our eyes, which they are led to employ, and thus we shall arrive at the deeper motives which account for the ordinary forms of their activity, whether it be personal or social. Several chapters of the present volume are attempts to apply this method to comparatively simple cases.

It seemed to me that the results of these attempts confirmed the theory set forth in *Mental Functions*. Relying upon that, indeed, I have been able to account for several facts which up till now have either been unexplained, or else interpreted by means of hypotheses, which are merely possible, if not arbitrary. The two books therefore support each other, and both originate in the same endeavour to fathom the ways of thought and the principles actuating those whom we, very improperly, term " primitives "—beings who are both so far removed from, and so near to, ourselves.[1]

September 1921.

[1] Some portions of this book formed the subject of lectures given at the Lowell Institute, Boston, in November and December 1919.

CONTENTS

CHAPTER I

CHAPTER II

CHAPTER III

CHAPTER IV

CHAPTER V

2

CHAPTER X

CHAPTER XI

INTRODUCTION

I

AMONG the differences which distinguish the mentality of
primitive communities from our own, there is one which
has attracted the attention of many of those who have
observed such peoples under the most favourable conditions—that is, before their ideas have been modified by
prolonged association with white races. These observers
have maintained that primitives manifest a decided distaste
for reasoning, for what logicians call the " discursive operations of thought " ; at the same time they have remarked
that this distaste did not arise out of any radical incapability
or any inherent defect in their understanding, but was
rather to be accounted for by their general methods of
thought.

The Jesuit missionaries, for instance, who were the first
to see the Indians dwelling in the eastern parts of North
America, could not help speaking of this. " We are forced
to the conclusion that the Iroquois are incapable of reasoning
like the Chinese and other civilized races to whom we set
forth the belief in God and His truth. . . . The Iroquois
is not influenced by reason. His direct perception of things
is the only light which guides him. The incentives to
belief which theology is accustomed to use in order to
convince the most hardened free-thinkers are not listened
to here, where our most profound truths are declared to
be lies. They usually believe only what they see." [1] A
little further on the same priest adds : " The truths of the
Gospel would not have seemed admissible to them had they
been founded on reason and good sense alone. Since these
people are wanting in culture and breeding, something

[1] *Relations des Jésuites* (edit. Thwaites), lvii. p. 126 (1672–3)

plainer and more tangible was required to make an impression on their minds. Although there are minds among them quite as capable of scientific thought as those of Europeans, yet their up-bringing and their need to hunt for a living has reduced them to a state in which their reasoning power does not go beyond what pertains to their bodily health, their success in hunting and fishing, their trading and their warfare ; and all these things are like so many principles from which they draw all their conclusions, not only as regards their homes, their occupations, and their way of life, but also their superstitions and their deities."

Comparing this passage with the previous one, we obtain the elements of a fairly precise description of the mentality of the Iroquois as it relates to the point we are considering. The essential difference between these " savages " and unbelievers who are more civilized than they, is not the result of an intellectual inferiority peculiar to them ; it is an actual state which, according to the Jesuit fathers, is explained by their social condition and their customs. The missionary Crantz says the same of the Greenlanders : " Their whole stock of ingenuity is exerted in the employments necessary to their existence, and whatever is not inseparably connected with those employments, forms no subject of their reflection. We may therefore describe their character as consisting of simplicity without stupidity, and good sense uncultivated by the exercise of reason." [1] Let us rather put it thus—" uncultivated in following a chain of reasoning which is in the slightest degree abstract." For it is not to be doubted that the Greenlanders, when following the avocations necessary to their existence, do reason, and that they employ means which are sometimes complicated, in order to arrive at the ends they are seeking. But these mental processes are not independent of the material objects which induce them, and they come to an end as soon as their aim has been attained. They are never exercised on their own account, and that is why they do not seem to us to rise to the level of what we properly

[1] D. Crantz : The History of Greenland, i. p. 135 (1767).

term "thought." A modern observer who has lived among the Esquimaux of the North, has drawn attention to this fact. "All their ideas," says he, "centre round the whale fishery, hunting, and eating. For anything beyond that, thought, to them, is generally a synonym for boredom or annoyance. 'What are you thinking about?' I said one day, when out hunting with an Esquimau who appeared to be deep in thought. My question made him laugh. 'Oh, you white people, you are always thinking so much! We Esquimaux think only of our stores of food; shall we have enough meat for the long winter or not? If the meat is enough, we have no need to think about anything else. As for me, I have more food than I really need!' I realized that I had offended him in attributing any 'thoughts' to him."[1]

The first people to study the natives of South Africa have made statements fully bearing out the opinions of the writer just quoted. Here again the missionaries testify that "they only believe what they see." "In the midst of the laughter and applause of the populace, the heathen inquirer is heard saying: 'Can the God of the white men be seen by our eyes? . . . and if *Morimo* (God) is absolutely invisible, how can a reasonable being worship a hidden thing?'"[2] It is the same among the Basutos too. "I will go up to the sky first and see if there really is a God," said a poor Mosuto proudly, "and when I have seen him, I'll believe in him."[3] Another missionary lays stress on the lack of serious thought and the absence of reflection generally noticed among these people (the Bechuanas). "To them thought is dead, so to speak, or at any rate they cannot raise it above the things of sense; . . . they are boors whose god is their belly."[4] Burchell writes in the same way about the Bushmen: "Those whose minds have been expanded by a European education, cannot readily conceive the *stupidity*, as they would call it, of savages in everything beyond the most simple ideas and the most

---

[1] Kn Rasmussen, *Neue Menschen*, pp. 140–1.
[2] *Missions évangéliques*, xxiii. p. 82 (1848). (Schrumpf.)
[3] Ibid., xiv. p. 57 (1839). (Arbousset.)
[4] Ibid., xxvii. p. 250 (1852). (Frédoux.)

uncompounded notions, either in moral or in physical knowledge. But the fact is, their life embraces so few incidents, their occupations, their thoughts, and their cares are confined to so few objects, that their ideas must necessarily be equally few, and equally confined. I have sometimes been obliged to allow Machunka to leave off the task, when he had scarcely given me a dozen words, as it was evident that exertion of mind, or continued employment of the faculty of thinking, soon wore out his powers of reflection and rendered him really incapable of paying any longer attention to the subject. On such occasions, he would betray by his listlessness and the vacancy of his countenance that abstract questions of the plainest kind soon exhausted all mental strength and reduced him to the state of a child whose reason was yet dormant. He would then complain that his head began to ache." [1] . . . But the same traveller, speaking of these Bushmen in another passage, says: " Their character possessed nothing of dullness or stupidity ; but, on the contrary ; they were lively enough ; and on those topics which their peculiar mode of life brings within their observation and comprehension, they often showed themselves both shrewd and quick." [2]

In them, therefore, as in the Iroquois, the distaste for the discursive processes of thought did not proceed from constitutional inability, but from the general customs which governed the form and object of their mental activity. Dr. Moffat, a missionary who spent many years in South Africa and spoke the native language fluently, tells us the same thing about the Hottentots. " It is extremely difficult, adequately to conceive of the extent of the ignorance even of their wise men, on subjects with which infants are conversant in this country. Yet it cannot be denied, in spite of general appearances, that they are acute reasoners, and observers of men and manners." [3]

[1] W. J. Burchell : *Travels into the Interior of Southern Africa*, ii. p. 295 ·1822). Also : " No sooner have we begun to ask him questions about his language than he becomes impatient, complains of headache, and shows that he finds sustained effort of such a kind impossible."—Spix und Martius, in *Reise in Brasilien*, i. p. 384.
[2] Ibid., ii. pp. 54-5.
[3] R. Moffat : *Missionary Labours and Scenes in South Africa*, p. 237 (1842)

Another missionary says of these same Hottentots:
" Our friends in Europe would certainly regard the examples
we could give of the mental sluggishness of these people
in thinking, grasping, and retaining, as absolutely incredible.
Even I, who have known them for so long, cannot help
being surprised when I see how tremendously difficult it
is for them to lay hold of the simplest truths, and above
all, to reason anything out for themselves—and also how
quickly they forget what they have taken in." [1]

What they are lacking in is the power of applying their
minds generally to other things than those which appeal
to their senses, or pursuing other ends than those whose
immediate and practical utility they perceive. " Campbell,
in his little tract on the *Life of Africaner*, says : ' Being
asked what his views of God were before he enjoyed the
benefit of Christian instruction, his reply was that he never
thought anything at all on these subjects ; that he thought
of nothing but his cattle.' " [2] Africaner, who was a powerful
chief and a very intelligent man, admitted the same to
Dr. Moffat.

When intercourse with Europeans had obliged the South-
African natives to make some attempt to analyse their
thoughts (which was quite a new thing to them), it was
natural that they should instinctively have tried to reduce
such efforts to a minimum. In every case in which their
memorizing power, which is really excellent, could relieve
them of the effort of thinking and reasoning, they did not
fail to make use of it. Here is an instructive example.
" The missionary Nezel said to Upungwane : ' You heard
the sermon last Sunday, tell me what you remember of
it. Upungwane hesitated at first, as Kafirs always do,
but later on he reproduced all the principal ideas, word for
word. Some weeks after, the missionary, looking at him
during the sermon, saw that he was apparently not listening,
but was busy cutting a piece of wood. When the sermon
was over, he asked him, ' Well, what did you remember.
to-day ? ' The native took up his piece of wood, and working
from his notches, reproduced one idea after another." [3]

[1] *Berichte der rheinische Missionsgesellschaft*, p. 363 (1865).
[2] R. Moffat : vide supra, p. 124.
[3] Dr. Wangemann : *Die Berliner Mission im Zululande*, p. 272.

This tendency to substitute recollection for reasoning
wherever possible, is seen even in the children, whose mental
habits are naturally modelled on those of their parents.
We know that native children, especially where missionaries
have succeeded in establishing schools, learn almost as
quickly and well as our own, at least up to a certain age,
when their development proceeds more slowly, and then
stops short. Pastor Junod has noted the following points
about the Thonga of South Africa. " The children succeed
better when the effort is one of memory, and this explains
why they are much more at their ease when learning the
English weights and measures, those complicated systems
of reductions, than when put to the metric system, which
seems so much more simple and rational. The English system
requires a perfect committal to memory of the relation
between the various measures—yards, feet, and inches ;
gallons, pints, and gills ; pounds, ounces, and grains—and
these being once mastered, all work becomes purely mechanical. This is what natives like, whilst in the metric system
there is one idea pervading the whole, and a minimum of
reasoning is necessary for its use ; the necessity for this
very minimum explains the unpopularity of the metric
system amongst the native pupils ; and the difficulty in-
creases ten times when they come to problems and have
to solve them without having been told whether addition
or subtraction is necessary. So arithmetic, when workable
by the agency of memory, seems to them an easy and
agreeable study. When requiring reasoning it is a painful
occupation." [1] Exactly the same thing has been noticed
in the Barotse. " Our Zambesi boys, like the Basutos
and South Africans in general, are very fond of arithmetic.
They know of nothing superior to figures ; arithmetic is
the science of sciences, the incontestable criterion of a good
education. Do you know the mazes of English arithmetic
with its old-fashioned but none the less revered system
of weights and measures ? Our Zambesians delight in it.
Talk to them about pounds, farthings, pence, ounces, drams,
etc., and their faces light up and their eyes shine, and in
a moment the calculation is performed, if it is a question

    [1] H. A. Junod : *The Life of a South African Tribe*, ii. p. 152.

of calculation. . . . It is strange how the most exact of sciences may become an admirable piece of machinery. But give them a problem of the very simplest kind, yet one which requires a little reasoning out, and they are up against a stone wall. ' I am beaten,' they say, and they think that they are thereby relieved of any mental effort. I notice this fact as by no means peculiar to the Zambesi boys." [1] " Among the Namaquas, if it is a question of thinking, it is extremely difficult to get the children to understand anything, whilst they show themselves past masters in anything which can be learnt mechanically, and which does not require either thought or reflection." [2] Similarly, on the Niger, " the Mossi does not know how to get at the reason of things, and though our own little ones reason things out and sometimes embarrass us by their questions, a Mossi never asks himself, ' How does that happen ? Why is it that way and not any other ? ' The first explanation is enough for him. This want of reflection is the reason why his civilization is so retarded . . . and that accounts, too, for his lack of ideas. Conversation with them turns only upon women, food, and (in the rainy season) the crops. Their circle of ideas is very restricted but is capable of growth, for the Mossi may be considered intelligent." [3]

To come to a conclusion as far as the African races are concerned, we quote the actual words of the missionary W. H. Bentley, who was a keen observer, and who summed up his experience as follows : " An African, whether negro or Bantu, does not think, reflect, or reason if he can help it. He has a wonderful memory, has great powers of observation and imitation, much freedom in speech, and very many good qualities ; he can be kind, generous, affectionate, unselfish, devoted, faithful, brave, patient, and persevering ; but the reasoning and inventive faculties remain dormant. He readily grasps the present circumstances, adapts himself to them and provides for them ;

[1] *Missions évangéliques*, lxxvi. pp. 402–3 (1901) ; cf. ibid., lxxvii. p. 346 (1897). (Béguin.)
[2] *Berichte der rheinischen Missionsgesellschaft*, p. 230 (1880) ; (Missionär Schröder : *Reise nach dem Ngami-See*.)
[3] P. Eugène Mangin, P.B. : "Les Mossi." *Anthropos*, x–xi. p. 325.

but a carefully thought out plan, or a clever piece of induction is beyond him." [1]

Perhaps it will not be superfluous to illustrate this incapability of reflection by a concrete example. I borrow it from Bentley's own narrative. "It was a very long while before we found out the reason for this keen desire to learn to read and write. The natives, when they carried produce to sell on the coast, took it to the buying store of the factory. When it was weighed or measured, the agent made a few marks on a piece of paper. They then took the 'book' to the agent in charge of the barter store, and he handed out the payment. . . . They concluded that if they could write, they need not trouble to take produce to the factories, but they had only to make a few marks on a piece of paper (as the first agent did), and on presentation of it at the "fetish"—as the barter store of a factory is called—they would obtain all they wanted. Hence, the desire to know how to read and write in San Salvador.

"There was no idea of theft in the case. An African never thinks a matter out if he can help it ; this is his weak point, it is characteristic. They never recognized any similarity between their own trading and the coast factory. They considered that when the white man wanted cloth, he opened a bale and got it. Whence the bales came, and why and how—that they never thought of. Everyone said that the cloth was made by dead men under the sea. The whole thing was so hopelessly mixed with the magic and occult, that their ideas only went as far as they could see. The presentation of the marked paper, without a syllable spoken, caused the cloth to be handed over, so they said, 'Let us learn to mark paper like that.'" [2]

Quite recently Wollaston remarked on the same naïve behaviour in New Guinea. "Before starting they (the porters) were shown the knife or axe or whatever it was that they would receive for their labour, and at the end they raced back to Parimau. . . . Some of the less energetic people in the village, when they saw that their friends received a knife or an axe by merely presenting a small

[1] Rev. W. H. Bentley : *Pioneering on the Congo*, i. p. 256 (1900).
[2] Ibid., i. p. 159–90.

piece of paper to the man in charge of the camp at Parimau, thought that they might easily earn the same reward, and they were rather astonished to find that the small scrap of paper which they handed in, produced nothing at all or only a serious physical rebuff. But they were so childlike in their misdemeanours that we could not be seriously angry with them." [1]

There was not the least idea of trickery in this. Bentley, who had had more experience than Wollaston, realized this clearly and explained it well. It is but one sign among a large number, and a more striking one than many others, of that habit of mind which makes the primitive " stop short at his earliest perception of things and never reason if he can anyhow avoid it."

It would be easy to quote numerous observations of the same kind, referring to other uncivilized peoples, in South America, Australia, and so on. " To follow the course of a Melanesian's thought," says Parkinson, " is no easy task. Intellectually, he stands very low in the scale. Logical thought, in nearly every case, is an impossibility to him. What he does not directly grasp through his senses, is witchcraft or magic agency ; to reflect upon it would be only labour lost." [2]

In short, the entire mental habit which rules out abstract thought and reasoning, properly so-called, seems to be met with in a large number of uncivilized communities, and constitutes a characteristic and essential trait of primitive mentality.

II

Why is it that primitive mentality shows such indifference to, one might almost say such dislike of, the discursive operations of thought, of reasoning, and reflection, when to us they are the natural and almost continuous occupation of the human mind ?

It is due neither to incapacity nor inaptitude, since

[1] A. R. Wollaston : *Pygmies and Papuans*, p. 164 (1912) ; cf. C. G. Rawling : *The Land of the New Guinea Pygmies*, pp. 166–7.
[2] R. Parkinson : *Dreissig Jahre in der Südsee*, p. 567.

those who have drawn our attention to this feature of primitive mentality expressly state that among them are " minds quite as capable of scientific thought as those of Europeans," and we have seen that Australian and Melanesian children learn what the missionary teaches them quite as readily as French or English children would do. Neither is it the result of profound intellectual torpor, of enervation and unconquerable weariness, for these same natives who find an insuperable difficulty in the very slightest abstract thought, and who never seem to take the trouble to reason, show themselves on the contrary, observant, wise, skilful, clever, even subtle, when an object interests them, especially when it is a case of obtaining something they very much desire.[1]

The observer who recently remarked on their " stupidity " goes into ecstasies over their ingenuity and their taste. We must therefore not take the word " stupidity " literally. Or rather, we must ask ourselves whence this apparent stupidity arises, and what are its determining features.

As we have seen above, it has been explained by the very missionaries who have testified to the primitives' dislike of the very simplest logical process. The explanation they give has been derived from the fact that the primitives whom they have studied never thought, and never wanted to think, of more than a very few things— those necessary to their subsistence, their flocks and herds, their game, fish, etc. The mental habits they would thus acquire would become so pronounced that all other things, especially if abstract in their nature, would be powerless to arrest their attention. " They only believe what they see ; their ideas go no further than the regions of sense ; what is not directly perceived is not thought," and so on.

But this statement does not settle the question. If the observations reported are correct, as they seem to be, it tends rather to complicate it. Firstly, we do not see why the pursuit of interests which are entirely material, or even

[1] " You can always trust a New Guinea man to make rapid deductions from what he sees, and there is very little that concerns himself that his eye misses. . . . It sometimes seems uncanny how they know things." H. Newton : *In Far New Guinea*, p. 202 (1914).

why the limited number of the ordinary objects of thought, should necessarily result in the incapability of reflection and the distaste for reasoning. On the contrary, such specialization, and the concentration of the mental powers and the attention on a small number of things to the exclusion of others, ought rather to bring about a kind of definite and precise adaptation, mental as well as physical, to the pursuit of them ; and this adaptation, being partly intellectual, would involve a certain development of ingenuity, reflection, and skill in arriving at the means best calculated to attain the desired end. This is in fact what often happens.

That, side by side with this adaptation, primitives manifest an almost insuperable indifference with regard to matters bearing no visible relation to those which interest them, is frequently matter of painful experience to the missionary. But the incapability of understanding the Gospel message, and even the refusal to listen to it, are not of themselves sufficient proof of the primitives' distaste for logical thought, especially when we remember that these same primitives exhibit considerable mental activity when the subject of thought interests them, when it deals with their cattle or their wives, for instance.

Moreover, is it not rash to account for this dislike by their exclusive attachment to the objects of sense, since the missionaries show us that, in other respects, primitives are the most fervent believers one can find ? We cannot rid their minds of the belief that an infinite number of invisible beings and actions are actually real. Livingstone tells us that he often found matter for wonder in the incontrovertible faith of the negroes of South Africa in beings whom they had never seen. Wherever observation has been sufficiently careful and prolonged, wherever it has come to an end by reason of the natives' excessive reticence with respect to sacred things, it has revealed the existence of an almost illimitable field of group ideas relating to things not perceptible to sense, such as invisible powers, spirits, souls, *mana*, and so on. Most frequently, too, it is not an intermittent faith, like that of so many devout Europeans, who have certain days and special places for their religious exercises. The primitive makes no distinction between this world and the other, between what is actually present to sense, and what is beyond. He actually dwells with invisible spirits and intangible forces. To him it is these that are the real and actual. His faith is expressed in his most insignificant as well as in his most important acts. It impregnates his whole life and conduct.

If then, primitive mentality avoids and ignores logical thought, if it refrains from reasoning and reflecting, it is not from incapacity to surmount what is evident to sense, nor is it because such mentality is exclusively attached to a very small number of objects, and these of a material kind only. The very witnesses who insist upon this trait of the primitive mind also authorize and even oblige us to reject such explanations. We must therefore look elsewhere. And if our search is to meet with any success, we must present the problem in terms which render an exact solution possible.

Instead of imagining the primitives whom we are studying to be like ourselves and making them think as we should do in their places—a proceeding which can only lead to hypotheses, at most merely probable, and nearly always false—let us on the contrary endeavour to guard against our own mental habits, and try to discover, by analysing their collective representations and the connections between these, what the primitives' way of thinking would be.

As long as we assume that their minds are orientated like our own, that they react as ours do to the impressions made upon them, we assume, by implication, that they *should* reason and reflect as ours do with regard to the phenomena and entities of the known world. But we agree that as a matter of fact they neither reason nor reflect thus, and to explain this apparent anomaly we make use of a number of different hypotheses, such as the feebleness and torpidity of their minds, their perplexity, childlike ignorance, stupidity, etc., none of which take the facts sufficiently into account.

Let us abandon this position and rid our minds of all preconceived ideas in entering upon an objective study of primitive mentality, in the way in which it manifests itself in the institutions of uncivilized races or in the collective ideas from which these institutions are derived. Then we shall no longer define the mental activity of primitives beforehand as a rudimentary form of our own, and consider it childish and almost pathological. On the contrary, it will appear to be normal under the conditions in which it is employed, to be both complex and developed in its own way. By ceasing to connect it with a type which is not its own, and trying to determine its functioning solely according to the manifestations peculiar to it, we may hope that our description and analysis of it will not misrepresent its nature.

PRIMITIVE MENTALITY

CHAPTER I

THE PRIMITIVE'S INDIFFERENCE TO SECONDARY CAUSES

I

WHEN confronted by something that interests, disturbs, or frightens it, the primitive's mind does not follow the same course as ours would do. It at once embarks upon a different channel.

The uninterrupted feeling of intellectual security is so thoroughly established in our minds that we do not see how it can be disturbed, for even supposing we were suddenly brought face to face with an altogether mysterious phenomenon, the causes of which might entirely escape us at first, we should be convinced that our ignorance was merely temporary ; we should know that such causes did exist, and that sooner or later they would declare themselves. Thus the world in which we live is, as it were, intellectualized beforehand. It, like the mind which devises and sets it in motion, is order and reason. Our daily activities, even in their minutest details, imply calm and complete confidence in the immutability of natural laws.

The attitude of the primitive's mind is very different. The natural world he lives in presents itself in quite another aspect to him. All its objects and all its entities are involved in a system of mystic participations and exclusions ; it is these which constitute its cohesion and its order. They therefore will attract his attention first of all, and they alone will retain it. If a phenomenon interests him, and he does not confine himself to a merely passive perception of it without reaction of any kind, he will immediately conjure up, as by a kind of mental reflex, an occult and invisible power of which this phenomenon is a manifestation.

" The view-point of the native African mind," says Nassau, " in all unusual occurrences, is that of witchcraft. Without looking for an explanation in what civilization would call *natural* causes, his thought turns at once to the supernatural. Indeed, the supernatural is so constant a factor in his life, that to him it furnishes explanation of events as prompt and reasonable as our reference to the recognized forces of Nature."[1] John Philip, the missionary, speaking of " Bechuana superstitions," says: " Everything in a state of ignorance " (i.e. before the instruction given by the missionaries) " which is not known, and which is involved in mystery " (that which cannot be accounted for merely by perception), " is the object of superstitious veneration, where second causes are unknown, and invisible agency is substituted in their places."[2]

The mentality of the natives of the Solomon Isles suggests the same reflection to Thurnwald. " In considering any matter, they never go beyond simply registering the facts. The profound causal connection is, in theory, entirely lacking. The non-comprehension of the connection between phenomena is the source of their fears and of their superstitions."[3]

Here, as so frequently happens, we must distinguish between the fact reported and the interpretation given to it. The fact is that the primitive, whether he be an African or any other, never troubles to inquire into causal connections which are not self-evident, but straightway refers them to a mystic power. At the same time observers, whether missionaries or others, give their explanation of this fact, and in their opinion, if the primitive immediately has recourse to mystic powers, it is because he does not trouble to inquire into causes. But why does he not trouble to do this? It really is the other way about. If primitives do not think

---

[1] Rev. R. H. Nassau : *Fetichism in West Africa*, p. 277 (1904).
[2] Rev. John Philip : *Researches in South Africa*, ii. pp. 116–17 (1828).
[3] R. Thurnwald : " Im Bismarck Archipel und auf den Salomo Inseln."
Zeitschrift für Ethnologie, xlii. p. 145.

of seeking causal connections, if, when they do perceive them or have them pointed out, they consider them as of slight importance, it is the natural consequence of the well-established fact that their collective representations immediately evoke the instrumentality of mystic powers. It follows that the causal connections which, to us, are the very framework of Nature, the basis of its reality and stability, are of very little interest in their eyes. " One day," said Bentley, " Whitehead saw one of his men sitting in the cold wind on a rainy day. He advised his going home and changing his wet cloth for a dry one, but he said: ' It does not matter. People do not die of a cold wind; people only get ill and die by means of witchcraft.' "[1]

From New Zealand, too, a missionary writes in an almost identical strain. " A native came to me, apparently in a deep decline. He also had caught cold and had not taken care of himself. The natives are not in the least aware of the causes of their diseases. They ascribe to Atua everything that gives them pain. The deluded man said Atua was within him, eating his vitals."[2]

To a mind thus orientated, and wholly absorbed in preconceptions of a mystic nature, what we call a cause, that which we consider accountable for what occurs, could not at most be more than an opportunity or, rather, an instrument which serves the occult powers. The opportunity might have been afforded by something else, and the instrument have been a different one, but the event would have taken place just the same, for all that was necessary was for the occult power to come into play without being prevented by a superior force of the same nature.

II

From among the many examples that occur to us, let us take one of the most familiar ones. In all uncivilized races everywhere, death requires to be explained by other than natural causes. It has frequently been remarked that when they see a man die, it would seem as if it might be the

[1] Rev. W. H. Bentley : *Pioneering on the Congo*, ii. p. 247 (1900).
[2] *Missionary Register*, August 1917. (Ramsden.)

very first time such a thing had happened, and that they could never before have been witnesses of such an occurrence. " Is it possible," says the European to himself, " that these people do not *know* that everybody must die sooner or later ? " But the primitive has never considered things in this light. In his eyes, the causes which inevitably bring about the death of a man in a certain (fairly definite) number of years —causes such as failure of the bodily organs, senile decay, diminution of functioning power—are not necessarily connected with death. Does he not see decrepit old men still alive ? If, therefore, at a given moment death supervenes, it must be because a mystic force has come into play. Moreover, senile weakness itself, like any other malady, is not due to what we call natural causes ; it, too, must be explained by the agency of a mystic force. In short, if the primitive pays no attention to the causes of death, it is because he *knows* already how death is brought about, and since he knows *why* it happens, *how* it occurs matters very little. Here we have a kind of *a priori* reasoning upon which experience has no hold.

Thus, to borrow examples from inferior races in parts where the influence of the white man had not yet been felt, in Australia (in Victoria) " death is at all times by them attributed to human agency. When any black, whether old or young, dies, an enemy is supposed, during the night, to have made an incision in his side and removed his kidney fat. Even the most intelligent natives cannot be convinced that any death proceeds from natural causes." [1]

Neither the body of the sick man, nor his corpse after death, bears the slightest trace of the incision, but the Australian aborigine does not consider that any reason for doubting that it took place. What other proof of it than death itself is necessary ? Would death have occurred if someone had not taken away the fat from the kidneys ? Moreover, this belief does not involve any idea of a physiological rôle attributed to the fat ; it is simply a question of a mystic act brought into operation by the mere presence of the organ which is its agent.

According to the notes furnished by Thomas Petrie;

[1] Hugh Jamieson : *Letters from Victorian Pioneers,* p. 247.

Dr. W. E. Roth says: " During the first years of European colonization, in the Brisbane district . . . nearly all aches, pains and diseases were ascribed to the quartz crystal in the possession of some medicine-man (*turrwan*). This crystal gave its owner supernatural powers. The spirit of the *turrwan* used to put the crystal into the victim, who could only be cured by getting a medicine-man to suck it out again ; thus a medicine-man could make an individual sick even when he was miles away, and ' doom ' him, so to speak." [1] " At Princess Charlotte Bay, all complaints of a serious nature, from malaria to syphilis, are ascribed to the action of a particular charm . . . formed of a pointed piece of human fibula stuck with wax on to a reed spear. It is believed that when the spear is thrown in the direction of the intended victim, the shaft remains in the hands of the thrower, while the bone splinter travels across the intervening space, becomes lodged in the victim's body—the wound immediately closing without leaving a scar—and so causes sickness or disease." [2]

Generally speaking, when a man dies, it is because he has been " doomed " by a sorcerer. " The predestined victim may depart as usual on some hunting expedition . . . when he suddenly feels something at his leg or foot, and sees a snake just in the act of biting him. Strange to say, this particular kind of snake will now immediately disappear. . . . By this very process of invisibility the person bitten recognizes that some enemy has been pointing the *mangani* at him, and that through this form of it he is sure to die ; nothing can possibly save him. He makes no effort to apply a remedy, loses heart, gives way, and lies down to die." [3]

Spencer and Gillen say, too: " All ailments of every kind, from the simplest to the most serious, are without exception attributed to the malign influence of an enemy in either human or spirit shape." [4] " Death by accident," says Howitt, " they can imagine, although the results of what we should call accident they mostly attribute to the effects of some

[1] Dr. W. E. Roth : " Superstition, Magic, and Medicine." *North Queensland Ethnology*, Bulletin 5, nr. 121, p. 30 (1907).
[2] Ibid., nr. 138.
[3] Ibid., nr. 147.
[4] Spencer and Gillen : *The Native Tribes of Central Australia*, p. 530 (1899).

evil magic. They are well acquainted with death by violence, but even in this they believe, as among the tribes about Maryborough (Queensland) that a warrior who happens to be speared in one of the ceremonial fights has lost his skill in warding off or evading a spear, through the evil magic of someone belonging to his own tribe. But I doubt if anywhere in Australia, the aborigines, in their pristine condition, conceived the possibility of death merely from disease. Such was certainly not the case with the Kurnai." [1] " If a man is killed in battle, or dies in consequence of a wound, he is supposed to have been ' charmed.' " [2] "Although the Narrinyeri are so often exposed to the bite of poisonous snakes, they have no remedy for an accident of this kind. Their superstition induces them to believe that it is the result of being bewitched." [3]

This attitude of mind is not peculiar to Australian tribes only. It is to be found occurring almost uniformly among uncivilized peoples who are widely removed from each other. That which does vary in their collective representations is the occult power to which they ascribe the disease or death which has supervened. Sometimes a wizard is the guilty person, sometimes it is the spirit of a dead man, sometimes powers which are more or less definite or individualized, ranging from the vaguest representation to the definite deification of a disease like smallpox. That which is similar, we might almost say identical, in these representations, is the preconnection between the illness and death on the one hand, and the invisible power on the other, which results in the comparative disregard of what we call natural causes, even when these are self-evident.

I shall give a few significant examples of this unanimity of idea. " Natives," says Dr. Chalmers, " never believe in being sick from anything but spiritual causes, and think that death, unless by murder, can take place from nothing but the wrath of the spirits. When there is sickness in a family, all the relatives begin to wonder what it means. The sick

[1] Rev. A. W .Howitt : *The Native Tribes of South-East Australia*, p. 357 (1904).

[2] A. Meyer : " Encounter Bay Tribe," in Woods' *The Native Races of South Australia*, p. 199 (1879).

[3] Rev. G. Taplin : *Manners, Customs, etc., of the South Australian Aborigines*, p. 49 (1879).

person getting no better, they conclude something must be done. A present is given ; perhaps food is taken and placed on the sacred place, then removed and divided amongst friends. The invalid still being no better, a pig is taken on to the sacred place and there speared and presented to the spirits." [1]   It is the same in (German) New Guinea. " According to the Kai, nobody dies a natural death." [2]

Among the Araucans, " all deaths save those caused by battle or combat, were supposed to be the effects of super-natural causes or sorcery. If a person died from the results of a violent accident it was supposed that the *huecuvus* or evil spirits had occasioned it, frightening the horse to make it throw its rider, loosening a stone so that it might fall and crush the unwary, temporarily blinding a person to cause him to fall over a precipice, or some other expedient equally fatal. In the case of death from disease, it was supposed that witchcraft had been practised and the victim poisoned." [3]   Grubb says the same thing about the Chaco Indians. " Death is invariably supposed by the Indian to result from the direct influence of the *kilyikhama*, (spirits) either proceeding from their own desire to injure, or induced through the medium of a witch doctor." [4]   Dobrizhoffer gives the same testimony as far as the Abipones are concerned. [5]

Similar beliefs, too, may be found to exist in nearly all the primitive peoples of the two Americas.

In South Africa we find the exact equivalent of what has been noted in Australia. " It is held to be possible for a man to give over a certain man, who has gone to hunt, to a buffalo, or elephant, or other animal. The wizard is believed to be able to ' charge ' the animal to put the man to death ! ... And so when it is announced that a certain person has been killed in the hunting-field, some of his friends will remark : ' It is the work of enemies ; he was given over to the wild beast.' " [6]

[1] Rev. J. Chalmers : *Pioneering in New Guinea*, pp. 329–30 (1902).
[2] R. Neuhauss : *Deutsch Neu-Guinea*, iii. p. 140 ; cf. ibid., iii. pp. 466 et seq.
[3] R. E. Latcham : "Ethnology of the Auracanos," *Journal of the Anthropological Institute* (henceforward referred to as *J.A.I.*), xxxix. p. 364.
[4] W. B. Grubb : *An Unknown People in an Unknown Land*, p. 161 (1911).
[5] M. Dobrizhoffer : *An Account of the Abipones*, ii. pp. 83–4 (1822).
[6] J. Mackenzie : *Ten Years North of Orange River*, pp. 390–1 (1871).

Bentley expresses the same idea in very definite fashion. " Sickness and death are considered by a Congo to be quite abnormal ; they are in no way to be traced to natural causes, but always regarded as due to sorcery. Even such cases as death by drowning or in war, by a fall from a tree, or by some beast of prey or wild creature, or by lightning— these are all in a most obstinate and unreasoning manner attributed to the black art. Somebody has bewitched the sufferer, and he or she who has caused it is a witch." [1]

As far back as the seventeenth century Dapper had testified to the same beliefs in Loango. " These poor benighted creatures imagine that no accident ever happens to a man which is not caused by the *moquisies*, that is, his enemy's gods. For instance, if somebody falls into the water and is drowned, they will tell you that he has been bewitched ; if he is devoured by a wolf or a tiger, it is because his enemy, by virtue of his magical powers, has been transformed into a wild beast ; if he falls from a tree, if his house is burnt down, if the rainy season lasts longer than usual, it is all due to the magic powers of some bad man's *moquisies*. It is only waste of time to try and drive this foolish idea out of their heads ; it is simply exposing oneself to their contempt and ridicule." [2]

In Sierra Leone, " no death is natural or accidental, but the disease or the accident by which it is immediately caused is the effect of supernatural agency. In some cases it is imagined that death is brought about by the malign influence of some individual who employs witchcraft for that purpose ; in other cases it is supposed that death is inflicted by the tutelar demon of someone on whom the deceased . . . was practising incantations. It is most usual to assign the former cause for the sickness and death of chiefs, and other people of consequence and their connections ; and the latter for those of any of the lower class." [3]

Finally, in (German) East Africa, " to the Dschagga there

[1] Rev. W. H. Bentley : *Pioneering on the Congo*, i. p. 263 (1900).
[2] O. Dapper : *Description de l'Afrique*, p. 325 (1686).
[3] Th. Winterbottom : *An Account of the Native Africans in the Neighbourhood of Sierra Leone*, i. pp. 235–6 (1803).

is no such thing as a natural death. Disease and death are always the result of witchcraft."[1]

Here we will conclude the enumeration of corroborative testimonies, for these might be prolonged indefinitely.[2]

III

From disease and death to mere accidents is an almost imperceptible transition. The foregoing facts show that primitives, as a rule, do not perceive any difference between a death which is the result of old age or of disease, and a violent death. They are not so " unreasoning " (to borrow Bentley's expression) as not to notice that in the one case the sufferer dies more or less gradually, surrounded by his own folks, while in the other he perishes suddenly, devoured by a lion, for instance, or struck down by an enemy spear. This difference, however, is of no interest to them, for from their point of view neither the illness on the one hand, nor the wild beast or spear on the other, is the actual cause of death ; these are merely the agents of the occult power which willed the death, and which might equally well have chosen any other instrument to bring it about. Therefore every death is an accidental one, even death from illness. Or to put it more precisely, no death is, since to the primitive mind nothing ever happens by accident, properly speaking. What appears accidental to us Europeans is, in reality, always the manifestation of a mystic power which makes itself felt in this way by the individual or by the social group.

In a general way there is no such thing as chance to a mind like this, nor can there be. Not because it is convinced of the rigid determinism of phenomena ; on the contrary, indeed, since it has not the most remote idea of such determinism, it remains indifferent to the relation of cause and effect, and attributes a mystic origin to every event which makes an impression on it. Since occult forces are always felt to be present, the more accidental an occurrence seems

---

[1] A. Widenmann : " Die Kilimandscharo-Bevölkerung," in Petermann's *Mitteilungen Ergänzungsheft*, 129, p. 40 (1889).

[2] Cf. *Les Fonctions Mentales dans les Sociétés Inférieures*, pp. 314-28.

to us, the more significant it will appear to the primitive mind. There is no necessity to explain it ; it explains itself, it is a revelation. Most frequently, indeed, it serves to explain something else—at least in the form in which this type of mind troubles about an explanation. But it may become necessary to interpret it, if no definite preconception has provided for this.

Dr. Roth tells us that the natives of the Tully River had resolved to kill a certain man from Clump Point for the following reasons. " On the previous Sunday's *prun* (meeting) he had thrown a spear high up against a tree, whence it had glanced sharply downwards, imbedding itself in the neck of an old man with fatal results. The unfortunate thrower of the spear happened to be a ' doctor,' and nothing would satisfy the deceased's tribesmen but that it was some of his witchcraft which was responsible for the death. Mr. E. Brooke, who was with me at the time, did his best to explain that it was a pure accident, but it was no good. After taking sides, the fight commenced amongst these excited savages, with the result that the ' doctor ' was ultimately speared (non-fatally) in the knee." [1] In this typical case it was difficult, and indeed practically impossible, for the natives to listen to reason. First of all they had to satisfy the dead man, whom there would have been good reason to fear had he not been avenged ; in any case, therefore, they were obliged to put someone to death, and nobody could be more suitable than the one who (whether voluntarily or involuntarily mattered little) had been the cause of the misfortune. Moreover, the missionary would never have succeeded in making them understand that it was simply a case of accident. They would inevitably have asked, why, when the spear rebounded, did it fall exactly on the old man's neck, and not just in front or just behind him ? Why should it happen to belong to a medicine-man ? And as for the absence of any deadly intention on the part of the culprit, how was that to be proved ? It could only be presumed, and a presumption cannot weigh against the fact. Besides, it might have been intentional on his part without his even knowing it. Wizards

[1] W. E. Roth : *North Queensland Ethnography*, Bulletin 4, nr. 15.

are not necessarily aware of the baleful influence they exert. This one might, indeed, in all good faith deny his, but to the natives' minds his denial would be worthless.

In New Guinea, when hunting one day, a man was wounded by one of his comrades' spears. " His friends came and asked him who it was that had bewitched him ; for there is no room for ' accidents ' in the Papuan scheme of things. . . . They all pestered him to tell them the name of the man who had thrown the spell upon him, for they were sure that the spear wound was not enough to cause death, and they had quite made up their minds that he was going to die, and kept telling him so. . . . Although he was conscious almost to the last, he had made no answer to the questions of his friends, nor told who had bewitched him, and now their anger was diverted to the people of Oreresan, and the man who had thrown the spear." [1]   Thus, they laid the blame on this man only as a last resort, and in default of ascertaining the cause of death, they used him as a makeshift, as it were.   If the wounded man had given the least indication respecting the perpetrator of the witchcraft, the man who had injured him would have remained immune from punishment ; he would be regarded merely as the agent of the wizard, and as little responsible for the injury as the spear itself.

On the other hand, the slight nature of the wound does not prevent them from declaring it to be mortal.   What actually kills the wounded man is not the destruction of the tissues by the spear, but witchcraft ; he dies because he has been condemned, or as the Australian natives say, " doomed."   There we have a life-like presentment of the preconception which makes the very idea of accident inconceivable to the primitive mind.

In New Guinea, again, " a tree falls ; it is a witch who caused it to do so, although the tree may be quite rotten, or a gust of wind may break it off.   A man meets with an accident ; it is the (action of) *werabana*." [2]

Very similar cases have been noted in other undeveloped races ; in Central Africa, for instance.   " In 1876 an Akele

[1] Rev. A. K. Chignell : *An Outpost in Papua*, pp. 343–5.
[2] Rev. Bromilow in G. Brown : *Melanesians and Polynesians*, p. 235 (1910).

chief, Kasa, was charged by an elephant he had wounded, and was pierced by its tusks. His attendants drove off the beast ; the fearfully lacerated man survived long enough to accuse twelve of his women and other slaves of having bewitched his gun, thus causing it only to wound instead of killing the elephant." [1]

" During a hunting expedition, a somewhat influential chief named Nkoba was overtaken by a wounded female elephant who, lifting him from the ground with her trunk, impaled him on one of her tusks. . . . Terrible was the wailing of his adherents. . . . The whole district was assembled before the *nganga nkissi*, who was to pronounce whether the elephant was possessed of the devil or had been bewitched by some enemy of the dead chief, or whether it was a case of *Diambudi nzambi*, the will of the Great Spirit." [2]

In both these cases the rank of the victim demands that his death shall be avenged, and anyhow there is a very strong presumption in favour of the idea of witchcraft. Why should the chief's gun have missed fire ? Assuredly a malevolent influence must have been exerted upon it. In the same way, too, the wounded elephant would not have killed the other chief if someone had not " delivered him over." The greater the misfortune and the more exalted the person subjected to it, the more inadmissible is the possibility of an accident.

Most frequently it does not even occur to the native mind. Thus, " a canoe from Vivi, with six people in it, was descending the river (Congo). . . . As they rounded the point upon which afterwards our Underhill station was built, the canoe was caught in a cauldron, filled, and sank. . . . The natives . . . decided that the *witchcraft*, which caused so terrible an accident was no ordinary witchcraft, and must be met accordingly. Three witches must die for each man drowned, so that eighteen more must be put to death because of the accident which had caused the drowning of six men ! In that district deaths of important men, or under extraordinary circumstances, were so met." [3]

[1] Rev. R. H. Nassau : *Fetichism in West Africa*, p. 86 (edit. of 1904).
[2] H. Ward : *Five Years with the Congo Cannibals*, p. 43 (1890).
[3] Rev. W. H. Bentley : *Pioneering on the Congo*, i. p. 411.

" A man enters a village, puts down his gun, which goes off and kills a person. The gun is claimed by the friends of the deceased. It is worth several slaves, and the owner may be as anxious to redeem it as he would have been to redeem his brother. When there is no gun to pledge, the homicide is put in a slave-stick and retained just as in murder. Some native authorities take a more lenient view of homicide. Instead of seizing the party or his gun, they pronounce him quite blameless, and go to the sorcerer to discover the bewitcher who has been the real cause of the death. They hold that it is this being that must bear the whole of the responsibility. They use a simile here that is borrowed from hunting customs. The hunter that first wounds a buck claims it, even though it be ultimately brought down by another man. The man that brings the buck down is only the finder, as it were, of another man's game ; so the homicide only found or brought down the victim that the witch had already destroyed ; he is not the cause, but the occasion of the death. Some insist that although the homicide may protest his innocence and affirm that he is the victim of some witch, he must pay damages all the same. I once saw two men tried for a disturbance committed while they were drunk. The person that had supplied them with beer was also brought up, and was afraid that he should be supposed to have bewitched the beer. A still deeper terror hovered over his speech. ' Perhaps he himself and his beer were both bewitched, and used as a cat's paw by some other person.' " [1]

It is evident that to minds so constituted the theory of an accident would be the last that would present itself, or rather that it would never present itself. If it is suggested to them, they will reject it, because they are certain that what we call " accidental," has a mystic cause, and that they must fathom it unless it is at once revealed.

" A short time ago, chief Kanime of the Ovambi tribe ((German) West Africa) was having an ox prepared for work. Just as they were about to pierce its nostrils, the animal tossed its horns and put out a native's eye. They said at once that the man who had lost his eye had been bewitched.

<hr>

[1] Rev. Duff Macdonald : *Africana*, i. pp. 172–3.

They consulted the wizard, and as he had to discover who had woven the spell, he indicated one of Kanime's servants as the guilty party. When condemned to death, this man ran away, but Kanime pursued him on horseback, overtook him and killed him." [1]

The following year " one of my neighbours, in good health and cheerful mood, went off to hunt for frogs, of which they are very fond. When throwing his spear, he gave himself a deep wound in the arm, lost a great deal of blood, and finally died of hemorrhage. . . . Three days later the wizards began to inquire who had bewitched this man. I objected to this, but they told me : ' If we don't find the *omulodi* and put him to death, perhaps we shall all die.' By request of the missionaries, the chief intervened, but shortly afterwards he took advantage of their absence to have the culprit put to death." [2]

This explanation of most accidents is so natural to these African tribes that even in places where the missionaries have been endeavouring to combat it for a long time, they are unable to convince the natives. Observe the complaints made by Dieterlen in 1908 about the Basutos. " Last month lightning struck the house of a man I know ; it killed his wife, injured his children, and burned all his belongings. He knows quite well that lightning comes from the clouds, and that no man's hand can reach the clouds. But he was told that the flash of lightning was sent him by a neighbour who bears him a grudge ; he believed it, he does so still, and will continue to believe it. Last year locusts descended in swarms on the fields of the young chief Mathé-a-lira, a man who has been fairly well educated in the school, and has often frequented the religious services in our churches. What does *that* matter ? He ascribed this plague of locusts to the enchantments of his brother Tesu, who is disputing the rights of seniority and the succession to the throne of the Leribe district with him."

" About a fortnight ago a young widow, living about a kilometre away, died of an internal complaint, probably due to her own loose conduct. This disease was given her

[1] *Berichte der rheinischen Missionsgesellschaft*, p. 242 (1895).
[2] Ibid., p. 213 (1896).

by a man whom she had refused to marry, when giving her a handful of hemp to smoke. Her mother is a Christian, and I explained to her that such a thing was not possible. She did not believe me, and she cherished a feeling of hatred for the man whom she regarded as the murderer of her child." [1]

Even if the accident should be a fortunate instead of a fatal one, the primitive's reaction to it will be the same. He will see in it the instrumentality of mystic forces, and generally he will be frightened by it. Any unusual joy or success is suspicious. "It often happens," says Major Leonard, "that two friends go out fishing together, and one of them, either by accident or, it may be, better management, secures a much greater haul of fish than the other. Unfortunately, however, it is an act by which he unconsciously lays up for himself a store of evil that is fraught with danger to his life ; for on their return to the town the unlucky one immediately goes and consults . . . the witch doctor, as to the reason of his friend's having obtained a larger haul than himself. The " doctor " at once attributes the cause to magic. So the seed of strife and death is sown, and the warm-hearted friend is suddenly changed into an active enemy who strives his utmost to procure the death of one that until so recently was to him as of his own flesh and blood." [2]

"I was at Ambrizette," says Monteiro, "when three Cabinda women had been to the river with their pots for water ; all three were filling them from the stream together, when the middle one was snapped up by an alligator, and instantly carried away under the surface of the water, and of course drowned. The relatives of the poor woman at once accused the other two of bewitching her, and causing the alligator to take her out of their midst ! When I remonstrated with them, and attempted to show them the utter absurdity of the charge, their answer was: 'Why did not the alligator take one of the end ones then, and not the one in the middle ? ' And out of this idea it was impossible to move them, and the poor women were both obliged to

[1] *Missions évangéliques*, lxxxiii. p. 311.
[2] Major A. G. Leonard : *The Lower Niger and its Tribes*, p. 485 (1906).

take *casca* " (i.e. ordeal poison). " I never heard the result, but most likely one or both were either killed or passed into slavery." [1]

Monteiro does not realize that to the native mind what has occurred cannot be accidental. First of all, alligators would not have attacked these women of their own accord. Therefore, someone must have incited this one to do it. Then, too, it knew exactly which woman to drag under the water. She was " delivered over " to him. The only thing to find out was *who* had done it. . . . But the fact speaks for itself. The alligator did not touch the women on each side, he took the middle one, therefore the two others must have delivered her over. The ordeal they had to undergo was not so much for the purpose of clearing up a doubt which scarcely exists, as of revealing the actual origin of the witch-craft within them, and exerting upon it a mystic influence which would henceforward render it incapable of injuring others.[2]

Here is a similar fact reported from the same locality. " The same evening, on an up-river voyage, Ewangi was snatched from his canoe by a crocodile, and seen no more. Word of the tragedy was brought to Dido's town. War canoes were despatched. One of the men who were with Ewangi in the canoe at the time of his death, and the man off whose beach the crocodile lay, were arrested, charged with witchcraft, and doomed to death." [3] In fact, *there is no such thing as chance.* The idea of accident does not even occur to a native's mind, while on the contrary the idea of witchcraft is always present. Ewangi then was " delivered over." There is no need to inquire who did it ; those who

---

[1] J. J. Monteiro : *Angola and the River Congo*, i. pp. 65–6 (1875).

[2] Vide infra, chap. viii. pp. 235-6.

[3] G. Hawker : *The Life of George Grenfell*, p. 58 (1909). The same re-action is to be noted at Nias, where the missionaries whose boat caused it are held responsible for an accident. In the natives' eyes, the victims have been " delivered over," and satisfaction must be made. Two of them had been drowned in the night when returning to land, after a visit to the *Denninger*, the Mission boat. " At first it seemed as if the people had taken the matter quietly, but they came back again afterwards making the most impossible demands. They required that the captain and the cook of the boat should be handed over to them so that, in their persons, they might avenge the deaths of the two men drowned, and they had already threatened to take reprisals on the Sisters at Telok Dalam, if the sailors were not given up to them."—*Berichte der rheinischen Missionsgesellschaft*, p. 153 (1885).

accompanied him, and whom the devourer spared, or else the man on whose beach it lived, were assuredly the guilty parties.

IV

To be able thoroughly to understand the natives' mind in this matter, we ought to remember that, according to their account, crocodiles and alligators are harmless by nature. Man has nothing to fear from them.   It is true that in certain places where they abound, and where accidents very frequently occur, the natives are gradually abandoning this idea, and precautions are taken.   In (German) East Africa, for instance, " since there are an incredible number of crocodiles, it is not safe to draw water from the river Ruhudge direct, but a kind of palisade is erected, and the water is drawn up to the top of the very precipitous bank, by means of vessels hung on to long bamboo poles." [1]   The same method is pursued on the upper Shiré, on the Quanza River.[2] But this is an exceptional case.   As a rule, the natives do not hesitate to approach the river banks, or even to bathe in the neighbourhood of the crocodiles.   Moreover this feeling is shared by a certain number of Europeans.   Bosman had already written: " The whole time I have been here, I have never heard of a crocodile devouring either man or beast. . . . There are a terrible number of these animals in all the rivers of the country . . . I would not venture into the water, although I have never heard of any accident of this kind." [3]   During a two years' stay in the Cameroons, Von Hagen knew of only three cases in which men had been attacked by crocodiles, although the natives bathe and swim in the river, and during the dry season they splash about in the lagoons.[4]   The same belief obtains on the west coast of Africa.   " It is said that in the river Gallenhas (between Sherbro and Cape Mount) where alligators are in great abundance, there was not an instance on record of

[1] Fr. Fülleborn : *Das deutsche Njassa und Ruwumagebiet, Deutsch Ost Africa,* ix. pp. 185, 541.
[2] J. J. Monteiro : *Angola and the River Congo,* ii. p. 123.
[3] W. Bosman : *Voyage de Guinée,* 14e lettre, pp. 250–1.
[4] G. von Hagen : *De Bana,* Bässler-Archiv, ii. p. 93 (1911).

any person being hurt by them, although the natives were much in the river until a few years ago, when a slave ship blew up opposite its entrance." [1]

Bentley was of opinion that if the necessary precautions were taken there was not much risk of danger from this source. " Crocodiles are very timid creatures and will not venture easily into danger. The shouting and splashing and frolicking of some dozen or more African boys bathing is quite enough to keep the crocodiles at bay. But if one of them should venture into the water alone, an accident is possible." [2] Should such an accident happen, how will the native explain it ? Will he place it to the score of his own imprudence, or will he change his opinion of the habits of the crocodile ? Will he think that it is an accident ? He certainly would do so, if he reasoned as we do. As a matter of fact, he does not even imagine such a thing. He has his explanation all ready, and it is something altogether different. " In districts where crocodiles are common," says Bentley, " the witches are believed sometimes to turn into crocodiles, or to enter and actuate them, and so cause their victim's death by catching him. Where leopards are common, the witches may become leopards. The natives often positively affirm that a crocodile, of itself, is a harmless creature. So thoroughly do they believe this, that in some places they go into the river . . . to attend to their fish-traps without hesitation. If one of them is eaten by a crocodile, they hold their witch palavers, find and kill the witch, and go on as before.

" At Lukunga, one of the stations of the American Baptist Mission, a great crocodile came up out of the river to attack the Mission pigsty in the night. The pig smelt the reptile and began to make such a noise that Mr. Ingham, the missionary, got up ; when he found the cause he shot the crocodile. In the morning he skinned it, and found in the stomach the anklets of two women. They were at once recognized as belonging to women who had disappeared at different times, when fetching water. I was at the station

[1] T. H. Winterbottom : *An Account of the Native Africans in . . . Sierra Leone*, i. p. 256 (1803).
[2] Mrs. H. M. Bentley : *The Life and Labours of a Congo Pioneer*, p. 34 (1900).

a few days after, and one of my Congo workmen, who was with me, warmly denied that the crocodile ate the women. He maintained that they never did so. ' But what about the anklets ? Were they not proof positive that in this case the crocodiles had eaten the two women ? ' ' No, he caught the women and handed them over to the witch, who worked through him ; as for the anklets, it must have been his fashion to take them as his perquisites ! ' What can be done," adds Bentley, " with such a devil-possessed brain as this ? " [1]

Bentley is shocked at what he considers unheard-of obstinacy in denying the evidence. But it is something quite different. It is simply one individual case of that " impermeability to experience " which is a characteristic of the native mind, when preoccupied with collective representations. According to these representations, in which second causes are negligible (the real cause being of a mystic nature), the crocodile, which acts in such an unusual way and devours a man, cannot be an animal like others; he must be the agent of a wizard, or the wizard himself.

" Great numbers of alligators are bred in the creeks and rivers, which frequently carry off . . . the persons of the natives, yet such is their superstition, that when a circumstance of that kind happens, they attribute it to witchcraft ; and are so infatuated that they will not be at the pains to enclose those parts of the rivers where their women and children are continually washing, and from whence they are frequently taken." [2]

On the upper Zambesi " it is said that there are doctors who give crocodile-medicine. If anybody steals the cattle of one of these medicine-men, the doctor goes to the river. When he gets there he says : ' Crocodile come here ; go and catch the man who has killed my cattle.' The crocodile understands. When morning comes the doctor hears that a crocodile has killed someone in the river. He says : ' It was the robber.' " [3]

Thenceforward, every fresh accident, instead of shaking

[1] Rev. W. H. Bentley : *Pioneering on the Congo*, i. pp. 275–6 ; cf. ibid., i. p. 317.

[2] John Matthews : *A Voyage to the Sierra Leone River*, p. 50 (1788).

[3] E. Jacotet : *Études sur les langues du Haut Zambèze, III, Textes Louyi* p. 170, Publications de l'école des Lettres d'Alger, xvi. (1901).

the native's conviction, will only serve as a fresh proof of
it.   He will seek out and punish the witch, and the European's
reprimands will seem more than ever absurd to him.   " Two
men had been taken by crocodiles.   Now, they maintain
that it is not the custom of the crocodiles to take men.
Therefore they were witch-crocodiles, and the chief, the owner
of the district, had witched the men away. . . . Of course
he declared his innocence, but was compelled to drink the
ordeal poison to prove it ; and the scoundrel of a doctor
had arranged a fatal dose. . . . We could do nothing." [1]

Collective representations exactly like these have been
verified in New Guinea (Woodlark Island).   " Maudega,
a woman of Avetan, in Murua, had been on a visit to the
neighbouring village of Nabudau, and on her return had
brought back with her the daughter of Boiamai, the Nabudau
chief.   The child was unfortunately taken by a crocodile,
and in revenge Boiamai, with his son and some other men
of his village, killed Maudega and three of her relations. . . .
On the trial, the son made the following statement.   ' It
is true we killed those people. . . . Maudega took my sister
away to her village, and while she was there she bewitched
an alligator and made it come out of the water, and take
away my sister and eat her.' " [2]   The idea of an accident
did not even occur to the minds of the victim's family.   The
crocodile *could* only be an agent.   A little further on, Murray
relates that " crocodiles are a great danger to the runaway,
and a belief is gaining ground in a part of the Papuan Gulf
that the crocodiles are in league with the Government,
based upon the fact that a prisoner escaping from gaol was
severely lacerated by one of these creatures while crossing
a river. . . . Still the crocodiles are by no means all under
Government control ; the great mass of them remain faithful to the sorcerers and will not attack a man unless bidden
by a sorcerer to do so.   I had to cross a river once which
was reputed to be full of crocodiles, and I asked an old man
with me if he was not afraid.   He said that he was not.
" A crocodile won't touch you," he explained, " unless someone has made *puri puri* against you, and if someone has

[1] Rev. W. H. Bentley : *Pioneering on the Congo*, i. p. 317.
[2] J. H. P. Murray, *Papua*, pp. 128–9 (1912).

made *puri puri* against you, you are a lost man in any case—
he will get you somehow—if not with a crocodile, then in
some other way. So the crocodiles do not really matter."[1]
Thus the danger lies elsewhere, and from the reptile himself
there is nothing to fear. If he should attack the traveller,
it is because the latter has been " delivered over " to him.

If we try to determine *how* the native mind represents
the relations between the witch and the reptile to itself,
we come up against an almost insurmountable difficulty.
His thought is not subject to the same logical exigencies as
our own. It is governed, in this case as in many others, by
the law of participation. Between the wizard and the crocodile the relation is such that the wizard becomes the
crocodile, without, however, being actually fused with him.
Considered from the stand-point of the law of contradiction, it must be either one of two things : either the wizard
and the crocodile make but one, or they are two distinct
entities. But prelogical mentality is able to adapt itself
to two distinct affirmations at once. Observers do indeed
sense this quality of participation, but they have no means
of expressing it. Sometimes they insist on identity, sometimes on the distinction between the two beings ; the very
confusion in their language is significant. Thus " the
balogi (wizards) are credited with the power of transforming
the dead into snakes, crocodiles, etc. This transformation
is usually effected with the crocodile, therefore this monster,
though not a god, nor even a spirit, is respected and feared.
He is at one with the person who effects the change ; between
them there is, as it were, a secret pact, a complete understanding. The person will order the reptile to go and seize
a certain individual, and it will go, and make no mistake. . . .
What we have just said explains why, when anyone has been
carried off by a crocodile, the first thing to do is to find the
mulogi who despatched the monster, and there is always
a guilty person to be found. His fate is quickly decided."[2]
Among the Bangala, " no crocodile would have done it unless
it had been instructed to do it by a *moloki* (witch) or unless

[1] J. P. H. Murray, *Papua*, pp. 237–8.
[2] P. Eugène Hurel: " Religion et vie domestique des Bakerewe."
Anthropos, vi. p. 88 (1911).

the *moloki* had gone into the animal and made it commit the outrage." [1] Thus the missionary considers the two hypotheses separately, while to the native mind, in a way that is incomprehensible to us, they are but one.

In Gaboon (French Congo) " the superstition about the man-tiger," says M. le Testu, an excellent observer, " is no less obscure than that of the magic charm involved. It appears in two different forms. In the one case the tiger (a leopard or panther, be it understood) who is the author of the crime, is a real animal belonging to a person, obedient to him, in carrying out his orders ; such a tiger is passed on to his heirs like any other piece of personal property. So-and-so, they say, has a tiger. In the other case, the animal is but an incarnation of some sort ; they do not even know whether it is a man who has taken the form of a beast, the beast being merely a sign, or whether there really has been an incarnation, properly so called, of a man in an actual animal. . . . The idea these natives have of a man-tiger is extremely vague." [2]

Major Leonard presents the matter rather differently. " The old woman of Utshi was accused of the death of Oru, by projecting her spirit-soul into the crocodile that devoured him, and not, as might be supposed, by converting herself, body and all. For the impossibility of this, in this particular instance, at all events, was clearly demonstrated by the fact that five other women were similarly accused. From the native stand-point it is possible for a number of spirits to be attached to one object, or to project themselves into the body of one animal, although it is, as a rule, unusual for them to do so." [3]

But here is the story of a native from his own lips : " Perhaps when the sun is overhead to-day, you may be drinking palm wine with a man, unconscious that he is possessed of an evil spirit, in the evening you hear the cry of ' *Nkole! Nkole!* ' (crocodile) and you know that one of these monsters, lurking in the muddy waters near the river

[1] Rev. J. H. Weeks : " Anthropological Notes on the Bangala of the Upper Congo River," *J.A.I.*, xxxix. pp. 449–50.
[2] G. Le Testu : *Notes sur les coutumes. Bapounou dans la Conscription de la Nyanga*, pp. 196–7.
[3] Major Leonard : *The Lower Niger and Its Tribes*, p. 194 (1906).

bank, has grabbed a poor victim who had come to fill a water jar. At night you are awakened from your sleep by the alarmed cackling in your hen-house, and you will find that your stock of poultry has been sadly decreased by a visit from a *muntula* (bush cat). Now . . . the man with whom you drank palm wine, the crocodile who snatched an unwary villager from the river bank, and the stealthy little robber of your hens are one and the same individual, possessed of an evil spirit." [1] Participation is very clearly suggested here. To the native it is quite enough that he feels it to be real, he does not ask himself how it comes to pass.

V

As there is no such thing as chance, and as primitives moreover do not trouble to examine the conditions which bring about or do not bring about a phenomenon, it follows that whatever is unusual or unexpected is received by them with more emotion than surprise. The idea of the unusual or extraordinary, though not defined in the same way as it is with us, is nevertheless very familiar to the primitive mind ; it is one of those notions which are both general and concrete, such as *mana, orenda, psila,* and so forth, which I have defined elsewhere. [2]

The unusual may occur with comparative frequency, and the primitive's disregard of second causes is, as it were, compensated by an ever alert attention to the mystic meaning of everything that strikes him. Therefore observers have frequently remarked that the primitive, who properly speaking, is astonished at nothing, is nevertheless very emotional. His absence of intellectual curiosity is accompanied by extreme sensibility to the appearance of anything which takes him by surprise.

Again, among unusual phenomena, we must distinguish those which occur but rarely, but yet already have a place in the collective representations, from those which make their appearance without any prevision whatever. The birth of

[1] E. J. Glave : *Six Years of Adventure in Congo Land,* p. 92 (1893).
[2] *Les Fonctions Mentales dans les Sociétés Inférieures,* pp. 147–8.

twins, for instance, is a comparatively rare phenomenon but at any rate it is known to occur. In nearly all uncivilized peoples it gives rise to a series of rites and ceremonies ; an authoritative preconception decides how it is necessary to act in such a case, so as to avert the dangers of which this phenomenon may be the sign or the cause. It is the same thing with solar or lunar eclipses. But when the native is faced by phenomena which are entirely unexpected, the demeanour to be maintained is not thus decreed beforehand. When this happens, (and it occurs fairly often), how is primitive mentality affected by it ? It is not taken unawares. It immediately recognizes in such phenomena the manifestation of occult powers (spirits, souls of the dead, magic influences, and so on), and it explains them, as a rule, as the presage of great misfortune.

CHAPTER II

MYSTIC AND INVISIBLE FORCES

I

FROM what has been set forth in the preceding chapter we seem better able to understand why primitive mentality fails to seek for what we call the causes of phenomena. This lack of curiosity does not arise from intellectual torpor or from mental weakness either. Strictly speaking, it is no lack ; in the language of the Schools, it has not a " deficient " or ' negative " reason ; it has an actual and positive one. It is the direct and necessary consequence of the fact that primitives live, think, feel, move and act in a world which, in a great many ways, does not coincide with ours. Therefore many of the questions raised by our experience of life do not exist as far as they are concerned, since these are answered beforehand, or rather, because their system of representations is such that these questions possess no interest for them.

I have explained elsewhere our reasons for considering this type of mind as " mystic " and " prelogical." It is difficult to give an exact definition of it. The European mind—even when most imaginative, as in the case of poets and metaphysicians—is profoundly positive, when compared with the primitive mind. To adapt ourselves to an attitude so opposed to that which is natural to us, we should have to do violence to our most ingrained mental habits, without which, as it seems to us, we could not think at all.

To the primitive mind his preconnections, which are no less imperative than *our* need to trace every phenomenon back to its causes, establish without any possibility of doubt, the direct transition from such-and-such a sense-impression to such-and-such an invisible force. Or rather, it is not even a transition, for that term, though suited to our discursive operations, does not exactly express the primitive's mental functioning, which seems more like direct apprehension or intuition. At the very moment when he perceives what is presented to his senses, the primitive represents to himself the mystic force which is manifesting itself thus. He does not " infer " the one from the other, any more than we " infer " the meaning of a word from its sound in our ears. According to Berkeley's shrewd observation, we really do understand the meaning at the time we hear the word, just as we read sympathy or anger in a person's face without first needing to see the signs of such emotions in order to interpret them. It is not a process accomplished in two succeeding moments, it takes place all at once. In this sense, then, preconnections amount to intuitions.

Undoubtedly this kind of intuition does not make it possible to perceive the invisible or touch the intangible ; it cannot have the effect of giving sense-perception of what is outside the realm of sense. But it does give implicit faith in *the presence and agency* of powers which are invisible and inaccessible to the senses, and this certainty equals, if it does not surpass, that afforded by the senses themselves. To the prelogical mind these elements of reality—much the most important in his eyes—are no less matters of fact than the others. It is these which give the reason for what occurs. Strictly speaking, it is even better not to say that what happens needs explanation, for at the very moment when it happens prelogical mentality immediately forms an idea of the invisible influence which is being manifested thus. It is, indeed, when this is in question that we may say that to the primitive the surrounding world is the language of spirits speaking to a spirit. It is a language which his mind does not remember ever having learnt, but which the preconnections of its collective representations make quite a *natural* one.

From this point of view, the primitives' experience must appear more complex and richer in content than our own. At first this idea seems almost absurd when we compare the apparent poverty of their mental life with the activity of ours ; have we not ourselves said that as often as they can they avoid thinking, and is not the simplest act of reflection an almost intolerable effort to them ? The paradox, however, may be justified, and it becomes permissible when we add that their " direct " experience is in question. Our experience is the sum-total of a comparatively small number of data and an infinitude of inferences. That of the primitive mind on the other hand contains but a small proportion of inferences ; but it contains many direct data to which we deny objective value, although in the primitive's eyes they are as real as, even more real than, those afforded by the senses.

It is indeed the superabundance of these mystic data, and the existence of dominating preconnections between the data afforded by the senses and the invisible influences, which make the inferences that serve to develop our experience, needless in his case. They, too, prevent the primitive mind from adding to its mental stores by means of its experiences. When anything new presents itself to us we realize that we have to seek for an explanation of it, and that the number of our problems is going to increase at the same time as our knowledge is enlarged. The primitive, on the other hand, in the presence of anything new, knows already everything he needs to know. In any unusual event he immediately perceives the manifestation of an invisible force. Moreover, the primitive's mind is not, like our own, orientated to cognition, properly so called. It knows nothing of the joys and advantages of knowledge. Its collective representations are always largely emotional. The primitive's thought and his language are but slightly conceptual, and it is in this respect that the distance which separates his mind from ours may perhaps most easily be estimated.

In other words, the mental life of primitives (and consequently their institutions), depend upon this essential primary fact that in their representations the world of sense and the other make but one. To them the things which are unseen cannot be distinguished from the things which are seen. The beings of the unseen world are no less directly present than those of the other ; they are more active and more formidable. Consequently that world occupies their minds more entirely than this one,

and it diverts their minds from reflecting, even to a slight
extent, upon the data which we call objective. What is
the good of fathoming these, since life, success, health,
the order of Nature, everything in fact depends upon mystic
forces at all times ? If human effort can accomplish anything,
must it not first of all endeavour to interpret, settle, and,
if possible, even induce the manifestations of these forces ?
That is in reality the course pursued by the primitive in
attempting to develop his experience.

II

The invisible forces which persistently preoccupy the
primitive's mind may be briefly arranged in three categories,
which, however, frequently overlap. These are, firstly, the
spirits of the dead ; secondly, the spirits (taking the word
in its widest sense) which animate natural objects (of the
animal and vegetable worlds), inanimate objects (such as
streams, rocks, sea, mountains, manufactured things, etc.),
and lastly, charms or spells due to the agency of sorcerers.
Sometimes the line of demarcation between these categories
is very finely drawn. Thus in Loango, according to Pechuël-
Loesche, the medicine-men co-operate with the spirits ani-
mating fetish objects, but on no account would they have
anything to do with the spirits of the dead, whom they
greatly fear. Elsewhere the distinction is less definite (or the
investigations less exact), and the transition from the spirits
of the dead to other invisible beings seems scarcely perceptible. Everywhere, or nearly everywhere, however, among
inferior races, these mystic influences are direct data, and
the preconnections in which they occur as the predominating
factor, impose themselves on the collective representations.
The fact is well known, and I shall confine myself to a few
examples only.

In the Papuan tribes of (German) New Guinea, which have
just been so carefully studied in the book published by
Dr. Neuhauss, " witchcraft plays a more important part
than the fear of ghosts. If it does not rain, or rains too
much, if the crops are not good, if the coco-nut trees do
not yield, if the pigs die, if hunting and fishing bring no

results, if the earth trembles, if a high tide sweeps through the coastal village, if disease or death supervene—natural causes are never enough to account for these things ; there is always witchcraft at work somewhere." [1] According to the Kai, nobody ever dies a natural death. Even in the case of old people they maintain that death is wizardry, and it is the same thing in all misfortunes that may occur. Has a man had a fatal fall ? A wizard made him fall. Has another been wounded by a wild boar, or bitten by a snake ? It was a wizard again. He, too, working from a distance, can make a woman die in childbed, and so on.[2]

In a similar way, in most primitive communities witchcraft is ever lying in wait, as it were, to work ill and inflict injury. There is a " perpetual possibility " of sorcery which seizes every opportunity to manifest its power. The number of such opportunities is an indefinite one, and it is impossible for thought to imagine them all beforehand. It is at the very moment of action that the witchcraft shows itself ; when it *is* perceived, the mischief is already done. Therefore the perpetual uneasiness in which the primitive lives hardly allows him to forecast, and try to prevent, the misfortune which is about to happen to him. His apprehension of witchcraft never leaves him, but he is no less assuredly its victim. This is one of the reasons, and by no means the least important, which explains the rage felt by primitives for the wizard, when he is unearthed. It is not merely a question of reprisals for the past enchantments these people have suffered from, the number and extent of which they do not even know. They desire further, and above all, to destroy beforehand those which the wizard might use against them in future. The only means of doing this which is within their power is to kill the sorcerer—generally by throwing him into the water or by burning him—a proceeding which at one stroke annihilates the evil spirit dwelling in and operating through him.[3]

Innumerable are the enchantments which the wizard may employ. If he has " doomed " an individual, he will

---

[1] R. Neuhauss : *Deutsch Neu Guinea*, i. pp. 445–6.
[2] Ibid., iii. p. 140.
[3] Vide infra., chap. viii. p. 236.

sometimes take possession of something belonging to him which, through participation, *is* himself (for instance, his hair or his nail-parings, his excreta or urine, his footprints, shadow, likeness, name, and so forth), and by certain magic arts practised upon this part of him, the wizard will compass his death. Sometimes he will sink his canoe or make his gun misfire, or at night, during his slumber, he will cut him open and rob him of his vital principle by taking away the fat of his kidneys. Sometimes he will " deliver him over " to a wild beast, a snake, or an enemy. Or again, he will cause him to be crushed by a falling tree or by a rock which breaks away when he is passing—and so on *ad infinitum*. If necessary, the wizard will change himself into an animal. We have seen that in Central Africa the crocodiles which carry off human victims are not ordinary reptiles, but the docile agents of witches, or even witch-crocodiles. In British Guiana, " a jaguar which displays unusual audacity in approaching men will often unnerve even a brave hunter by the fear that it may be a *Kanaima tiger*. ' This,' reasons the Indian, ' if it be but an ordinary wild beast, I may kill with bullet or arrow ; but what will be my fate if I assail the man-destroyer—the terrible Kanaima ? ' Many of the Indians believe that those Kanaima animals are possessed by the spirits of *men* who have devoted themselves to deeds of blood and cannibalism " [1]—(a belief similar to that which we have had attested in Central Africa, where the sorcerer is dreaded as a cannibal also). According to Dobrizhoffer, the Abipones used exactly the same expressions as these Indians of British Guiana. The Araucans, " if they notice any unusual act of bird or beast, immediately conclude that it is possessed. A fox or puma that prowls round their hut by night, is a witch who has come to see what she can steal. On driving it away they take care to do it no bodily harm for fear of reprisals. . . . Everything not immediately explicable by natural and visible agency is put down either to evil spirits or to witchcraft." [2]

According to Guevara, the Araucan " attributes every-thing out of the common which he sees, or which happens

---

[1] Brett: *The Indian Tribes of Guiana*, p. 374 (1868).
[2] R. E. Latcham : " Ethnology of the Araucanos," *J.A.I.*, xxxix. pp. 350-1.

to him, to the intervention of malevolent spirits or supernatural causes. Whether it be an unsatisfactory harvest,
an epidemic among his cattle, a fall from his horse, illness
or death . . . it is always caused by wizards. The length
of a man's life, and the misfortunes which overtake him during
its course, rest with them." [1] The number and variety of
amulets, talismans, formulæ, and practices of every kind
by which, making use of a little everywhere, they try to
protect themselves as far as they can from all possible forms
of witchcraft, show how much this idea of sorcery obsesses
the minds of uncivilized races, and it is even found among
peoples who are more highly developed.

When loss or misfortune does occur, one thing is certain,
and this is that some occult influence has been at work.
But it is often difficult to discover what it is. Considering
the actual event in itself, the fruitless chase, the illness that
has occurred, the drought that has stripped the fields, etc,
there is nothing in it to indicate whether it is the work of
a wizard, or the dead who are displeased, or malevolent
spirits who are énraged. In most of the observations we
have just quoted, as in many others, the expression used is
" wizards or malevolent spirits." In fact, malevolent spirits
may be in the employ of sorcerers, or vice versa ; sometimes
the sorcerer himself, without being aware of it, is animated
by an evil spirit. Then the two representations overlap
each other. But there is this difference between them,
that the wizard is necessarily an individual, a member of
the social group or of a neighbouring one, the representation
of whom is therefore clear and distinct, while that of the
spirits, so long as they are not the spirits of the dead (ghosts),
is always more or less vague and elusive, varying with the
communities in which they are observed. The representation
varies, too, within these communities according to individual
imaginings, and the classes to which the individuals belong.

Between the clear conception of spirits who are, as it
were, real *daimones* or divinities, each of whom has his
name, attributes, and frequently his religious following,
and the representation, both general and concrete, of an indwelling power in objects and beings, such as the *mana* (unless

[1] T. Guevara : *Folklore araucano*, p. 22.

this force is individualized), there is room for an infinitude of intermediate forms, some fairly definite, others more fleeting and vague, with outlines that are less distinct, though none the less real to a mentality which is but slightly conceptual, in which the law of participation still predominates.

Most of the mystic forces manifesting themselves in Nature are both diffuse and individualized. The necessity of choosing between the two forms of representation is never imposed on these primitives ; it does not even occur to them. How can they define their answer to questions which they never think of asking themselves ? The word " spirit," although too precise a term, is the least cumbersome that we have to denote those influences and agencies which continually surround primitives.

As time passes and the missionaries penetrate further into the mystery of the ordinary thoughts of those among whom they live, the more clearly does this mystic orientation reveal itself. We notice it in their descriptions, even when the terms used suggest the idea of more clearly defined representations. For example, " with these undesirable denizens of the spirit-world," says Father Jetté, " the Ten'a may be said to have an almost continual intercourse. They hold themselves liable to see or hear them at any time. Any unusual noise, any fancy of their imagination, quickly assumes the shape of a devil manifestation. If a black, water-soaked log, under the action of the current, bobs up within their view, and disappears, they have seen a *nekedzaltura*. If they hear a whistling in the woods, somewhat unlike the cries of birds that are familiar to them, a *nekedzaltura* is calling them. No day passes in an Indian camp without someone reporting that he or she has heard or seen something of the kind. . . . " The manifestations of the devil's presence are as familiar to the Ten'a as the blowing of the wind or the singing of the birds." [1] In another passage this same missionary had already remarked : " The intensity as well as the extent of their devil-belief is beyond our conceptions. Their imagination is always on the alert to descry some devil moving about in the dark or in the broad

[1] Fr. Jetté : " On the Superstitions of the Ten'a Indians," *Anthropos*, vi. pp. 721–2.

daylight, as the case may be, and no caprice of the unruly fancy is too strange for them to believe. Hence, to hear them talk, one would think that they are constantly in touch with the devil, and that they have seen it hundreds of times."[1] For the word "devil" substitute those vaguely defined spirits we have just been considering, and Father Jetté's description fully agrees with the many others which insist upon the presence of more or less diffuse mystic forces everywhere in the primitive's world.

III

Speaking of a Bantu tribe, a careful observer tells us "It is of the utmost importance for students of the sociology of these people to try and realize the reality and closeness of the influence of the ancestral spirits upon the daily life of the native, and unless an ethnologist has been in daily contact with the people, and striven to understand their point of view, it is difficult for the weight of this to be felt to a full extent."[2]

We might say the same about most inferior races. The Jesuit Fathers of New France often laid stress upon the position which the dead occupied in the minds of the Indians. And Codrington, when remarking on the Melanesian languages, expresses the same idea in a striking way. "When a native says that he is a man, he means that he is a man and not a beast. The intelligent agents in this world are to his mind the men who are alive, and the ghosts, the men who are dead, the *ta-maur* and the *ta-mate* of Motu. . . . When white men first appear to Melanesians they are taken for ghosts, dead men come back ; when white men ask the natives what *they* are, they proclaim themselves to be men, not ghosts."[3]

In the same way, among the Chiriguanos of South America, when two men meet, they exchange the following greeting : "Are you alive ? " "Yes, I am alive." And the author

[1] Fr. Jetté : "On the Medicine-men of the Tena," *J.A.I.*, xxxvii. p. 159.
[2] C. W. Hobley : "Further Researches into Kikuya and Kamba Religious Beliefs and Customs," *J.A.I.*, xli. p. 432.
[3] R.H. Codrington : *Melanesian Languages*, pp. 82–8 (1891) : cf. R. H. Codrington : *The Melanesians*, p. 21.

adds : " Other South American tribes have the same way of addressing each other, e.g. the Caingua, who are also Guaranis. " [1]

In short, as I have shown in another place, the dead are alive, at least for a certain time ; they are living beings of a different kind from ourselves, beings in whom certain participations are ruptured or at least impaired, but who only by slow degrees cease to belong to their social group. To understand the primitives' mentality, we must first of all rid our minds of our own idea of death and the dead, and try to replace it by that which dominates their collective representations.

In the first place, the moment of death is not the same to them as it is to us. We believe that death takes place when the heart ceases to beat and the breathing stops entirely. Most inferior races, however, hold that death takes place at the moment when the tenant of the body, which has certain traits in common with what we call the soul, definitely leaves it, even if the physical life has not yet become extinct. That is one of the reasons which explain the hasty burials which are so common. In the Fiji Islands, " the process of laying out is often commenced several hours before the person is actually dead. I have known one take food afterwards ; and a second who lived for another eighteen hours. All this time, in the opinion of a Fijian, the man was dead. Eating, drinking, and talking, he says, are the involuntary actions of the body—of the empty shell as he calls it, the soul having taken its departure." [2]

Nassau has heard the negroes of West Africa talk in a similar fashion. " It has frequently occurred that even intelligent natives, standing by me at the side of a dying person, have said to me : ' He is dead.' The patient was indeed unconscious, lying stiff, not seeing, speaking, eating or apparently feeling ; yet there was a slight heartbeat. I would point out to the relatives these evidences of life. But they said : ' No, he is dead. His spirit is gone, he does

---

[1] " Domenico del Campana. Notizie intorno ad Ciriguani." *Archivio per l'antropologia*, xxxii. p. 100 (1902).

[2] Th. Williams : *Fiji and the Fijians*, p. 161 (1858) ; cf. p. 195. The wives of a chief are strangled whilst he is still alive, in order that they may follow him to death.

not see, nor hear, nor feel; that slight movement is only the spirit of the body shaking itself. It is not a person, it is not our relative ; *he* is dead.' And they began to prepare the body for burial. A man actually came to me on Corisco Island in 1863 asking me for medicine with which to kill or quiet the body-spirit of his mother, whose motions were troubling him by preventing the funeral arrangements." [1]

In any case, if the soul has definitely left the body and death has taken place, the dead man is not separated from his relatives on that account. On the contrary, he remains near his body, and the care which they bestow upon his mortal remains is inspired by the feeling of his presence, and the risk that would be run if he were not treated according to the customary rites.

With certain primitive peoples, it is not permissible to bury dead persons not belonging to the social group, in the soil which it owns. " Their creed forbids," says Pechuël-Loesche, "that the stranger should be buried in the locality, for by doing this they would be giving his soul a home, and who knows what it might not do ? " [2] And he tells the story of a Portuguese, who, by way of exception, had been buried in Loango ; whereupon there had been a period of drought, and the body was exhumed and thrown into the sea. In the story told by Cavazzi, the veracity of which has so often been questioned, we find a similar feature. " The faithful were desirous of interring a missionary within the church itself, but certain heathens who up to that moment had concealed their lack of faith, opposed this so strongly that the king himself, fearing the defection of the others, considered it wiser to dissimulate . . . and the body was thrown into the sea." [3] In the Ashanti country, the king conceals the death of the child of a missionary whom he has imprisoned. " In order to prevent disaster in his country, this superstitious king, not desiring to have a white person buried near his dwelling, had the child embalmed, so that he could restore it to its parents when he set them free." [4] A Kafir chief, desiring to express his attachment to a missionary

[1] Rev. R. H. Nassau : *Fetichism in West Africa*, pp. 53-4 (edit. of 1904).
[2] Dr. Pechuël-Loesche : *Die Loango Expedition*, iii. 2, pp. 210-11.
[3] Cavazzi : *Istoria descrizione de'tre regni di Congo, Matamba ed Angola*, p. 569.   [4] *Missions évangéliques*, xlv. p. 280 (1870).

who refused to leave the country, and to thank him for this, said to him : " You must die here ; and if your bones whiten here, you will be asked for—a man never dies without being inquired for." [1] That means, you belong to us, you are part of our social group, which needs you, and naturally after your death you will form a part of it as you do now.

It is so much the more necessary to render the customary dues to those just dead because they are, as a·rule, evil-disposed and ready to do harm to the survivors. It matters little that they have been kindly and amiable when alive. In their new state their disposition is quite otherwise ; they are irritable and vindictive, perhaps because they are un-happy, weak, and suffering, while their bodies are decomposing. Thus, " Ouasinpareo was one of those men who have such a happy disposition that they live peaceably with everybody. According to the natives, he had never killed anyone, and if he had eaten human flesh, his spear had never dealt the victim his death-blow. What conclusion did the savages draw from that ? Exactly the opposite of what would have occurred to our minds. They thought that Ouasinpareo, having been kindly during his life, would necessarily be malicious after death. Events confirmed this superstition of theirs, for two or three natives, overcome by age and disease, died shortly after him. ' You see,' said the natives to us, ' how bad Ouasinpareo has become ?' And immediately the two priests in the district made it their duty to chase to the open sea the *ataro*, phantom, soul, spirit of Ouasinpareo, which, they said, was prowling about the shore." [2] In the same island, the Pia would never consent to the burial, in their midst, of a missionary who had died of illness. The reason they adduced was that his *ataro*, never having killed anybody during his lifetime, would be certain to slay several people after death ! [3] In British New Guinea, " the intentions of the ghost towards living humanity are always evil, and his visits are feared by the people." [4]

[1] Letter from Rev. Gladwin Butterworth, Kaffraria, *Wesleyan Missionary Notices*, ix. p. 192 (1851).
[2] L. Verguet : *Histoire de la première mission catholique au vicariat de Melanésie (San Christobal)*, p. 154.
[3] Ibid., p. 281 (note).
[4] R. W. Williamson : *The Mafulu Mountain People of British New Guinea*, p. 269 (1912).

The same belief obtains in West Africa. " No matter how well-disposed a person has been in this existence, and in spite of the fact that he is regarded as a good spirit, it is recognized that unless, on the one hand, he is propitiated by his people, and on the other, pleased with the behaviour or attitude of his people towards himself, he is quite capable, not only of neglecting, but of injuring their interests." [1] And among the Bana of the Cameroons, " however good the dead man had been whilst alive, as soon as he is dead his soul thinks of nothing but doing harm." [2]

The malevolent influence of the ghost may be exercised in a hundred different ways. The survivors have a special dread that he will try to carry off one or more of them with him ; he feels lonely and forsaken ; he misses his own friends, and therefore wants to have them near him. Should one of them just at this time fall ill and die, all know whence this fresh blow comes. Moreover, those recently dead have a mystic influence on all natural phenomena, and especially on those which are the chief concern of the social group. " Physical phenomena (as heavy storms), when taking place about the time when a person dies, or is being buried, are regarded as being caused by the deceased person ; hence, when a storm threatens to break during the funeral festivities of a man, the people present will call the beloved child of the deceased . . . to stop the rain. The lad steps forward towards the horizon where the storm is rising, and says : ' Father, let us have fine weather during your funeral cere-monies.' " [3] " A few hours after the death of a young man whom I knew, a furious storm broke on the town, blow-ing down plaintain trees and working great havoc in the farms. It was stated in all seriousness by the old folk that the storm had been sent by the spirit of Mopembe——the lad's name." [4]

Therefore, when the funeral rites are not performed as they ought to be for the one who has just died, he is able to punish the whole tribe. He can prevent the rain from falling, and

[1] Major A. G. Leonard : *The Lower Niger and Its Tribes*, p. 187 (1906).
[2] G. von Hagen : "*Die Bana*," Bässler-Archiv, ii. p. 109 (1911).
[3] Rev. J. H. Weeks : " Anthropological Notes on the Bangala of the Upper Congo River," *J.A.I.*, xl. p. 383.
[4] Ibid., p. 373.

reduce the survivors to a state of despair. This results in inevitable conflicts with the missionaries, who are anxious to put a stop to these pagan practices. Here is a characteristic example. " A female member of our society, on embracing Christianity, had been put away by her heathen husband, and for some years they lived in a state of separation from each other, he having another wife, with whom he lived till his death. . . . No sooner had this event occurred, than the master of the kraal to which the man belonged laid hold of the woman, and compelled her, in common with the other wife, to undergo a heathenish process, which is deemed necessary to appease the wrath of some imaginary being who, if not thus propitiated, would be sure to revenge himself by withholding the necessary supplies of corn next season." The missionary intervened. " The old persecutor, . . . so far from making any concession, persisted in asserting that he was only doing what he considered necessary to conserve the interests of the Baralong nation." [1]

IV

At all costs, therefore, the ghost must be placated. His demands vary according to the race to which he belongs, and his place in the social group. In the case of a child of tender years, a slave, a woman of the people, a poor devil of no consequence, a young man not yet initiated, the ghost remains after death much what the living being was, and nobody troubles much about it. Those who cared for the living mourn the dead, but nobody is afraid of such as these. The medicine-men, chiefs, fathers of families, old men who are still active and revered, however—in short, all important people, are far from ceasing to be important when they die. To the influence which the dead man exercised by virtue of his own power, his personal *mana*, must be added the mysterious and tremendous effect produced by his condition as a ghost. He can do much to harm the living, but they can do nothing, or next to nothing, to him. There is no doubt that in certain communities they do sometimes try

[1] Letter from Rev. James Cameron : *Wesleyan Missionary Notices*, vi, January 1848.

to render him inocuous by mutilating his body, reducing it to a liquid state, chasing away or mislaying his spirit. But, as a general rule, it is considered wiser to act in such a way as to secure his favour, that is, to satisfy his requirements. " The chief reason why the native tries to acquit himself creditably in his funeral obligations often is his fear of provoking the malevolence of the dead, whose vengeance seems more formidable to him than that of a living enemy."[1]

Among the Australian aborigines, for example, and in a good many other uncivilized races, the relatives of the dead man, either to secure his favour, or merely to avert his wrath, have to find the man who " doomed " him, and put him to death also. If this rule were strictly followed, it would soon lead to the total extinction of the peoples in question. Considering their low birth-rate, and the great mortality among children, if every adult death were necessarily followed by one or more others, the social groups would soon be reduced to nothing. In reality, it is only the deaths of really important persons which are thus avenged, and in certain cases this vengeance is a mere formality. Spencer and Gillen have described in great detail the Arunta punitive expeditions called *kurdaitcha*.[2] Very similar ones are to be found elsewhere. But the men who have taken part in them often return to camp without having killed anyone. No formal explanation of this is either asked or vouchsafed. The women and the other members of the group are convinced that the requisite satisfaction has been obtained, and probably even those who have taken part in the expedition end by believing it also.

" Tradition," says Eylmann, " demands that every murder shall be avenged. I am convinced that this vengeance is but rarely effected, since as a rule there is a dread of arousing the hostility of the alleged murderer. Appearances must be saved, however. . . .When the warriors return without having touched a hair of the criminal's head, the dead man is obliged to consider himself appeased since, according to

---

[1] E. Eylmann : *Die Eingeborenen der Kolonie Süd Australien*, p. 227.
[2] Spencer and Gillen : *The Native Tribes of Central Australia*, pp. 476 et seq. (edit. of 1899).

all appearances, his relatives have done all that they could to avenge his death." [1]

Is it certain, we may ask, that the dead man does allow himself to be thus duped, and may not this fraud have disastrous consequences to those taking part in it ? As a matter of fact, the primitive mind does not perceive any real fraud in it. In certain cases, of course, it is the death of the guilty man alone that can completely satisfy his victim. Most frequently, however, the punitive expedition itself possesses a value and an effect that suffices, whether the criminal be put to death or not. It acts as a placatory rite, appeasing the dead man's resentment and consequently allaying the survivors' anxiety. This is what Taplin recognized. " Generally they cannot catch him" (the author of the crime) " and often they do not wish it. Arrangements are forthwith made for a pitched battle, and the two tribes meet in company with their respective allies. . . . If there is any other cause of animosity between the tribes . . . there will be a pretty severe fight with spears. If, however, the tribes have nothing but the dead man to fight about, they will probably throw a few spears, indulge in considerable abuse of each other, and then some of the old men will declare that enough has been done. The dead man is considered to have been appeased by the efforts of his friends to avenge his death by fighting, and the two tribes are friendly again. In such a case the fight is a mere ceremony." [2]

Missionaries in (German) New Guinea have clearly demonstrated the close relation subsisting between the ghost and his group, and the care taken by the survivors to satisfy him. " The neighbouring groups consider it their duty to visit the grave, and this visit serves at the same time as an assertion of their innocence. If the men of any village hold aloof, it is because their consciences are not clear." [3] As a matter of fact, witchcraft loses its power as soon as the wizard touches his victim ; he is therefore obliged to avoid the sick man's presence, and consequently he dare not show his sympathy

[1] Eylmann : *Die Eingeborenen, etc.*, p. 242.
[2] Rev. G. Taplin : *The Narrinyeri Tribe*, p. 21 (edit. of 1879).
[3] R. Neuhauss : *Deutsch Neu Guinea (The Neighbourhood of King William Cape)*, iii. pp. 258–9.

by visiting him. " When death has taken place, he cannot witness the funeral ceremonies because he would run the risk of being unmasked as the wizard. The Kai believe that as soon as his mortal enemy draws near, the corpse on his bier spits out the betel-nut placed between his lips, or gives some other sign of a similar nature. This explains the suspicions felt by the relatives of a dying or dead person, with regard to those who do not visit him when sick, or attend his funeral." [1]

" In any case, the survivors must at least let the wizard feel the weight of their anger. . . . Relatives who fail in this duty are punished by all kinds of misfortune. Their crops fail, their pigs and their dogs die, their teeth begin to decay. That is the vengeance of the departed spirit. The " little " spirit (for the Tami distinguish between a great and a little spirit) remains near the grave until worms have begun to destroy the body." [2] The native therefore has the most urgent reasons for placating the ghost, but it is only in the days which immediately succeed death that this fear is really active. By degrees, as time passes, he becomes reassured, and finally " it depends upon the dead man himself, whether the funeral ceremonies are prolonged or not. If he gets abundance of game from the hunters belonging to his village, the obsequies will last a long time. If he does not get any, or but a small amount, his memory is soon effaced. The bereaved partner can marry again : the funeral rites would not prevent that." [3] The essential thing is to avenge the death immediately it has taken place. " It is nearly always a death which causes wars among the Kai. To be able to live in peace, the wizard or wizards must be put to death, and all their relatives exterminated. The dead man's ghost demands vengeance ; if it is not forthcoming, his relatives will suffer for it. Not only will he deny them any success in the chase ; he will send wild boars to lay waste their fields, and will cause all kinds of misfortunes. If any troubles arise in the interval, if the rain fails, if sickness supervenes on account of chills, or if men should cut themselves, they recognize that the ghost is taking vengeance.

[1] R. Neuhauss: *Deutsch Neu Guinea* (*Kai*), iii. p. 134.
[2] Ibid. iii. p. 519.   [3] Ibid. (*Kai*), iii. p. 83.

Thus the native finds himself in a most embarrassing dilemma.
If the fear inspired by the vengeance of formidable spirits
were not stronger than his dread of man, if, moreover, he
were not attached to his most prized possessions and to his
pigs, the Papuan, at any rate the Kai, would never undertake a campaign." [1]

If he discovers, in a neighbouring tribe, the wizard who
has compassed the death, and kills him, a war will be the
result. He weighs very carefully beforehand the exact
amount of harm this can do him, and he makes his arrangements in full cognizance of the matter. If the dead man
should be incensed against him, however, everything is to
be feared ; whatever misfortunes the Papuan may have
anticipated, yet others may overwhelm him at the moment
when he least expects them. Evil for evil, he prefers the
one which is both known and definite, and all the more
because, if his plans are to succeed, the active assistance of
the ghost is indispensable.

Similarly, at Bougainville, " it is above all the spirits
of the dead who intervene in men's lives to help or injure
them. Therefore men appeal to their ancestors for support . . .
they present them with offerings, sacrifice to them, and so
on." [2]

Perham, a careful investigator of the Dyaks of Borneo,
has shown how close is the brotherhood uniting the living
and the dead, and the mutual services they render each
other. " The dead are believed to build houses, make paddy
farms, and go through all the drudgery of a labouring life,
and to be subject to the same inequalities of condition and
of fortune as the living are here. And as men help each
other in life, so death, they think, need not cut asunder the
bond of mutual interchange of kindly service ; they can
assist the dead with food and other necessaries ; and the
dead can be equally generous in bestowing upon them
medicines of magical virtue, amulets, and talismans of a
kind to help them in the work of life." [3]

In this passage, Perham notes that the dead form a

[1] R. Neuhauss: *Deutsch Neu Guinea (Kai)*, pp. 62–3.
[2] R. Thurnwald : " Im Bismarck Archipel und auf den Salomo Inseln,"
Zeitschrift für Ethnologie, xlii. pp. 132–3.
[3] H. Ling Roth : *Natives of Sarawak*, i. p. 213.

community just like the living, and that between them there is an interchange of mutual service, each having need of the other. But then it is a case of the dead who are thoroughly established in their new state, all the funeral rites having been duly carried out. In the transition period which the dead man goes through, starting from the moment when life ceases, he makes special demands, among the Dyaks as well as in other races. To these the living cannot turn a deaf ear, for fear of inciting his anger and drawing down great misfortunes upon themselves.

That is, as we know, one of the reasons for the head-hunting which is so common in Borneo and the adjacent regions. Like the Kai of New Guinea, the native is faced by a dilemma. He must either bring back, from an expedition undertaken for the purpose, one or more heads, or he must submit to the dead man's vengeance, which will fall, not on himself alone, but upon his relatives and all the members of his group, and like the Kai, he will choose the lesser of two evils. Here is a characteristic example. " On one occasion Lingir, a chief of one of the Sareta tribes, appeared at Sarawak with his head shaved, and in his most desolate and ragged attire, but attended by thirty-three boats, to request permission of the Rajah to attack the Dyaks of Lundu or Samarhand ; he gave as his reason for the strange request that his brother had died, and that he could not celebrate his funeral until he had somehow obtained a head. . . . Lingir, of course, was unsuccessful in his application to Sarawak, and being desired to return immediately with his fleet, he captured the heads of four unfortunate fishermen, with whom he fell in, on his return." [1] This chief was not unaware that if the Rajah were informed of this fact—which was more than probable—he would have to answer for his deed, and that things might turn out very uncomfortably for him, but he preferred to run the risk of this rather than go back home without having procured what was absolutely necessary to satisfy his dead brother's ghost.

A similar custom seems to have existed in the Cameroons. " The death of chiefs," says Mansfeld, "seems formerly

[1] Hugh Low : *Sarawak*, pp. 215–16 (edit. of 1896).

to have given rise to a kind of guerilla warfare. When an old chief died in a village which we will call A, two or three men went to a village, B, about three leagues away, and lying in ambush, killed (without any provocation whatever) two men of the village, returning home with their skulls. Naturally the people of B took their revenge." [1]

In communities which are rather more civilized than the preceding, such as the Bantus and other South African tribes, for instance, the relations between the living and the dead are no less close, but they appear to be better organized, and they tend to create a kind of ancestor-worship, although, strictly speaking, its practice differs in some important points from what we know as such.

The dead are alive, there is no doubt of that. " What are you doing here ? " asks Hahn of a Namaqua woman he meets on the veld.—" My friend," she replies, ' do not laugh at me. I am in distress ; through the drought and the Bushmen we have lost a large number of sheep and cattle, and I am going to the grave of my father who died out hunting. I am going to weep and pray there ; he will hear my voice and see my tears, and then he will assist my husband, who has gone to hunt ostriches. Then we shall be able to buy goats and cows again, and give our children something to eat.'

" ' But your father is dead,' said I, ' how can he hear you ? ' ' It is true that he is dead,' she answered, ' but he is only sleeping. When we Hottentots are in distress we always go and pray at the graves of our relatives and ancestors ; that is one of our most ancient customs.' " [2]

Who are these living dead ? It is extremely difficult, almost impossible, for us to form any satisfactory idea of them. The representations vary in different communities, according to their constitution and the degree of civilization they have attained. Moreover, almost everywhere we find that the person who has just died passes more or less rapidly through a series of transitory states before he arrives at a

---

[1] A. Mansfeld : *Urwald Dokumente. Vier Jahre unter den Crossflussnegern Kameruns*, p. 158.
[2] Th. Hahn : *Tsuni Goam*, pp. 112–13.

comparatively definite condition, whence he will emerge, either by a fresh death, or by a return to the land of the living. These representations will very often prove irreconcilable ; we know that the emotions enter very largely into them, that primitive mentality troubles very little about logical coherence, and finally, nowhere do we find any collections of representations which are coeval and constitute a system. On the contrary, everything leads us to think that some of them are extremely ancient, and others, more or less compatible with these, have been built up on these foundations in the course of the centuries. Those which we ascertain as existing to-day are a kind of amalgam, a residue, as difficult for us to analyse as is the stratification of a terrain of which we know the surface only.

The profound obscurity thus surrounding the very nature of these representations is increased by the action of the investigators who make these observations. They collect them with preconceived ideas about the after-life and the immortality of the soul. They do not suspect the difference between our conceptual thought and the thought of primitives, which is but slightly so ; and their observations, thus perverted, remain in any case incomplete, and often worthless. The word " soul " and the current ideas about " the relation between the soul and the body " cause inextricable confusion.

Since the law of participation governs the representations relating to the intercourse between the living and the dead, the latter are present as well as absent in, and solidary with, though independent of, the decaying body ; the ghost, a few days after death, is to be found both in his grave in the neighbourhood of the house he died in, as well as on the way to the place of shadows, if he has not already arrived there.

Those who, when living, held high rank, and carried out important functions continue to do so after their death, although they may have been succeeded in office. In many Bantu tribes, for instance, dead chiefs still protect their group when necessity arises ; they secure for it, as they formerly did, the required rain and the regular change of seasons. Frequently they remain the owners of their cattle, which cannot be taken away from them, and special guards are assigned to the flocks and herds. They are followed into the other world by a certain number of their wives and their slaves, by objects stamped with their personality, and so forth. In a general way the dead, in varying degrees, form an integral part of the social group, and the individual member does not feel himself entirely separated from them. He has duties with respect to them, and in these he finds as little to wonder about as in those that bind him to the living.

The Mossi of the Niger have symbolized in a very striking way this continual presence of the dead man in his social group. From the moment of death until the final obsequies, someone has to represent the dead man, and to undertake the part he played when in the flesh. "Every Mossi who dies a natural death, whether it be man, woman, child, or chief, survives in the person of the *kourita*. In the case of a married man, the *kourita* or *koutoarsa* (who imitates the deceased) is a woman belonging to his family, usually the wife of one of his younger brothers, who bears a certain resemblance to the dead man. She is selected by the family, sometimes even by the dying man. She takes the dead man's clothes, his blanket, his hat, his old shoes, his bangles and his rings; she wears his belt and his hunting-knives, bears about his staff, his pick-axe, and his *doré*; she carries his assegai, point downwards. She walks like the man she is representing, and tries to imitate him in everything; she continues his life in the midst of his family. If the dead man was usually accompanied by a child carrying his saddle-bag, the *kourita* will have her child following her, and carrying the same saddlebag, but turned inside out. If the deceased was leprous, and had lost his fingers, she will behave as if she had none; if he loved laughter, she will laugh; if he was a grumbler and always wrangling, she will not change his disposition. The dead man's children will call her father, the wives will claim her as their husband and prepare the mealie-bowl for her. If the deceased was a *naba* (chief) they will call her *naba*; if not, they will give her the name that belonged to him.

"She will continue to act thus until the day of the *kouri*

(the second part of the funeral ceremonies). On that day she shaves her head like the other members of the family, and her part is over. She retains the name of *kourita*, however, and when the dead man's things are divided she receives a garment in exchange for his clothes, which she returns ; if the heir is generous and the inheritance allows of it, she may receive some cattle, sometimes a child. The *kourita* will now die sooner than if she had not carried out this rôle, they say, because the shades of dead ancestors will come and fetch her ; therefore the performance of this part is seldom sought after." [1] Thus, as long as the Mossi is not definitely separated from his group by the performance of the final obsequies, the survivors see him, and he finds himself in ordinary intercourse with them in the person of the *kourita*. It is the real presence of the invisible made visible.

Callaway, who has left us such valuable documents respecting the Zulu beliefs, admits that " their theory is not very consistent with itself nor very intelligible. . . . They say the shadow—that evidently cast by the body—is that which will ultimately become the *itongo* or spirit when the body dies. In order to ascertain that this was really the meaning, I asked, ' Is the shadow which my body casts when I am walking, my spirit ? ' The reply was ' No, it is not your *itongo* or spirit ' (evidently understanding me to mean by " my spirit " an ancestral guardian spirit watching over me and not my own spirit), ' but it will be the *itongo* or ancestral spirit for your children when you are dead.' They say that the long shadow shortens as a man approaches his end, and contracts into a very little one. When they see the shadow of a man thus contracting, they know he will die. The long shadow goes away when the man is dead ; and it is that which is meant when it is said ' The shadow has departed.' There is a short shadow which remains with the corpse and is buried with it. The long shadow becomes an *itongo* or a spirit." [2]

It is of the first importance to know how the *itongo* is

[1] P. Eugène Mangin, P. B. " Les Mossi," *Anthropos*, xi. pp. 732-3 (1914).
[2] Rev. C. H. Callaway : *The Religious System of the Amazulu*, p. 126 (note) (1868). Cf. The long and the short spirits of the New Guinea Papuans, in Neuhauss : *Deutsch Neu Guinea*, iii. p. 518.

disposed towards the survivors. The ordinary honours have been paid to the dead, his obsequies have been conducted in accordance with the customary rites—if the *itongo* gives no sign of life, the survivors are uneasy and try to find the reason for this silence. Most frequently, however, the *itongo* does give some sign of satisfaction to his relatives, either by dreams in which they behold him, or by showing himself to them in the form of a snake creeping into the house. These *itongo* snakes are very different from others. " Those which are men are known by their frequenting huts, and by their not eating mice, and by their not being frightened at the noise of men ; they are always observed not to be afraid of the shadow of a man ; neither does the snake that is an *itongo* excite fear in men, and there is no feeling of alarm as though there was a wild beast in the house ; but there is a happy feeling, and it is felt that the chief of the village has come." [1]

" They wait impatiently for the presence of these reassuring snakes. If a snake is observed on the grave, the man who went to look at the grave says on his return: ' Oh, I have seen him to-day basking in the sun on the top of the grave.' So then if the snake does not come home, or if they do not dream of the dead, they sacrifice an ox or a goat, and it is said he is brought back . . . home. And if they do not dream of him, though the snake has come home, they are troubled and ask ' How did this man die ? We do not see him, his *itongo* is dark.' " (There is a suspicion of witchcraft). " They go to a ' doctor,' if he is the chief man of a large village, but nothing is done for the poor." [2]

The trouble taken to retain connection with the *itongo* is thus clearly shown, and this trouble is prompted by the feeling of power possessed by the spirit—a power upon which the health, prosperity, and the very life of the inhabitants of the village depend. As we have just seen, every ghost is not an *itongo*. The *amahlosi* do not all of them become *amatongo*, but only those who are dead chiefs ; in the world of spirits the *itongo* occupies a rank which is superior to

---

[1] Rev. C. H. Callaway : *The Religious System of the Amazulu*, pp. 198–9.
[2] Ibid., pp. 141–3 ; cf. Dr. Wangemann : *Die Berliner Mission im Zulu-lande*, p. 17.

ordinary *ihlosi*.   In addition to the *amatongo*, who are common
to the tribe, each family has its special *itongo*.   " Our father,
whom we know," say they, " is our whole life."   He is regarded
as a kind of tutelary genius of the family.[1]   If it migrates,
and the *itongo* does not show himself in the new home, they
have to go and look for him.   They break off a branch of
the wild mulberry-tree, and carry it to the old home.   There
they offer a sacrifice, and sing the *itongo's* favourite song,
that he may say to himself : ' Of a truth my children feel
themselves forsaken, because I do not go with them ! '
Then they drag the mulberry-branch along the ground to
the new home, hoping that the *itongo* may follow its track,
or else explain in a dream why he does not come." [2]

Whatever the honour and consideration which the living
may lavish on their *itongo*, he must remain worthy of it,
however.   If he neglects to secure their prosperity, and
misfortune overtakes them, they will first of all redouble
their appeals for help ; but later on their tone changes,
and they tell the *itongo* the naked truth.   " Their father
is a great treasure to them even when he is dead.   Those
of his children who are already grown up know him thoroughly,
his gentleness and his bravery.   And if there is illness in
the village, the eldest son lauds him with the laud-giving
names he gained when fighting with the enemy, and at the
same time lauds all the other *amatongo*. . . . The son reproves
the father, saying : ' We for our parts may just die.   Who
are you looking after ?   Let us die, all of us, that we may
see into whose house you will enter.   You will eat grass-
hoppers, you will no longer be invited to come anywhere,
if you destroy your own village.' " [3]

In the Kafir's eyes nothing is more precious than his
cattle.   He retains possession of them after his death, and
if he thinks that folks are not giving him all the honour due
to him, he can take his revenge by inflicting all sorts of
misfortunes on the cattle, and even on men themselves. . . .
" Thus, to the Zulu, side by side with the world of sense, there
exists a world of spirits, which he imagines as continuing

[1] Dr. Wangemann : *Die Berliner Mission im Zululande*, p. 16.
[2] Ibid., pp. 17–18.
[3] Rev. C. H. Callaway : *The Religious System of the Amazulu*, p. 145.

to live in close connection with the former, and which he fears all the more because these spirits, though unassailable by men, have the power of doing them harm at all times. For the world of spirits, therefore, the Zulu has the feelings which a superior force inspires, and he serves them because he fears them, although his language about them, even the way he addresses them, is not always very respectful." [1]

Similar ideas and beliefs are found in Central and Western Africa. I will give a few examples only. Among the Adio of the Upper Congo, the dead man makes his wishes known by means of a dream. "From the moment the sleeper awakes, the claims of the departed must be satisfied, everything else being postponed, otherwise all sorts of accidents and mischance will occur. People will break all the vessels or utensils they want to make use of ; if they desire to make beer, for instance, it will go bad ; if they are trying to cook something, their pots will break, and so on."

"Some ghosts, in order to show themselves to their living relatives, will take on the form of a large, but harmless snake called *rumbo*. This snake is visible only to the relative to whom the deceased wishes to appear, and this appearance always occurs near the grave." [2] In Dahomey, "the son is constantly united in thought with his deceased parents. He speaks to them every day and asks their protection. Should any misfortune befall him, he hastens to them and tries to enlist them on his side by the offerings he brings to their tombs. They will listen favourably to his entreaties and will intervene for him with the Great Master common to them all." [3]

Here is a circumstance noted in a Bantu tribe in East Africa, which shows how closely the interests of the living are intermingled with those of the dead, and their effect upon each other. "If a young unmarried man is killed away from his village, his *muimu* or spirit will return there and speak to the people through the medium of an old

[1] Dr. Wangemann : op. cit., pp. 14–15.
[2] A. Hutereau : " Notes sur la vie familiale et juridique de quelques populations du Congo belge," *Annales du Musée du Congo belge*, Série III. *Documents ethnographiques*, i. p. 50.
[3] A. Le Hérissé : *L'ancien royaume du Dahomey*, pp. 99–100.

woman in a dance and say: ' I am So-and-so speaking, and
I want a wife.' The youth's father will then make arrangements to buy a girl from another village, and bring her to
his, and she will be mentioned as the wife of the deceased. . . .
She will presently be married to the brother of the deceased,
but she must continue to live in the village where the deceased had his home.

" If at any time the corporeal husband beats or ill-treats
her, and she in consequence runs away to her father, the
muimu of the deceased will come and pester the people of
the village and they will have bad luck; it will probably
ask, through the usual medium, why his wife has been ill-
treated and driven away. The head of the family will
then take steps to induce the wife to return for fear of the
wrath of the spirit of the deceased son." [1] The latter,
therefore, present though invisible, takes part in all that
occurs among the living. When his wife is ill-treated by the
corporeal husband who has been given her, it is not upon him
alone that the ghost will take vengeance. The consequences
of such a misdeed threaten to react upon the entire social
group, and its chief hastens to avert them by endeavouring
to satisfy the dead man. The solidarity of the group is
such that at any moment its prosperity may depend upon
the conduct of one or another of its members with respect
to the dead.

It may happen that a ghost's wishes are unreasonable. In
such a case the survivors do not consider themselves bound
to defer to them. " If a spirit were to come saying: ' I
want calico,' his friends would just say that he was mad, and
would not give it. ' Why should he want calico? What would
he do with it? There was calico buried with him when he
died, and he cannot need more again.' But if the request
is at all reasonable (as when an old hunter asks animal food)
it will be quickly attended to, and personal taste carefully
consulted. . . . If a spirit asks a house, they will build him
one." [2]

---

[1] C. W. Hobley: " Further Researches into Kikuyu and Kamba Beliefs
and Customs," *J.A.I.*, xli. p. 422 (1911).
[2] Rev. Duff Macdonald: *Africana*, i. p. 94.

V

Besides those who have recently died and the dead whose memory is still green, whose features, disposition, and habits the survivors recall, with whom they converse in dreams, and even (if Miss Kingsley is to be believed) when wide awake, we have to take into account those more distant dead who disappeared long ago from among the living, but who nevertheless exercise considerable influence upon their fate. Meinhof has rightly laid stress upon the gradual transformation of ghosts into ancestors. " After a certain time the soul loses its human characteristics more and more, and becomes a spirit. Then these spirits become the object of actual adoration, and are represented as friendly or inimical according to their disposition. To the native of Eastern Africa this fusion of spirits in mass becomes a terrible force which inspires him with surpassing dread. The Schambala call it *muzimu*. This *muzimu* does not possess a personality like a man, nor is it the spirit of any particular man ; it is the power which is the source of all misfortunes, a power which it is imperative to placate." [1]

The Wachaga tribe define this distinction very explicitly. In their *kirengo* (a kind of catechism taught to the young men who have recently been circumcized), the eighth chapter treats of " unknown " dead chiefs, and the tenth refers to those who are known. " When Kizaro is no longer known to anyone, the circle containing his name is deleted from chapter ten, and inserted in the chapter which relates to the unknown chiefs. This custom has a bearing on the religious beliefs of the Wachagas. The souls of the dead, say they, remain in the land as long as there are any persons who have known them and who, on that account, offer sacrifices to their manes ; but when the manes no longer have any friend on earth who sacrifices to them, they withdraw from the district, and go and inhabit a strange and unknown country." [2]

It would be difficult to over-estimate the importance of these ancestors to the daily life of many of the Bantu tribes. " Our ancestors see us," say the natives. " They

[1] C. Meinhof : *Afrikanische Religionen*, pp. 39–40.
[2] P. E. Meyer, C.S. Sp. : " Le Kirengo des Wachaga, peuplade bantoue du Kilimandjaro," *Anthropos*, xii–xiii, pp. 190–1.

behold all that we do ; if we are bad, and do not faithfully observe the traditions they bequeathed us, they send us the *kombo*. *Kombo* means famine, warfare, any unforeseen misfortune whatever." [1]

Of the complex feelings which ancestors inspire, fear is the predominating one. They are exacting, and one can never be sure of having satisfied them. In order that the prayers addressed to them may be heard, they must be supplemented by liberal offerings. Everything is done as if their good-will were purchasable. " The *marimo*," says another missionary, " are fairly often incensed against the living, and send disease, drought, famine and death to man and beast. Therefore they must be pacified, and their favour purchased by offerings. . . . Here is the prayer addressed by the Ba-Nkouma to their *suikwembo* (ancestral spirits) when presenting an offering—' O you, our former fathers and mothers, why do you say that we deprive you of food ? Here is the ox you want ; eat it, sharing it with our ancestors who died both before and after you ; with those whom we know and the others who are unknown to us.' (This is, in fact, the collective mass of ancestry, the nameless and impersonal spirit-fusion of which Meinhof speaks.) ' Give us life, give good things to us and our children, for you have left us on earth, and it is clear that we shall leave our children too. Why are you angry with us ? Why do you despise this village which is your own ? It was you who gave it us. Send away, we entreat you, all the evil spirits who cause us sufferings, all the bad colds, and all the illnesses. Here is the offering we bring you, and by means of it we present our supplication to you.' " [2]

Junod has clearly set forth the nature of the unvarying relations subsisting between the tribe and its ancestors These rest upon the principle of *do ut des*, allied with the feeling that a higher power dwells in the ancestors. They may be entreated, supplicated, cajoled, but they cannot effectively be compelled.

" Their goodwill secured by this offering, the gods (that

[1] P. Jeanneret : " Les Ma-Khaça," *Bulletin de la Société de Géographie de Neuchâtel*, viii. p. 138 (1895).
[2] E. Thomas : " Le Bokaha." (N.E. Transvaal). *Bulletin de la Société de Géographie de Neuchâtel*, viii. pp. 161-2, (1895).

is, the ancestors) will vouchsafe their descendants an abundant harvest (for it is they who cause the products of Nature to mature and ripen) ; they will authorize them to fell the trees, and then, when they fall, the mighty trunks will do no harm to anybody. . . . (If on the other hand they were to be cut down without the gods' permission, accidents would be sure to happen.) These sacrifices therefore are essentially preventive in their nature. By giving the manes something to eat, and *overwhelming them with presents*, it is possible to secure that events shall follow their customary course with success, and that no misfortune shall disturb established prosperity. . . . There are, too, *expiatory* sacrifices destined to appease the angry manes . . . sacrifices which aim at ending quarrels by reconciliation, etc." [1]

The prayers addressed to ancestors are often mingled with reproaches. These are given what they appear to demand, but they are made to feel that they ask too much and that, according to the familiar saying, folks get nothing for their money. This, for instance, is a prayer for a sick child. " You, our gods," (ancestors in general) " and you, So-and-So, (one particular ghost) " here is our *inhamba* (offering). Bless this child and make him live and grow ; make him rich, so that when we visit him, he may be able to kill an ox for us. . . . You are useless, you gods, you only give us trouble. For although we give you offerings, you do not listen to us ! We are deprived of everything ! You, So-and-so " (naming the god to whom the offering must be addressed, according to the order given by the *astragali*, that is, the god who is angry and has induced the other gods to do harm to the village by making the child ill), " you are full of hatred! You do not enrich us. All those who succeed, do so by the help of other gods ! Now we have made you this gift. . . . Call your ancestors, So-and-so, call also the gods of this sick boy's father, because his father's people did not steal his mother ; these people of such-and such a clan came in the daylight " (to pay the fair price for the wife). " So come here to the altar. Eat and distribute amongst yourselves our ox ! " (usually a hen).[2]

[1] H. A. Junod : *Les Ba-Ronga*, pp. 394–5.
[2] Ibid. : *The Life of a South African Tribe*, ii. p. 368.

The tone of this prayer is scarcely polite. Junod draws attention to the fact that as a rule these prayers do not show any very deep religious feeling, and that in any case they are absolutely lacking in respect. During the sacrifice " the natives laugh, speak in a loud voice, dance, sing obscene songs, even interrupt the priest with their remarks, and insult each other about family matters. The officiant himself sits on the seat designated by the bones, and speaks in a monotonous way, looking straight in front of him in utter indifference. There is nothing in his demeanour which denotes fear or even respect. If the gods were indeed real old people, still living, he could not address them with more familiarity." [1] But let misfortune come, let drought and famine afflict the country, and the supplications will become devout and humble. The familiarity with which ancestors are often treated, arises in part out of the constant communication the people have with them. They still form a part of the social group, whose prosperity and very life depend upon their good pleasure, and from whom they themselves receive food and presents. In this sense, then, they may be regarded as habitual visitants from another world. But to the Bantu, that other world cannot be distinguished from this one. The living appeal to their dead, and the dead need the living. In every individual consciousness the collective representations concerning the vicinity of these dead, their power, their influence on others, or on natural phenomena, are so constantly remembered and hold so important a place that they form a part of his very life.

VI

The all-pervading presence of spirits, witchcrafts, and enchantments ever threatening in the background, the dead so closely connected with the life of the living—this ensemble of representations is an inexhaustible source of emotion to the primitive, and it is to this that his mental activity owes its characteristic features. It is not only mystic, that is, at all times orientated to occult forces : it is not only pre-

[1] H. A. Junod : *The Life of a South African Tribe*, ii. p. 385.

logical, that is, indifferent as a rule to the law of contradiction: it is more than this; the causality it pictures to itself is of a type differing from that familiar to us, and this third characteristic is indissolubly bound up with the other two.

As we understand it, the connection between cause and effect necessarily unites phenomena in time, and conditions them in such a way that they are arranged in a series which cannot be reversed. Moreover, the series of causes and effects are prolonged and intermingled to infinity. All the phenomena of the universe, as Kant says, have universally reciprocal influence; but however complex the system may be, the certainty we have that these phenomena are always arranged in causal series, is the very foundation, to our minds, of the order of the universe, and, in short, of experience.

The primitive's mind views the matter very differently, however. All, or nearly all that happens, is referred by him, as we have just seen, to the influence of mystic or occult powers, such as wizards, ghosts, spirits, etc. In acting thus, his mind doubtless obeys the same mental instinct as that which guides us. But instead of both cause and effect being perceptible in time and nearly always in space, as in our case, primitive mentality admits only one of the two conditions to be perceptible at one time; the other belongs to the sum-total of those entities which are invisible and imperceptible to sense.

It is true that to the primitive's mind the latter are no less real and no less directly perceptible than the former, and this very fact is one of the characteristics peculiar to his mentality; but the causal connection between these two heterogeneous conditions will differ profoundly from that which we should imagine it to be. One of these conditions—that which we call cause—has no visible link with the beings and the circumstances of the world perceived by sense. It is extra-spatial, and consequently, in one aspect at least, extra-temporal. It does undoubtedly precede its effect; it will be the resentment felt by a dead man, for instance, that will cause him to inflict such-and-such a disaster upon the survivors. But, nevertheless, the fact that the mystic forces which are " causes," remain invisible and imperceptible to ordinary observation, makes it impossible to fix them in time and in space, and often does not allow of their being individualized. As visitants from an inaccessible region they float around, they radiate, so to speak ; they surround on all sides the primitive, who finds nothing extraordinary in feeling them to be present in several places at the same time. The world of experience thus formed in the primitive mind may appear richer than ours, as I have already remarked, not only because this experience comprises elements which ours does not contain, but also because its constitution is different. To primitive mentality these mystic elements seem to involve a supplementary dimension unknown to us, not exactly a spatial dimension, but rather a dimension of the sum-total of experience. It is this peculiar quality of experience which allows primitives to regard as quite simple and natural, forms of causation which we cannot imagine.

To prelogical mentality, cause and effect present themselves in two forms, not essentially different from one another. Sometimes the collective representations impose a definite preconnection ; for example, if a certain taboo is infringed, a certain misfortune will be the result, or inversely, if such-and-such a misfortune supervenes, it is because such-and-such a taboo has been violated. Or again, the fact which is apparent may be related to a mystic cause in a general way ; an epidemic is raging, and it may be due to the wrath of ancestors, or the evil work of a wizard ; this can be ascertained, either by divination, or by making the persons suspected of witchcraft submit to trial by ordeal. In either case there is a direct relation between cause and effect. It admits of no intermediate links, or at any rate, if it does recognize them, it regards them as negligible, and pays no heed to them.

When we say that a death has been caused by poisoning, we imagine a number of phenomena which have followed in definite order upon the introduction of poison into the system. In the body it will have acted, for example, on a certain tissue, certain digestive organs ; this action will have reacted on the nerve-centres ; then the respiratory organs will have become involved, etc., until finally the whole of the physiological functioning will be found to have ceased. To the primitive mind, if the poison proves effective, it is solely because the victim has been " doomed." It is between death on the one hand and the fatal influence of witchcraft on the other that the connection is established, and all the intermediary phenomena are quite unimportant. They are only produced by the will and, above all, by the power of the magician. Had he desired it, they might have been quite different. It is not even a process that he sets in motion. The idea of such a process, which would necessarily develop from a given moment, involves a clear conception of the determinism of certain phenomena, and primitive mentality has no such conception. Its place is supplied by the representation of obedient and docile agents, such as the crocodile which carries off the victim pointed out by the witch. It is certain that the crocodile is going to carry him off, but this is not because the man has exposed himself imprudently to the animal's attack. On the contrary, according to the primitive, if the crocodile were not acting as the witch's agent, it would do the man no harm.

In the same way paralysis, acute pain, and even death produced by poisoning, are by no means the necessary effect of the poison in the body, but the means chosen by mystic powers to slay their victim.

We now perceive the fundamental reason which accounts for the primitive's indifference towards the search for secondary causes. His mind is accustomed to a type of causality which obscures, as it were, the network of such causes. While these constitute the links and chains which stretch throughout time and space, the mystic causes to which primitive mentality nearly always turns, being extra-spatial and even at times extra-temporal, exclude the very idea of such links and chains. Their influence can only be direct. Even if it be produced at a distance (as so often happens in cases of witchcraft), and if its effect is not perceived till after a certain lapse of time, it nevertheless does not fail to be represented—or, to put it more accurately, to be felt— as producing itself without any intermediary.

The connection (which is altogether mystic) and most frequently we must add, the preconnection, links the occult power to the effect produced, however distant this may be. The question *how* it does this, hardly ever presents itself to a mind of this kind. At the same time, the direct nature of mystic causality equals, and even goes beyond, what we call evidence, whether it be of the senses, or rational or intuitive. The very essence of a preconnection is to be unquestioned and incontestable. When natives find Europeans refusing to believe in it, they pity them, or else they recognize that what means a good deal to themselves means nothing to white people. A very sound conclusion, but not in the sense in which they mean it.

The predominance of this kind of mystic and direct causality in their minds helps to give their mentality as a whole, the characteristics which make it so difficult for us to enter into their thought. For evidently time and space are not exactly the same to them as they are to us—I mean to us in daily life, and not in philosophic or scientific thought. Can we imagine what our familiar idea of time would be if we were not accustomed to consider phenomena as bound together in the relation of cause and effect ?

It is because to us these phenomena are arranged, without our having to think about them at all, in series which cannot be reversed, with definite and measurable intervals between them ; it is because effects and causes appear to us as if arranged in order in surrounding space, that time, too, seems to us to be a homogeneous quantum, divisible into parts which are identical with each other, and which succeed each other with perfect regularity. But how is time represented in minds which disregard these regular series of phenomena in space, and which pay no attention, at least deliberate attention, to the unalterable succession of cause and effect ? Having no support, it can but be indistinct and ill-defined. It rather resembles a subjective feeling of duration, not wholly unlike the *durée* described by Bergson. It is scarcely a representation.

Our idea of time seems to us to be a natural attribute of the human mind. But that is a delusion. Such an idea scarcely exists where primitive mentality is concerned, for that sees the direct causal relation between the given phenomenon and the extra-spatial occult power.

As Hubert has shown,[1] primitive mentality is much more conscious of time according to its qualities than it conceives of it by its objective characteristics. " The negroes who live more in the interior of the country," writes Bosman, " distinguish time in a curious way, namely as happy and unhappy. There are some districts where the long happy time lasts for nineteen days, and the little one " (for you must know that they differentiate them thus) " seven days ; between these two periods they reckon seven days that are unlucky, and these really are their holidays, for then they do not travel, nor begin a campaign, nor undertake anything important, but remain quietly at home doing nothing." [2] In this we recognize the classical distinction between the *fasti* and *nefasti*. Periods and salient points of time are characterized by the manifestations of the mystic powers which occur in them ; it is to them, and almost entirely to them, that primitive mentality clings. Certain investigators have expressly noticed this. Thus, " what we Europeans call the past, is linked to the present, and this in its turn is connected with the future. For, believing as these people do in a life of two existences which are continuous, merging one into the other as the human does into the spiritual, and back again as the latter does in the former, time for them has in reality no divisions as it has for us. Equally so, it has neither value nor object, and for this reason is treated with an indifference and a contempt that is altogether inexplicable to the European." [3] This remarkable passage of Major Leonard's is somewhat obscure, probably like the very representations which he desires to give an idea of. But they are the representations of minds which live as much in the world of invisible realities as in that which we call objective reality.

What has just been said of time applies equally well to space, and for the same reasons. Space which we think of as absolutely homogeneous—not the space of the geometri-

---

[1] Hubert et Mauss : *Mélanges d'histoire des réligions*, pp. 197 et. seq.
[2] Bosman : *Voyage de Guinée*, p. 164 (edit. 1705).
[3] Major A. G. Leonard : *The Lower Niger and Its Tribes*, p. 181.

cians alone, but the space implied in our current ideas, appears to us like a background of canvas, unconcerned with the objects which are traced upon it. Whether phenomena are produced in this or that region of space, in the north or south, above or below, on our right or on our left, makes, we think, absolutely no difference to the phenomena themselves ; it merely allows us to place, and often to measure, them. But such an idea of space is possible only to minds accustomed to the consideration of a series of secondary causes, which in fact do not vary, whatever the region in space wherein they appear. Let us imagine minds quite differently orientated, engaged primarily and almost entirely with occult forces and mystic powers whose agency is manifested in a direct way. These minds will not picture space as a uniform and immaterial quantum. On the contrary, to them it will appear burdened with qualities ; its regions will have virtues peculiar to themselves ; they will share in the mystic powers which are revealed therein. Space will not be so much imagined, as *felt*, and its various directions and positions will be qualitatively differentiated from one another.

In spite of appearances, homogeneous space is no more a natural datum of the human mind than homogeneous time. Undoubtedly the primitive moves in space exactly as we do ; undoubtedly when he desires to throw his projectiles or to reach a distant goal, he knows as we do, and sometimes better than we do, how to calculate distances rapidly, to retrace a path, and so on. But action in space is one thing, and the idea of space quite another. It is the same thing here as in causation. Primitives constantly make use of the actual relation of cause to effect. In their construction of implements, for instance, or of traps, they often make proof of an ingenuity which implies a very careful observance of this relation. Does it follow that their idea of causation is like ours ? To arrive at such a conclusion we should have to admit that the possession of a means of activity is the same as being able to analyse it, and as a reasoned knowledge of the mental or physiological processes which accompany it. We have but to formulate such an assumption to see that it is untenable.

When we describe the experience of primitive mentality as being different from our own, it is a question of the world formed for them by their collective representations. From the point of view of action, they move in space as we, and as the animals, do ; they attain their ends by means of instruments, the use of which involves the actual connection between cause and effect, and if they did not conform to this objective connection, they, like ourselves (and like the animals), would immediately perish. But what actually makes them human beings is that the social group does not rest satisfied to act in order to live. Every individual member has a representation of the reality in which he is living and acting, absolutely in accordance with the constitution of this group. In fact, their minds cling to it above all for other reasons than the objective relations upon which practical activity and industry are established.

Thus it is that in primitive mentality, which is wholly mystic and prelogical, not only the data, but even the limits of experience fail to coincide with our own. Bergson's well-known theory which requires us to conceive of time as a homogeneous quantum by fusing living duration and space, which is such a quantum, does not seem applicable to primitive mentality. It is only in races which are already somewhat developed, when the mystic preconnections become weak and tend to be dissociated, when the habit of paying attention to second causes and their effects is growing stronger, that space becomes homogeneous in the representations, and time tends to become so too. Thus the limits of our experience are sketched little by little, are strengthened and become fixed. Much later, when reflection leads us to make these ideas our own, we are tempted to believe that they are its constituent elements—innate, as the philosophers used to say. The observation and analysis of the collective representations of inferior races are far from confirming this hypothesis.

CHAPTER III

DREAMS

THE world of experience, as a whole, does not present itself to the primitive mind as it does to us. It is not only that its framework differs somewhat, since time, space, and causation are imagined, and above all felt, in a different way ; its data also, are more complex, and in a certain sense more copious. The world we see provides primitives, as it does us, with a collection of realities perceptible to sense, but in their minds others are added, or rather intermingled, with these—data arising out of the mystic forces always and everywhere present, and these are by far the most important. How are these to be collected, how can they be induced if they are long in coming, how should they be interpreted, and classified ? These are functions which the primitive mind must perform, and their collective representations show us how very complex they are. We perceive, then, that the intellectual torpor, lack of curiosity, and indifference which so many investigators have declared as existing in primitive communities are nearly always more apparent than real. As soon as the agency of mystic powers is involved, these dormant minds awake. They are then no longer indifferent or apathetic ; you find them alert, patient, and even ingenious and subtle.

Undoubtedly the course they pursue does not lead, as ours does, to the formation of concepts and to scientific knowledge, with an illimitable field before it in which to advance. It very quickly attains its end, or it comes to nothing. Moreover, most of the collective representations which engage its attention are of a markedly emotional character, and the preconnections established between them are often prelogical in their nature and impervious to experience.

7

What it behoves the primitive to understand above all is the agency of the mystic forces by which he feels himself surrounded. These forces, from their very nature, are invisible and imperceptible. They only reveal themselves by more or less explicit manifestations, and these vary both in their significance and in their frequency. It will be necessary, therefore, to learn to discern, collect, and understand them. We have already seen that all which appears unusual, fortuitous, extraordinary, striking, or unforeseen is interpreted as a manifestation of occult powers. But there are other means, more direct, and certainly more regular, by which these powers make known what is going to happen, and, as it were, warn the individual or the social group. Of such a nature are dreams and good and bad omens. When these manifestations are not forthcoming of themselves, the primitive mind exercises its ingenuity to induce them; it invents methods of procuring them (such as dreams which are instigated, processes of divination, ordeals, etc.), and thus it arrives at various data which find a place in the scheme of primitive experience, and contribute, in no small degree, to making this puzzling to us.

I

To the primitive mind, as we know, the seen and the unseen worlds form but one, and there is therefore uninterrupted communication between what we call obvious reality and the mystic powers. Nowhere perhaps is this more directly and completely brought about than in dreams, in which man passes from the one world to the other without being aware of it. Such is in fact the ordinary idea of the dream to primitive peoples. The "soul"[1] leaves its tenement for the time being. It frequently goes very far away; it communes with spirits or with ghosts. At the moment of awakening it returns to take its place in the body once more. If witchcraft or accident of any kind hinders its return, illness and speedy death are to be feared. At

[1] I use this expression in default of another, better adapted to the representations of primitive mentality.

other times, it is the spirits of the dead, or even other powers, which come and visit the soul in sleep.

Thus the dream brings to primitives data which in their eyes are equal to, perhaps even more valuable than, the perceptions of the preceding day. To accept these data as authoritatively as they do others, they have no need of the " natural philosophy " with which Tylor and his school endow them. Neither are they the dupes of a gross psychological fallacy. They are quite well able to differentiate between their dream and the perceptions of the previous day, and they dream only when they slumber. But they are not in the least astonished that their dreams should bring them into direct relation with forces which can neither be seen nor touched. They are no more surprised at possessing such a faculty than they are at being endowed with sight and hearing. It is undeniable that this faculty cannot be exercised at will, nor is it permanent, like the senses. But is it not quite natural that mystic forces should themselves decide whether to grant or to refuse intercourse ? Moreover, a dream is not so rare a circumstance as to conflict with everyday experience. Among many inferior races, where all pay great attention to dreams, people ask each other about their dreams every morning, exchange their experiences, and interpret the dreams ; there is always somebody or other who has had a dream.

The Homeric idea that " Sleep is the twin-brother of Death " doubtless has a very far-off origin. To primitives, it is literally true. According to them, as we know, the man who has just died continues to live, but under new conditions. He does not take himself off at once, but remains in the neighbourhood, and continues to influence his social group, which is conscious of his presence and cannot be indifferent to him. His " soul " has left his body, but the body has remained, and as long as it is not entirely decomposed, the relations between the dead man and his group are only partially ruptured. In the same way, when a sleeping man dreams, his soul leaves his body, and until it returns he is in a state which is exactly like that of a man recently dead. Sometimes primitives express this

---

[1] Vide E. B. Tylor : *Primitive Culture*, 4th edit., 1903.

idea in a striking way. Thus, in (German) West Africa, " to dream" (*drokuku*) means " to be half dead." " In the dream, the soul leaves the body and goes away to the land of phantasy where, in a moment, it seems to see and to possess things ; but these do not allow themselves to be retained. . . . Nevertheless, these spirits are regarded as real. For instance, if one has seen in a dream anyone who has been dead a long time, he really has been in communication with him. In a dream we see real objects, happenings which ' pass for real,' and the soul which is for the ·time being freed from the body speaks and acts as it does in the daytime when it is in the body. The sole difference lies in this ; in the dream it has its being, not in the seen but in the unseen world."[1] We could not better express the idea that both worlds equally form part of his experience.

The Maoris of New Zealand have no other conception of the dream than this. " This old lady," writes Elsdon Best, " once said to me, ' I am inclined to believe that old persons who die regain their youth in the *reinga*. Because I went to the *reinga* last night (i.e. she had had a dream, and I saw Kiriwera (an old woman recently dead), and she appeared quite young and nice-looking.' " When a native says that he has been to the *reinga*, he means that he has been dreaming. " An old man said to me : ' I was at the *reinga* last night and saw my old friend—who has long been dead. I could tell from his appearance . . . that it will be a fine day.' "[2]

Colenso had already noticed the same thing. " They believed in the truth of dreams, of which they had many kinds, both bad and good. . . . All were firmly believed to be remembrances of what they had seen in the *reinga* or unseen world (or place of the departed), whither the spirit was supposed to have been during the sleep of the body." [3]

Lastly, not to multiply evidence, similar beliefs are to be found in North America. " They are also guided to a great extent by their dreams, for they imagine that in the night they are in direct communication with the spirits

[1] J. Spieth : *Die Ewestämme*, p. 564.
[2] Elsdon Best : " Maori Eschatology," *Transactions of the N.Z. Institute*, xxxviii. p. 236 (1905).
[3] W. Colenso : *On the Maori Races of New Zealand*, p. 60 (1865).

which watch over their daily occupations." [1]   The Indians
of New France, who always attached so much importance
to dreams, thought of them in exactly the same way.
" Being unable to conceive how the soul functions during
sleep, when it brings things that are far off or altogether
absent, before it, they are persuaded that the soul leaves
the body when it is asleep, and itself goes and finds the
objects in the dream in the places where it sees them, and
that it returns to the body towards the end of the night,
when all the dreams are scattered." [2]

What is seen in dreams is, theoretically, true. To minds
which have but slight perception of the law of contradiction,
and which the presence of the same thing in various places
at one and the same time does not perturb in the least,
what reason is there for doubting these data more than any
others ? Once having admitted the idea which primitive
mentality forms of sleep and of dreams, since nothing seems
more natural to him than the communication between the
seen and the unseen worlds, why should he mistrust what
he sees in dreams any more than what he sees with his eyes
wide open ? He would be even more inclined to believe
in the former because of the mystic origin of these data,
which makes them all the more valuable and reliable.   There
is nothing about which one can feel more sure than about
things revealed in dreams.[3] In Gaboon, " a dream is more
conclusive than a witness." [4]

But are there no dreams which are incoherent, ridiculous,
and manifestly impossible ? To primitive mentality the
law of contradiction does not exercise the same influence
on the connection of ideas as it does on ours.   Moreover,
primitives do not accord belief to all dreams indiscriminately.
Certain dreams are worthy of credence, others not.   Thus, the
Dieri " distinguish between what they consider a vision and
a mere dream.   The latter is called *apitcha*, and is thought
to be a mere fancy of the head." [5] Among the Indians of

[1] L. M. Turner : *The Hudson Bay Eskimo*, Report of Bureau of American
Ethnology (Smithsonian Institute), xi. p. 272.
[2] *Relations des Jésuites*, liv. p. 66 (1669–70).
[3] A. C. Haddon : *Head-hunters, Black, White, and Brown*, p. 57 (1901).
[4] G. Le Testu : *Notes sur les coutumes Bapounou, dans la Circonscription
de la Nyanga*, p. 200.
[5] Rev. A. W. Howitt : *The Native Tribes of South-East Australia*, p. 358.

New France " those who have the gift of dreaming a good deal do not pay attention to all their dreams indiscriminately ; they distinguish between the false and the true, and the latter, they say, are rather rare." [1]

With this reservation, the primitive has no doubt of the truth of the dream. That which dreams announce will take place, what they reveal has already happened. To quote but one or two examples taken from some of the Australian peoples. " If a man dreams that he will find a swan's nest in some particular spot, he visits the place with the expectation of finding it. If he dreams that something serious happens to him, as, for example, that he is mortally wounded in battle, and if, afterwards, he is wounded, he says : ' I knew that this would take place, for I dreamt it.' . . . If a man is told by a friend that he had a bad dream about him, this will make him very miserable and ill for a long time. If a dog shows agitation while asleep, that is a sign that he dreams of hunting kangaroos, and that he will kill one the next day ; and so confident is his master in the dog's dream, that he will go out with him the next day to help him." [2]

Whether it be a question of a past event, or of an occurrence some long way off, the primitive is no less certain. " One day I heard a great cry at the wurleys (huts). I went up and found the women wailing with their faces blackened and hair shorn off. An old man sat in the midst, with a despairing look on his face. I inquired the reason for all this, and learned that the old man had dreamt that someone at Tipping had put a *ngadhungi* to the fire to work his death. . . . Some of the young men assured me that he would die unless someone went to Tipping to stop the sorcery, so I sent off a party in the boat in compliance with their wishes. Next day they returned and said that they could find no sorcery, and so it was concluded that there must be a mistake somehow, and the old man got well." [3]

Facts like this have frequently been noted in inferior

[1] *Relations des Jésuites*, x. p. 170 (1636). (Le Jeune.)
[2] J. Dawson : *Australian Aborigines*, p. 52. (Melbourne, 1881.)
[3] Rev. G. Taplin : *The Narrinyeri Tribe*, p. 135.

peoples widely separated from each other. In Sumatra, a Battak, from the vicinity of Lake Toba, not being able to understand how it was that white people could predict the solar and lunar eclipses, opined that they were revealed to them in dreams.[1] In New Zealand, in 1830, a missionary relates that " a man and woman have just been murdered under the pretext that they had bewitched several persons who have died lately. Some other woman dreamt that such was the case, and this dream was sufficient in the eyes of a native." [2] In Central Africa, a voyage undertaken in a dream is reckoned as an actual voyage. " I visited the chief again, and was surprised to find him sitting outside dressed in European clothes. He explained that during the night he had dreamed he was in Portugal, England, and a few other places, so on rising he had dressed up in European fashion, and told his people he had just returned from the white man's country. All who went to see him, young and old, had to come and shake hands, and bid him welcome back again." [3]

In French Congo, a man against whom trial by ordeal has been pronounced, and who does not imagine that it can fail in its finding, admits that he may have committed the act imputed to him in a dream. " I heard a man who was thus accused reply : ' I will pay, because as a matter of fact, I might have killed him when I was asleep ; but I have no conscious knowledge of it." [4]

II

Just as objects seen in dreams are real, so actions committed in dreams entail responsibility, and their authors may be taken to task about them. In New Guinea, for instance, " the man who dreams that a woman is declaring her love for him, believes that she really has a penchant for him. . . . Among the Kai, if a man dreams that he commits himself with his friend's wife, he is punishable.

---

[1] *Berichte der rheinischen Missionsgesellschaft*, p. 231 (1911).
[2] *Missionary Register*, Williams, p. 467 (October 1830).
[3] Rev. F. S. Arnot : *Bihé and Garenganze*, p. 67.
[4] G. Le Testu : *Notes sur les coutumes Bapounou, dans la Circonscription de la Nyanga*, p. 201.

If his dream should be made known, he has to pay a fine, or at any rate he will be violently vituperated."[1]

A man is even responsible for what another has seen him do in a dream. One can imagine what complications this may lead to. Here are some of the quaintest. "At Mukah (Borneo) I met Janela. . . . He said the reason of his coming here was that his daughter was about to be fined in Luai, because her husband had dreamt she had been unfaithful to him. Janela brought away his daughter."[2] At Borneo again, "a man" says Grant, "came to me officially and asked for protection. The case was this. Another man of the same village dreamed that the complainant had stabbed his father-in-law, who lay ill in the house. The defendant believing this, threatened the complainant with vengeance, should the sick man die. The plaintiff therefore appealed for protection, stating that he had not struck the sick man, and that if his ghost had done so during his sleep he knew nothing about it, and was not therefore responsible for the deed. It so happened that I was attending the sick man."[3]

From this story it appears that the accused man does not absolutely deny the deed imputed to him; he does not even seem to doubt the accuracy of his accuser's dream. He grants that in sleep he *may* have done that of which they are accusing him, and maintains that his "soul" is alone responsible. Both accuser and accused may be acting in good faith. They admit as a self-evident fact that what appears in dreams is real, difficult as it seems to us to reconcile it with the rest of their experience.

On this point nothing is more instructive than the facts collected by the missionary Grubb from the Lenguas of Grand Chaco. "An Indian," says he, "dreamt that he was eating a *kala* (water-fowl) and said that on waking he had heard the screeching of these birds in the swamp near by. In the morning he informed his neighbours that his young child, who was with his mother at another village,

---

[1] R. Neuhauss : *Deutsch Neu Guinea (Kai)*, iii. p. 113.
[2] H. Ling Roth : *Natives of Sarawak*, i. p. 232 (1896).
[3] Ibid., i. p. 232.

had been awake most of the night. A superstition prevails that a man who has a young child should not eat this bird because, if he does, his child will be sleepless during the succeeding night. In this case it is evident that the cry of this water-fowl in the night had given rise to his dream, and holding this superstition, he concluded that, as in spirit he had eaten of it, so his child that night had suffered for his rash act." [1] Thus the Indian does not differentiate between an action taking place in a dream and an action which had occurred in daylight on the previous day. Both forms of experience were equally valid to him.

It may happen that the primitive sees in dreams circumstances which are to occur later ; these circumstances are both prospective, because he foresees their happening, and they are also retrospective, because he has seen them in a dream, and having seen them thus, to his mind they have already taken place. Such a thing is an impossibility to minds governed, as ours are, by the law of contradiction, for they have a clear representation of time unfolding in a unilinear series of successive moments. How can the same event occupy two different places in this series, at a distance from each other, and thus belong both to the past and the future ? Such an impossibility, however, puts no strain upon prelogical mentality. Not that it accommodates itself to gross mental disorder, as people so frequently maintain, but because the world of its experience, more complex than our own, admits the simultaneity of data which cannot be coexistent either in time or space with us. It is only in this way that we can understand facts of the kind related by Grubb. " The Indian," says he, " has implicit faith in dreams and allows them to control his actions. . . . Poit . . . had been greatly impressed by a dream which he had related to some Indians many weeks before he attempted my life, the gist of which was that I met him in an open space in a forest, accused him of misappropriating my property, and with a gun shot him. This dream he took as a secure warning of what would happen, and from the Indian point of view, if he could not otherwise avoid the catastrophe he had perforce to endeavour to

Rev. W. B. Grubb : *An Unknown People in an Unknown Land*, p. 132.

turn the tables on me, and as far as possible deal with me as he dreamt I dealt with him." [1]

In committing his attempt at assassination, the Indian does not consider himself the aggressor. That is the part he attributes to Mr. Grubb. What he has seen in the dream is real ; therefore it is Mr. Grubb who has attacked him, and the Indian's attempt is merely legitimate defence. Does he regard the event he has seen in his dream as past or future ? Evidently he considers it a future occurrence, since he has not yet sustained Grubb's shot and been wounded by him. But it has happened nevertheless, and therefore his reprisals are justified.[2]

The event I am about to relate involves yet greater difficulty, unless we admit that the experience of these Indians is arranged in a setting more elastic than our own, and allowing, at one and the same moment, of data which to our minds would be mutually exclusive " This man arrived at my village from a place about a hundred and fifty miles off. He asked me for compensation for some pumpkins which I had recently stolen from his garden. I was thoroughly surprised, and told him I had not been near his village for a very long time, and so could not possibly have stolen his pumpkins. At first I thought he was joking, but I soon perceived that he was quite serious. It was a novel experience for me to be accused by an Indian of theft. On my expostulating with him, he admitted quite frankly that I had not taken the pumpkins. When he said this I was more bewildered still. I should have lost patience with him, had he not been evidently in real earnest, and I became deeply interested instead. Eventually I discovered that he had dreamed he was out in his garden one night, and saw me, from behind some tall plants, break

---

[1] Rev. W. B. Grubb : *An Unknown People in an Unknown Land*, p. 275.

[2] The Island of Flores has recently furnished a similar case. " Everything the mind takes cognizance of in a dream is regarded as absolutely real, even if facts manifestly contradict it. One man has been assassinated by another, because the latter had seen him kill his sister in a dream. On awaking, he could easily have assured himself that his sister was alive, but that did not seem to be necessary. He took his vengeance first. When brought before the judge and informed that his sister was still living, he did not hesitate to maintain in all good faith that he was within his rights."— Van Sachtelen : *Endeh (Flores)*, p. 129. *Mededeelingen van het bureau voor de bestuurszaken der buitengewesten, bewerkt door het Encyclopædisch Bureau*, Aflevering xiv. (1921).

off and carry away three pumpkins, and it was payment for these that he wanted. ' Yes,' I said, ' but you have just admitted that I had not taken them.' He again assented, but replied immediately : ' If you had been there, you would have taken them,' thus showing he regarded the act of my soul, which he supposed had met his in the garden, to be really my will, and what I should actually have done had I been there." [1]

This conversation throws a ray of light on the mental functioning of the Indian. Grubb thinks that he has proved to him the impossibility of regarding his dream as real, and he explains the Indian's persistency by attributing to him the belief that the mind's intentions are the same as its deeds. But at the same time he recognizes that the Indian maintains that he has met Mr. Grubb's soul in his garden. The latter does not in fact doubt that he has seen the missionary himself. When Grubb asserts that he was a hundred and fifty miles off at the time, the Indian concurs in the statement. Yet the logical incongruity between the two is not enough to make him abandon the statement based on his dream, and he maintains both facts, particularly the one which rests upon what he saw with his own eyes while dreaming. He prefers admitting implicitly what the Schoolmen call the ' multipresence ' of the same person, to doubting what seems a certainty to him. That is the necessary result of his experience which, beyond and above the realities which we term objective, contains an infinity of others belonging to the unseen world. Neither time, nor space, nor logical theory, is of use to us here, and this is one of the reasons which cause us to regard the primitive's mind as " prelogical."

The multipresence implicitly admitted by the Indian just cited is not an isolated case. In a great many primitive peoples the natives thus picture to themselves the multi-presence of the man who has just died, who, to the European's great perplexity, inhabits the tomb where his body lies, and at the same time is haunting the neighbourhood where he passed his life. The contradiction in this is not perceived, and as a rule, calling attention to it does not suffice to bring it to an end.

[1] Rev. W. B. Grubb : *An Unknown People in an Unknown Land*, pp. 129-30.

III

Among the South African races which are somewhat more developed, there is perpetual obsession on the subject of witchcraft. On the other hand, they maintain continual intercourse with the dead, not only with those whose memory is still vivid, but also with the accumulated mass of " ancestors." It is quite natural, therefore; that dreams should assist this intercourse, and be also of use in unmasking wizards. This fact is confirmed by many investigators. The dream reveals the enemy's secret plots. Among the Kafirs, " a short time previous to the death of Gaika, that chief sent a messenger to an old woman, formerly one of his concubines, but who was then living at the (Mission) station, informing her that he had dreamt about her on the preceding night, and that he wished to see her at his kraal. She declined the invitation. . . . On the following day, three chiefs waited on Mr. Chalmers, and soliciting a private interview, informed him in a low tone, that the woman whom they had come to demand had bewitched the chief with the hair of a goat, together with some old rags. . . ." [1]

" A man dreams that an attempt has been made to take his life by one whom he has always regarded as his true friend. On awaking he says: " This is strange ; a man who never stoops to meanness wishes to destroy me. I cannot understand it, but it must be true, for ' dreams never lie.' Although the suspected friend protests his innocence, he immediately cuts his acquaintance." [2]

Callaway relates a very similar characteristic, giving it very nearly in the native's language. " Sometimes there is a man who is acting with the secret intention of injuring another without his suspecting it, and without his knowing anything about him, he being his friend. But if he hears in a dream a voice saying to him, ' So-and-so is pretending merely to be your friend. Do you not see that he will kill you ? What do you think he means by saying such-and-such a thing ?' (alluding to something he has said)

[1] A. Steedman : *Wanderings and Adventures in the Interior of South Africa*, i. pp. 229-30 (1835).
[2] Rev. J. Tyler : *Forty Years Among the Zulus*, p. 108 (edit. of 1891).

he remembers it and exclaims, 'Yes, surely, So-and-so may hate me on that account.' And he begins to separate from him, and to be on his guard. . . . And if he says to him: 'So-and-so, now you keep at a distance from me. What is it? What difficulty has arisen between us?' the other puts him off." [1]

The native does not hesitate between his friendship and his dream. Surprised he may be, but he does not doubt. The dream is a revelation coming from the unseen world, and to disregard it would be folly. The petty African potentates turn these warnings to account. "If Casembe dreams of any man twice or thrice he puts the man to death, as one who is practising secret arts against his life." [2] The wizard who is unmasked in a dream is killed immediately.

From various passages in Callaway's work, we find that the dreams which reveal danger proceed from the dead. "If in your sleep you dream of a beast pursuing you, trying to kill you, when you wake you wonder and say: 'How is this that I should dream of a wild beast pursuing me?' And if in the morning they are going to hunt . . . you go knowing that you are in jeopardy; you know that the *itongo* brought the beast to you, that you might know that if you do not take care, you may die. If you go to the hunt you are on your guard. Perhaps you do not go. . . ." [3] And again, yet more explicitly: "Black men steadily affirm that the *amatongo* (plural form of *itongo*) help them; they do not say so from what diviners have said, but from what they have themselves seen. For instance, when they are asleep, a dead man appears, and talks to one of them, and says: 'So-and-so, it is well that such-and-such be done in this village,' telling them that something will happen." [4]

It is evident that all dreams are not equally easy to interpret, and also that the Kafirs, like all races who regulate their actions by dreams, have been led to distinguish between good and bad dreams; between those which are reliable and those which are untrue. "People say summer dreams

---

[1] Rev: C. H. Callaway: *The Religious System of the Amazulu*, p. 164; cf. p. 228.
[2] Rev. D. Livingstone: *Last Journals*, i. p. 277 (1874).
[3] Rev. C. H. Callaway: *The Religious System of the Amazulu*, pp. 228 et seq.   [4] Ibid., pp. 178–9.

are true, but they do not say they are always true ; they say that summer dreams do not usually miss the mark. But they say the winter is bad, and produces confused imaginations, that is, very many unintelligible dreams. . . . A dream that is said to be sent by the *itongo*, is one which comes with a message from the dead, inquiring why such-and-such a thing is not done. For example, among black men, if one has an abundant harvest, sometimes the head of the village dreams that it said to him : ' How is it, when you have been given so much food, that you do not give thanks ? . . . . And he immediately commands his people to make beer, for he is about to sacrifice." [1]

Here we have the type of dream which is reliable ; it is a demand made by the dead, who desire to be rewarded for the services they have rendered. Their claim seems just as natural as the form in which it is presented. It is an incident of everyday life, like the reminder of a creditor that payment of a debt is due. The only difference is that the creditor presents himself during the day, and the *itongo* speaks at night, either in his own or in his ancestors' name, through the medium of the dream.

It frequently happens that when all the missionary's efforts to induce a native to change his faith have proved ineffectual, a dream suddenly determines him to take the step, especially if the dream is repeated several times. For example, among the Basutos, " what plays the chief part in the conversion of the Mosuto ? . . . The paramount rôle is played by the dream. . . . To make him definitely decide, there must be something out of the common, a Divine intervention (as he regards it) which strikes his imagination. . . . If you ask a heathen who has heard the Gospel, when he will be converted, he will answer in the most matter-of-course way : ' When God speaks to me.' " [2] " It is very remarkable to find how many people here attribute their conversion to a dream. . . . This would be confirmed by most, if not all, of our missionaries. The dream plays a great part in the early religious life of the blacks. M. Mondain recently told me of a kind of vision

[1] Rev. C. H. Callaway : *The Religious System of the Amazulu*, pp. 238 et seq.
[2] *Missions évangéliques*, lxx. pp. 341–2.   (Marzolff.)

which led to the conversion of a Malagasy wizard. At Lessouto, occurrences of this kind are frequent, and hundreds of Christians in these parts heard the first appeal of their conscience in the form of a dream." [1]

" Augustus, a Mashona boy here, told me that the Lord had called him to be converted four years ago, but that he would not listen to his voice. I thought that by the voice of the Lord he meant the Gospel message, but he meant a dream in which he had seen a dazzling light and heard a voice saying: ' You must become a Christian.' A few days after our conversation the native had another dream of the kind, and he became converted." [2] Similarly, the chief Sékoate told a missionary: " I have been dreaming for a long time that I always see missionaries. Let them come, and I shall treat them as I treated the Boers." [3]

Merensky, like Wangemann, states that it is often dreams alone which can overcome the natives' hesitation. " Very frequently to heathens who were wavering, the dream was the deciding factor. . . . Among those who are inquiring and yet hesitating, these dreams occur so regularly that one day, at the end of the lesson, Podumo asked us in the presence of the other catechumens how we could explain the fact that he had not yet had any dreams, although he had been anxiously inquiring, and praying a good deal. The content of these dreams often seemed to our minds to have no significance whatever, but the natives thought differently, and their dreams frequently made a lasting impression upon them." [4] Podumo's argument and his anxiety are significant. If God desires his conversion, why does He not say so ? And if He wanted to tell him anything, would He not speak to him in a dream, as the *amatongo* do ?

In Central Africa, dreams have similar meanings. To give but one example : " The Azande of the Upper Congo believe that during the night the dead make their wishes known to the living. Dreams are quite authentic to them,

1 *Missions évangéliques*, lxviii. i. pp. 114–15. (Rambaud.)
2 Dr. Wangemann : *Die Berliner Mission in Koranna Lande*, p. 207.
3 A. Merensky : *Erinnerungen aus dem Missionsleben im Süd Ost Afrika*, p. 94.
4 Ibid., pp. 152–3.

and they are convinced that when they see a dead relative in a dream they really have a conversation with his ghost, and in its course he gives advice, expresses satisfaction or displeasure, and states his aspirations and desires. It may happen that in this way the dead man expresses his need of a slave to look after him. Then the natives consult the *benget* and if the oracle predicts misfortune should the dead man's wishes not be acceded to, they break the arms and legs of a slave and lay him on the grave, where he succumbs to his injuries and starves to death. If it be impossible to sacrifice a slave, one of the dead man's widows is thus immolated." [1]

IV

The influence of the dream in the daily life of primitive peoples has nowhere been more fully set forth than in the *Rélations des Jésuites* of New France. Not that they have set themselves the task of studying or describing dreams. If the missionaries do speak about them, it is because they force themselves upon their attention ; they are to be met with everywhere, and these dreams of the Indians prove either the most invincible obstacle to the success of the mission, or its most valuable resource ; finally, the Jesuits cannot sufficiently express their astonishment at all that their dreams make the Indians do. "The dream is the oracle that all these people consult and defer to, the prophet who predicts their future, the Cassandra who warns them of the dangers that threaten, the physician-in-ordinary of their illnesses, the Esculapius and the Galen of the whole country ; in short, their most absolute ruler. If a chief pronounces one thing, and the dream another, the chief may shout himself hoarse ; it is the dream that will be obeyed. It is their Mercury in travels, their steward at home ; it often presides over their councils ; their trading, fishing, and hunting are usually undertaken by its consent, and apparently only to afford it satisfaction ; they negotiate nothing so important but that it will be willingly renounced

[1] A. Hutereau : "Notes sur la vie familiale et juridique de quelques populations du Congo belge," *Annales du Musée du Congo belge*, Série III. *Documents ethnographiques*, i. p. 93.

at the instance of some dream. . . . The dream is, in fact, the chief God of the Hurons." [1]

" The Iroquois," says another Jesuit priest, " have, strictly speaking, but one divinity, which is the dream ; they submit to it and follow all its orders most implicitly. The Tsonnontouens are much more attached to it than the others ; their religion respecting it is most precise ; whatever it may be that they believe they have done in a dream they feel absolutely obliged to carry out immediately. The other tribes are content to pay attention to their most important dreams, but this one, which is said to live more circumspectly than its neighbours, would consider it was guilty of a great crime if it did not heed every one of them. That is all the people think of ; they never talk about anything else, and their huts are all peopled with their dreams." [2]

It seems impossible to express more strongly and impressively the unvarying influence of invisible powers in the life and conduct of the Indians, and the predominance of mystic elements in their experience. The dream is the medium by which these mystic elements manifest themselves, and its revelations are not only accepted by the Indians as unhesitatingly as are the data afforded by sense, but they are moreover the object of religious devotion. The terms divinity, god, oracle, religion, flow unceasingly from the Jesuits' pens when they are writing of dreams. It is not simply a question of advice, hints, friendly suggestions, official warnings conveyed by dreams ; it is nearly always definite orders, and nothing can prevent the Indian from obeying them. " If overnight they have dreamt that they must kill a Frenchman, woe to the man whom they meet in a secluded spot next day." [3] " If our dreams were not true, *theirs* were, and they would die if they did not carry them out. According to this, our very lives depend upon the dreams of a savage, for if any of them dreamt that they had to kill us, they would infallibly do so if they could. One of them told me that once upon a time he had dreamt that a certain Frenchman had to be killed before the speaker

[1] *Relations des Jésuites*, x. p. 170 (1636). (P. Le Jeune.)
[2] Ibid., liv. p. 96 (1669–70).
[3] Ibid., iv. p. 216 (1626). (P. Lalemant.)

could be cured of a disease that was threatening him, and he had sent for him." [1]

Why is it so absolutely necessary that the Indian should obey the orders given him in a dream, or, to put it more precisely, why, when once awake, must he carry out what he has seen done in a dream ? This question has been put to the Jesuit fathers many times. They always give the same answer. It is a question of life or death to the Indian. If what he has seen in a dream is not realized, he will die ; not only when the dream has suggested some action of his own, but also if he has been merely a spectator, and others have done the deed, for then these must carry it through. However extraordinary or exacting the demand of the dream may be, they have no choice but to submit to it. " It would be cruelty and a kind of crime not to grant a man what he has dreamed of. For such a refusal might cause his death ; hence it comes about that some find themselves despoiled of everything, without hope of its return, for whatever they may give, nothing will be given to them unless they themselves dream, or pretend to dream, of it. Usually however, they are too conscientious to make use of pretence, for that, in their opinion, would be inviting all sorts of misfortune. There are, however, some who throw overboard their scruples, and enrich themselves by means of fabricated tales." [2]

If the Indians really had the feelings the fathers describe, such a piece of trickery would be extremely rare. " The dream is a divinity to savages, and their respect for it is not less than ours for the most sacred things. Everything that they dream must be accomplished unless they are to incur the hatred of all the dreamer's relatives, and expose themselves to the consequences of their rancour." [3]

We might imagine that this pressing need to bring about what has been seen in dreams is peculiar to the Indians of New France. It is, however, to be found in other communities which are widely separated from each other, and its existence must rest upon a fundamental idea in the

[1] *Relations des Jésuites*, v. p. 160 (1633). (P. Le Jeune.)
[2] Ibid., xlii. pp. 164-6 (1655-6).
[3] Ibid., li. p. 124 (1666-8). (P. Bruyas.)

mentality of such peoples. The Barotse of South Africa "believe in dreams; a woman often comes asking for a handful of millet, because she has dreamt that she is going to have some sickness if a certain person does not give her a handful of grain." [1]

In Kamchatka, "if a man desires the good graces of a young girl, it is quite enough to say that he has dreamed she looked favourably on his suit; she then considers it a mortal sin to deny him, for if she did, it might cost her her life. If somebody wants a *kuklanda* or a *barka*, or any other object that he is too poor to acquire for himself, he has only to say: 'I had a dream last night; I was sleeping in So-and-so's *kuklanda*, and immediately the other says: 'Take it, it is mine no longer,' because he is firmly persuaded that if he does not give it his life will be forfeit." [2]

In this case it is not the dreamer himself who will die if the dream is not "fulfilled," as it is with the North-American Indians, but the one whom the dreamer has seen; but however important this difference may be from other points of view, it does not prevent the necessity in both cases of "fulfilling the dream" from appearing absolutely imperative. Something similar is to be found at the present day in the Kurds of Asia Minor. "They are convinced that if their conscience is clear (that is, if they have offered up the evening prayer and performed the ablutions ordered in the Koran before lying down to rest) their soul enters into such an intimate relation with the angels of Paradise that it is in a kind of celestial beatitude, and then knows all that it needs to know by means of the dreams which Allah vouchsafes them as a token of his goodwill, or (if their soul is in a state of sin) of his vengeance. When they awake, they have not the slightest doubt but that their soul has really seen what was presented to it in the dream. Consequently, thus firmly and blindly persuaded, they act with a kind of fatalism which makes them veritable scoundrels, and real scourges to their country. If they have dreamt of something that they covet and are trying to obtain, they do not rest till it has been given up to them,

---

[1] L. Decle: *Three Years in Savage Africa*, p. 75.
[2] G. W. Steller: *Beschreibung von dem Lande Kamtschatka*, p. 279 (1774).

nolens volens ; if they have seen in their dream some animate
being, object, or benefit belonging to others (especially to
Christians) they give themselves no rest till they have
become the masters of it, even if to satisfy their fatal ambition
they are obliged to have recourse to armed force, murder,
or pillage ; should they dream of an enemy or of a Christian
(always regarded as an enemy to their religion) they must
seize the first occasion that offers to put him to death or
plunder his estate. Thus to these madmen dreams nearly
always form the dominating motive of their crimes and
their impostures." [1]

The difference of social conditions between Indians
and Kurds suffices to explain why what the former do from
friendly motives often becomes an occasion for crime and
murder in the Kurds.   But, even with this difference,
we see the similarity in the obligation to act thus, and still
more clearly when we remember the cause which the Jesuits
attribute to this imperative need. Why must dreams be
" fulfilled " at all costs ? " Because," says Charlevoix,
" according to the Iroquois, every illness is a desire of the
soul, and people only die when their desire is not fulfilled." [2]
The Jesuits of the seventeenth century expressed themselves
very definitely on this point. " Now they believe that
the soul makes known these natural desires by dreams
as well as by words, so that when these desires are satisfied
it is pleased, but if its desires are not granted it grows angry,
not only because its body has not obtained the benefit
and prosperity it desired to procure for it, but often because
it actually revolts against it, causing it to suffer from diverse
maladies, and even death. . . . In consequence of these
erroneous opinions, most Hurons take great pains to note
their dreams and to provide their souls with what they have
revealed to them during sleep." [3]

Similarly, " they have a sure and infallible belief that if
they have dreamed of something and have failed to carry
it out, some misfortune which was mysteriously expressed

    [1] Abbé Jos. Tfinkdji : "Essai sur les songes et l'art de les interpréter en
Mésopotamie," *Anthropos*, viii. pp. 506–7 (1913).
    [2] P. F. X. de Charlevoix : *Journal d'un voyage dans l'Amérique
septentrionale*, iii. pp. 369–70 (1744).
    [3] *Relations des Jésuites*, xxxiii. pp. 188–90 (1648–9).

in the dream will befall them. I have even noticed that when these savages were in good health, the majority of them took very little trouble about obeying the directions given in dreams, but the moment they became ill they were convinced that there was no more potent remedy to cure them and save their lives than the carrying out of all that they had dreamed." [1] At least, however, when their illness had not been the work of a wizard.[2]

The Jesuit father's last remark leads us to infer that those dreams which must inevitably be " fulfilled " were, as a rule, the dreams of sick people or dreams which caused illness to be dreaded. The examples reported are usually of this nature. " A woman who was very ill in Onnontaghe had dreamt that a black robe was necessary in order that her recovery might be brought about, but the recent cruel massacre of our fathers by these savages having deprived them of any hope of procuring one from us, they had recourse to the Dutch, who made them pay a heavy price for the worn-out habit of Father Poncet, who had been robbed of it some time before by the Annienhronnons. The woman, who attributed her recovery to the possession of this, would not part with it for the rest of her life. . . . Last summer, when a woman was unable to procure in Quebec a French dog of the kind of which one of her nephews had dreamed, she undertook a second journey of more than four hundred miles, in spite of snow, ice, and very rough roads, to go and find the animal so ardently desired, in the place to which it had been taken." [3]

But it sometimes happens that a dream must be " fulfilled " without there being any question of illness involved. The Jesuits themselves give many instances of this. " Not long ago a man in the city of Oiogen in his sleep one night saw ten men plunging into a frozen river, entering it by one hole made in the ice, and coming out by another. On awaking, the first thing that he did was to prepare a great feast and invite ten of his friends. They all accepted, and soon began to make very merry. . . . Thereupon he

[1] *Relations des Jésuites*, liv. p. 100 (1669–70).
[2] Ibid., xxxiii. p. 198 (1647–8).
[3] Ibid., xliii, p. 272 (1656–7).

related his dream, which did not surprise them in the least, for they all prepared to put it into execution immediately. They therefore went to the river, broke the ice, and made two holes, about fifteen feet from each other. The divers removed their garments, and the first led the way ; jumping into one of the holes, he had the good luck to come out by the other ; the second did the same, and all the others with the exception of the tenth, were equally fortunate ; he, however, paid the penalty for all, since he could not manage to emerge, and perished miserably under the ice." [1] To determine the Indian's ten friends to risk their lives thus, the dream must have been an expression of " the soul's desire," which it was impossible to disobey for fear of dire penalties ; yet we are not told that there was any question of the Indian's being ill at the time.

The same remark applies to the dreams which were of special interest to the proselytizing missionaries. Like the Bantus of whom we have spoken, the Indians seldom decided to change their faith until they had dreamed that they did so, or at any rate, until a dream had required them to do so. " ' I am quite ready to adopt your faith and become a Christian, although I do not want to,' said one of these poor heathen to us, ' if my dream tells me to do it.' As a matter of fact, nothing seems difficult to them, when it is a question of obeying a dream." [2]

Then there is a final difficulty, and it is one which the Jesuit fathers do not seem to have troubled about. What, exactly, *is* this soul which makes known to them in dreams what it desires, and whose wishes are orders which must be carried at all costs ? The term " soul " is very vague. Can it bear the same meaning to the Jesuits' minds as it does to the collective representations of the Indians ? The latter, they tell us, admit the existence of at least two souls in every man. One of them is something like a vital principle, and its fate follows that of the body ; the other has its dwelling in the body during life, but leaves it at the moment of death. It was pre-existent to it, and survives it. Between this second soul, the inhabitant of

---

[1] *Relations des Jésuites*, xlii, pp. 150–2 (1655–6).
[2] Ibid., xxiii (1642) ; cf. xli, p. 142 (1653–4) ; lvii, pp. 194–5 (1672–3).

the body, upon which the well-being and the very life of a man during his existence on earth depend, and his tutelary genius, his guardian angel, his " personal god " (as Powell expresses it), his protector, or his particular totem, there is a connection which investigators have never been able to make clear, and which doubtless is not intended to become so. This close connection or participation probably does not go so far as fusion or identity of the two entities.[1] It is such, however, that the Indian feels himself to be entirely dependent upon this " spirit " (genius) which at all times can make him happy or unhappy. There is no greater misfortune for him than to incur its displeasure. If the Indian alienates it, he will certainly perish.

Let us admit that the dream is the expression of this " spirit's " will, and at once the respect, fear, and the need of rendering immediate obedience so frequently and so strikingly shown by Indians, find a simple explanation. It would be a kind of crime to refuse to give, or to do for any one of them what his *tutelary genius* requires.

Now as a matter of fact, the terminology of the Jesuit fathers is somewhat vague, and it may happen that in their reports the personal totem of the Indian is not differentiated from his soul. Charlevoix expressly declares : " In Acadia, nothing that a sick man asks for is denied him, because the desires he expresses while in this state are orders given by his tutelary genius." [2]

In a great many cases, illness is a sign to the Indian that his tutelary genius is offended, or displeased because something he desires is not being done, and he is therefore threatening to abandon him, a proceeding which would infallibly cause his death. How is he to know what the

---

[1] Durkheim, who has made a prolonged study of the idea of the soul held by Australian races, regards it both as a personal principle and as the totem of the whole clan. He arrives at the conclusion that " the soul, generally speaking, is only the totemistic principle embodied in each individual. . . . It is necessary to share it and divide it among them, and each of these fragments is a soul." On the other hand " the ideas of totem and of ancestor are so near to one another that they are sometimes confused. . . . And if the ancestor is thus confused with the totemistic spirit, it must be the same with the individual soul which is so closely connected with the ancestral soul "—*Les formes élémentaires de la vie religieuse*, pp. 355–67.

[2] P. F. X. de Charlevoix : *Journal d'un voyage dans l'Amérique septentrionale*, iii. p. 367.

desire is, and how he can appease the 'genius'? The latter alone can indicate it, and he makes it known in a dream, which it is imperative to obey faithfully. This hypothesis is all the more tenable because it is always in a vision or dream—whether this be spontaneous, or whether it be solicited or induced in any way—that the Indian has first perceived his guardian spirit. He has no other means of knowing him, and he is therefore quite ready to believe that dreams, or at any rate, some dreams, are communications from his tutelary genius, whose revelations will usually be made thus, and we know that the Indian stands in an unvarying and permanent relation to his personal totem. " He must respect it, follow its advice, merit its favour, put his whole confidence in it, and dread the effects of its wrath if he neglects to carry out his duties with regard to it." [1]

To conclude this subject, I am going to relate a circumstance noted in the Chippeway Indians. It is the story of partial disobedience to a dream, and it seems absolutely to confirm our interpretation of the matter.

" The evening previous to the departure of the band, one of them, whose *totam* (totem) was a bear, dreamed that if he would go to a piece of swampy ground, at the foot of a high mountain, about five days' march from my wigwam, he would see a large herd of elks, moose, and other animals; but that he must be accompanied by at least ten good hunters. When he awoke, he acquainted the band with his dream, and desired them to go with him; they all refused, saying it was out of their way, and that their hunting grounds were nearer. The Indian, having a superstitious reverence for his dream (which ignorance, and the prevalence of example among the savages, carries to a great height), thinking himself obliged to do so, as his companions had refused to go with him, went alone, and coming near the spot, saw the animals he dreamed of; he instantly fired, and killed a bear. Shocked at the transaction and dreading the displeasure of the Master of Life, whom he conceived he had highly offended, he fell down

[1] P. F. X. de Charlevoix: *Journal d'un voyage dans l'Amerique septentrionale*, iii. pp. 346-7.

and lay senseless for some time ; recovering from his state of insensibility, he got up and was making the best of his way to my house, when he was met in the road by another large bear, who pulled him down, and scratched his face. The Indian, relating this event at his return, added, in the simplicity of his nature, that the bear asked him what could induce him to kill his *totam* ; to which he replied that he did not know he was among the animals when he fired at the herd, that he was very sorry for the misfortune, and hoped he would have pity on him ; that the bear suffered him to depart, told him to be more cautious in future, and acquaint all the Indians with the circumstance, that their *totams* might be safe, and the Master of Life not angry with them. As he entered my house, he looked at me very earnestly, and pronounced these words, ' Beaver ' (the Indian name of Long) ' my faith is lost, my *totam* is angry, I shall never be able to hunt any more.' " [1]

[1] John Long : *Voyages and Travels of an Indian Interpreter and Trader,* pp. 86–7 (1791).

CHAPTER IV

OMENS

I

AFTER dreams, which form one of the most important components of the primitive's mental experience, bringing him as they do into direct relation with the unseen world, come omens, which also furnish him with data concerning the influence of the mystic forces by which he feels himself surrounded. Omens are thus revelations which are produced spontaneously, and in most cases, the preconnections existing between his collective representations enable the primitive to interpret them at once without needing to reflect upon them. Such a bird is heard on the left ; such an animal crosses his path during a march ; the lucky or unlucky meaning of the omen is apprehended at the very moment of its occurrence. Then, according to circumstances, the primitive pursues the course embarked upon with renewed courage, or abandons his attempt. In acting thus, he is only acting in accordance with the data afforded by experience, among which omens hold high rank ; and his case is somewhat akin to that of the physician who is guided in his prescriptions by what the symptoms reveal the state of the patient to be.

The noting of omens was a custom of ancient times, and it was specially practised in the Roman republic, where it was an official institution. Our reading of Latin authors has familiarized us with the custom. We should be wrong, however, if we were to admit, without previous examination of the matter, that what was true of omens in classical times is necessarily so of the omens of primitive peoples. Our best method will be to study first of all the omens of the primitives, as if we knew nothing of those of the ancients or their theories about them. It may be that on the other hand the analysis of data collected from primitive peoples will shed fresh light on the omens of classical races, and help us to understand them better. If the comparison has not been anticipated in the course of this survey itself, it will be all the more pregnant of results.

Let us leave aside for the moment the Greek and Roman omens, and fix our attention on those which the primitives note. In order to understand them thoroughly, and to enter into the state of mind which induces them, it will be necessary to make two preliminary observations.

1. Omens announce, for instance, that the enterprise upon which a man is about to engage will succeed or fail, or indeed they may give warning of a more or less imminent danger which he had not suspected. In that way they differ from other revelations constantly perceived by primitive man. Everything at all out of the common is, as we know, a revelation to him. Every accident is a revelation, for there is nothing fortuitous, and the slightest departure from ordinary occurrence shows that occult forces are at work. But such revelations most frequently relate to the past. They make known, for example, that magical practices have been exercised upon a certain person, that taboos have been infringed, that the dead are dissatisfied because their wishes have been disregarded, etc. Such omens are but one species of a genus that contains many others, and these are the revelations relating to future events. As such, they are of capital importance, since the future is still a matter of contingency, and the knowledge of the past is important to the primitive mainly because of its bearing on the present moment, or on the future.

We know, however, that the primitives' minds do not represent time exactly as ours do. Primitives do not see, extending indefinitely in imagination, something like a straight line, always homogeneous by nature, upon which events fall into position, a line on which foresight can arrange them in an unilinear and irreversible series, and on which they must of necessity occur one after the other. To the primitive time is not, as it is to us, a kind of intellectualized intuition, an " order of succession." Still less is it a homogeneous quantity. It is felt as a quality, rather than represented. If two events are due to succeed each other at a certain interval of time, the primitive certainly does perceive the second as being relatively future to the first, but he does not clearly distinguish the intermediary conditions which separate them, unless indeed (which rarely happens), these points should be of exceptional interest to him. In short, a future event, as a rule, is not situated at any particular point on the line of futurity ; it is vaguely represented and felt as something to come.[1]

2. This mental peculiarity in primitives is, as we have seen, connected with their habitual consideration of a causality which is of mystic type. If to them the line of time does not prolong itself indefinitely in the direction of the future, as it does to us ; if on the contrary it stops short almost at once, it is because it is not subtended by the interlinked chain of events formed by antecedents and consequents. Primitive mentality does not trouble to ascend or descend the series of conditions which are themselves conditioned. Their mentality, like ours, starts as a rule from the direct data afforded by the senses, but it immediately abandons what we call objective reality, in order to try and discover the mystic cause, the occult invisible power manifested by a change in the sense-impression. Very often, indeed, this occult power is indicated to it in advance by the preconnections between its representations. The lack of capacity to conceive of a future which is regularly arranged, and indifference to the search after secondary causes, are but two aspects of the same mental condition.

Hence arise the capital importance and the peculiar function of omens in the life of primitives. To minds like ours, accustomed to perceive a fixed order in nature, to reckon upon and deal with this order, to make their hopes and fears depend on it, what can omens be ? Merely

[1] This is one of the principal reasons for that " lack of foresight " so often observed and deplored by those who study uncivilized peoples. It is undoubtedly also due to other causes of a social and economic order ; but it proceeds mainly from the mental habits of primitives. They have but a confused notion of future time, as their languages show, for these are relatively lacking in expressions relating to degrees of futurity. Hence arises a kind of myopia which prevents them from clearly locating what is a little way ahead, and this evidently is not conducive to foresight, even were they otherwise inclined that way.

signs indicating beforehand what this order of Nature will assuredly bring about by virtue of that determinism which regulates the series of cause and effect. Supposing these signs did not occur, or if they did occur and nobody should see or notice them, there would be no change in the events, the effects would be the same, provided the causes still obtained. Omens therefore remain something outside the series of natural phenomena. But as these series are often very long and complicated, and our power of rational foresight is very weak, we like to imagine that a friendly power lifts the veil shrouding the future, and straightway shows us the end of the series. It is a sort of gracious compliance which satisfies our impatience to know, and it does not change or modify any of the conditions.

Primitive mentality, however, is not thus equilibrated by the conception of a fixed order of the universe. The type of causality which it habitually conceives is quite different. Consequently, for the primitive omens will assume a different importance. As the manifestations of mystic and occult powers, which alone are causes, they play an essential part in the production of that which they announce. It is not their only function to reveal what will happen; what they reveal would not take place without them. The future which the omens predict being *felt* as direct and real, they are *felt* to determine it at the time when they manifest it. Here the law of participation intervenes, and the abstract analysis of this mental process could make it entirely intelligible only by misrepresenting it. It is far better to let the facts speak for themselves, interpreting them by the light of the preceding observations.

II

The custom of noting omens and regulating conduct by them is met with in many uncivilized peoples. But nowhere does it seem to be more fully developed than among the Dayaks and most other native tribes of Borneo. It is here that we shall find the most favourable conditions for the study of omens. The evidence at our disposal is abundant, and it is usually concordant, while some of it, notably that of Perham and Nieuwenhuis, is extremely valuable.

Perham has ably demonstrated the authority recognized as belonging to omens, and the power attributed to them by native tribes. " This involved system of life is thoroughly believed in as the foundation of all success. Stories upon stories are recounted of the sicknesses and of the deaths that have resulted from disregard of the omens. You may reason with them against the system, but in the co-incidences which they can produce for them they have a proof positive of its truth ; and to them an accidental coincidence is more convincing than the most cogent reasoning. . . . All the cases in which the event has apparently verified the prediction are carefully remembered, whilst those in which the omen has been falsified are as quickly forgotten." [1]

This selection of theirs, which is made quite unconsciously and in all good faith, is facilitated by the fact that " this system . . . is most elaborate and complex, involving un-certainties innumerable to all who are not fully experi-enced in the science, and the younger men have constantly to ask the older ones how to act in the unexpected coin-cidences of various and apparently contradictory omens." [2]

There can be no question here of entering upon an ex-position, however brief, of this system and the casuistry which it induces. Suffice it to say that omens for all the circumstances of life, whether individual or social, are furnished by seven different birds, besides a certain number of animals (the stag, moose-deer, gazelle, and armadillo), three kinds of insects, the lizard, bat, python, cobra, and sometimes also the rat. " All these creatures may afford omens in different ways, and consequently, inasmuch as they have this power, they are called birds (*burong*) ; obtaining omens from them is called *beburong*." Omens are derived from the flight of birds, the cries of animals, the direction whence they come or which they follow, and so on. . . . In this respect the similarity to the Roman auguries is most striking.

[1] Rev. J. Perham, quoted by Ling Roth : *The Natives of Sarawak*, i. p. 195. [2] Ibid., i. p. 191.

Many witnesses affirm that in default of favourable omens or in face of sinister ones, an enterprise will not be undertaken, or, if already begun, will be abandoned. For instance, " the Kenyah of Tanah Putih wished to make use of our stay to build a boat. But on entering the forest (to fell a tree) they met a *hisit* (bird) which whistled to the left of them, and they turned right about. Half an hour afterwards they returned and felled a tree, but at the moment it fell they again perceived an unfavourable augury. They left the tree lying, and gave up all idea of their boat." [1]

In the same way, from the very first moment of starting a journey, the omens must be favourable, or else it will be abandoned. " Their attitude seemed really inexplicable to me, but I was immediately told that there could be no question of our starting, seeing that one of their omen birds, a *hisit* moreover, had just flown over the house and had even entered by the roof. That was the most fatal sign of all for the beginning of a journey ; therefore it would be necessary to observe a *melo njaho* (a general taboo) for four days, and then study the birds again. . . ." [2]

The more difficult or dangerous the enterprise, the greater the need of favourable omens. " They tell me that several villages wished to take part in this journey, about five hundred men in all, but it was necessary for each village to study the birds on its own account. For an expedition of this kind they did not think it wise to be satisfied with less than ten different favourable auguries. Since most of the natives found something or other unfavourable in the series, they were obliged to retrace their steps." [3]

If the decree which the omens yield is thus supreme, it is not only on account of their being considered infallible predictions. The reason goes deeper yet. A favourable omen is a positive support with which one cannot dispense. It does not simply announce success ; it secures it. It is an indispensable guarantee for it, a *sine qua non*. It is not enough that there should be no unfavourable augury ; it is absolutely necessary that favourable ones should present themselves. Wanting these, nothing can be done,

[1] A. W. Nieuwenhuis : *Quer durch Borneo*, ii. p. 441.
[2] Ibid., i. p. 417.   [3] Ibid., ii. p. 425.

even should doing nothing prove disastrous. Thus, before beginning to sow the seed, it is absolutely essential to have heard one particular bird on the right, or to have seen another on the left, etc. If it were only a question of being informed whether the harvest would be good, one might resign oneself, *faute de mieux*, to work on in uncertainty, especially when time is pressing, and the season for sowing will soon be over. Nevertheless, the natives will not begin as long as the necessary auguries are not forthcoming, and this is because the bird omens of themselves have a magic virtue which assures a good harvest at the same time as they predict it. If these omens have not made their appearance, neither will the good crop.

Perham's evidence on this point is very explicit. " It may possibly require a month to obtain all those augural predictions which are to give them confidence in the result of their labours. The augur has now the same number of twigs or sticks as birds he has heard, and he takes these to the land selected for farming, and puts them in the ground, says a short form of address to the birds and Pulang-gana, cuts a little grass with his *parang*, and returns. The magic virtue of the birds has been transferred to the land." [1] It is because the magic virtue of the birds is indispensable to the fertility of the soil that the natives are obliged to await their good pleasure before beginning to cultivate.

The following fact is no less significant : " When visiting the sick, birds on the road are desired, as possessing some power for health. And here I may mention another way of communicating the virtue of the good omen to the object. When a Dayak hears a good bird on his way to a sick friend, he will sit down and chew some betel-nut, sirih leaf, lime, tobacco and gambier for his own refreshment, and then chew a little more and wrap it in a leaf and take it to his friend; and if the sick man can only eat, it will materially help the cure, for does it not contain the voice of the bird, a mystic elixir of life from the unseen world ? " [2]

The Dayak therefore not only brings the sick man the assurance that he will recover, but at the same time he

---

[1] H. Ling Roth : *Natives of Sarawak*, i. p. 192.
[2] Ibid., i. pp. 194–5.

provides him with a valuable remedy, carefully procured, and derived from the magic virtue of the bird. " The *burong malam* is an insect, so called because it is generally heard at night ; it is specially sought after on the warpath as the god of safety and victory. It is altogether a good genius as the *nendak* is among the birds. And in farming it is equally valued. A man heard it on one occasion in a tree on his farmland, late in the morning, and dedicated an offering to it at the foot of the tree, which was afterwards regarded as sacred and was not felled with the rest. And he had his reward in an abundant harvest." [1]

It is evident that the insect is not treated like a messenger bringing good news, but like a power, almost a divinity, whose continuance of favour is sought. The tree is spared, because by a sort of participation the good influence of the insect which rested upon it has passed into it. The tree is now impregnated with this virtue, and it, in its turn, impregnates the Dayak's land.

" When travelling on the river the Kenyahs hope to see *Isit* (the spider-hunter) fly across from left to right as they sit facing the bow of the canoe. When this happens they call out loudly : ' O *Isit*, on the left hand ! Give us long life, help us in our undertaking, help us to find what we are seeking, make our enemies feeble !' They usually stop their canoes, land on the bank, and then making a small fire, say to it : ' Tell *Isit* to help us.' Each man of the party will light a cigarette in order that he may have his own fire, and will murmur some part at least of the usual formulas." [2] This invocation is also a prayer, and undoubtedly it is to the bird itself that the Kenyah addresses it.

It will not surprise us therefore to find Perham writing of a *bird cultus*. " The object of the bird cultus is like that of all other rites : to secure good crops, freedom from accidents and violence and diseases, victory in war, and profit in exchange and trade, skill in discourse, and cleverness in all natural craft. I say bird *cultus*, for it rises from observance of omens into invocations and worship

[1] Rev. J. Perham : " Sea Dayak Religion," *Journal of Straits Branch of Asiatic Society*, No. 10, p. 232 (1911).
[2] Hose and MacDougall : *The Pagan Tribes of Borneo*, ii. pp. 58–9.

of birds. . . ." (Here follows a lengthy extract from a Dayak hymn.) "The birds are here contemplated as in company with the Dayak, ordering his life and giving effect to the labour, and the invocation and the offering are to impetrate their favour. Another function in which the cultus of these winged creatures comes out distinctly is the festival which is described as *mri burong makai*, giving the birds to eat, that is, giving them an offering. It may be said to be a minor festival in honour of Singalang-Burong, and of his sons-in-law, the omen spirit birds." [1]

These are not the ordinary birds we know. Even if we conceive of them as endowed with mystic powers, our idea of them does not in any way correspond with that formed by the Dayaks. We cannot fail to perceive, first and foremost, their objective characteristics in the image our minds form of them. We visualize the characteristic shape of their bodies, their wings, beaks, movements on the ground and in flight, and so on ; and on these we superimpose the idea of their mystic properties. But to the Dayak's mind these properties, which he considers of incomparable importance, conceal all the others. In the omen bird he sees first of all the sacred being, the mystic power upon which his lot depends. Here we find that special form of abstraction which I have described elsewhere,[2] a form for which there is scarcely any analogy in our thought, which is primarily conceptual.

"These birds," says Perham, "are forms of animal life possessed of the spirit of certain invisible beings above and bearing their names" (this is a significant trait, for the name is not merely a designation ; the identity in the name implies an actual participation, an identity of being), "so that when a Dayak hears a *beragai*, for instance, it is in reality the voice of Beragai, the son-in-law of Singalong Burong ; nay more, the assenting nod or dissenting frown of the great spirit himself." [3]

To minds like ours it is one of two things. Either the birds are the mouthpiece of invisible beings whose will

[1] H. Ling Roth : *The Natives of Sarawak*, i. pp. 196–7.
[2] *Les Fonctions Mentales dans les Sociétés Inférieures*, pp. 124–8.
[3] H. Ling Roth : *Natives of Sarawak*, i. p. 200.

they make known, and from whom they are distinct, or else they are the incarnation of these invisible beings, who have in this way made themselves perceptible to the senses. These two incompatible ideas cannot both be true, and we must choose between them ; but the Dayak does not find any difficulty in admitting them both at once. In his representations the one does not exclude the other. He has a direct understanding of certain participations which relegate logical exigencies to the second place. To him, " to be " in this sense means " to partake of the same essence." The birds *are* invisible beings from on high, just as the Bororo of Brazil *are araras* (red parrots).[1]

III

Hence it is quite natural that to the Dayak idea sacred birds should not only announce events, but should also bring them about. As the mouthpiece of invisible beings, they predict ; as these invisible beings themselves, they operate. To them, therefore, prayers and invocations will be addressed, they will be the objects of worship. This fact, described, as we have already seen by Perham, has also been noted in many of the tribes of Borneo by Hose and MacDougall, but they interpret it differently. They do not think, as Perham does, that in the natives' eyes the omen birds really possess the mystic power which controls events. The proper function of these birds would seem to be to act merely as the messengers of the gods, and it is by a kind of abuse and usurpation of the rôle that more important powers are attributed to them. " The custom of approaching and communicating with the gods through the medium of omen birds seems to be responsible in a large measure for the fact that the gods themselves are but dimly conceived, and are not felt to be in intimate and simple relations with their worshippers. The omen birds seem to form not only a medium of communication, but also, as it were, a screen which obscures from the people the vision of their gods. As in many analogous instances, the intercessors and messengers to whose care the messages are committed assume in the eyes of the people an undue importance ; the god behind the omen bird is apt to be almost lost sight of, and the bird itself tends to become an object of reverence, and to be regarded as the recipient of the prayer and the dispenser of the benefits which properly he only foretells or announces." [1]

• Hose and MacDougall make frequent references to this idea. "We think it probable," they say, "that in this case the Kenyahs have carried further the tendency we noted in the Kayans to allow the omen birds to figure so prominently in their rites and prayers as to obscure the gods whose messengers they are ; and the Bali Flaki (a kind of hawk) has in this way been driven into the background, and more or less completely taken the position of a god whose name even has been forgotten by many of the Kenyahs, if not by all of them." [2]

Elsewhere, too : " Although the Kenyahs thus look to Bali Flaki to guide them and help them in many ways, and express gratitude towards him, we do not think that they conceive of him as a single great spirit as some of the other tribes tend to do ; they rather look upon the hawks as messengers and intermediators between themselves and Bali Penyalong, to whom a certain undefined amount of power is delegated. No doubt it is a vulgar error with them, as in the case of professors of other forms of belief, to forget in some degree the Supreme Being, and to direct their prayers and thoughts almost exclusively to the subordinate power, which, having concrete forms, they can more easily keep before their minds. They regard favourable omens as given for their encouragement, and bad omens as friendly warnings. We were told by one very intelligent Kenyah that he supposed that the hawks having been so frequently sent by Bali Penyalong to give them warning, had learnt how to do this of their own will, and that sometimes they probably did give them warning or encouragement independently without being sent to them." [3]

[1] Hose and MacDougall : *The Pagan Tribes of Borneo*, ii. pp. 9–10 (1912) ; cf. ii. p. 75.
[2] Ibid., ii. p. 15.   [3] Ibid., ii. pp. 57–8.

The interpretation suggested by Hose and MacDougall for the fact that they themselves have noted makes an ingenious hypothesis, and the analogy they bring forward may make it appear probable. More than once, indeed, it has happened that a divinity has paid the price of his remoteness, and has found himself supplanted as an object of worship by mere intermediaries who are nearer to men, more familiar with them, and more accessible to their imagination. But are we to conclude from this general remark that such an evolution has taken place in the natives of Borneo ? If the omen birds of Borneo began by being nothing but messengers and intermediaries, Hose and MacDougall do indeed explain how it is they have become powers which are invoked and adored on their own account. But the precise question to determine is whether this transformation has ever taken place, and whether the functions of omen birds have ever been other than they are to-day. Has any other witness ever explicitly presented them as messengers and nothing more ? Hose and MacDougall do not maintain such to be the case, and nothing in Perham's report leads us to imagine it. Neither Nieuwenhuis nor other investigators thoroughly worthy of belief say anything of the sort. The hypothesis seems more or less venturesome. It appears to have been suggested by the well-known tendency to discover in the mentality of inferior races the processes which we observe in our own.

Finally—and this is a point which again controverts the Hose-MacDougall hypothesis—in Hardeland's excellent grammar of the Dayak languages, we find that omens are considered as persons. " The Dahiang omens furnished by birds, snakes, etc., are personalities (*biti*) to the Dayaks. They have their abode in the sea of clouds." [1] They are then blended with those " invisible beings from on high " of which Perham speaks.

When an important enterprise is in question it is necessary, as we have already seen, to obtain a great number of favourable omens—omens which are themselves highly important, and which proceed from the highest of the mystic powers.

[1] A. Hardeland : *Grammatik der Dayakschen Sprache*, p. 368.

If there should not be a sufficient number of these, and of the class required, must the enterprise be abandoned ? To avoid such an extreme measure, the natives of Borneo try to influence these powers. The means which they set in motion are themselves naturally of a mystic character.

Frequently a whole series of rites, ceremonies and inhibitions will be indispensable. For instance, it may be a question of deciding which of the Kayan fields shall be cultivated in any particular year. " If, during three days, no evil omens have been observed, there is sufficient encouragement therein to proceed to the last stage of felling the heavy timber, and to incite the entire household to co-operate in the search for further requisite auguries. . . . All the families remain secluded in a long veranda, or in their small private rooms, and sit all day long quite still, smoking and talking ; not a soul is allowed to leave the house, or at most to go further than the bank of the river, excepting two men designated as the *laki-niho* (hawk-men), whose duty it is to look for a hawk called *niho*. While these hawk-men are engaged in this search, no one may call them by their true names ; even an accidental infringement of this rule is punished by a fine. . . . It is the custom of some households for the *laki-niho* not to return to the house during the whole three days' search for omens ; at such times they build in the jungle, near the clearing, a small hut which they indicate to be *permantong* (taboo) by putting up outside it two poles . . . whereon the bark is stripped . . . at intervals." [1]

The choice of two men specially engaged in the search for sacred birds, the precautions of which they are the object, the inhibitions to which they have to submit, very closely recall the ceremonies customary in New Guinea (Wanigela River)[2] to assure success in the hunting of dugong. The similarity of the processes employed permits us to conclude that the ends pursued are the same. The natives of New Guinea hope in this way to exercise a magical influence on the dugongs, that they may make their nets safe and

    [1] W. H. Furness : *The Home Life of the Borneo Head-hunters*, pp. 161–4 (1902).
    [2] R. E. Guise: "On the Tribes inhabiting the Mouth of the Wanigela River, New Guinea," *J.A.I.*, xxviii. p. 218.

guide the boats from which they harpoon. The Kayans in the same way believe that they can exercise a mystic influence on hawks which will induce them to appear and furnish favourable omens, that is, to give the help without which it would be useless to try and cultivate the soil.

Should one of these omens be forthcoming, the native immediately thanks the bird, who then becomes in his eyes not only the herald, but also the author, of the benefit thus announced. This is a thanksgiving which natives never neglect. " As soon as one of these favourable omens is seen, the hunters build a fire, a signal to the birds and animals, conveying thanks for their services." [1]

" As we rounded the turn of the river we came to a sudden pause. The advance guard of the five canoes had hauled up to the shore. On a narrow sandy bank an excited crowd of warriors were kindling a fire and putting up poles and arches of sticks cut along their whole length into curled shavings—a bird of good omen had been seen on the right side ! . . . The fire, an unfailing messenger from men to the omniscient Omen-givers, now announced to the birds that their favour was greatly appreciated." [2]

" That morning we saw on a branch projecting over the river a beautiful bird called *burong papu* by the natives. . . . It is . . . one of the birds whose appearance is considered a good omen by the Dayaks, especially if they are starting for a . . . head-hunting expedition. But to meet it is always a sign of good luck, and my Dayaks asked me to allow them to stop a little while in token of respect, to which I readily consented. They stopped rowing, and remaining a few minutes quite still with their paddles lifted, and then cheerfully resumed their labour." [3]

Dr. Nieuwenhuis had an opportunity of observing the same thing. " Quite close to us, on the right, they heard the cry of the *isit*. The bird was thus predicting a successful journey. In conformity with custom, Kwing Iran had to disembark and smoke a cigarette." [4] (The smoke carries the native's thanksgiving to the bird.)

[1] W. H. Furness : *Borneo Head-hunters*, p. 4.
[2] Ibid., p. 78.
[3] O. Beccari : *Wanderings in the Forests of Borneo*, pp. 328-9 (1904).
[4] A. W. Nieuwenhuis : *Quer durch Borneo*, i. p. 351.

IV

The facts just recorded and examined shed a good deal of light on the nature of omens. The signs thus given by birds or certain animals are not only indications, warnings, announcements of what is about to happen. They are at the same time the causes of them. In these birds and animals the primitive's mind perceives mystic powers upon which the events they foretell depend. Does the power to produce these events belong to them wholly and as of right ? Are they alone the vehicles of it ? Are they to be considered as transmitting agents, themselves possessing a portion of the power while exercising the influence they represent ? These are questions which the primitive does not ask himself in any clear and precise fashion, and questions which, if asked, he would not answer in any uniform way.

There is no reason to suppose that representations of this kind are necessarily identical everywhere. In proportion to the degree of development attained by a people, the notions of religion received from neighbouring groups, or from conquered or conquering races, the idea of individualized deities will be more or less prominent, and the birds or animals which furnish omens will appear more or less distinctly as the ministers or messengers of these gods. Hose and MacDougall, as well as Nieuwenhuis, have pointed out differences in this respect between the tribes in Borneo itself.

Without denying the variations which necessarily result from the diversity of social structure, we may affirm that the more we find, in any given uncivilized race, the characters peculiar to primitive mentality, the more distinctly will its omens present the features we have stated above. The bird or animal furnishing them is not invoked simply as the bearer of good tidings ; it is besought, adored, and thanked as the dispenser of gifts which are indispensable and which can be procured from it alone. To a mind of this kind, therefore, the omen is not a mere sign, it is at the same time a cause. Or, to put it more clearly, in such circumstances the mind does not differentiate between sign and cause. Perhaps it has no notion of a sign which is purely a sign, at any rate when the realities of the invisible world enter in any degree into its representation. Undoubtedly, certain primitives are very well able to turn natural signs to account. Very often, for instance, if it is a question of recognizing the scarcely perceptible tracks made in the ground by a special animal or person, if it is a case of prognosticating a change of weather, and so forth, natives have amazed Europeans by their sagacity. But then we are dealing with connections which have been made familiar to them through experience, education, and considerations of practical utility. Then they make use of a memory which is often " phenomenal," and apply a degree of attention which is all the more powerful because it has few other objects. But when it becomes a question of signs which manifest the presence of mystic forces, their mental orientation is absolutely different. The signs take on a mystical significance. It is no longer possible to distinguish between " sign " and " cause." Omens are an excellent example of this, and unusual circumstances, such as we have already treated of, form others.

Which of these two elements is it that predominates in the eyes of the primitive ? The omen predicts and produces the event of which the bird is the herald and the author. But does it predict it because it produces it ? Or, indeed, as is generally believed, does it seem to produce it because it predicts it ? In such a case the illusion would be the result of a well-known psychological law ; when the master is too far off, and cannot be readily imagined, the ministers who interpose themselves, and who *are* in evidence, receive the homage primarily intended for him. If we are guided by our own experience, this latter conjecture would seem natural enough. But it does not appear to tally with the mental experience of the primitive, for to him prediction is not in fact differentiated from production. We have many proofs of this besides those we have found in omens, properly so called. Thus, with the Indians of New France, " from what we have told them about solar and lunar eclipses (of which they stand very much in awe) they imagine that we govern them ; they think we know everything that is about to happen, and that we arrange it

With this idea in mind they apply to us to find out whether their crops will be good, to know where their enemies are, and in what force they will attack." [1]

" In Kamchatka the natives thank the wagtails for the spring and summer because they think these birds bring the seasons with them." [2] These wagtails are also omen birds, and to them is attributed the power to produce the spring they announce. All the circumstances of this kind, of which there are a great many, are easy to interpret when we refer them to the type of causality familiar to primitive mentality. In default of any idea of the causal relation of antecedent and consequent, the transition from the invisible mystic power to its visible effects is a direct one.

The Indians have no idea of the astronomical conditions upon which the solar or lunar eclipses depend. But they know that white people are mighty wizards, whose power cannot be measured ; why should not their sorceries be exercised on the sun and moon ? In fact, the missionaries do predict the precise day and hour of the eclipses. How could they do this, if they did not cause them ? To comprehend a prediction which is merely the knowledge of an event about to occur, it is necessary to have been able to conceive the concatenation of secondary causes which culminates in the event appearing at a given time and place. But if there is no notion of this sort at all, it is very difficult to imagine that he who can predict is not he who produces, except in a case where the mystic powers have confided their intentions. A similar mental process must have been employed in the case of a woman in South Africa, who was accused of sorcery and threatened with death because she had nursed very carefully, and cured, a certain disease. It had been concluded that it was she who had caused it. How could she have known how to make it disappear if she had not been the one to make it come ? Directly it becomes a question of mystic agency, knowledge is not differentiated from power, and power is the condition of knowledge.

The Hose-MacDougall hypothesis already recorded was

---

[1] *Relations des Jésuites*, xvii. p. 118 (1639–40). (Le Jeune.)
[2] G. W. Steller : *Beschreibungen von dem Lande Kamtschatka*, p. 280.

therefore not merely gratuitous; it presented the case
as exactly contrary to its real bearing. It is not because
the sacred birds announce events that the natives end by
believing that they produce them; on the contrary, as
Perham clearly perceived, the natives believe that the
birds *make* the success or failure of the undertakings, and
that is why omens are infallible signs of what will happen.
Thus omens are at once predictions, promises, and guarantees.
They may be trusted, because the birds or animals to which
they are due have shown through them their goodwill
and their favour at the same time as their prophetic power.
In the acts of thanksgiving addressed to them, the gratitude
of the natives is not given to the heralds of good tidings
merely, but first and foremost to the protecting powers who
assure the success of their undertakings.

Thus, to the primitive mind, the omen is primarily a
cause, but at the same time it is a sign because it is a cause.
As the characteristics peculiar to his mentality grow pro-
portionately weaker, the mystic type of causality ceases
to dominate it almost entirely, time and space come to be
felt less as qualities, and realized more as ideas, and finally,
the attention fastens more and more closely upon the objective
series of cause and effect. By an inevitable consequence
the omen tends to conform to these changes of idea. It
becomes more and more of a sign and less and less of a
cause, until at length the primitive no longer understands
how it could ever be a cause.

Between these two extreme positions there are many
intermediate ones. The omen will lose its power little by
little as the mind attaches itself more to the consideration
of secondary causes. It will become more and more restricted
to its function as a sign by which is revealed, not the agency
of a mystic power any longer, but the event in which a
given series of cause and effect is to culminate. Nevertheless, one mental habit does not disappear entirely and all
of a sudden in presence of another which tends to take
its place. On the contrary, both are in existence for some
time before their incompatibility is discovered. It may
even happen that the old custom is not entirely superseded
by the new. The French peasant, for instance, knows in

a general but superficial way what climatic, physical, and chemical conditions are necessary to secure an abundant harvest. He will none the less continue to believe it to be due also and above all to the goodwill and favour of mystic powers. He doubtless no longer imagines their agency to be a direct one, or as independent of time or space, nor does he consider it in any way unique. But he still attributes to these powers ability to direct the chain of events as they desire.

It is thus that omens continue to possess a certain value, although they are no longer recognized as possessed of a causality of their own. They remain signs of what will happen. If they no longer produce it, they still announce it; and if they announce it as accredited messengers, they still participate in the respect inspired by powers whose intentions and decrees they make known. At this stage the study and the interpretations of omens still preserve a religious character. At a subsequent period this respect degenerates into superstition. The good man who is so annoyed at having seen a spider this morning, because a spider is " a sign of bad luck," does not believe that the spider will cause the bad luck it foretells. He is merely annoyed with it for announcing it. Into this resentment there enters a lively residue of the old idea of the omen, when it was both sign and cause, and " sign " because " cause." Such signs as these are divested of their causality little by little, but as long as they remain really signs, some remnant of their earlier mystic power remains attached to them.[1]

---

[1] On this point the missionary Jetté utters a significant statement. " Omens," says he, " as observed by our Ten'a, imply an obscure idea of causality, inasmuch as the omen is taken not merely as foreboding what is going to happen, but as being in some measure instrumental in bringing it about. The same is true, as observation shows, of the omens observed by superstitious whites ; for in their case, as well as in that of our savages, it is taken for granted that the avoidance of the omen averts the calamity. A sea-captain, for instance, who takes care not to sail on Friday, a guest who declines to sit the thirteenth at the dinner-table, implicitly assert that by suppressing the ill-omened circumstance they will avert the forthcoming misfortune, and evidently establish between the two a relation of cause to effect, which it is absurd to suppose."—R. F. Jul. Jetté : " On the Superstitions of the Ten'a Indians," *Anthropos*, vi. p. 241.

Absurd, indeed, from the point of view of our mentality, which involves a consideration of the determinism of natural phenomena, but not absurd from the standpoint of prelogical mentality, which is mystical by nature, and pays no heed to anything but the direct causality of occult forces.

CHAPTER V

OMENS—(continued)

I

WHEN the primitive observes an omen that is favourable he is filled with gratitude. He feels encouraged to take action, strengthened in his resolve, and sure of success. He puts forth all his energies, and very frequently, in fact, he does succeed.

But when he observes an unfavourable one, what will he do ? Whenever possible, he will refrain from action. He will not make a start, or, if already *en route*, he will return home. He will abandon the enterprise he has begun. We have seen how the native of Borneo gives up a journey because the auguries are unfavourable, leaves the tree, which he had selected for his canoe and felled with great difficulty, lying on the ground, and so on.

It may happen that renunciation is not always possible.[1] If the omen which predicts disaster is encountered when the travellers are already far from home and near the meeting-place ; if they have already joined issue with the enemy ; if their fields are ploughed and their seed sown, what are they to do then ? A whole system of casuistry has had to be evolved to meet such cases, and give a favourable inter-pretation to bad omens, or at any rate to neutralize them. The native has been obliged to make a plan, or rather a multiplicity of plans, to overcome them, lest they bring about the misfortune they announce.

[1] It appears as if the search for favourable omens were always obligatory for those who take the initiative in any undertaking. But if, under the pressure of circumstances, they have to act at once, they are forced to abandon it. Nieuwenhuis has noticed this fact. " Before undertaking any enterprise whatever, the Kenyah seek for good omens as conscientiously as the Bahau do, but should this search conflict with the needs of the moment, they venture to disregard the omens. If danger threatens, if, for instance, the enemy is in ambush in the neighbourhood, the Kenyah no longer pay attention to omens."—Nieuwenhuis : *Quer durch Borneo*, ii. p. 487.

First of all they may consider that the decision arrived at admits of appeal, and they may seek for a favourable augury without being discouraged by the fact that the one that has appeared is of the contrary kind. That is the simplest thing, and such a plan of action is most frequently adopted. When at length the good omen desired does present itself, it nullifies those which have gone before ; therefore they act at once, lest a fresh augury, and this time an unfavourable one, should make its appearance and once again enjoin withdrawal. Or again, the fatal omen may be tested by divination. " The worst of all omens is a dead beast of any kind, especially those included in the omen list, found anywhere on the farm. It infuses a deadly poison into the whole crop, and will kill someone or other of the owner's family within the year. When this terrible thing happens, they test the omen by killing a pig, and examine the appearance of the liver immediately after death. If the prediction be confirmed, all the rice grown on that ground must be sold ; and, if necessary, other rice bought for their own consumption. Other people may eat it, for the omen only affects those at whom it is directly pointed." [1]

This last characteristic depends upon the causal relation implied in the apprehension of the omen being qualitatively *felt* in the connection between its expressions, without at the same time being represented generally. Here we have one of the many different forms in which the very slightly conceptual nature of the primitive's collective representations betrays itself, and it is to be met with in many inferior races. Thus, in the Upper Congo, " the landing of a hippopotamus in a town might be an omen of war for one family, and have no significance for another ; a flood might be a sign of famine and trouble to one family and not affect another ; a huge tree floating freely down river might be an augury to one town of sickness and many deaths, and be entirely disregarded by another." [2]

" There is another way," adds Perham, " of escaping the effects of omens less vicious than the foregoing. Some

[1] Rev. J. Perham : " Sea Dyak Religion," *Journal of the Straits Branch of the Asiatic Society*, No. 10, pp. 231–2.
[2] Rev. J. H. Weeks : " Anthropological Notes on the Bangala of the Upper Congo River," *J.A.I.*, xl. p. 376 (1910).

men by a peculiar magic influence, or by gift of the bird-spirits, are credited with possessing in themselves, in their own hearts and bodies, some occult power which can over-come bad omens (*penabar burong*). These men are able, by eating something, however small, of the produce of the farm, to turn off the evil prognostications. Anything grown on it which can be eaten, a bit of Indian corn, a little mustard, or a few cucumber shoots, is taken by the wise man ; and he quietly eats it raw for a small consideration and thereby appropriates to himself the evil omen which in him becomes inocuous, and thus delivers the other from the ban of the *pemali* or taboo."[1]

This operation throws a strong light on the nature of the omen. If it were the mere announcement of misfortune communicated by a superior power, would not the native first of all address himself to this power and try to induce it to avert the calamity, or apply to its representatives if he knew any ? The Dayak does not think of doing that. To one mystic power he opposes another, superior to it. The omen is not averted ; it is fought and overcome.

But the most usual method employed, when circumstances permit of it, is the prevention of the sinister omen from making its appearance. In order not to hear the cry of a bird of evil omen, for instance, the natives will make such a commotion that the bird's cry, even if uttered, will not be heard by anyone.

" When setting up the posts of a farm or of a house, they beat gongs and make a deafening noise to prevent any birds from being heard."[2] Naturally this is *after* they have obtained the favourable auguries without which they would not risk beginning to build a house. " When we were all seated, the gongs redoubled and trebled their din, to drown all sounds of evil portent while the rites take place."[3] Sir Spenser St. John had already noted this custom. " To hear the cry of a deer is at all times unlucky, and to prevent the sound reaching their ears during a marriage

[1] Rev. J. Perham : " Sea Dyak Religion," *Journal of the Straits Branch of the Asiatic Society*, No. 10, p. 232.
[2] Rev. J. Perham, quoted by Ling Roth : *The Natives of Sarawak*, i. p. 195.
[3] Furness : *The Home Life of the Borneo Head-hunters*, p. 33.

procession gongs and drums are loudly beaten. On the way to their farms, should the unlucky omen be heard, they will return home and do no more work for a day." [1]

Perham regards practices of this kind as contradictory. He argues that if the Dayaks really believe that the bad omen exerts a sinister influence on the ceremony that is taking place, it is not averted in any way by their preventing the portent from being noticed. The sound of their gongs and drums cannot hinder the stag from having bayed, or the *isit* from having whistled on the wrong side, etc. To refuse to recognize a fact does not prevent its actually happening. Although it may not be perceived it nevertheless exists, and it produces its usual effect none the less. But in the first place, that which is contradictory has no terrors for the primitive mind. We know that it readily accommodates itself to that, especially when under the influence of a fairly powerful emotion, and in the circumstances we are investigating the Dayaks have a capital interest in evading bad omens. They have a passionate desire that such shall not appear.

In the second place, it is not as a herald that the sinister omen is formidable, but as a cause, a force, or at any rate the vehicle of a force. Moreover, by virtue of the law of participation primitives do not clearly differentiate between a force and its expression. If therefore they succeed in hindering the latter from conveying the malignant power to its destined end, if they arrest its course, they also paralyse it and prevent its efficacy. The power is nullified, just as we have found it was when a man endowed with special magic virtue ate a grain of rice grown on the field threatened by an evil omen. This process therefore is not mere inconsistency and child's play; it is an effectual parrying of the blow. It is a weapon which the Romans did not fail to employ, to the great dismay of those who recount the history of divination. [2]

To evade evil portents all subterfuges are allowable. For example, " if the hawk appears on the wrong side` when

---

[1] Quoted by A. C. Haddon : *Head-hunters, Black, White, and Brown,* p. 386.
[2] Bouché-Leclercq : *Histoire de la divination dans l'antiquité,* iv. p. 137.

men are paddling a few days away from home and nearing another village, they immediately turn the boat right round and pull to the bank and light a fire. By turning round they put the hawk on the right side, and being satisfied in their own mind they proceed on their journey as before."[1] Such conduct would be silly and childish if the hawk were simply bringing bad news, if it were merely announcing what was to happen, for the " trick " played by the Dayaks would not alter anything. But if the hawk is the vehicle of a mystic force, a good or an evil one, according to the direction it comes from, it is not foolish to change this direction if one can, and make it favourable instead of unlucky. As far as the mystic powers are concerned, it is an operation analogous to that of the engineer who reverses the steam valve when he desires to go in a contrary direction to that which he has just been pursuing. The thanksgivings addressed to the hawk show the earnestness and the sincerity of the Dayaks, who interrupt their navigation to be able to light the thanksgiving fire, and who would not dare to play a prank on the sacred bird.

If at all costs the sinister portent must be prevented from making its apearance, the natives will try to discover an infallible method of accomplishing this. Thus " to perceive bad omens on the very first day of cultivation is particularly unlucky, for if they are met with on the morning of that day, rice cannot be cultivated for a whole year ; only potatoes and maize may be planted. To avoid such a catastrophe, the native will choose the night hours to go first to the field which he is to cultivate."[2]

Here, again, is it a harmless prank which should raise a smile ? Most assuredly not, to the native's mind. It is on the contrary a really serious plan, and one that can entirely paralyse the baneful influences which might prohibit the cultivation of rice for a whole year. It is, as it were, putting a formidable foe out of action.

If the vexatious event has occurred and seems likely to last, the best thing is to entreat the omen birds to put an end to it. In a variety of ways the natives try to induce

[1] A. C. Haddon : *Head-hunters, Black, White, and Brown*, p. 387.
[2] A. W. Nieuwenhuis : *Quer durch Borneo*, i. p. 161 ; cf. i. p. 387.

them to pursue a more kindly course. If need be, they threaten them.

" At the end of five days, during which the freshet acquired daily and nightly new strength from heavy thunder-storms, the omen birds, the guides and guardians of these people, were harangued and alternately cajoled and threatened. At one time a fruitless attempt was made to deceive them. The whole party disembarked, and donning their spears and parangs, made a wide circuit in the jungle, so as to make the birds believe that the canoes were not going home, but were on an ordinary hunting expedition.

" Once Tama Bulan, while sitting in our canoe, shook his fist at a bird perched on a bough near by, and upbraided it for not causing the rain to cease. When he observed our interest in the proceedings, his face broke into an em-barrassed smile, and he poked me in the ribs, and said, chuckling : ' Tuan does not believe in the birds, does he ? He thinks Tama Bulan is crazy.' " [1]

After reading this, it seems difficult to maintain that the birds' function is merely to announce what will happen. The natives act as if they were persuaded that the cessation of the rain depends upon the birds.

If the original idea of the omen be such, and to the native mind it really is an active agent as well as a revelation of the future, we shall not be surprised to find that nearly all uncivilized communities manifest a desire to rid them-selves, whenever possible, of the creature which is the harbinger of woe. To the Borneo Kayans " all the snake *aman* are bad omens, and in the case of a Kayan seeing *batang lima* (*Simotes octolineatus*) he will endeavour to kill it ; should he fail to kill it, then ' look out ! ' " [2]

In New Zealand, too, " if a traveller should see a lizard in the path before him, he would know the creature had not come there of its own accord, but had been sent by an enemy as an *aitua* (evil omen) to cause his death. He therefore at once kills the reptile, and craves a woman to step over it as it lies in the path. By this means the evil omen is averted." [3]

[1] W. H. Furness : *The Home Life of the Borneo Head-hunters*, p. 28.
[2] A. C. Haddon : *Head-hunters, Black, White, and Brown*, p. 391.
[3] W. H. Goldie : " Maori Medical Lore," *Transactions of the New Zealand Institute*, xxxvii. p. 18 (1904).

The expressions used in this recital are very characteristic. The evil omen is sent not merely to announce the death
of the native who sees it, but to " cause " it. By killing
the lizard, the blow is warded off. Steller presents things
as somewhat different in Kamchatka. " The natives regard
lizards as spies and emissaries sent by the ruler of the lower
world to seek out men and tell them they are about to die.
Therefore they notice lizards carefully, and when they see
one they spring upon it with their knives and cut it in pieces
so that it may not make any report about them. If it
should escape them they are greatly concerned, and expect
death at any moment, and as this may, indeed, sometimes
happen as the result of imagination, or even as a mere
coincidence, this belief of theirs gains ground." [1] Here
it would seem as if the lizard were nothing but a messenger.
But if so, why should the native consider himself safe if he
has killed it ? How would the destruction of the messenger
announcing his death prevent that death from taking place ?
This action of his must be explained like that of the Dayak
who beats the drum so that the bird of evil omen may not
be heard. The lizard is no mere bearer of news, any more
than was the bird ; he is the instrument of the power which
is being exerted, and in destroying the instrument the
power is impeded. If the lizard is killed it cannot make
any report about the destined victim, who is henceforward
sheltered from the malevolent force which chose the lizard
as its agent.

In Upper Congo, " the mournful hooting of the owl,
heard at midnight by a villager, is a message that death
is stealing silently towards the huts waiting to select a victim,
and all who hear the call will hasten to the neighbouring
wood and drive the messenger of ill tidings away with sticks
and stones." [2]

The reason for such action, which is also met with
elsewhere, proceeds from what has gone before. The owl is
not merely a messenger ; it causes the death its hooting
announces. By chasing it away, therefore, death is averted.
Conversely, however, by attracting it, disaster would be

[1] G. W. Steller : *Beschreibung von dem Lande Kamtschatka*, pp. 198–9.
[2] Glave : *Six Years of Adventure in Congoland*, p. 91.

brought about, and he who commits a crime of this kind, if discovered, would be severely punished. " In South Africa," says Dr. Wangemann, " there is a bird called the honey-bird, which, when it finds honey and cannot get at it by itself, calls out until someone pays attention to its cries. . . . If this bird goes into a kraal, the Kafirs regard it is a great misfortune for the owner. One day a honey-bird flew right into Umhala's kraal and alighted on his assegais. That was the signal for a great scare. ' Gasela has bewitched me,' exclaimed Umhala, and he immediately summoned all his followers to begin a war. The terrified Gasela took refuge with the missionaries, who succeeded in settling the matter amicably," [1] In spite of all appearances, Umhala believed that he had been " doomed " by Gasela. The latter might have caused him to die in a hundred different ways ; he might have " delivered him over " to an elephant, a lion, a crocodile, or have afflicted him with some mortal disease, etc. He chose another agent ; he sent Umhala a bird of evil omen which flew right into his kraal and alighted on his assegais, and Umhala felt himself undone. Thus in this case the evil omen, that is to say the honey-bird, possesses the same mystic power as the crocodile or lion, to which the victim would have been " delivered over," would have had.

II

In nearly all uncivilized communities observers have noted a special type of omen which proves very alarming to primitives, and determines them to make the most desperate efforts to combat the disaster its appearance seems to threaten. Such omens are to be found in facts or events which are unusual, or in individuals who are more or less teratological, like the *monstra* and *portenta* of the Romans. As a rule, these omens are distinguished by a special name. In (German) East Africa, for example, *wuhenu* really means something strange, unwonted, bizarre ; lt is the word used for an omen, when the spirits who desire to produce a certain effect or kill a certain man send their messengers to announce

[1] Dr. Wangemann : *Die Berliner Mission im Zululande*, p. 86.

the fact." [1] What is to be done when an omen of this kind appears? The universal plan is to cancel it as quickly as possible. To guard against that which the monster portends, it must be made to vanish. This would be a childish absurdity, if the monster were merely announcing disaster.

"In the Waschamba tribe, if a child presents itself feet first in childbirth, it is killed." [2] If a goat is seen to be devouring its excreta, a fact so extraordinary is the work of a wizard (*utschai*), and the animal must be sacrificed. . . "Again, if a goat in first giving birth has twins, there is witchcraft in it, and both goat and kids must be destroyed. . . . Should a dog devour his excreta he must be killed, for he is the prey of a sorcerer." [3]

Hobley has described in some detail how the Kikuyu of East Africa act in many similar circumstances. I will quote a few instances only. "If a cow, in grazing, happens to twist her tail round a tree, she is *thahu*; she must be killed at once. Her owner offers her in sacrifice; the older men receive the backbone, and the young warriors the neck."

"There is a white bird called *nyangi*; . . . if one is seen to settle on a cow, and the cow is not killed, the owner of the cow will be *thahu*, and will die. The cow must be killed there and then and the meat divided up. . . . no person belonging to the village must eat of the meat. . . . The herd of cattle also need to be purified. . . . If a cow's horn comes off in a person's hand, the animal is *thahu*, and is slaughtered. . . . If a bull or bullock leaves the herd while it is grazing and comes home alone, and stands outside the village digging at the refuse heap with its horns, it is seen to be *thahu*, and is forthwith killed by the owner. . . . If a goat is giving birth to a kid, and the head appears first and the body is not born quickly, it is said to be *thahu* and is slaughtered by the owner. . . . If a woman bears twins the first time she has children, the twins are *thahu*, and an

[1] J. Raum : " Die Religion der Landschaft Moschi," *Archiv für Religionswissenschaft*, xiv. p. 173 (1911).
[2] A. Karasek-Eichhorn : " *Beiträge zur Kenntniss der Waschambaa*," Bässler-Archiv, i. p. 118 (1911).
[3] Ibid., iii. pp. 103–6.

old woman of the village, generally the midwife, stuffs grass in their mouths until they are suffocated, and throws them out into the bush. . . . If a cow or goat bears twins the first time, the same practice is observed." [1]

The animal which is *thahu* on account of the unusual manner of its birth, or wqich shows itself to be so by some unwonted and extraordinary, and therefore suspicious, circumstance ; the child who is born in an unusual posture ; and finally twin births, are not merely sinister portents announcing misfortune to be imminent. To the mind of the East African Bantu, creatures who are *thahu* are a menace to their owner, their family, and the whole village. Either by their state or their actions they betray that they are imbued with a malevolent principle, a mystic force, whose influence will be a fatal one, unless some means be employed to get rid of it by destroying them. " If in the act of birth the presentation be not normal, or if there should be a twin birth, it is a terrible misfortune. However this calamity may happen, a veritable reign of terror ensues ; everybody flees, for they fear that at the very sight of the mother the body may begin to swell, and the victim may die then and there." [2]

The same customs, founded on the same beliefs, prevail in British East Africa. " If a child is born feet foremost, it is smothered. The reasons given for this practice are that if the infant is permitted to live, their crops will all wither up from drought, their cattle will die, and many other evils befall them." [3]

With the Wawangas, " if a fowl lays an egg at night, it is killed and eaten ; otherwise it is believed that one of the children in the hut will fall sick." [4]

In an island in Lake Victoria Nyanza, " immediately after their birth twins are placed in a vessel of clay and exposed in a valley. . . . Children who cut their upper teeth first must be killed as soon as the fact becomes generally

[1] C. W. Hobley : " Kikuyu Customs and Beliefs," *J.A.I.*, xl. pp. 43–5.
[2] Fülleborn : " Das deutsche Njassa und Ruwumagebiet," *Deutsch Ost Afrika*, ix. pp. 353–4.
[3] Captain Barrett : " Notes on the Customs and Beliefs of the Wa-Girama," *J.A.I.*, xli. pp. 22, 32.
[4] K. H. Dundas : " The Wawanga and Other Tribes of the Elgon District," *J.A.I.*, xliii. p. 47.

known, otherwise they will be the cause of great disaster
to the village. . . . On the other hand, they neither expose
nor kill the aged, infirm, idiots, or even criminals." [1]

Among the Hottentots in South Africa, " if hens begin
to crow like cocks, they are caught and killed, or they are
chased till they die. If this is not done, their owner will
assuredly die." [2] " If a goat," says Mackenzie, " climbs
upon the roof of a house, it is speared at once ; it has
' transgressed,' gone beyond what is proper in a goat, and
would bewitch its owner if it were not put to death. . . ."
It is the same thing if a cow beats the ground with its tail
during the night. " This is a very serious matter. It is
an offence which has got a special designation. The cow
is said to be *tiba*, and this implies that she is no longer a
mere cow ; she is bewitched, and she only waits her opportunity to bring disease or death upon her owner or his
household. A man who is rich in cattle would not hesitate
to spear such an animal at once. A poorer man will proceed
with the cow next morning to the missionary or to a trader
and offer her for sale." [3] Here we see that it is no case of
prediction nor of mere announcement of misfortune. The
animal sacrificed has committed an unusual, we might almost
say culpable, act, and by committing it has revealed that
there exists within it a malevolent principle which, for
want of a better term, is called witchcraft (*sorcellerie,
Zauber*). In order to escape from the fatal effect of this
principle the animal must be killed ; otherwise the village
remains exposed to the gravest dangers.

With his usual clearness and penetration, Junod has
accounted for the conduct of the Ba-ronga and their neighbours in similar circumstances. " The arrival of two or
three infants at a birth is considered by the Ba-ronga a
great misfortune, a stain upon them, on account of which
they must undergo very special rites. . . . It is true that
the customs relating to twin births vary in the different
clans. If they are put to death in certain tribes, in others
their arrival is regarded as a piece of good luck. . . . But

[1] Franz Paulssen : *Rechtsanchauungen der Eingeborenen auf Ukarra,*
Bässler-Archiv, i. p. 41 (1913).
[2] Th. Hahn : *Tsuni Goam*, p. 90.
[3] J. Mackenzie : *Ten Years North of the Orange River*, p. 392 (1871).

there is always a certain connection between the birth of twins and the rainfall." [1]

In a more recent work, Junod writes :—

" Abnormal children, such as twins, children who have died before the *boha puri* rite, in some clans also children who cut their upper teeth first, partake in this noxious character. They are a calamity for the whole land, as they are in connection with the mysterious power of Heaven, and so they prevent the rain from falling. The great remedy for the evil, the only means of counteracting its influence, is to bury these children in wet ground. Should this not have been done, the chief must order these little corpses to be exhumed and buried near the river." [2]

Probably the most fatal sign of all is that which manifests itself at the teething period. Livingstone has not failed to remark this. " If a child cuts the upper front teeth before the lower, it is killed, as unlucky ; this is a widely spread superstition. When I was amongst the Makolo in 1859 one of Sekeletu's wives would not allow her servant's child to be killed for this, but few would have the courage to act in opposition to public opinion as she did. In Casembe's country if a child is seen to turn from one side to the other in sleep it is killed. They say of any child which has these defects ' he is an Arab child,' because the Arabs have none of this class of superstitions, and should an Arab be near they give the child to him ; it would bring ill-luck, misfortune (*milando*) . . . on the family." [3] " At Likwangwa, a royal tomb surrounded by a little village, . . . I found a child whose upper teeth had come through before the lower ones. Its father, anxious to save it from the terrible fate awaiting such children, had hidden it for eight years. But an enemy had told Kalonga of the circumstance, maintaining that this child was the cause of all the disasters and deaths which had occurred in the village. . . . When I saw the father I told him to bring the child to us as soon as possible, but alas ! he arrived a few days later in great distress to tell us that they had strangled his son

[1] H. A. Junod : *Les Ba-ronga*, pp. 412–20.
[2] Ibid., *The Life of a South African Tribe*, ii. pp. 296–7.
[3] Rev. D. Livingstone : *Last Journals*, i. pp. 276–7.

and thrown him into the lake." [1] Another missionary tells us : " A *kinkula* inspires almost as much dread in negroes as a *kiva* (ghost). They call a child that cuts its upper teeth first a *kinkula*, a child of woe. If he were allowed to grow up, his inevitable destiny would be to bring ruin upon his whole family. That is why he must be destroyed mercilessly and immediately. Generally it is old women who take this duty upon themselves . . . and the custom is carried on in secret even to this day. . . . In other tribes, those on the eastern side of Lake Nyassa, for instance, twins are dreaded as being *kinkula*, and they are killed." [2]

On several occasions Major Delhaise observed the same occurrences in the case of the neighbouring tribes living in Belgian Congo, and the description he gives tallies with the preceding ones.

" They call the children whose upper teeth are cut first *kiliba* (kiliba-kitabwa), *kinkula* (kilemba). They are children of woe ; they are often killed, either by throwing them into the water, or by exposing them to wild beasts. The mother herself, shamed at having given birth to such a monstrosity, carries out the sentence. Sometimes she employs some old shrew to do it, and occasionally mother-love wins the day, and the child is kept. Later on it will be sold into slavery. It is such a child that causes all the misfortunes that occur in the village, for it has the evil eye. . . . The father of a *kiliba* is continually twitted with the fact, and held up to universal derision for having begotten such a being." [3] In the immediate neighbourhood, among the Wahorohoro, " if the upper teeth make their appearance first, the mother takes her child to the bank of the river and leaves it there. In the night it will be carried off by the wild beasts which come down to drink. If the mother were to conceal her child, it would be chased, not only from the village, but from the entire neighbourhood, and it could only live where the history of its birth (*sic*) was unknown. As in the Wabemba tribe, such a

---

[1] A. and E. Jalla : *Pionniers parmi les Marotse*, pp. 245-6.
[2] P. Alois Hamberger : " Nachtrag zu den religiösen Ueberlieferungen und Gebräuchen der Landschaft Mkulwe," *Anthropos*, v. p. 803 (1910).
[3] Delhaise : *Notes ethnographiques sur quelques peuplades du Tanganika* (*Wabemba*), pp. 8-9.

reprobate is called a *kiliba*, and superstition attributes all the misfortunes occurring in the village to his agency. The natives declare that every time a *kiliba* loses a tooth, one of his nearest relatives dies. The father of a *kiliba* is keenly ridiculed by the members of his family for having given them a *kiliba* as a relative." [1] Finally, in the Warega people, the infant is no longer immolated, but it is treated as a pariah. " When the upper teeth appear first, the terrified wife informs her husband, and he announces the fact to the whole village. It is a disaster for the village, and the child is called a *dino*. The natives at once put up an isolated hut for the reprobate, for he can no longer live with others, and he will be solitary for the rest of his life. His food is prepared separately, and nobody may share his meal. When grown up he may mingle with the rest of the group, but he is always derided and abused. It very often happens that such treatment affects his character, and he becomes melancholy and misanthropical. Any woman who consents to live with him must submit to the same fate. The *dino* must not touch seed that has been prepared for planting, for if he does the harvest will be entirely ruined. Neither can he eat bananas from a plantation in full bearing, or all the fruit would go bad. In short, he has " the evil eye." [2]

III

The comparison of the abnormal child with the possessor of the " evil eye " is informative. Like the *jettatore*, the child which has cut its upper teeth first has revealed in this way that he, too, is the embodiment of a noxious principle, the effects of which will make themselves felt by all in his neighbourhood. To protect themselves against this, he must be destroyed, though in certain tribes it is sufficient to remove or isolate him. The treatment meted out to these abnormal children, or to children that are considered such, seems to Europeans horrible and unnatural in its cruelty. But to the native mind there is no cruelty

[1] Delhaise: *Notes ethnographiques sur quelques peuplades du Tanganika (Wabemba)*, p. 34.
[2] Ibid., p. 154.

in it. In their eyes it is merely a measure undertaken for the public safety, for if the malevolent principle is not put out of action, disease and death will be let loose. There can be no hesitation therefore, but rather than kill the unfortunate infant it will be given to the Arabs. It will be all right if the social group is no longer in contact with it.

It may happen that at first nothing reveals the presence of this malevolent principle in an individual. His birth and dentition may both have been normal, and it is only in the course of time that his true nature discloses itself. " Among the Kitui section," writes Hobley, " certain persons are found who are believed to be congenitally unclean and bearers of ill-luck ; if such a person counted people or live-stock he would by thus doing bestow ill-fortune, and the people or stock would probably sicken and die. They state they have no reason for suspecting a person beforehand, but if any untoward sickness occurs they are often apt to pitch upon someone as a scapegoat. The accused is called up and requested to spit upon the sick person or beast ; it is believed that this will exorcise the curse." [1]

From this description it is not easy to decide whether it is a question of an abnormality, a *jettatore* or a witch. On the one hand, the malevolent principle is considered to be congenital ; this trait is also met with in other " Jonahs," and in abnormal children, those who are " unclean," to use Hobley's striking expression. But on the other hand, in the last case quoted the abnormality is not perceptible, nothing makes it manifest. It remains in the " chrysalis " state, as it were, until the outbreak of disasters all around him induce people to suspect that such an individual bears the cause of them within his personality ; and that is exactly how the *jettatori* are recognized.

Finally, when such individuals are required to spit upon sick people in the hope of curing them, their neighbours are following the usual course pursued by primitive peoples to deliver a victim from the power of witchcraft, if it be still possible. When a wizard has been unmasked and compelled to confess, he is taken to the man whom he has bewitched and compelled to undo his mischief. The

[1] C. W. Hobley : *Ethnology of the A-Kamba*, p. 165.

transition from the abnormal infant to the sorcerer, as well as from the *thahu* animal to the sorcerer, is an unconscious one.

Thus a strong light is thrown upon the nature of these *monstra* and also upon that of witchcraft. To understand how the primitive's mind instantly and completely identifies abnormality with witchcraft, we must modify our ideas of both very considerably. This point may be regarded as achieved, and it will further our comprehension of the ordeal.[1]

Similar facts have also been noted in West Africa, among negroes who are not Bantus. On the Upper Niger, for instance, " a cock crowing at an unusual hour of the night means death in the family, unless the cock be immediately killed." [2] " If it happens," says Major Leonard, " that during childbirth the infant comes out of the womb feet foremost—the event which is referred to as *mkoporo-oko*, i.e. bad or evil feet—it is regarded in the same light as twin-birth, and the unfortunate mother is accorded exactly the same treatment." [3]

In Togoland, " if a child cuts its upper teeth before the lower, it is a *busu*, which means that when grown up it will see and do all sorts of alarming things." (The German word used is *hexen*, which signifies to bewitch.) " That is why children of this sort used to be sold, or even drowned. The same course was pursued with children who were born with teeth." [4] Here the likeness borne by these children to witches is an explicit one. Their abnormality reveals their future evil-doing and the power which henceforth imbues them. In Dahomey, purifying rites were considered to meet the case. " Similar ceremonies " (i.e. to those carried out in the case of twins) " took place for the *agosou*, infants which were born feet first, and the *ouënsou*, infants born head first, but with upturned faces." [5] Among the Ashantis, the child who was suspect was he who betrayed any

[1] Vide infra., chap. viii., p. 249.
[2] A. F. Mockler-Ferryman : *Up the Niger*, p. 141 (note 4) (1892).
[3] Major A. G. Leonard : *The Lower Niger and its Tribes*, p. 461 (1906).
[4] P. Franz Wolf : " Beitrag zur Ethnographie der Fo-Neger in Togo," *Anthropos*, vii, p. 86 (1912).
[5] A. Le Hérissé : *L'ancien royaume du Dahomey*, p. 235.

malformation in the hand. " . . . . If a child is born luckily, that is, without any excrescence on the little finger, for this would be considered a sixth finger, and would condemn him to death." [1] In Madagascar " at this very time, January 1907, people are whispering that a monster, half ox and half child, has been born in the Ankeramadinika forest, and that all sorts of calamities are to be feared in consequence, and it is hardly worth while to make any special effort or to work hard. . . . Even last year, the Bara of the south buried alive children who were born on Thursdays." [2]

All these facts proclaim a practice which prevails throughout the world, and not in Africa alone, of getting rid of children who exhibit certain abnormalities. It exists even in peoples who are highly developed. We may say in a general way that there is a desire to eliminate at the outset those individuals who are not likely to be as healthy and vigorous as others, and who in their turn would not have children capable of being defenders of the city. This was the explanation given in Lacedemonia, and accepted by the Spartans, whose history is known to us. But assuredly it was not motives of this kind that gave rise to the custom. Wherever we find children of tender years, or at birth, being sacrificed, it is not on account of any physical blemish which will prevent them from becoming healthy adults ; but very frequently it is by reason of some mystic defect which makes them a menace to the social group. The child who was suffocated or exposed to wild beasts, because it was born feet foremost, or because it had cut its upper teeth first, might otherwise be perfectly sound and well-developed. In vain might it give promise of becoming a healthy and vigorous member of the social group ; that would not save it from immediate death ; whilst children who were puny, but showed no suspicious abnormalities, were spared, and continued to struggle on as best they might. If among the adults of an uncivilized community we find very few, or practically no individuals exhibiting any physical peculiarities (which is not always the case), we must not conclude that the others were got rid of at

---

[1] Ramseyer und Kühne : *Vier Jahre in Asanti*, p. 157.
[2] *Missions évangéliques.* lxxxii. i. p. 298. (Mondain.)

birth. In these races infant mortality is very high. It will first of all carry off the children of weakly constitution, and least capable of resisting disease and unhygienic conditions. But these peoples do not deliberately get rid of children as abnormalities, except those who for mystic reasons are considered a menace to the community. Possibly, too, if we knew exactly which were the children condemned at birth by the Lacedemonians, we should find that in the Greek city they were chosen on the same principle.

The abnormalities presented by man or beast, by the *monstra* or the *portenta* therefore, must be compared with unusual and isolated circumstances on the one hand, and on the other with omens. Like the latter, they not only announce the future, the event about to happen ; they determine it, or to put it more precisely, they make it happen. There is a direct connection between the appearance of the abnormal child and the misfortunes which it will cause later on, should it survive. It matters little that these misfortunes are not to happen for some time ; we know that to the primitive mind a future calamity is felt both prospectively and as already present in the preconnection which refers it to the appearance of the abnormal child. And just as the omen bird by its mystic agency produces the benefits expected from his song or his lucky flight, so the cock which crows at the wrong time, or the child who is born with teeth, is a " harbinger of woe " in the full sense of the word. His abnormality has revealed the malevolent principle with which he is imbued. His " transgression " has betrayed the indwelling of this principle, which is a constant menace to his own family and to the whole social group.

CHAPTER VI

THE PRACTICES OF DIVINATION

OF all the direct data which their experience affords, primitives are chiefly interested in those which proceed from the unseen world, and reveal to them the orders issued by the mystic powers dwelling therein. The prosperity of the social group, the health and very existence of each one of its members, depend at all times on the good or bad influences exercised upon them. As long as they are uncertain whether one of these mystic forces may not be effectively engaged against them, they cannot hope that any enterprise they undertake will prosper. Hence the need of assurance that these powers are on their side, and that their venture will be successful.

How are they to make sure of this ? The unseen powers do undoubtedly manifest their presence frequently, and the primitive is given to seeing them everywhere. Many ordinary occurrences, and nearly all unusual circumstances, bear the import of revelations to him, and he is always ready with an explanation of them. Nevertheless, dreams, omens, and other indications of a like nature may be wanting at the very moment when most needed ; when, for instance, it is necessary to come to an important decision or make a difficult choice. How can he overcome such an impediment ? To calculate the chances carefully and systematically, and try to think out what will happen, and make plans accordingly, is hardly the way in which primitive mentality proceeds. Such a course does not even occur to it. If the primitive did think of it he would never take the trouble, for he would consider it useless. In his view events depend upon mystic powers, and according to their disposal matters will be arranged. Should they be favourable, he will take action, and should they disapprove, nothing can be done, and he must wait, if possible, in the hope of moving them or winning them over. Above all, it behoves him to find out what he has to rely on, and if no revelation occurs spontaneously, it must be induced.

With such a stimulus to urge him forward, the primitive shows himself remarkably ingenious and fertile in expedients. Taking the word divination in its widest sense, we may employ it to designate the sum-total of the direct or indirect processes which primitive mentality brings to bear on the discovery of that which interests it so strongly. I shall first of all examine into those forms of divination which are interrogatory, and consist of direct questions addressed to the powers of the invisible world.

I

Through the agency of the dream the living man communicates in the simplest and easiest way with the dead, and with mystic powers in general. When asleep, his condition very closely resembles that of a dead man. The barrier which separates him from the dead in his waking hours is lowered for a moment, and he sees and hears them, talks with them, makes demands of them, and receives theirs. But the dream is not produced at any given time, nor every time that it is needed. The primitive therefore will endeavour to induce dreams, and he will succeed in doing this.

The greater the importance which a community attaches to its dreams, the more will this method of divining be employed. The Indians of New France who, according to a Jesuit father, " make their dreams their god," made use of this method constantly. When a dream was desired, fasting was the ordinary means of supplication. " They fast in honour (of their gods) when they want to know the issue of a certain event. I have felt compassion at seeing some of them, who had a certain combat or hunting expedition in view, spend seven days in succession, taking hardly any food, and resolutely continuing in this course until they had had the vision they desired, or seen a herd of elk or a troop of Iroquois in flight, or something of that kind. A dream of this nature is all the more likely to occur when the mind is vacant, and the body exhausted by fasting, and there is nothing else to think about all day." [1]

Is it merely in order to ascertain whether they will succeed that the Indians thus prosecute their fast until the dream they consider necessary has made its appearance ? We have already seen with what profound religious fervour they carry out all that the dream demands of them. We know, too, that the primitive believes that omens not only announce but also cause events to happen, and the dream is an omen. That which the Huron takes so much pains to induce before he starts out to fight or hunt is therefore something altogether different from a mere revelation of what will happen. It promises and guarantees success and victory. If the Huron does not succeed in seeing in dreams a herd of elk or deer, it is because, in spite of his fasting, the mystic essence of these animals remains hostile to him. And if that be so, what is the good of hunting ? He will not encounter the prey he desires, for it will remain invisible ; or if it is perceived, it will not come within range. If, on the contrary, these animals do appear to the Indian during his sleep, such a dream is a guarantee that the animals' mystic essence has relented, and that the hunt will be successful. Fortified by this assent, he starts upon his quest.

The divination thus practised by these Indians, in the form of a dream which they induce, includes both an attempt to discover whether the success desired will be attained, and an effort to make sure of it. We can also see in it a prayer, for these same Indians think that when the missionaries pray they are pursuing exactly the same ends as they themselves are when striving to induce dreams. In this respect the following story is significant : " As our little company was waiting till I had finished my office, the native who was our guide, impatient at my being so long on my knees in a place remote from the noise of the hut, approached me, and, believing I had had some revelation, or received the gift of prophecy, begged me in all seriousness to tell him what was about to befall us that

[1] *Relations des Jésuites*, 1. p. 290 (1666-7).

day. ' You speak to God, you direct the sun's path, you
are a priest, and you are clever, and we must believe that
He who has made everything has granted your prayer ;
tell me, then, whether we shall kill many elks and beavers
to feast you with to-day, after the amount of fatigue and
want you have undergone hitherto.' I was somewhat taken
aback at this speech. . . ." (The priest replies by a little
disquisition on the ways of Providence.)

"Entirely taken up with the idea that God spoke
familiarly to priests, this native did not hide his chagrin,
especially when I had told him that I did not know of any
place where we might find beavers, bears, or elks, and that
we must trust ourselves entirely to the care of the Divine
providence. ' Then I,' said he, ' am something more than
a priest, for God has spoken to me in my sleep, and He
has told me that before noon to-day we shall undoubtedly
kill both elks and beavers in abundance, and be able to
feast.' . . ." [1]

Thus we can account for the fact that even young
children are made to fast, in the hope of obtaining the
desired dream. " In order to save the trouble of making
a fire, or to husband their food, or to accustom their children
not to eat anything until evening, they make them fast
like dogs, telling them that they will dream of the manitou-
sturgeon, the bear, deer, or something of that kind, and
this will enable them to spear the sturgeon or shoot the
bear ; and if they are not yet old enough to go spearing
or hunting, they (the women) do not hesitate to make them
fast, assuring them that the hunters and fishers will be
successful if they dream. These little children have an
overwhelming desire to kill some animal or spear some
fish, whence it follows that if a dreamer once succeeds,
they put all their confidence in the dream." [2] The Jesuit
father here tells us explicitly what it is they want to see
in the dream induced : it is the " manitou-sturgeon, bear,
etc." That is what I have called the mystic essence of
the creature, whose acquiescence is indispensable to the
success of the chase. It is not therefore simply a question

[1] P. Le Clerc, récollet : *Nouvelle relation de la Gaspésie*, p. 375 (1910).
[2] *Relations des Jésuites*, lvii. pp. 272–4 (1672–3).

of divination, as we understand the term, but also of a request and a prayer, especially if one allows the influence exerted on the power to which it is addressed to be an integral element in the idea of the prayer.[1]

Before playing games of chance, the natives have recourse to the same process of divination. " There are some who always fast for some days before playing ; the previous evening they all meet in a hut and make a feast for the purpose of finding out what the issue of the game will be. . . . They used to choose someone who had dreamt he would win to pass the dish." [2] Thus they fast to try and dream of what they will win, just as they do to try and see in a dream their game or their foes ; and a dream of this nature is equal to the possession of a charm which will assure success. Listen to this again : " A group of young men who have blackened their faces " (which is a war measure) "enters our hut in the evening, telling us they have come to sleep in the chapel so that God may appear to them during the night and promise to deliver them from their enemies." [3] These young men desire to obtain from the God of the missionaries a favour like that they have just been asking of the manitou-sturgeon, bear, stag, etc. The priest does not tell us whether this night of prayer had been preceded by ceremonies calculated to bring the desired dreams, but judging from the custom usually followed in such cases, we shall not be wrong in assuming this to be so.

In order to induce a dream, Indians frequently have recourse to fasting. " They (the Hurons) believe that fasting makes their sight extraordinarily acute, and gives them the power of seeing things which are absent and far away." [4] There are dreams which mean nothing, and on the strength of which one would take no risks. The dream following on a period of fasting has a mystic value. It is, of necessity, reliable, it is, properly speaking, a vision. In such a state, the Indian " sees " the people and things of

---

[1] Compare with this a weighty observation made by Codrington. " It is certainly very difficult, if not impossible, to find in any Melanesian language a word which directly translates the word ' prayer,' so closely does the notion of efficacy cling to the form employed."—*The Melanesians*, pp. 145-6.

[2] *Relations des Jésuites*, x. p. 188 (1636). (P. Le Jeune.)

[3] Ibid., lviii. p. 50 (1672-3).

[4] Ibid., liv. pp. 140-2 (1669-70).

the invisible world. He hears these people speak and he converses with them. Fasting has rendered him able to receive these visions. It possesses purifying powers, and (to make use of the expression given by Hubert and Mauss) it makes him pass over from the profane to the sacred sphere. It even exercises an influence on the beings of the unseen world.

Supposing, for example, it is required to obtain, by means of an induced dream, the information which the Indian desires more than anything else in the world—the revelation of what is to be his guardian spirit, his personal totem—this, say the fathers, is the way they " create the divinity."

" When a child has reached the age of ten or twelve, his father teaches him, and gives him the instructions necessary to find out who is henceforth to be his god. First of all he makes him fast for several days, so that with his mind free he may the more readily dream when asleep. For it is then that this chimerical god will reveal himself, so that all the natives' ingenuity and endeavour are exercised in an endeavour to see during sleep something out of the common, which will henceforward hold the place of god to them." [1] The essential function of the dream is to let the young Indian know that a certain mystic power has consented to become his personal totem, just as it would reveal that the manitou-elk was willing to allow the elks to be hunted and caught. This is therefore not a purely divining process ; it must not be differentiated from the rites and ceremonies which precede it, and which are destined to assure its veracity and virtue.

Even to-day, among the North American Indians who have preserved their original traditions, facts similar to those related by the Jesuit fathers of the seventeenth century are to be observed. Here is one, taken from the Hidatsa: " When my father was about thirty years of age, all the men of the five villages went to hunt buffaloes. The young men on this hunt killed the bear whose claws you see here. My father then thought he had a chance to 'find his god.' So he asked them to skin it with the paws and skull entire.

[1] *Relations des Jésuites*, x. p. 206 (1636). (P. le Jeune.)

He then took off all his clothes. He then pierced the dead bear's nose with his knife, and put a rope through the hole. He then had a man pierce the muscles of his back in two places; he thrust a stick between and fastened a rope to the stick so that my father might drag the bear's head and skin. All day until evening my father dragged the bear's skin in a lonely place. At evening he came towards camp. Something caught, as if the bear's skin had been snagged on something. At the same time he heard a sound like a live bear, ' sh, sh, sh.' He looked back, and the bear skin had stretched out with its legs as it lay on the ground, as if it were alive. He then came back to the camp, and then the other men released him from the bear skin. That night he dreamt the bear showed him how to cure sick people. He was to sing a mystery song, which the bear taught him, and to take the piece of buffalo-felt and hold it out towards the sick man, when the sick man would recover." [1]

The pain which the Indian Hidatsa voluntarily undergoes in carrying the bear skin is equivalent to fasting, and both have the same magical efficacy. A recent observer of the Blackfeet describes similar occurrences. " When an Indian desired to know the later course of his life, or to receive knowledge that would be of value to his tribe, he went off alone upon the plains, or to a remote region among the Rocky Mountains to fast and pray, sometimes for many days, that he might receive a dream or vision. If he was worthy, a message would be transmitted from the sun, through some animal, or supernatural being, whose compassion had been excited by his fasting and exhausted condition. The revelation, and with it the gift of power, generally came in a dream through the medium of one of the same powerful animals, such as the buffalo, beaver, wolf, or grizzly bear, which were believed to have supernatural attributes, or through one of the personified natural forces, such as the Thunder Chief, Windmaker, etc." [2]

[1] Pepper and Wilson : " An Hidatsa Shrine and the Beliefs respecting it," *Memoirs of the American Anthropological Association*, ii. p. 305.
[2] W. MacClintock : *The Old North Trail*, pp. 352–3 ; cf. Dorsey : " Siouian Cults," *Bureau of American Ethnology, Smithsonian Institute*, Report XI, pp. 392–3.

The Jesuit fathers had indeed noted that the animals which show themselves in dreams to the Indians are not regarded by them as the same beasts as those they meet while hunting. The former belong to the unseen world, and are endowed with mystic powers. The discussions which used to take place between the fathers and the medicine-men reveal this. " Father Mermet resolved to put to confusion, in the presence of the natives, one of those charlatans who worshipped the bull as his great manitou (his tutelary genius). After having led him on unconsciously until he owned that it was not the bull he worshipped, but the bull-spirit below the earth, which inspires all bulls, and restores life to his followers when sick, he asked him whether other animals, such as the bear, for instance, which his companions worshipped, were not also inspired by a manitou below the earth. ' Undoubtedly they are,' replied the charlatan. ' But if that is so,' the missionary went on, ' men, too, must have a manitou who inspires them.' ' Most certainly they must,' replied the charlatan." [1]

In many other communities the natives resort to an incited dream in order to be able to communicate with their guardian spirits, just as the North American Indians do. The *nyarong* (spirit-helpers) described by Hose and MacDougall, as known to the Ibans in Borneo, are regarded in the same way. " Perhaps only one in a hundred men is fortunate enough to have a secret helper, though it is ardently desired by many of them. Many a young man goes to sleep on the grave of some distinguished person, or in some wild and lonely spot, and lives for some days on a very restricted diet, hoping that a secret helper will come to him in his dreams." [2]

These same natives of Borneo believe that the most infallible remedies are revealed in dreams. The dream itself, as Perham shows, has healing power through the vision it brings. " To *nampok* is to sleep on the tops of mountains with the hope of meeting with the good spirits of the unseen world. . . . A year or two ago, a Rejang Dayak, afflicted with some disease, tried several hills to obtain a cure, and

[1] *Relations des Jésuites*, lxvi. pp. 236-8.
[2] Hose and MacDougall : *The Pagan Tribes of Borneo*, ii. p. 92.

at length came to Lingga, and was guided by some Dayaks of the neighbourhood to Lingga mountain. He offered his sacrifice, and laid down to sleep beside it, saw an *antu* (spirit) and returned perfectly cured." [1]

Finally, in many Australian tribes where the natives attach the greatest importance to dreams, those which are induced are at once methods of divination, requests for help addressed to the powers of the unseen world, and a guarantee that what they have desired to see in the dream will be realized. That is what is testified by W. E. Roth, one of the most acute investigators who has ever lived among the Australian aborigines of North Queensland. " On the Bloomfield River," he says, " the natives will tell one another what they have dreamt, and either interpret it themselves, or discuss it with others. It is here that a native may set his mind on dreaming that his enemy will die—and with satisfactory results. The Tully River blacks . . . can go to sleep and make up their minds to dream that a certain enemy is dead—and he will die ; . . . if their women dream of having children put inside them they may beget them ; if some crime is committed, the culprit, as in many other districts, can be discovered in a dream." [2] This custom can only be understood if the natives believe the dream they solicit has itself an actual mystic influence. Sleep permits them to enter the unseen world, and the dream they obtain testifies that the forces of this world are favourable to them and will grant them their requests.

Thus during sleep there are established participations which are not very comprehensible to us, and which Roth has illustrated in some very striking passages. " On the Tully River, whenever a man (or woman) stretches himself for a sleep, . . . or on arising in the morning, he mentions in more or less of an undertone the name of the animal, etc., by which he is called, or belonging to his group division . . . if there is any particular noise, call or cry connected with such name, he may mimic it. The objects aimed at in carrying out this practice, which is taught by the elders

---

[1] Rev. J. Perham, quoted by H. Ling Roth : *The Natives of Sarawak*, i. p. 185 ; cf. O. Beccari : *Wanderings in the Forests of Borneo*, p. 158.

[2] W. E. Roth : " Superstition, Magic, and Medicine," *North Queensland Ethnography*, Bulletin 5, No. 106 (1906).

to the youngsters as soon as they are considered old enough to learn such things, are that they may be lucky and skilful in hunting, and be given full warning as to any danger which might otherwise befall them from the animal, etc., after which they are named. If a man, named from a fish, thus regularly calls upon it, he will be successful in catching plenty on some future occasion should he be hungry. If a native neglects to call the thunder, rain, etc., provided, of course, they are his namesakes, he will lose the power of making them. Snakes, alligators, etc., will never interfere with their namesakes (provided they are thus always called upon) without giving a warning. . . . If the native neglects to do so it is his own fault if he is bitten or caught. . . . If people were to call upon others than their namesakes . . . it would bear no results either for good or ill to him. . . . On the Proserpine River, the native, before going to sleep, calls upon one or other of the names of the animals, plants, or other objects connected with his particular primary group division. . . . In reply to inquiries, the reason given me is that when called upon they warn the people, who have summoned them, of the advent of other animals, etc., during sleep." [1]

There are, therefore, induced dreams, as well as omens, which in the course of time have lost their early significance as mystic causes, and merely retain their value as sign and prediction. Before asking their dreams, whether spontaneous or induced, simply to reveal the future, the natives have tried to procure by their means the protection of the unseen powers, and success in their undertakings. In the attention paid by many communities nowadays to dreams, as omens, there is more or less of a survival of the deeper mystic value originally attributed to them.

Almost everywhere in early times the dream was a guide always followed, an infallible counsellor, and often even, as in New France, a master whose orders must not be disputed. What could be more natural, therefore, than to try and induce this counsellor to speak, to consult this master and solicit his advice in circumstances of difficulty?

[1] W. E. Roth: "Superstition, Magic, and Medicine," *North Queensland Ethnography*, Bulletin 5, No. 74.

Here is a typical example of such a case quoted by Duff Macdonald, the missionary :—

" The chief takes his departure. We pressed him to send his boy to school, and he said : ' I will dream about it.' He tells us that the Magololo chiefs are much guided by dreams. After some talk on the subject, we gave him a parting present, with the view of inducing a favourable dream." [1]

From the missionary's satirical comment, we feel that he regards these words of the chief as a subterfuge. Since he has no desire to send his son to the Mission school and does not care to say so frankly, he tries to get out of the difficulty by promising to dream about it. It is not easy to decide whether the idea of gaining time enters at all into the reply given, but at any rate it is probable that this answer expresses in all sincerity the chief's state of mind. Should he defer to the missionaries' request and confide his son to them, he is risking something which has never been done before—he is breaking with tradition, and undoubtedly his ancestors will be annoyed ; who can tell what the consequences of their displeasure may be ? Before exposing himself to it, he desires to talk with them and ask their advice ; he will then know whether they consent, or whether they disapprove of his son's entering the white man's school.

Can there be any better way of finding out what they think about the matter ? The European would have said: " I will think about it." The Magololo chief replies: " I will dream about it." The one reflects on the probable consequences of his decision ; the other in dreams consults his ancestors, who, although dead, still form a part of the social group and hold its fate in their hands, and whom he must on no account offend.

II

Even when solicited and induced, the dream may fail to appear. The primitive will then have recourse to other means of communicating with the powers of the unseen

[1] Rev. Duff Macdonald : *Africana*, ii. p. 101.

world. The simplest and most effective of these, whenever it is possible, is direct interrogation. It is employed in the case of the dead whose relations with the living are not entirely ruptured, and especially for those who have but recently died, for these, as a rule, are not very far away. The presence of the corpse, whether in the charnel-house, or in the neighbourhood, or just placed in the tomb, is considered the same as that of the deceased. If, therefore, the native is desirous of learning anything from him, he will ask him about it. He certainly no longer speaks, but he still hears, and there are many ways of obtaining his reply.

The interrogation may even take place before death (as *we* understand it) has occurred ; that is, in the interval in which the " soul " inhabiting the body has already quitted it, whilst the dying man has not stopped breathing, nor his heart ceased to beat. To the primitive, as we know, this dying man is already dead, and that explains why so many poor unfortunate wretches are hastily buried while still alive. " When a man is sick and about to die, all the family assemble together, and no fire is allowed in the house for fear that it might frighten the *tabaran* (spirit). They believe that the sick man is *ongi*, that is, taken possession of by a *tabaran*, and they proceed to ask him all kinds of questions. The answers are communicated by the voice of the patient, but it is the *tabaran* who speaks, and not the sick man. The questions are: ' Who are you ? Who *agagara'd* you ? Speak at once, or we will burn you with fire.' " [1]

This account is not very clear, but it seems to show that the dying man's family (to whom he is already dead) ask him questions to which the *tabaran* must reply. In the province of Victoria, in Australia, the relatives notice the limbs of the dying man, for their movements reveal the direction in which to look for the criminal, and indicate where vengeance is to be exercised.[2] Nevertheless, at such a time the persons present are as a rule exclusively occupied with the rites which have to be performed at the moment

---

[1] George Brown : *Melanesians and Polynesians*, p. 197 (edit. of 1910).
[2] Stanbridge : " On the Aborigines of Victoria," *Transactions of the Ethnological Society*, i. p. 299 (1861).

of death. So far from venturing to retain the dead man, they frequently betray a lively sense of fear, and desire nothing so much as to be speedily relieved of his presence. They therefore take care not to ask him anything. They will do this later on, when the first critical hours are over.

Among primitive peoples, where death is never, or hardly ever, " natural," the dead man's relatives are anxious to know who really is responsible for the witchcraft of which he has been the victim. No one knows this so well as the victim himself, and none can more certainly reveal it. By putting this question to him, the survivors accomplish a twofold aim. They unmask the wizard whose murderous activities are a constant menace to the social group, and at the same time they show the dead man that they have not forgotten the task of avenging him. They thus protect themselves from the anger which would not fail to fall upon them should he feel himself neglected.

In the Narrinyeri tribe, " the first night after a man has died his nearest relative sleeps with his head on the corpse, in order that he may be led to dream who is the sorcerer that caused his death. The next day the corpse is elevated on men's shoulders on a sort of bier called *ngaratta*. The friends of the deceased then gather round, and several names are called out, to see whether the mention of them will produce any effect on the corpse. At last the nearest relative calls out the name of the person of whom he has dreamed, and then an impulse towards him on the part of the dead body is said to be felt by the bearers, which they pretend they cannot resist, and consequently they walk towards him. This impulse is the sign by which it is known that the right name has been called out." [1]

The same interrogation, but a still more direct one, is addressed to the dead man in New Britain. " On the night following his death, the friends of the deceased would all assemble outside the house, and some sorcerer (*tena agagara*) would call out and ask the spirit of the deceased the name of the person who had bewitched him. When no answer was received, the *tena agagara* would call out

[1] Rev. G. Taplin : *The Narrinyeri Tribe*, pp. 19–20 ; cf. an identical passage in Eylmann : *Die Eingeborenen der Kolonie Süd Australien*, p. 229.

the name of some suspected person, and all around would listen intently for an answer. If none came, another name would be called, and this was repeated until a sound, like that made by tapping the fingers on a board or mat, was heard either in the house or on a pearl shell held in the hand of the *tena agagara*, after a certain name was called out ; this was then taken as conclusive evidence of guilt." [1]

Thus the corpse may of his own accord denounce the author of his death, during the preparation of the funeral ceremonies. " The person who sews up the apertures of the corpse runs some risk if he does not provide himself with good string ; for if the string should break it is attributed to the displeasure of the deceased, who is supposed to make known in this manner if he has been charmed by him. . . . If the . . . needle should not be sufficiently sharp to penetrate the flesh easily, the slightest movement, caused by pressing the blunt point into the flesh, is supposed to be spontaneous motion of the corpse, and to indicate if the sewer is the guilty person." [2]

" When the body is removed from the heads of the bearers and lowered into the grave," among the people of the Dieri, " conclusions are drawn as to the locality in which the person who has caused the death lives, from the direction in which the body falls from the heads of the two men who hold it." [3] In the Wurunjerri tribe, " when there was no medicine-man there to tell them who had killed him, it was the practice when digging the grave to sweep it clean at the bottom and search for a small hole going downwards. A slender stick put down it showed by its slant the direction in which they had to search for the malefactor." [4]

In this case, as in the preceding one, the information received is evidently the dead man's reply to the interrogations of the living. They are seeking a sign which shall be a revelation, and when this sign is forthcoming it is the dead man who has spoken. It is the same with the natives observed by Dawson. " When the offending tribe is not

[1] George Brown, *Melanesians and Polynesians*, p. 385–6.

[2] H. E. A. Meyer : " The Encounter Bay Tribe," in Taplin's *South Australia*, p. 200.

[3] A. W. Howitt : *The Native Tribes of South-East Australia*, p. 448.

[4] Ibid., p. 458.

otherwise revealed, the question is decided, after the body
has been put up into the tree, by watching the course taken
by the first maggot which drops from the body and crawls
over the clean-swept ground underneath. If the body
has been buried, the surface of the ground is swept and
smoothed carefully ; then the first ant which crosses it
indicates the direction of the tribe which caused the death
of the deceased." [1] Is this ant the very soul of the dead
man, or merely sent or directed by him ? It is hard to
say, if only on account of the enormous difficulty which
always confronts us when we make use of the term " soul "
to express the collective representations of primitives. It
is just as well that the subject under consideration at the
moment does not necessitate our deciding between these
hypotheses. It is enough for our purpose that, in the
primitive's mind, the ant exercises the same function as
the maggot. The latter undoubtedly bears a very close
relation to the body whence it has just fallen. The direction
it takes answers the question which the survivors have put
to the dead man.

Sometimes this question may remain unanswered for
months. " The corpse is carried about from camp to camp
for a long period, many months maybe, indeed until such
time as the deceased tells his brother, uncle, etc., who it
was that " doomed " or put him to death. But should he
not choose to tell, his relatives will find out for themselves,
by means of hair-twine made from hair removed from the
corpse. As this is being . . . rolled and stretched along
the thigh, the names of suspected persons are called aloud ;
the name at which it breaks is that of the person who
committed the deed." [2] The method thus employed is as
good as an interrogation of the deceased. We know that
to the primitive mind the hair and beard, as well as the
saliva, nail-parings, excreta, undigested food, etc., all form
an integral part of the personality. The twine made from
the dead man's hair thus " participates " in his nature,
just like the worm which has issued from his corpse. In
a neighbouring tribe (in the Brisbane district), it is the

---

[1] J. Dawson : *Australian Aborigines*, p. 68. (Melbourne, 1881.)
[2] W. E. Roth : *North Queensland Ethnography*, Bulletin 9, No. 4.

bones,[1] and in Moreton Bay and the territory behind it, it is his skin [2] which is asked to reveal the murderer. At Cape Bedford the information is obtained in a slightly different way. At a given moment of the funeral ceremonies " the deceased's brother . . . ties up the corpse in the trough quite firmly, puts it on his head and stands up. Then he runs away from there as fast as he can, being dragged along by the corpse's spirit, and on the very spot where the man was originally ' doomed ' the trough falls off." [3]

The aborigines of Western Australia have not been subjected to the same close study as the preceding, nevertheless, facts quite similar to those just quoted have been observed there. For example, in the Watchandies, " the space for some distance around the ground is cleared of bushes, stones, grass, etc., and then carefully swept so as to render the surface perfectly even and uniform. After this it is visited every morning and narrowly examined, to discover whether any living thing has passed over it. In course of time the tracks of some creature are sure to be detected (even those of a small insect, as a beetle, are held sufficient for the purpose), and the direction taken by this object indicates the whereabouts of the tribe to which the enchanter belongs." [4]

According to Bishop Salvado, " if they cannot discover any family or individual whom the deceased has offended, they pick up and throw into the air a handful of dust, or they notice the direction taken by the smoke, and according to the way the wind blows either of these, they hasten to avenge the death of their relative or friend. . . . So, too, if while digging the grave a little earth happens to fall to one side, that is the side from which the *boglia* (witchcraft) has come." [5] This last observation is probably somewhat imperfect. It is assuredly not the dust or the smoke which really gives the natives the indication they are seeking.

[1] W. E. Roth : *North Queensland Ethnography*. Bulletin 9, No. 13.
[2] J. D. Lang : *Queensland*, pp. 360-1. (Story of the Rev. K. W. Schmidt, of the German Mission, Moreton Bay.)
[3] W. E. Roth : *North Queensland Ethnography*, No. 5.
[4] A. Oldfield : " The Aborigines of Australia," *Transactions of the Ethnological Society*, iii. p. 246 (1865).
[5] R. Salvado : *Mémoires historiques sur l'Australie*, pp. 332-3.

The dust and smoke must in some way "participate" of the dead man's personality, and it is *he* who, by their means, answers the question proposed.[1]

In most primitive peoples, where it is an imperative duty to avenge the death of any man, we find the family of the deceased addressing themselves to him, as they do in Australia, in order to discover the guilty person, and employing the same or very similar methods to obtain a reply. We might quote innumerable instances, but I shall relate a few only, some of which were noted in peoples dwelling in the neighbourhood of the Australian continent, and others in African races.

In New Mecklenburg, "if someone happens to die, and it is suspected that he has fallen a victim to witchcraft, the natives appeal to the dead man's spirit to tell them who the murderer is." [2] The following is one of the methods they employ. "Into the dead man's empty hut, across the matting partition, they insert the end of a bamboo pole, to which they have fastened a pork-bone. The group of men called upon for this office hold the pole balanced on their hands without pushing it in any way. Then they call out in turn the names of all the natives. Until the murderer's name has been pronounced, the bamboo sways backwards and forwards each time, but at the guilty person's name it is drawn inside the hut, and with such a violent jerk that the men can no longer keep hold of it." [3] The spirit of the dead man has seized upon it, and he thus gives the indication they desire.

The natives of (German) New Guinea are no less anxious to satisfy their dead friends by drawing down vengeance on the guilty person. "In order to unmask him, the dead

---

[1] Such at least is the idea affirmed to exist among the Dayaks of Borneo. "The ascent of the smoke is carefully watched by the assistant relations, who draw from its perpendicular direction an augury favourable and satisfactory to them. Should, however, the smoke ascend, from wind or other causes, in a slanting manner, they depart, assured that the *antu*, or spirit, is not yet satisfied ; and that soon one or other of them will become his prey." (Hugh Low : *Saraw ̇k*, pp. 262–3.) It is quite clear that, according to their idea of the matter, it is the dead man himself who gives the smoke its direction.

[2] P. G. Peekel : *Religion und Zauberei bei dem mittleren Neu Mecklemburg*, p. 128.

[3] Ibid., p. 131.

man's ghost comes to their aid. There are many different methods. The first consists in making use of a trick to make the dead man tell his friends the name of his murderer. . . . Or the ghost may show his relatives the way to the wizard's village. . . . Or again, a drum and stick may be hung on the grave, and in the night the dead man uses it, as he goes to the village of the wizard whose whereabouts he thus reveals." [1]

In West Africa the dead man is sometimes asked a direct question. For instance, on the Guinea coast, " some of the men raise the corpse on their shoulders in the presence of the priest, and then ask him : ' Did you not die from such and such an accident ? ' If it is so, the men are obliged by some occult force or other to make the corpse give an inclination of the head in the direction of the man who has asked the question, and it is exactly the same as if he had said yes ; in the other case, they remain motionless." [2] In Togoland " they fasten a stick to the hand of the dead man, and the priests and priestesses take him twice all round the streets of the town. The one whom the corpse indicates (according to them), is suspected of having caused the death, and must submit to ordeal by poison." [3]

Other tribes in Togoland employ a slightly different method. " They have recourse to *the most certain*, they ask the dead man himself. To this end, shortly after the death, some friends of the dead man, from five to ten in number, and all of them fellow-members of his totem, meet together. Those who put the questions take a rod about five feet in length and stand on one side. One of them then goes down on his knees, and the rod is placed on his head, one end in front and the other behind. Then he rises, and from this moment he is no longer an ordinary man ; he has, according to them, become the dead man himself. One of the older men among the questioners then makes the necessary inquiries of the dead man, who gives an affirmative reply by raising his head and shoulders, and a negative one by inclining backwards. They say then

---

[1] R. Neuhauss : *Deutsch Neu Guinea*, iii. pp. 143-4 (*Kai*).
[2] W. Bosman : *Voyage de Guinée*, 13e lettre, p. 227.
[3] A. Plehn : " Beiträge zur Völkerkunde des Togogebietes," *Mitteilungen des Seminars für orientalische Sprachen*, iii. p. 97.

that he is 'far away.'"[1] Finally, in Sierra Leone, "when anyone dies . . . before the corpse is carried out for interment, it is generally put upon a kind of bier composed of sticks formed like a ladder, but having two flat pieces of board for the head and feet to rest upon. This is placed upon the heads of two men, while a third, standing before the body and having in his hand a kind of reed called *cattop*, proceeds to interrogate it respecting the cause of its death. He first advances a step or two towards the corpse, shakes the reed over it, and immediately steps back. He then asks a variety of questions, to which assent is signified by the corpse impelling the bearers, as is supposed, towards the man with the reed, while a negative is implied by its producing a kind of rolling motion."[2] Thus the dead man undergoes a regular interrogation.

III

A great many primitive peoples dread contact with the dead. They are considered dangerous and even contagious ; it is feared that they may draw other members of the social group after them to the place whither they have gone. While rendering them the customary dues, and even deploring their loss sincerely, the natives are anxious to drive them away, that is, to rupture, as speedily and as thoroughly as they can, the relations between them and the living, at any rate during the period which follows hard upon the death. The carrying out of the funeral rites secures the normal decomposition of the corpse, and when that has taken place the dead man is definitely separated from the group of the living by the second obsequies, the existence of which, or at least traces of it, is so frequently maintained. Robert Hertz has fully illustrated and analysed this whole class of facts.[3]

There are other primitives who, on the contrary, maintain constant intercourse with their dead, even those but recently

---

[1] Franz Wolf : " Beitrag zur Ethnographie der Fo-Neger in Togo," *Anthropos*, vii. p. 300.
[2] Th. Winterbottom : *An Account of the Native Africans, Sierra Leone*, i. pp. 236–8 (1803).
[3] R. Hertz : " La représentation collective de la mort," *Année sociologique*, x. pp. 50 et seq.

departed. We undoubtedly find among these peoples a good many of the collective representations and complex sentiments which have so often been described. They do believe, however, that they need their dead, and they hope to be able to procure their goodwill, since they, in *their* turn, cannot do without the living. Thus between the living and the dead, duly settled in their new estate, but still members of the social group, there is an exchange of kindly offices, founded on the give-and-take principle.

In these communities, therefore, the living will practise divination by means of the dead. But this will not only be to learn from them what they could not find out otherwise ; they will also ask them for advice, guidance, service, and support. They will try to consult them in a dream, and in default of a dream they will employ other methods. " I was once present," says Perham, " at the death of an old man, when a woman came into the room and begged him, insensible though he was,[1] to accept a brass finger-ring, shouting out to him as she offered it, ' Here, grandfather, take this ring, and in Hades remember I am very poor, and send me some paddy medicine [2] that I may get better harvests.' A Dayak acquaintance had made a good memorial covering of an unusual pattern for the grave of his mother, and soon fell ill, in consequence, some said, of his ghostly work. So he slept at her grave, feeling sure she would help him in his need ; but neither voice nor vision nor medicine came " (through her revelation, be it noted), " and he was thoroughly disappointed. He said to me, ' I have made a decent resting-place for my mother, and now I am ill and ask her assistance, she pays no attention. I think she is very ungrateful.' This belief in reciprocal good offices between the dead and the living comes out again in those cases where the remains of the dead are reverently preserved by the living. On every festive occasion they are presented offerings of food, etc., in return for which these honoured dead are expected to confer substantial favours upon their living descendants." [3]

[1] From the natives' point of view, therefore, he was already dead.
[2] A charm for rice.
[3] Rev. J. Perham, quoted by H. Ling Roth : *The Natives of Sarawak*, i. p. 211.

The natives' widespread custom of carrying about with them the bones (particularly the skull or lower jawbone) of those who have recently died is doubtless due to the same idea. In certain cases, the practice ministers to their desire to feel the actual presence of these absent members of the social group, so that they may be able to ask their help and advice. For instance, in the western islands of the Torres Straits, " whenever they were in trouble they used to take the skull of a relative, put fresh paint on it, and cover it with scented leaves, then they would speak to it and ask advice from it. When they went to bed they would put the skull on their sleeping-mat beside their heads, and if they dreamt, they thought it was the spirit of their dead friend talking to them and advising them what they should do. As they believed all this, it was by no means strange that they liked to keep and preserve the skulls of their dead relatives." [1]

Certain natives of Dutch New Guinea (Doreh) preserve skulls thus, decorating them, and calling them *korwars*. The spirit of the dead is believed to dwell in these, and " a Papuan will never fail to consult the dead man's soul in the *korwar* on every important occasion. He sits down in front of it, tells it of his plan, and asks its support. If at this time any special sign should be noted, if, for instance, the *korwar* should make a movement, due to any external circumstance, the Papuan considers that he has received an affirmative reply, and quietly proceeds to carry out his project. We can understand, therefore, that these *korwars* are constantly being consulted, even about the most insignificant trifles. To give an example : one day a Papuan's hand swelled up without any apparent cause ; what could be more natural than to ask the *korwar* to explain the reason ? It seemed to reply to the inquiry by an unfavourable sign, which clearly showed that the dead man's soul was displeased, although the native could not imagine how he had incurred this displeasure. He examined his conscience very carefully . . . and suddenly remembered that he had neglected his brother's widow, so he hastened to repair this omission. There was a fresh consultation of the *korwar*,

[1] A. C. Haddon : *Head-hunters, Black, White, and Brown*, pp. 182–3.

and this time the Papuan received a favourable sign, and was completely convinced that the dead man's soul no longer bore him a grudge." [1]

From such consultations of the oracle, to divination by means of it, is an easy transition. The ancestor's skull is no longer interrogated personally, so to speak, but it retains its mystic power, and this makes it a worthy instrument for what *we* call divination. But in order to make use of it thus, certain conditions are requisite. " A duly decorated skull, when properly employed, became a divining *zogo* of remarkable powers and was mainly used in discovering a thief, or a stolen article, or a man who had by means of sorcery made someone sick. But this could only be done by *bezam le,* or members of the shark clan, who were also members of the Malu fraternity. All who engaged in this hunt went in the early evening to the *zogo* house, and one of the *zogole* [2] took . . . the mask and put it on, repeating a certain formula. After leaving the house, the *zogole* carried the skull in front of them, and all marched with a particular gait till they heard a kind of grasshopper, called *kikoto,* and they rushed in the direction from which the noise proceeded. One particular *kikoto* was believed to guide the men to the house of the offender. Should the man lose the right direction the *kitoto* would wait for him to come up. . . . Ultimately they were led to the house, and this must, of course, according to their ideas, be the house of the malefactor." [3]

As we see, the success of the operation depends upon the use of the skull, and this is reserved for men of a certain clan, members of a special fraternity. The skull is not an instrument to be used by the first comer. On the other hand, the presence within it of a powerful dead man, though perhaps no longer explicitly represented, is yet strongly felt.

Among peoples who are rather more advanced, consultation of the dead, which often takes place through the medium of dreams, does also take on other forms, in which the dead man, whose interest the survivor desires to secure

[1] O. Finsch : *Neu Guinea und seine Bewohner,* pp. 105–6.
[2] The plural form of *zogo.*
[3] A. C. Haddon : *Head-hunters, Black, White, and Brown,* pp. 91–2.

for a certain enterprise, is directly addressed, without his presence having to be materialized by means of his body or skull. An offering will be brought to the dead, he will be invoked, and the survivors will speak to him just as if he were present. Facts of this kind are of daily occurrence. The bystanders who witness them do not pay any particular attention to them, so accustomed are they to resort to the same expedient on similar occasions. The intervention of invisible beings in the affairs of daily life seems to them the most natural thing in the world. In the Cameroons " the Jaunde rises from his couch in the darkness of the night, for he has seen in a dream one of his dead relatives, who, before returning to the kingdom of his ancestors, made a most important communication to him. But the sound of the drum can penetrate even to the *totolan* (kingdom of the dead). The native seizes his drum, or even makes use of the big village drum, and begins to " talk " with the dead. His neighbours go to sleep again quietly, as soon as they have heard that the communication is not intended for the living." [1]

Thus everybody considers it indispensable, when about to undertake anything, to assure himself first of all that the influential dead of the social group are in favour of it. " When a man intends to set out on some expedition, he goes to the chief of his village and tells him. The chief presents an offering to the spirit of his predecessor. This offering consists of a little flour, which he puts down very slowly at the top of his bed, or he may go to the verandah of the house of his deceased brother. As he puts down the offering he says the words : ' My son is come, he goes on a journey, enlighten his eyes, preserve him on his journey, may he return unscathed. Please, please, let him undertake the journey, and be very successful.'

" If the flour do not fall so as to form a cone with a fine point, there is a bad omen, and the journey is deferred. The remedy for this state of matters is to resort to the oracle . . . who will explain what is the cause of the bad omen. Probably the man will be told to ' try again.' If

[1] Nekes : " Trommelsprache und Fernruf bei den Jaunde und Duala," *Mitteilungen des Seminars für orientalische Sprachen*, xi. Abt. iii. p. 78.

the cone form beautifully on this occasion, then it will be clear that the god (the dead man) wanted him merely to delay for a day or two, and for some good reason; but if the cone still refuse to form, resort is again had to the oracle. The omen sets to work and finds that some deceased relative has a hand in this obstruction. . . ." [1]

But everything is not in order even when the flour has formed a cone with a good point. This first sign is not sufficient. "After the flour is put down, and has formed a shapely cone, the chief carefully covers it with a pot and leaves it all night. During the night he may have a dream about the journey, and this will decide his course. But if it is still undecided, he visits his offering early in the morning. Should he find that the cone of flour is broken down on one side, if it has not its proper point, the omen is bad. The flour is thrown away into the bush, the journey is forbidden by the spirit and cannot be thought of, and the result is an appeal to the oracle. But if the flour has preserved its conical form the omen is good, the divinity has accepted the present and granted the request. The village chief tells the man to go forth with confidence." [2]

A little further on Macdonald tells us that beer may be used instead of flour, and this serves both as offering and as oracle. " If when poured on the ground it sinks into one spot as it does in sandy soil, then the divinity receives it; but if it spread through the ground " (instead of being absorbed in one place only) " the omen is bad." [3] Thus what happens to the offering, at the same time indicates the dead chief's answer to the request made to him.

In this particular case the native desiring to undertake the journey does not consult one of his own forebears. He tells the village chief of his project, and the latter addresses himself to his dead predecessor. This is not merely because the dead chief is a powerful protector of whom the traveller may have need. By virtue of the close solidarity of the social group, nothing that one man risks is without interest to the rest. The one who has started on his journey may

[1] Rev. Duff Macdonald : *Africana*, i. pp. 76–7.
[2] Ibid., pp. 79–80.
[3] Ibid., p. 93.

have some adventure or other which will involve heavy responsibility for his family, clan, or tribe, and the group will have no right to shelve it. Therefore an individual is not allowed to depart without informing the chief, or rather, without the chief's being assured that the traveller may proceed on his way without mischance.

How can this assurance be obtained ? By a process which we might equally well describe as an offering, consultation, or divination. It is an offering, since the chief presents food to one of the powers of the unseen world, to a dead man (whom the missionary speaks of as a god). It is also a consultation, for the dead man is asked to say whether he approves of the projected enterprise. Finally, it is just as much a method of divination, since the form taken by the cone of flour (whether it is truncated or not) will inform the traveller whether his journey will be successful or not, and he will either set out or abandon his intention of doing so. We may even add that it is a prayer, in the ordinary sense of the word when used about primitives ; that is to say, a request for protection and assistance, paid for by an offering, with the more or less obscure notion of exercising influence on the power which is being entreated.

Elsewhere—among the Kavirondo of British East Africa, for instance—the offering is presented first, and then the divining process takes place, although this operation may actually be performed on the offering itself. " Another remedy for sickness is to catch alive a small animal called *ifukho*. The sick person and relatives assemble before the door of the hut. The person who caught the mole holds it up by one leg, and first the sick person, and then he himself, and then the others, each in turn spit upon it, saying : ' O our ancestors, help us and cause this mole to take away this sickness ; we have not got a sheep to give you, but accept this mole, which is as a sheep from the jungle.' " (The Kavirondo call the *ifukho* the wild sheep, although the animal bears not the slightest resemblence to a sheep.) " The live mole is then put into a hole in the ground, and an inverted pot is placed over it. If it now burrows its way out in the direction away from the house, the patient will recover ; but if in the contrary direction, he will die,

CHAPTER VII

THE PRACTICES OF DIVINATION (continued)

I

DIRECT communication with the forces of the unseen world is not always possible. The primitive has it in his power to find the most favourable conditions for such intercourse, and to solicit a dream or vision by appropriate rites and practices. But even with these, he is by no means sure of obtaining a dream, nor, even should he dream, that his dream will be the one desired. In the case of direct interrogation and intercourse, the unseen powers involved are of necessity represented as personages. But in a large number of cases the occult powers by whom the primitive feels himself surrounded, and whose views he desires to ascertain, cannot be invoked or interrogated, and he will then have recourse to other methods.

One of the forms of divination best known to us consists in examining the entrails, and especially the liver, of the victims sacrificed.

In Borneo, " divination by means of a pig's liver is resorted to on most important occasions. If anything special is wanted, they inquire of the pig. If they fear any enemies are coming, or ill luck or sickness, they ask the pig whether it is a fact that this will happen. They tell the pig not to mislead them, and to convey their message to the Supreme Being. The pig may even be told they are not going to kill it or eat it ; but the pig is killed the instant they have finished talking, lest the message should be altered by the pig if it knew it was to be killed." [1]

The plan of operation, which is a very simple one, is thus clearly sketched out. It is a case of consulting what Haddon calls here the Supreme Being, thereby meaning

[1] A. C. Haddon : *Head-hunters, Black, White, and Brown,* p. 337.

what I have more vaguely designated as the " mystic or occult powers," by addressing a definite question to them. The function of the pig sacrificed is to convey this message to them. Since they do not communicate directly with these powers, the victim is perforce the intermediary. The pig receives the question, transmits it, and the answer is inscribed on his liver. Haddon describes in detail how the Dayaks proceed. " A living pig with its legs tied was brought to the verandah. Aban Abit took a lighted brand and slightly scorched it, at the same time praying to the Supreme God, and the pig was asked to give the message to the god, who was requested to make his will known by means of the liver of the pig. When the scorching was over the suppliant kept the fingers of his right hand on the flanks of the pig so that he was in touch with the animal by this means, at the same time slightly prodding it with his fingers to make the pig aware of what he was saying. Finally, a spear was thrust into the neck of the pig, and as soon as all the kicking was over the side of the pig was ripped open, and the liver rapidly and dexterously extracted and placed on a dish. The old men crowded round and discussed the augury. The size and character of the various lobes of the liver, the appearance of the gall bladder, and the amount of fat and tendon, are objects of the closest scrutiny, and these all have a definite signification." [1]

This operation, as we see, is exactly like that recently described, in which the native of British East Africa asks counsel and protection of a dead chief, and reads his reply in the shape taken by a cone of flour. Here the pig's liver takes the place of the cone. But the care displayed that the pig's ill-will shall not falsify either question or answer, the precautions taken to secure his attention during the prayer, and the request that " God " will make known his will by means of the animal's liver, do not leave us in any doubt of the nature of the operation. It is a solicited omen. It asks for a revelation, and at the same time for a favourable one. Far from being a mechanical process, it comprises both a question and a prayer addressed to the powers upon whom the issue depends.

[1] A. C. Haddon: *Head-hunters, Black, White, and Brown*, p. 336.

Should the reply not be the one hoped for, it may happen that the question is propounded once more, and the prayer repeated, just as the appeal is made from an unfavourable omen to a fresh test. In Borneo, again, " priestesses cut the chicken's throat and at once looked for omens. Then the cockerel was sacrificed to provide food for gods and men. If the omens afforded by the first chicken were unfavourable, others would be killed until, by their means, success had been assured." [1]

Among the Polynesian peoples, who were more civilized than those of Borneo, the practices of divination were, properly speaking, indispensable. The success of their undertakings would depend entirely upon the powers of the unseen world. Should these not have revealed their intentions in any way, it was essential to be assured of them at all costs, before taking any risks, and also to try and conciliate them. To give only one example of these well-known facts, in Tahiti " the greatest importance was attached to the will of the gods ; if they were favourable, conquest was regarded as sure ; but if they were unfavourable, defeat, if not death, was as certain. Divination or enchantment was employed for the purpose of knowing their ultimate decision, and at these times they always pretended to follow implicitly supernatural intimation. . . . The success or failure was often chiefly augured from the muscular action of the heart or liver of the animal offered, or the involuntary acts and writhing contortions of the limbs of the human sacrifices in the agonies of death." [2] Here, again, the divination consists both of inducing a revelation and at the same time of appealing for support. The victim transmits the question and brings back the answer.

Father Alexis Arnoux has given in *Anthropos* a detailed description of the practices of divination prevailing in Ruanda ((German) East Africa). It helps us to understand the collective representations implied in divination. For instance, the victim whose entrails are examined is not merely an intermediary ; it serves at the same time as a *cause*, and this affords valuable confirmation of the interpretation

---

[1] A. W. Nieuwenhuis : *Quer durch Borneo*, ii. p. 179.
[2] Rev. W. Ellis : *Polynesian Researches*, ii. p. 502.

we gave of the omens furnished by birds.[1] " The words addressed in many cases," says Father Arnoux, " to the object furnishing the augury should be noted. As the perusal of these ' prayers ' will show, the natives suppose that the bull, sheep, etc., can modify at will their internal structure, or their mode of existence, upon the request of the diviner. They are persuaded that *Imana* (God) allows this transformation if He thinks fit. They are therefore equally sure that the victim which is being sacrificed is able to produce, as a *really efficient cause*, the happiness of an individual which would indicate in what sense the appellations which one hears should be understood. ' *Ub Imana, ub Imana.*' ' Thou art God, then be the God who cures.' " [2] (*Imana* represents what I have called the occult powers.) Subsequently a special prayer is addressed to the animal about to be sacrificed, and upon which it depends, at least partially, whether the answer requested will be a favourable one. " The diviner then takes a chicken in his right hand. He takes a mouthful of water, then pours this right into the chicken's beak ; this water, mingled with his saliva, actually furnishes the *imbuto.*" (In most methods of divining it is necessary that the inanimate object destined to furnish the reply should be brought into contact with saliva from the client's mouth.) " Then, to make sure of an auspicious augury, he speaks in a low voice in the chicken's right ear, so that, if necessary, he may modify his entrails, and make them ' white,' i.e. of happy omen." Father Arnoux then gives the text of the prayer, which is a very long one, specifying the appearance which the entrails must bear to satisfy the consultant.[3] The proceeding is the same when divining from the entrails of a ram.[4] When a special divination is taking place for the king's benefit, and a bull is being sacrificed, the animal, " standing up, is admonished by a *mukongori* (a special kind of diviner), who whispers into its ear, whilst other *bakongori* caress it to make it more attentive, and yet another holds it by the horns. They address a lengthy prayer to it, and tell

---

[1] Vide supra., chap. iv. pp. 126–38.
[2] P. Alexis Arnoux : " La divination au Ruanda," *Anthropos*, xii-xiii, p. 10.
[3] Ibid., pp. 30–3.
[4] Ibid., p. 36.

it exactly how its entrails should appear. ' Put the gall bladder on the right, etc.' Then, when they have thus spoken to the bull, the order is given, ' Knock the victim down and slay it.' " [1]

If divination is practised by means of the knucklebones, the natives attribute precisely the same rôle to them as to the animals sacrificed. They not only announce the ultimate result ; they also cause it to come about. " At the end of the third stage the wizard, scattering the ossicles (*nzuzi*), says: ' They are all listening attentively, they will answer like men ; ' " and in a note Father Arnoux says : " The *nzuzi* listen attentively and answer well. They hear our inquiries, and as far as I can judge by my powers of intuition " (it is the diviner speaking) " they answer correctly. They are yielding, like men." The part played by the diviner, therefore, is that of interpreter, since his expert knowledge enables him to make known the views of the *nzuzi*.[2]

Even when balls or pellets of butter are used for the divining process, similar prayers are addressed to them. The wizard, taking in his hand four butter-balls made the previous day or, at most, the day before, addresses the following brief exhortation to them. " Listen, butter, thou who art beautiful : do thou whiten, become yet whiter, grow absolutely white " (which means, be favourable to us). . . . " I will not let the ants have thee, and thou wilt refuse to let the enemy take me. . . ." Father Arnoux's note states : ' It is always supposed that the butter listens to the supplications of its clients, and changes accordingly." [3]

Should the method of divination practised have yielded a favourable result, the object which has " cast the lot " is used for making amulets, which are considered specially efficacious, and this is another proof of the effective causality attributed to it. The primitives admit that this object retains its beneficent influence, and seek to acquire its goodwill for themselves. " They are glad to make amulets," says Father Arnoux, " from butter, from which an auspicious

---

[1] P. Alexis Arnoux : " La divination au Ruanda," *Anthropos*, xii-xiii. pp. 39-43.
[2] Ibid., p. 18.   [3] Ibid., p. 51.

augury has been obtained. . . . Small pellets made from the fat of animals which have returned a favourable answer are placed under their pillows . . . or in a little vessel. These will secure peace for the dwelling possessed of such treasures. Amulets for use when they are about to sacrifice to the spirits (of the dead) are also made of such material. . . . A chicken which has yielded an auspicious augury is made into amulets held in high esteem." Finally, " amulets are made from sheep which are auspicious " (the parts used being chiefly the bones of their forefeet). " All these amulets are worn hung round the neck." [1] In the case of the bull which has been sacrificed for the king's special divination, they collect the bones from all parts, except the ankle-bones, which will be used, in part, for making amulets. . . . Sometimes they even burn the skin of the bull, but more often it is tanned and used on the royal bed, or even given to one of the court ladies, from whom a liberal recompense is expected in return. Whatever may be done with it, it is essential that the pieces shall be preserved, whether it be a drum skin, or part of a woman's clothing, since these pieces have been taken from a lucky bull, and form the very best amulets known." [2]

All these practices help us to understand how primitive mentality represents to itself the causative influence involved, as it believes, in divination. It finds no difficulty in the spontaneous constitutional change in the cockerel, sheep, bull, or even in such a substance as butter. How does this happen ? How is it conceivable or possible ? The primitive does not ask himself these questions, therefore he has no need to find or imagine an answer. The determinism of physical and physiological phenomena is absolutely unknown to him, and he is altogether indifferent to the relation of consequent to antecedent in the series of secondary causes. In his view the mystic cause, unless it runs counter to any other mystic power, disposes in a lordly fashion of what *we* call the facts of the case. It can transform these, if it desires to do so, to suit the purpose of the interrogator.

In South Africa, among the Bantus, " the knucklebones

[1] P. Alexis Arnoux, pp. 28, 35, 37.   [2] Ibid., p. 45.

play an enormous part. When an important decision is in question, natives will not resolve on any course without having consulted the magic bones, which will be certain to tell them which path to pursue. The chiefs resort to them in all misfortunes. If there is no rain, or some disaster is threatening, should strangers arrive in the country, or a warlike expedition be contemplated, they will call for their bone-thrower, who is always close at hand, and as a matter of fact the bones form their chief counsellor.[1] The German missionaries bear witness to the same fact. " The bones," says Merensky, " are indispensable to the Basuto wizard. . . . Frequently, when the chiefs seem to change their views or their course of action all of a sudden, without any apparent reason, or when in wartime they risk something which cannot succeed, or again, when they let slip a chance of injuring the enemy without profiting by it, the only explanation of these things is the reliance they place on this oracle of the bones. If it is a question whether a chief will welcome or dismiss a missionary, whether he will allow a stranger to cross his territory, or make him retrace his steps, the bones again play an enormous part." [2] Private individuals, as well as chiefs, have recourse to them. " If a man wishes to undertake a journey, or wants to know what to do in a case of illness, or should he be tormented by a desire to find out what has caused the death of a relative, he immediately consults the bones." [3]

Junod has clearly set forth the rules and principles of this method of divination, which allows of answers to all kinds of questions, and appears very amusing to him. " The diviner, or the consultant, will take twenty-five or thirty small bones in his hand, shuffle them well, rub them against one another, and then suddenly throw them down in front of him. Each of them possesses its own inherent significance, but this will be modified or intensified according to the way they scatter themselves on the ground. They therefore have to note the *side* on which the astragali fall,

[1] H. A. Junod : "L'art divinatoire chez les Ronga de la baie de Delagoa," *Bulletin de la Société de Géographie de Neuchâtel*, ix. p. 57 (1897).
[2] H. A. Merensky : *Erinnerungen aus dem Missionsleben in Süd Ost Afrika*, pp 42–3.
[3] H. A. Junod : ibid., p. 57.

the *direction* in which they are pointing, and finally the *position* they occupy with regard to each other." [1] We can easily see how many possible combinations there will be when all these things are taken into account.

Moreover, if the answer desired is not obtained at the first throw, they go on until it does come. "Possibly there will be a 'correspondence' between the way the bones fall and the case for which the consultation is made. For instance, if it is on account of a sick person, the astragalus representing that person has fallen in the negative position. Then the 'Word' has spoken. If there is no correspondence whatever, the bones are thrown again, one, two, or ten times! If they refuse to speak in the hut, the diviner will perhaps remove to the square, or to the bush, or behind the hut, until a clear answer is given." [2]

This persistence would be difficult to account for, if nothing but the desire to know what will happen were in question. But the bones do not reveal the future alone. "It is by means of the bones the Thongs believe they know what their gods think and wish." ("Gods" here signify "ancestors.") . . . "It is of the utmost importance to know what their gods think and do, as the very existence of the village, of the clan, and the welfare of every member of the clan depends on them. . . . They are the masters of everything : earth, fields, trees, rain, men, children, even of *baloyi* (wizards) ! They have a full control over all these objects or persons. The gods can bless . . . they can also curse, and bring any amount of mischief on their descendants " . . . (this last word proves that it is ancestors who are in question) "drought, disease, sterility, and so on." [3]

We can now readily understand the natives' constant recourse to the bones. Consulting them is as good as having a dream in which the ancestors make known their opinions and their desires. This method of divination is easier than dreams, for the bones are always at hand, and if one does not know how to interrogate them oneself, there is always an experienced diviner not far off who can do it. Should

[1] H. A. Junod: "L'art divinatoire chez les Ronga de la baie de Delagoa," p. 69.
[2] Ibid. : *The Life of a South African Tribe*, ii. p. 502.
[3] Ibid., pp. 360–1.

a difficulty confront the native, therefore, he need not say (as the chief did to the missionary Macdonald) : " I will dream about it." He has only to send for a bone-thrower, to learn from the astragali what his ancestors advise.

The revelations furnished by the bones and by divining practices in general thus procure for primitives the only extension of their experience which they are capable of appreciating or even imagining. It is a necessary one, for without it they would very often be at a loss. It is adequate, since it brings them a sure revelation of what the invisible powers have determined on, or what these wish them to do. The astragali " speak," and the native has but to receive their word, and this is their constant concern. " These practices," says Junod, " kill *in ovo* any serious attempt to use reason or experience in the practical life. Native tribes might have arrived at a useful and beneficial knowledge of the medical virtues of plants, if they had studied them properly. But what is the use of troubling themselves to study, when a single cast of the bones tells them what root must be taken to cure the disease ? " [1]

It is useless for the natives to know experimentally the properties of any particular plant, for this knowledge does not give them the idea of trying to find out what those of another well-known plant may be. These properties never seem to them sufficiently constant for the effects produced to depend upon them. Their effects are due rather to the invisible powers, and therefore the natives always come back again to the bones, since these furnish them with the surest information. " One day," says a Transvaal missionary, " I came across some men in a village who were engaged in throwing the bones on a mat spread out on the ground before them. I reminded them that it was a game of chance, and that they would do better to give up the custom. One of them said to me : ' But that is our book ; we have no other. You read in your book every day because you believe in it ; we do just the same, for we believe *our* book.' " [2]

[1] H. A. Junod : *The Life of a South African Tribe*, ii. p. 522.
[2] E. Thomas : " Le Bokaha," *Bulletin de la Société de Géographie de Neuchâtel*, viii. p. 162 (1895).

The reply is a striking one, and recalls the saying of the Jesuit missionary in New France, who declared that dreams were the Indian's Bible. The primitive mind knows no such thing as chance. What we speak of as accidental is to them fraught with mystic meaning. Throwing the bones, then, could not be blameworthy, or even a matter of indifference ; no other occupation could employ the time so well, or be more worthy of serious attention. Can the missionary do better than have intercourse with his God— the God who speaks to him in the Bible ? (To natives, a printed book is of a distinctly magical nature.) Well, then, their ancestors " speak " to the natives by the bones. Or rather, the Bible speaks, and the bones speak too. To consult them, therefore, is not doing anything that is absurd, or amusing oneself with childish games—not to risk anything without the approbation of the ancestors is being wise

II

It is not always as easy, as it is in South Africa, to discover to whom the natives are addressing their questions, and what is the nature of the assistance entreated. Nevertheless, the meaning of the divining practices remains the same, and those which are not difficult to explain give us enlightenment with regard to others which would prove enigmatical, if we could not perceive the transition from the one to the other.

Let us consider, for example, the methods of divination which are in daily use among the Papuans of New Guinea. " Before entering enemy territory, the Kai consults the oracle. He has recourse to it in the presence of any danger whatever, and according to the result of the consultation, he finds his fears confirmed, or he is at ease again. When the Kai warriors want to know whether they are threatened with an unexpected attack, a man will take a certain root, pronounce a magical formula over it, and bend it. If it should break, there is no danger ; but if it remains whole, the necessary precautions must be taken. Some vegetable produce must be boiled in a vessel over which certain incantations have been uttered ; and the side on which the water first begins to boil will be the direction whence danger may be apprehended. Or again, before beginning a campaign, all the weapons which are to be used are piled up on a hastily erected scaffolding, and on the top a war shell and an amulet are placed. Then the scaffolding is shaken until the shell falls down. Should it fall on the side nearest the enemy's village, it is an auspicious sign for the result of the expedition about to take place. Before the warriors start out, they use their united efforts to pull up a bush from the ground. If they have the good luck to free it from the soil with its roots unbroken, their attack will be successful. The following method of divination is one used in the most diverse circumstances. A staff to which a handful of grass is fastened is held by two men, who shake it violently backwards and forwards. If the grass falls off, the issue will be favourable ; but if it resists, it is a bad omen. To find out whether a sick man may hope for recovery or not, . . . they utter an incantation over a piece of the bark of a tree, and then pass this bark down the sick man's back. If it slips down with difficulty, as if it were fastened to the body, the worst must be expected." [1]

In a neighbouring tribe, the Jabim, " before undertaking an expedition, they try by means of an oracle to obtain some certainty as to its issue. They pronounce a magic formula over a certain onion, and then put it, with some leaves from a tree, over the fire in a vessel full of water. Men stand round to notice when the water bubbles. Before it begins to boil, they take some red paint and make a mark across the opening of the vessel. Half is then considered as belonging to the enemy, and the other half as belonging to their own tribe. The contents of the vessel begin to froth, and soon they are boiling. If it is their side which rises while bubbling, so that the liquid on the enemy's side overflows, and theirs, as it were, covers his, the omen is a favourable one. But should it happen the other way about, or should the contents of the vessel boil on both sides equally, then they stay at home." [2] Similarly,

[1] R. Neuhauss : *Deutsch Neu Guinea*, iii. pp. 132–3.
[2] Ibid., p. 317.

in the same district of (German) New Guinea, with the Bukaua, " before setting out, the expeditionary force tries to find out whether it is a favourable time to risk an attack. A vessel filled with plants of a pungent and bitter kind is placed· on the fire in the middle of the village square. When the water begins to boil, the band of warriors takes up its position on one side to wait till the froth overflows. Should it overflow on their side, it is a sign that the enemy is on his guard, and the expedition is given up. . . . If the contrary is the case, the warriors drink of the liquid, which will give them courage and hardihood." [1]

Missionaries have observed a large number of other practices of divination. All are of a magic kind. Whatever may be the creature or the object made use of, the diviners always begin by uttering some magical formula over it. That is a preliminary condition without which no valid result can be expected from the method employed. The first step, then, consists in establishing contact with the world of unseen powers, upon whom depends the success of the divination, as well as that of the undertaking to which it refers, and so the native does not differentiate between them. Thus he enters into the realm of what is " sacred." Then, and then only, may he put the question which is occupying his mind, and hope for an answer.

In the second place, the answer, as a rule, is given by a "yes " or "no," by a choice between two alternatives. Either the root bent over will break or it will remain whole ; either the water which boils over will be spilt on this side or on the opposite one ; either the handful of grass will fall off or it will remain fastened to the stick, and so on. Methods of this kind have the advantage of avoiding all ambiguity. It is certain that the unseen power interrogated will reply, and that its reply will be clear, since it is, so to speak, confined to two courses, one of which it is bound to choose. May not one fear to offend it by thus constraining it ? Neither the natives of New Guinea nor any other primitives appear to have the slightest scruple of this kind. Very often the powers in question are not possessed of a definite personality in their collective representations ;

[1] R. Neuhauss : *Deutsch Neu Guinea*, iii. p. 447.

the natives have both the idea and the vivid sentiment of a power, without any precise imagination where this is to be found. Moreover, even when it is a case of persons, properly so called, of the dead, for instance (with whom the Papuans of New Guinea maintain a constant intercourse without, however, as the missionaries tell us, addressing the questions put during the divining rites to them), the magic ceremony which began the operation has made communication with these dread powers both lawful and harmless. It has done more ; it has doubtless exercised such influence upon them that they cannot avoid the interrogation, and the issue of the event is indeed their answer.

Even the most complete description possible of the divining process does not disclose all its meaning. It necessarily leaves aside some of the essential features, which are the result of the peculiar nature of primitive mentality. Where we find symbolic relations merely, *it* feels a close participation. This cannot be expressed in our thought, nor even in our languages, which are much more conceptual than those of primitives. The term which would express it best in this connection would be the " momentary identity of substance." To take an example, a proceeding common to many of the tribes of (German) New Guinea consists in observing on which side the water begins to boil in a vessel containing certain magic herbs. It is not enough to say that the right side of the vessel " represents " the enemy, and the left the natives who are making the test. In a way which cannot be made objective to the understanding, nor expressed in language, but which is none the less real, the Papuans identify themselves and identify the enemy, with the respective sides. This side, says the missionary, " belongs " to them ; that is to say, it is theirs, just as their hands, limbs, head, and name are theirs, and " belong " to them. It is not simply theirs, it is they themselves. Whilst the test is being accomplished and they are following its progress with eager eyes, in passionate and often anguished ardour, they feel themselves to be personally engaged. It is something quite different from a symbolic representation, showing beforehand what is about to happen. It is the warriors themselves in the presence of their enemies. They are actual witnesses of their own victory or defeat.

This participation will lose some of its surprising and mysterious features when we compare with it the characteristics peculiar to primitive mentality which we have already indicated—the particular form which its experience takes, and especially the way in which it represents time and causality. We remember that, far from imagining events as linked together by a determinism which definitely binds antecedents to consequents, and shows them unfolding in an irreversible order, primitives do not see time as we do, stretching out like a straight line indefinitely before us. They therefore cannot give an exact location to future events on this line of time ; they simply *feel* them to be prospective, without seeing them arranged in immutable order, separated by intervals which must succeed each other. Their representation of the future consequently remains a vague one. On the other hand, the mystic powers who are constantly intervening in the visible world—themselves invisible—always exercise their influence in direct fashion. They are the only and the real causes of all things ; those perceived in the visible world being but instruments or opportunities. Consequently, as soon as the primitives form an idea of any action of the mystic powers, it is, in their eyes, from that very moment a real thing, even if it is not to manifest itself until later. Occurrences may therefore be both future and present at the same time. This simultaneity is not formulated in exact terms in the mind of the primitive ; it is simply felt. When the native who is noting, with an emotion which almost amounts to paroxysm, the movements of the boiling water, sees it overflowing on his side, he is at the same time present at his own victory. From this moment it is a reality to him, although it cannot take place until he has encountered the enemy. He is not only sure of conquering ; he has indeed, already conquered.[1]

[1] At Ruanda, in the course of a divining operation, " the bones say ' For the present, the inquirer may be reassured, but his good fortune will anyhow be but fleeting, for the *bazimu* are ready to begin the campaign. What am I saying ? They have already struck the first blow.' "—P. Alexis Arnoux : " La divination au Ruanda," *Anthropos*, xii-xiii. p. 13.

Commenting on this passage, Fr. Arnoux adds : " Here, the past appears

In this case, again, divination implies a prayer, in the sense in which the primitives pray ; that is to say, it makes an appeal to the unseen powers which is designed to have effective influence upon them. Undoubtedly, divination does first of all inform them of the chances of success. If, for example, the water boils over on the side which " belongs " to the enemy, they know that at this moment the invisible powers are favouring *him*. It may be that his wise men have more effective enchantments, that they are acquainted with more powerful incantations than theirs. In any case, they must pause, postpone the attack, try new charms, and begin the divining tests again, not risking anything until the answer vouchsafed is such as they wish it to be. When at length it is so, the successful issue of the test not only informs them that they may now proceed to action (just as the weathercock's new position announces that the wind has changed, and it is now safe to put out to sea). It certainly does that, but at the same time it does a good deal more : it promises a success which is already a reality. This is what gives divination its inestimable value in the eyes of the primitive. In the test which predicts his success he sees himself actually victorious. He must procure such a vision at all costs. Whether he receives it in a dream or obtains it from a divining process matters little. In both cases it is equally valid to him, and it responds to his ardent desire, not only to know whether he will conquer, but also to do so.

Similar proceedings may be noted in peoples who are further advanced in civilization than the tribes of New Guinea, but the mystic meaning of the divination has not entirely disappeared. Major Ellis, writing of the negroes on the west coast of Africa, says : " All seem to believe firmly in divination as a means of trying inferences concerning the course of future events. Without reasoning how it is done, they think that coming events are somehow foreshadowed by it." [1] These are remarkable words. The observer seems really to have recognized that the future

also to have the sense of the immediate future. ' You are so near to receiving the blow that you can regard it as already delivered.' "
  [1] A. B. Ellis : *The Ewe-speaking Peoples*, pp. 151–2.

occurrence announced is immediately felt as actually present, because to those interested, the test is already the event itself.

The same interpretation should doubtless be accorded to the following test, which is practised by the Bangala of the Upper Congo. " A saucepan of marsh or forest water is procured, and some medicine put into it. It is placed on the fire, to which none but the operators have access, and then after due time they say to the *likato* : " Will *they* kill us in the fight ? " If the water boils up and fills the saucepan, some of them will be killed, so they abandon the war ; but if the water keeps low, they ask : " Shall we kill some of them in the fight ? " Then if the water rises in the saucepan some of the enemy will be killed, and the war is prosecuted ; but if the water does not boil over, it shows that they will kill none of the enemy, consequently the fight is dropped. The test is put several times before they consider it satisfactory." [1]

Among the Zulus, certain practices of divination recall what we have noticed in the Papuans of New Guinea. " This custom," says Callaway, " is that of churning medicine in a pot of water. Two medicines are chosen, one to represent the chief, the other the, enemy. These medicines are placed in different vessels ; if that representing the enemy froths up suddenly whilst that representing the chief does not froth, they regard it as a sign that the enemy will prove too strong for them if they attack him at that time, and the army is not allowed to go out to battle. The same trial is represented again and again, it may be for months, or even years ; and the army is allowed to go out to battle only when the sign is reversed, and the chief's vessel froths up, and that of the enemy does not froth." [2]

As in New Guinea, the consultant here identifies himself with the object which represents him, and the future is felt to be actually real. At the very moment when victory is promised it is obtained. The battle is won ; it is a settled thing, and when, some weeks or even months later, it really

[1] Rev. J. H. Weeks : " Anthropological Notes on the Bangala of the Upper Congo River," *J.A.I.*, xl. p. 391.
[2] Rev. C. H. Callaway : *The Religious System of the Amazulu*, p. 441 (note 25) (1870).

does take place, it will be a mere formality, so to speak. Callaway expresses it exactly : " A chief does thus with his vessel, and he generally mentions what he is about to do before it is done, saying : ' Such-and-such will happen, and you will do so-and-so.' And so it is when the army is led out, the men look for a word to come from the chief to give them courage, that they may know what kind of people it is to whom they are going . . . (whether they are to be feared or no). . . . The chief is accustomed to say : ' You will not see any army. I say I have already killed So-and-so. . . . You will only take the cattle. There are no men, but some women.' The word of the chief gives confidence to his troops ; they say : ' We are going only ; the chief has already seen all that will happen.' " [1]

It is quite allowable to imagine that there may be some boasting in the words of the chief and his troops. But there is assuredly something else. The proof of it is that they never begin a campaign until the auspicious sign has made its appearance. It may have to be long waited for, but as soon as it is seen, all is won. The enemy is not *going to be* beaten ; he *is* already beaten. The chief has already slain such-and-such an enemy chief. The spear-thrust which will lay the enemy low is but the finishing-stroke of an event which from this very moment has actually occurred. The words which Callaway puts into the mouth of the Zulu chief exactly express what divination means to him and his people.

III

Divination " by alternative " takes various forms. Its object is nearly always the same, that of satisfying the need for the direction and protection of the invisible powers, to whom the questions and prayers are addressed. Thus, in the island of Mangaia, in Polynesia : " On the morning of the fatal day, the chief selected two beautiful *ariri* shells, one for himself and one for his adversary Koteateoru. Secret instructions were given for his forces to hide themselves

[1] Rev. C. H. Callaway: *The Religious System of the Amazulu*, pp. 342–3.

in a certain place. The narrow pathways between the deep taro swamps were obliterated. This done, the chief returned to look at his shells ; to his joy, the one representing his foes was turned upside down. He interpreted this as a sure omen of their destruction." [1] In the same way, in New Zealand, "in order to find out what the issue of a campaign will be, a young man takes a number of small sticks, one for each of the belligerent tribes. He levels a certain piece of land, and then sets up the sticks like nine-pins in two parallel rows to represent the two armies facing each other, and goes a little way off to see what the wind will do with them. If the sticks representing the enemy fall backwards, the enemy will be overthrown ; if they fall forward, he will conquer ; but should they fall to one side, the issue will be uncertain." [2] Sometimes the question is put directly in definite terms. In Motu Island, at the moment of fighting, "the chief catches his middle finger (*natugu*) and holding it says: '*Natugu, natugu*, shall I go or shall I stay ? Just speak, *natugu*.' He pulls the finger, and if it cracks he stays at home or returns. If there is no crack, he goes on." [3] Facts of this kind are extremely common in all latitudes.

Divination bears upon future occurrences of every kind. It will reveal whether a sick person will recover, what the sex of an unborn child will be, whether the harvest will be good, or the rain will fall. But it is often used for the mere discovery of something that is hidden, or the obtaining of important information about an event which has already occurred. For instance, someone wants to know whether a traveller, from whom there has been no news for a long time, is in good health, where something that is lost may be found, whether it has been mislaid or stolen, who has done a deed for which the social group is suffering, in which direction a beast which has wandered away from the herd is to be sought, and so forth. Now it is noteworthy that the processes employed in these cases, and in many other similar ones, do not essentially differ from those used when

[1] W. W. Gill : *Savage Life in Polynesia*, pp. 14–15 (1880).
[2] "Société de Marie." *Annales des Missions d'Océanie*, i. 94–5 (Lettre du P. Servant. 1841.)
[3] Rev. J. Chalmers : *Pioneering in New Guinea*, p. 304.

it is a question of ascertaining and securing a certain result in the future.

This resemblance is first accounted for by what has been said about the idea of time peculiar to primitive mentality, when it perceives or solicits omens, and interrogates the mystic powers upon which the future depends. To it the influence of these powers appears to be immediate, in the full sense of the word. It is exercised without any intermediary, and consequently *at once,* and the future event which will be produced by means of it is felt to be already here. If it be so, the same processes of divination will serve to ascertain the issue of the next campaign, as to find the horse which has disappeared during the night. Moreover, in the case of future events, the practices of divination imply a request for help and support, and even a prayer addressed to the unseen powers. These elements of divination are equally present when it bears upon matters that are past or objects that are hidden. Only instead of praying for a thing to happen—that is, for the unseen powers to make it a reality—the primitive asks that he may be enabled to see the object lost or the event which he did not witness, and that the power may reveal it to him *directly.* It matters little whether the event belongs to the future or to the past ; to primitive mentality it seems as if the field of operations of the unseen powers constitutes a comprehensive category, dominating those of time and space in which, to our minds, events are necessarily arranged in definite order. It is in this sense that the primitive's experience is more ample, if not richer in content than our own, for it can embrace more at one time. Its framework is less rigid, and allows of its comprising the seen and the unseen in the same reality, what we call the natural and the supernatural ; in a word, this world and the other. Hence we find characteristics which are common to all kinds of divination. Even should it not be a question of the future, its methods tend not only to find out what is at present unknown, but at the same time they endeavour to obtain the help of the powers which are able to lift the veil.

We can make this matter clearer by some examples.

In (German) New Guinea, " the co-operation of a wizard is of peculiar importance when the discovery of a thief is in question. If a robbery has taken place without its being possible to name the guilty person, the native resorts to the man who possesses a charm which will detect him. The wizard takes his axe and strikes at a creeper with it, pronouncing a name at each blow. If the axe hits the creeper, the name is that of an innocent man ; but if it fails to reach it, the man just named is the culprit. Or again, he takes a small branch with some leaves, pronounces some incantations over them, and strikes his left arm with the branch. If a leaf falls off, the man then named is not guilty, but if, in spite of the blow, all the leaves remain fastened to the branch, the man named at the moment is the thief." [1] Quite near this district, among the Kai, " when a robbery has taken place, the natives consult the oracle to find out who is the thief. There are various ways of proceeding. For instance, they fasten a coco-nut full of water to the end of a cord, and start a revolving movement with it, at the same time saying over the names of the inhabitants of the village. He at whose name the water is spilt is the guilty person. Or again, they put a stick in the ground and balance a pot upon it. They then call out all the names of the people in the village. As long as the robber's name is not uttered, the pot sways and threatens to fall off, but when the robber's name is pronounced, it recovers its equilibrium and remains motionless." [2] In the Bakaua tribe, neighbours of the Kai, " to discover a thief, the natives take a vessel, the bottom of which is painted with red stripes. A rod is stuck into the ground in the middle of the village square, and the upper surface, which is also striped with red, is perfectly smooth. One of the village people tries to balance the vessel on this surface, at the same time calling out the names of all the others in turn. The natives, who are exasperated by the theft, seat themselves round and watch the performance. The vessel seems constantly about to fall, but as soon as the name of the thief has been pronounced it stops swaying and remains

---

[1] R. Neuhauss : *Deutsch Neu Guinea*, iii. pp. 251–2 (Neighbourhood of King William Cape).   [2] Ibid., p. 127.

steady. Then they search the suspect's bag, and they go through his house from top to bottom. Whether the object stolen be found there or not, suspicion remains fastened on him, and the opprobrium of it is intolerable. The man is obliged to leave the village—if not for good, at any rate for a long time—until the matter has unconsciously passed into oblivion." [1]

In a case in which *we* should hold an inquiry, the Papuan " draws lots." But to him there is no " chance " in drawing lots. On the contrary, he is making an appeal to mystic powers, and the magic nature of the operation guarantees its infallibility. It always starts with rites which put the sorcerer, the bystanders, and all that is to be done, in touch with the unseen world. They are thus conveyed to the sacred realm, and as a consequence the revelation vouchsafed to them will perforce be reliable. It matters little whether experience confirms it or not. If the general notions here involved are analysed, we shall find that the methods employed are the natural result of the natives' mentality, and that they cannot fail to have firm faith in them.

Why are they inspired with such anger with the unknown thief, and so anxious to discover his identity ? Are they acting on behalf of a social law which demands that the violation of any right shall be followed by the pronouncement of a sentence ? Are they obeying an imperative feeling which requires that private property shall be respected ? But in communities like those of the Papuans, we know that the idea of ownership is different from our own. The number of things which may be possessed in turn by various persons is extremely small. Within the social group there is hardly any buying or selling, nor is there really any economic existence. If we subtract what is common property—the hunting grounds, for instance— every individual does indeed possess some things which are his ; but they " belong " to him in a mystic sense, giving this term a more profound meaning than ours. They participate more or less in his substance. They belong to him as do his head and his limbs, his wife and his children, his nail-parings, hair, skin, fat, excreta. The very clothing

[1] R. Neuhauss : ibid., pp. 471–2.

he wears, being moistened with his bodily perspiration, is a very part of him.[1] It is the same with the spear which he uses in hunting and his fishing net; whoever lays hands on them, touches him, and he who tries to take them from him is suspected of the most sinister designs. He who has become possessed of them, henceforth has the power of doing him the greatest possible harm, and his life is held at the robber's discretion. Into whose hands are these actual parts of his personality going to fall? Who knows whether the robber, or one of his accomplices, may not already have "doomed" him?

Among such peoples, therefore, a thief is not merely an "undesirable" member of the group, a lazy and unscrupulous fellow who wants to procure, without working for it, the fruit of others' labours. He may be that, and still more, a sorcerer of the very worst type, a virtual assassin. Moreover, to become possessed of things which he may put to such dread uses, he must already be engaged in the practice of magic. He makes himself invisible, he enters huts while their owners are asleep, he devotes himself to their undoing in a way they are quite unconscious of, etc. It is therefore absolutely essential to their safety that this dangerous malefactor shall be made known. But they will never succeed in discovering him unless they can meet the mystic forces he is employing with other and more powerful ones which shall overcome his.

Thus the natives do not think of an inquiry conducted according to the European idea of law. Such an idea would never occur to them, and even if it were suggested, they would not see any useful purpose to be served by it. What matters to them is to have a mystic hold on the unknown thief. Now if he is a member of their group, it will be possible to obtain such a hold. They can employ powerful means of magic to try and discover his name. If they are successful, they have him, and he will not escape them, for to primitives, the name serves not only to designate individuals; it is an integral part of the personality, it participates in it. If the name is disposed of,

[1] G. Landtman: "The Folk Tales of the Kiwai Papuans," *Acta societatis scientiarum fennicæ*, xlii. pp. 313–15; cf. ibid., p. 268.

the personality is mastered, and to deliver up the name of a man is to deliver him over. Hence the methods in use for the purpose of discovering the criminal. While the mystic operation proceeds—the swaying movements of a vessel full of liquid, over which enchantments have been uttered, for example—a man who is qualified to do so calls out in turn the names of all the members of the group. By so doing he brings them directly in touch with the mystic power which is acting, without any possibility of escape. The moment the name of the guilty person is pronounced, this contact with the unseen powers becomes a revealing process. The vessel ceases its swaying movement and remains still ; the thief is discovered. The natives do not dream of doubting the result, and they need no other test to corroborate the verdict.

Proceedings similar to these have been noted in nearly all parts of the world, in Australia, South, Central, and West Africa, etc. They are, as it were, a necessary consequence of the orientation of the primitive's mind. The coincidence of a certain name with the disclosure awaited, which they consider to be due to the intervention of occult powers, is as good as a revelation made by a dream, or a divination pronounced by the choice of an alternative, examples of which we have already given. However diverse the methods may be, its working is, at bottom, identical.

Frequently, too, instead of revealing the name of the guilty party, divination makes known the direction in which he is to be sought, or the place which must be visited if a missing object is to be found, and so on. Thus, in North Queensland, " a medicine-man can find to a certainty the direction whence the *ti* (sorcerer) came, by going out into the bush where he will throw certain charcoal-looking pellets into the air in the direction of the four cardinal points. These will remain suspended in mid-air unless thrown in the proper quarter, where only they will fall on the ground. I was informed that these pellets had been sucked by a medicine-man out of some other patient on a previous occasion." [1] In South Africa, " the Kafirs

[1] W. E. Roth : " Superstition, Magic, and Medicine," *North Queensland Ethnography*, Bulletin 5, No. 130.

use the praying mantis for the purpose of divination. If cattle are lost, if a doctor is needed, or anything of that sort, they get one of these insects on a blade of grass, and put it somewhere or other, no matter where. The insect seeks another place for itself, and the direction in which its head then points is the one in which the missing cattle will be found, or the doctor who is needed, etc." [1] Similarly, with their neighbours the Hottentots, a box is the instrument used. A bit of thread is soaked in grease and the end lighted ; it is placed in a closed box and held against the wind. The direction in which the smoke escapes tells the perplexed Hottentot where he must look for the animal which has strayed, or the travelling companion who has lost his way. [2] In these happenings, which are so common that there is no need to relate any more of them, everything occurs exactly as if the possible directions were enumerated in turn, just as we have seen the names of the natives were. But in this roll-call there was, at any rate in its inception, a mystic reason ; is there not also one in this search for directions ?

In the native's eyes, nothing happens by chance. If then the praying mantis or the smoke takes one direction in preference to all others, this semblance of a choice is a revelation ; that is to say, it supplies the answer to the question propounded, provided this has been couched in the proper mystic fashion. Moreover, if the name of a man, as an integral part of his personality, gives a hold on him, should not that region of space where he was born, and which he inhabits, the home of a social group, play an equal part ? Do not they, by their intimate participation, " belong " in the same way ? Are not the social group, the individuals composing it, and the region they occupy in space all united in a mystic bond which, like their names, can make them known ? [3] The primitives' representation of space, like that of time, as far as they have any special one, is above all " qualitative." Regions in space are not con-

[1] Fr. Ægidius Müller : " Wahrsagerei bei den Kaffern," *Anthropos*, i. p. 778.
[2] L. Schultze : *Aus Namaland und Kalahari*, p. 226.
[3] Spencer and Gillen, "The Native Tribes of Central Australia," pp. 303, 544.

ceived, nor really represented, but rather *felt* within complex masses, and each region is inseparable from that which fills it. Each participates in the real or mythical animals which live in it, the plants which grow there, the tribes inhabiting it, the tempests and hurricanes which visit it, and so on. The representation of a space that is homogeneous, to which we are accustomed, does not give the idea at all. The following circumstance, which occurred in Western Australia, may make this difference more perceptible.

A party of Europeans and aborigines taking part in an expedition was tormented by thirst. They examined all the water-holes, to see what hope there was of finding water, and the natives dug a kind of channel in the sand, and plunged a stick down it, lest perchance there might be some underground source. At the first pit made they found nothing ; at the second the end of the stick came up damp. The natives redoubled their efforts, and soon arrived at sand which was wet enough to stick to their hands when pressed. " It was now no longer necessary to carry the large pit any further down, as a much smaller hole dug in this bottom would serve our purpose. But now a difficulty arose in the minds of the natives, and one not at all appreciated by us. With them the question now was, in which corner of the larger pit the small one should be dug, so as to be sure of finding water ? while to us, not so influenced by imagination as they, it seemed perfectly immaterial, for water was evidently to be had, by sinking anywhere within the above space, for the whole of it was equally moist. But the black man never trusts to chance ; he must have a reason, good or bad, to guide him in every action ; and consequently they at once proceeded to discuss this knotty point in regular form. The first proposal was to dig it in the western side of the pit, for the sea being in that direction it was probable that water would be found towards that quarter ; but this plausible proposal was immediately scouted, and its author ridiculed on the ground that though water would be found in the direction suggested, yet coming from the sea it would be salt, and therefore unfit for drinking. The next proposal was that it should be in the eastern part of the pit, for the

14

reason that the Angaardies dwelling in that direction have plenty of *boolia* (magic power), and can make it rain whenever they please, consequently they are never short of this element. This proposal seemed to decide the matter, for they were on the point of digging . . . when an old man expressed a fear lest these much-dreaded Angaardies should turn sulky if their rights were thus infringed, and in revenge use their terrible powers of enchantment against the Watchandies, and thereupon this idea was at once abandoned. One sage proposed the north-west, for all the rain came from that quarter, and this suggestion would have been adopted, had not another proposed the south, contending that the whites coming from that quarter must have found plenty of water on their journey, consequently that desideratum was to be found in the specified direction. This compliment to ourselves carried the day." [1]

Primitive mentality thus attaches great importance to relations to which we pay no attention, but which, by some sort of participation, connect beings and things with the direction or the point in space where they are usually or actually to be found. The water will be found in the east, because that is the home of the Angaardies, those mighty magicians and rain-makers ; but the Angaardies in their turn participate in the quality which belongs to everything in the east. Again, water will be found in the south, because the whites, who have much magic power at their command, have come from the south ; thus there is a participation existing between the southern region and the whites, and this is represented partly by a quality peculiar to the whites, which is extended to that region, and partly by a property of the south which will be at the disposal of the whites. These connections, familiar as they are to primitive mentality, do not afford it material for reflection. The primitive mind never expresses them in a general or abstract way ; he feels them more than he thinks them. Just because he apprehends them directly, by a kind of intuition, he is guided by them in action without being consciously aware of them. His mind functions in a space which is qualitatively

[1] A. Oldfield : " The Aborigines of Australia," *Transactions of the Ethnological Society*, iii. pp. 282–3 (1865).

determined and more opulent in its properties than our own ; for if he knows nothing of geometrical properties, space on the other hand is endowed with qualities which are directly perceptible, and these it shares with all that occupies it.

Oldfield tells us again : " Every male " (of the Watchandie tribe) " is bound to visit the place of his nativity three times in the course of a year, but for what specific purpose I could not learn." [1]

Spencer and Gillen report similar customs among the natives of Central Australia. We know, too, that when several tribes meet together at a certain place, each tribe takes up its position on the spot which its mystic connections with a certain definite point in space assign to it. This fact has been noted in other places besides Australia, where it is very clearly evident. " I have often been struck," writes William Thomas, " with the exact position each tribe takes in the general encampment, precisely in the position from which their country lies according to the compass (of which they have a perfect notion). I have found this invariably the case, and latterly could form an idea on the arrival of the blacks what part they came from." [2]

A. R. Brown, who has made a recent study of three tribes of Western Australia, very clearly describes that participation which Oldfield had noted, half a century previously, in the same region. He says : " In the early days of the settlement of the whites in the country of this and neighbouring tribes the squatters made use of the natives as shepherds, and I have been told on several occasions that they found it at first impossible to persuade a native to shepherd the sheep anywhere except on his own part of the country. . . . It is impossible for a man to leave his local group and become naturalized or adopted in another. Just as the country belonged to him, so he belonged to it. If he left it he became a stranger, either the guest or the enemy of the man in whose country he

---

[1] A. Oldfield : " The Aborigines of Australia," *Transactions of the Ethnological Society*, iii, p. 252.
[2] William Thomas, in *Letters from Victorian Pioneers*, p. 96.

found himself. . . . The country now belongs to the white man, and the natives have to live where they can. But even now the attachment of a man to his own country has not been destroyed. Natives often express a wish to die and be buried in their own inherited hunting-ground." [1]

Thus to these Australian aborigines the idea of the social group comprises not only the living and the dead ; it has also other integral parts. The place the natives dwell in, the region of space in which their ancestors have lived, where they are living still (as the dead do live while waiting, in those totemistic centres described by Spencer and Gillen, until the opportunity occurs for them to be born again in the form of actual members of their group), all these enter into a man's representation of his social group. This intimate connection between the living, the dead, and the soil, has been thoroughly grasped by a missionary in British New Guinea. " The spirits of the dead, invoked to obtain success in hunting or fishing, are called upon in the very places where *they* have hunted and fished. And it seems as if this were the chief reason which induces the Kuni religiously to remember the names of their ancestors. When, during the course of my genealogical investigations, a native was unable to furnish me with the name of his grandfather or great-grandfather, the bystanders at once said to him : ' But then, what do you do when you are hunting ? ' " [2]

The intimate relation between the social group and its territory extends not only to the soil and the game which is found there ; all the mystic powers, spirits, forces more or less clearly conceived, that are concerned with it, have the same symbiotic connection with the group. Each of its members realizes what they are to him and he to them. When there he knows the mystic dangers which threaten him, and the supernatural support upon which he can reckon, but away from this region there is no support of any kind for him. Unknown, and so much the more terrifying perils surround him on all sides. It is no longer *its* air that he breathes, *its* water he drinks, *its* fruits he gathers and eats.

---

[1] A. R. Brown : "Three Tribes of Western Australia," *J.I.A.*, xliii. p. 146.
[2] P. V. M. Egidi, M.S.C. : "La religione e le conoscenze naturali dei Kuni (Nuova Guinea Inglese)," *Anthropos*, viii. p. 206.

They are not *its* mountains which surround him ; he does not tread *its* paths ; everything here is hostile to him, since it lacks those participations he is accustomed to feel. Hence arises his extreme reluctance to leave his own district, even for a short time. " It may be that the disinclination," says Newton, " to go away to another district for medical treatment is due to fear of the evil spirits of another place, who may have a special objection to intruders, and it is better to bear the ills one has. It seems, indeed, that the only good the spirits do to the inhabitants of a place is the negative one of making strangers fear to intrude, and this may also account for the objection natives in the olden days had to travelling far from home. Was it that the conservative instincts of the people and their objection to and fear of strangers made them attribute the same sort of feelings to the spirits, or was it that this fear made the people conservative ? Which is cause and which is effect ? These are the sort of puzzles one meets when one comes in contact with native races, whose minds and modes of thought no white man can understand." [1]

Not very far off, in (German) New Guinea, " two years ago there came to the missionary Hanke at Bongu a man from Bilibili, who addressed him on behalf of the people of his village, who had fled to the district of Rai. He begged him to intercede with the Government to allow them to return to Bilibili. In support of his request he stated : ' The spirits of our ancestors have come to Rai seeking us ; they were very angry, and scolded us, saying : " How could you desert the place where all our spirits dwell ? Who is there now to care about us ? " And then,' the man added, ' the spirits spat with contempt upon the new vessels which were even then not quite finished, and all these vessels are broken. And now, therefore, we are living as strangers among the people of Rai ; we have no fields of our own, and what is worst of all, we cannot make any pots and vessels for ourselves. Let us then return to our former home, that the spirits may no longer be incensed against us.' " [2]

---

[1] Rev. H. Newton : *In Far New Guinea*, p. 86 (1914).
[2] *Berichte der rheinischen Missionsgesellschaft*, p. 137 (1907).

It is difficult, therefore, for primitives to live elsewhere than on the land which makes a part of their social group, if we may put it thus. It is no less difficult for them to fight well away from home. Thus in New Zealand, " whatever degree of courage a tribe may possess when on their own ground, on quitting this it soon evaporates ; nor have they the least hesitation in admitting that this is the case. . . . They are in dread of surprises and attacks from all sides."[1] This fact is generally known, and many similar observations have been made.

By virtue of this same participation, the man who is exiled for all time from the place where his social group has its home, ceases to form a part of it. As far as it is concerned he is dead, more really dead than if he had simply ceased to live, and had received the customary funeral rites. This is the case, too, with prisoners of war who have been spared, and are adopted by the conquering tribe. Thus it is that permanent exile means the same thing as death. In Vura, one of the Solomon Islands, " a Christian had, in an outbreak of rage, so struck his wife as to break her jaw and cause her death in a few hours. The woman had, according to the testimony of her own people, exasperated him beyond endurance, and was continually making unfounded charges against him. They wanted, however, to take the law into their own hands and to kill him after the old fashion, as a matter of private revenge ; but the chiefs prevented this and . . . it was decided that transportation for life would be the most fitting punishment. With this sentence native public opinion entirely agreed ; the people considered that he would be *dead to them*."[2]

Here, again, is a symbolic African rite which allows the relation between the soil and the dwellers on it to appear. " When a Ronga comes back from Kimberley, having found a wife there, both bring with them a little of the earth of the place they are leaving, and the woman must eat a little of it every day in her porridge, in order to accustom herself to her new abode. This earth provides the transition between the two domiciles."[3]

[1] Wm. Brown : *New Zealand and its Aborigines*, p. 47 (1845).
[2] E. S. Armstrong : *The History of the Melanesian Mission*, p. 308 (1900).
[3] H. P. Junod : *The Life of a South African Tribe*, i. p. 47 (note).

All this illustrates how, in certain cases, divination makes use of a location in space, as it does of the name of a man. The location where the man may be found, the region of space in which he dwells, are " his," in the full sense of the word, like his limbs and his mind, since, to make use of Brown's forcible expression, he belongs to his country as it belongs to him. Hence, a man may be denounced by the location in space which he occupies, as well as by the marks left on the ground by his feet. It possesses the characteristic quality of his personality, or at any rate, of that of his group.

In time this process may lose its original meaning and become mechanical, and even end by being used on occasions which have nothing in common with its pristine signification. When in searching for the cattle which have strayed during the night the Hottentot is guided by the direction taken by a praying mantis, we may be of opinion that in this there is a form of divination exactly like those by coincidence and alternative which we have already studied. But in those, too, there was at first a mystic meaning. And perhaps, in the mind of the Hottentot, there may exist some obscure perception of the sense of participation, which we have found to be such a vital part of the collective representations of Australian aborigines.

If the object of the foregoing study were a survey of all the divining processes in use among primitive peoples, it would be a very incomplete one ; but I have only aimed at showing what the practices of divination (or those known as such) signify to primitives, what they expect from them, and how the same general ideas have led to the most diverse methods. For that purpose examples taken from the most undeveloped peoples known to us sufficed.

Many processes of divination of which I have not spoken are employed by them, and these might be analysed in the same way. Primitives, for instance, know how to utilize the services of mediums, for the purpose of communicating with the unseen world, and can hypnotize them. There is hardly anything about the phenomena ·familiar to spiritists of all ages and in all parts of the world that primitives do not know. Myers' *Phantasms of the Living* would afford them little surprise. Intercourse with spirits, especially those of the dead, forms a part of their daily experience. Though often in dread of it, they frequently risk courting it, taking due precautions. They can discern among their own people those " subjects " who are the most sensitive to occult and unseen influences, and the best fitted to receive communications from the world beyond. These subjects become diviners, seers, and wizards in the best sense of the word. It is to them that they turn when in need of any special revelation. The Esquimaux reserve all the divining processes for the medicine-man, the *angekok*. To carry them out, he puts himself into a state of hypnotic slumber, or cataleptic or ecstatic trance ; that is to say, he transports himself to the realm of the unseen powers and enters into communication with them. He sees and hears the dead ; he traverses, imperceptibly and instantly, immense distances on the wings of the wind, and so on. His experience is like that of a dream which is induced ; it is a privileged and infallible vision.

Primitives are also acquainted with divination, closely allied with the preceding forms, which is practised by means of a crystal, a mirror (when they possess one), the surface of water, etc. To quote one among countless examples, in Greenland, according to Crantz: " They pretend to find out whether a man, that has not come home from the sea in due time, is living or dead. They lift up the head of the nearest relation of the missing man with a stick ; a tub of water stands under, and in that mirror they behold forsooth the absent man either overset in his *kayak*, or sitting upright and rowing." [1]

Witch doctors and sorcerers are endowed, as a rule, with special clairvoyant powers. Their eyes see that which remains invisible to others. Thus they are " supermen " during their life, and very frequently after their death. They often have the ability to detect guilty persons by their appearance alone, and full confidence is placed in what they affirm. " It is interesting to note," says Dixon, speaking of the Shasta, " that shamans are supposed to

[1] D. Crantz : *History of Greenland*, i. p. 214 (1767).

have the power of telling at once whether a person has been wrong in any way. They are able to do this because, when they look at a person who has stolen, or done anything wrong, the person seems to the shaman to be, as it is phrased, ' covered with darkness.' " [1]

The characteristic peculiar to this clairvoyance, which plays so great a part in very many methods of divination, is its being both direct and intuitive. The reply to the question propounded is revealed to the diviner or the shaman in a single and indivisible act of vision. Callaway has discreetly laid stress on this point. " When anything valuable is lost they look for it at once ; when they cannot find it, each one begins to practise this inner divination, trying to feel where the thing is, for not being able to see it he feels internally a pointing, which tells him that he will go down to such a place, it is there, and he will find it. . . . At length he sees it, and himself approaching it ; before he begins to move from where he is, he sees it very clearly indeed, and there is an end of doubt. That sight is so clear that it is as though it was not an inner sight, but as if he saw the very thing itself and the place where it is ; so he quickly arises and goes to the place. If it is a hidden place, he throws himself into it, as if there was something that impelled him to go as swiftly as the wind. And, in fact, he finds the thing if he has not acted by mere head-guessing. If it has been by real inner divination, he really sees it. But if it is done by mere head-guessing, and only that he has not gone to such a place and such a place, and that therefore it must be in another place, he generally misses the mark." [2]

This is a very instructive description. It demonstrates clearly, by means of a practice with which the primitive is familiar, his distrust with regard to discursive operations and reasoning, and his preference for intuitive and direct apprehension. Discursive processes do not seem merely difficult and tedious to him ; he has another reason for avoiding them. He does not believe in them. Should

[1] R. B. Dixon : " The Shasta," *Bulletin of the American Museum of Natural History*, xvii. pp. 488-9.
[2] Rev. C. H. Callaway : *The Religious System of the Amazulu*, pp. 338-9.

CHAPTER VIII

ORDEALS

I

THE history of the Middle Ages familiarized us with those tests, closely connected with divination, which are called Judgments of God, or Ordeals. They were known, as Glotz [1] has so clearly demonstrated, to the Ancient Greeks. They are to be met with also among many primitive peoples. Nevertheless, it would be wiser to refrain from admitting prematurely that the data regarding them, furnished by widely differing communities, are identical. I shall not take for granted that the ordeals known to primitives constitute a special judicial process which gives the gods the option of saving a condemned person who may be innocent (as in the Greek usage), or which refers the decision of a trial to God (as in the Middle Ages). Leaving aside for the moment any preliminary definition, I shall confine myself first of all to analysing instances, and these I shall take preferably from African races, where ordeals play a considerable part in the life of the people, not prohibiting myself, however, from studying comparable conditions in other communities.

The feature which first of all impresses itself on the attention of observers everywhere is the absolute and invincible confidence, the unwavering faith of primitives in judgment by ordeal. Even in the seventeenth century, Italian missionaries on the Congo were already laying stress on this point. " I was absolutely amazed, and I could not persuade myself that any men, however great their ignorance, could really believe in such manifest trickery, and not admit even one of the many reasons the missionaries daily advanced against it. . . . But instead

[1] G. Glotz : *L'ordalie dans la Grèce primitive* (Paris, 1909).

of being convinced, they merely shrugged their shoulders, saying : ' It is quite impossible for our tests to fail us ; that can never be, it is quite impossible ! ' " [1]

The explorers and missionaries of to-day testify to the same firm faith in trial by ordeal. " The native thoroughly believes in its efficacy. My own porters have constantly offered to submit to the ordeal on the most trivial charges." [2] " All the natives," says Duff Macdonald, " believe that *mvai* (ordeal by poison) is infallible, while they know very well that the testimony of their countrymen is not so. . . . Here we encounter the most deeply rooted faith that these tribes have. If they believe in anything, it is in this ordeal. I once asked Kumpana of Cherasulo, ' What would you do if a man stole ivory and vomited the *mvai*, but was afterwards found selling the stolen ivory ? ' His reply was : ' If the man stole the ivory he would not vomit the *mvai*, the *mvai* would kill him.' I have made many similar suppositions to many natives, and though I carefully concealed my *petitio principii*, they at once pointed out that I was supposing cases that could never occur." [3] " The blacks are always ready to take the poison, and it is very rarely that an accused man will avoid, by flight, his obligation to submit to this proof. When conscious that they are innocent, they betray no fear of trial by poison." [4] " The blacks believe firmly that anyone who is assured of his innocence may drink the *m'bambu* in all confidence ; he will not die. For instance, one day when we were on an expedition, we missed a knife from our camping-place. At first we thought it had been stolen by one of the many natives who were squatting around our encampment, but even before we could formulate any accusation they one and all declared themselves willing to drink the *m'bambu* in order to prove their innocence. Of course we could not consent to that, and after a more thorough search, the knife turned up again." [5]

[1] Cavazzi : *Istorica descrizione de'tre regni di Congo, Matamba, ed Angola,* p. 97.
[2] L. Decle : *Three Years in Savage Africa,* p. 512 (1898).
[3] Rev. Duff Macdonald : *Africana,* i. p. 160.
[4] P. Pogge : *Im Reiche des Muata Jamwo,* p. 39.
[5] H. von Wissmann, *Wolf . . . Im innern Afrikas,* p. 144.

In a tribe of Basutos, " yesterday morning a woman from a neighbouring village came to tell me that she was about to undergo the ordeal of boiling water on a charge of witchcraft. Her nearest neighbour was a very bad woman who had made her life a burden for months, and was always accusing her of being a witch ; so that now she had offered to undergo the trial by water (that of soaking her hands in boiling water). My visitor was not in the least afraid of the test before her ; knowing herself to be innocent, she felt sure that the water would not scald her." [1]

In East Africa, it is the same thing. " The Kond is absolutely convinced of the infallibility of this test by ordeal," writes the missionary Schumann. " They respect anyone who has vomited the poison, and do him honour. Everybody drinks the *muavi* cup, big and little, men and women, the sole exceptions being the chiefs, who, if occasion requires it, do so by proxy " (not in any way because they fear the result of the ordeal, but because of the sacred nature of their personality). Merensky, too, says : " The Kond is always willing to submit to the ordeal. Drinking the *muavi* is such a favourite test of this kind here that you constantly hear the expression ' I will drink *muavi* (to prove the speaker to be right). They drink *muavi* not only to decide between innocence and guilt, but also because it affords an easy way of throwing light on a question of disputed rights. What is the use of troubling about laborious investigations when it is so easy to find out what to rely on by getting a verdict from the cup of *muavi* ! " [2] However, it is not from laziness, as we shall soon see, that natives resort to the trial by ordeal even when there is no question of crime.

Winterbottom relates the story of a young woman in West Africa who, being accused of witchcraft and knowing what awaited her if she denied it, prudently made up her mind to acknowledge it. She was not sold into slavery at once because she was enceinte, and she succeeded in

[1] *Missions évangéliques*, lxxxi. p. 31. (Th. Burnier.)
[2] Fülleborn : " Das deutsche Njassa und Ruwumagebeit," *Deutsch Ost Afrika*, x. pp. 309-10.

escaping to the care of the white people. " Such, however, was the darkness of their minds, and so far were they
from suspecting that any deceit and villainy were practised
that the woman, though persuaded of her innocence, said
no more than that ' the grigris were bad ' and that she
wished for an opportunity of drinking ' red water ' which
she was sure would cure her." [1]   And on the Lower Niger
" the belief prevails that the innocent alone escape, and
that only the guilty die." [2]   This accounts for the enormous
number of ordeals, and the victims, sometimes to be
reckoned by hundreds, on the death of a chief, or even
as a precautionary measure on his accession.

Whence comes this firm belief, which is so universal,
and which so shocks Europeans ?   How is it that the
black man, who is often so discreet and even subtle when
it is a question of protecting his interests, can be so blind
when his life is endangered by the ordeal ?   Does he not
see that in accepting these tests he is delivered over,
bound hand and foot, to the " doctor " who prepares the
poisoned cup, to the chief whose tool the doctor is, or to
his own enemies who pay the wizard for his services ?
When this very evident peril is pointed out to him, he
either shrugs his shoulders or he gets angry.   If emphasis
is laid on the absurdity of such a method of procedure,
he turns a deaf ear.   No argument prevails with him.

Instead of declaring this obstinacy to be ridiculous
and inconceivable, let us look back upon other courses
taken by primitive mentality which reveal faith of a
similar kind.   Let us recall, for instance, the story of the
Congo native who insisted on maintaining to Bentley that
crocodiles were harmless and never attacked human beings,
at the very moment when he was shown two women's
anklets found in the stomach of one of these reptiles ;
or the Ronga who consults the astragali to find out what
medicine is to be given to a sick man.   If we start from
the hypothesis that these primitives reason as we do,
represent to themselves as we do, the connection between

---

[1] Th. Winterbottom : *The Native Africans in Sierra Leone*, i. pp. 142–3
(1803).
[2] Major A. G. Leonard : *The Lower Niger and its Tribes*, p. 480.

cause and effect, I venture to say that we must at once give up the hope of understanding them. What they think and what they do, in that case, can but appear absurd and childish in our eyes. But if, instead of attributing to them our own habits of mind, we try to adapt ourselves to their mental attitude, indifferent as this is to the most obvious causal relation, and solely occupied with mystic and unseen forces, we shall find that their way of thinking and acting is the natural and even necessary outcome of this.

The European cannot help taking into consideration before everything else, the physiological effect of poison. Consequently, to his mind the effects of the test will vary according to the strength and the amount of the poison introduced into the system. If sufficiently strong, the dose will always prevail, whether the one who swallows it be guilty or innocent ; and if weak, it may do no harm to the worst of villains. The white man is amazed that the native should shut his eyes to such obvious truisms.

But the black man's point of view is altogether different here. The idea of what we call poison is not clearly defined in his mind. He doubtless knows by experience that certain decoctions may kill those who drink them. Nevertheless he is ignorant of the mechanical action of poison, and does not try to learn it ; he does not even suspect its existence. According to his view, if such decoctions prove deadly it is because they are the vehicle of mystic powers, like medicines which are used in illness, the efficacy of which is also to be explained thus. " Their drugs produce their effects," writes Nassau, " not as ours do, by virtue of their chemical properties, but through the existence of a spirit whose favoured vehicle they are." And in her turn Miss Kingsley says : " In every influence exerted, spirit acts upon spirit ; thus the spirit of the remedy influences the spirit of the malady." It is just the same in the case of the ordeal poison. Black people do not imagine its positive properties ; they only think about its mystic and direct quality. " They do not, however, consider this as a poison," says Winterbottom very rightly, " because they do not think it would be fatal if the person who drinks it were innocent,"[1] It is a kind of mystic *reagent*, and, as such, it is infallible. The native is so convinced of this that he will frequently take no precaution before submitting to the ordeal. He will not exercise the right that is his, of superintending the preparation of the poison, he will not examine the dose to see whether it is excessive, or the liquid too thick, etc. . . . What is the use, since the beverage does not act materially but spiritually, so to speak ? Whether a little more or less of it is swallowed, matters not. It is not upon that that the success of the test depends. " The accused, it is said, has a voice in the selection of the pounder, but so implicitly is the ordeal believed in that the natives think it is of little consequence who ' pounds ' it."[2]

II

As far as we have considered it, the ordeal seems to be a magical process designed to reveal without any possibility of doubt whether an accused person is innocent or guilty. The constant use which is thus made of it by certain peoples has appealed to the imagination of most observers. It is that to which they almost exclusively allude, not without expressing their surprise and disgust at the same time. But the ordeal is also employed in other circumstances, where it no longer has anything in common with judicial procedure. " It is no uncommon thing," says Bentley, " for natives to use the ordeal of poison to decide in other matters. A young woman, now living close to our Wathen station, took *nkasa* some years ago, when her uncle was ill, to find out whether he would recover or not ; at that time she was only twelve years old."[3] In the same neighbourhood the ordeal by boiling water was resorted to, to obtain a medical prognostication. " The doctor puts a vessel full of water and various ingredients on the fire, and when it boils, he plunges his bare hand into it, and withdraws it unhurt, to show that that is a

[1] Th. Winterbottom : *An Account of the Native Africans in the Neighbourhood of Sierra Leone*, i. p. 270 (1803).
[2] Rev. Duff Macdonald : *Africana*, i. p. 204.
[3] Rev. W. H. Bentley : *Pioneering on the Congo*, i. p. 278-9.

privilege reserved for his profession. Then over this water he mumbles his accursed enchantments, and as if he believed that it must obey him, he orders it to tell him whether the sick man will die or not ; then again plunging his hand into the boiling water, he withdraws it, and if it be scalded it is a sure sign of death ; if, on the other hand, it is unhurt, he is convinced that the invalid will recover." [1] In both these cases, is not the ordeal a form of divination similar to those which we studied in the preceding chapter, and should it not be explained in the same way ?

A test by means of the *muavi* may, like the practices of divination, also serve as a method out of a difficulty which suddenly presents itself. A man, whose like one has never seen before, a white man, makes his appearance ; who knows what he may be capable of, what magic powers he possesses, which misfortunes may be in his train ? Are they to let him set foot in their country ? " Lukengo held a great family council, and then he ordered them to make a cock take the poison *ipomea*, a large assembly of people being present ; if the cock vomited the poison, it would prove that I came as a friend, but if the cock died, I must be treated as an enemy." [2] " When you came here for the first time, ten years ago," said King Lewanika to Coillard the missionary, " the Barotse, who were suspicious as to your intentions, hastened to consult the bones, and to administer *muati* (a virulent poison) to several hens. Some of them died, the others recovered, and that accounts for the ambiguous messages that were sent to you. They did not dare openly to forbid you to set foot in the country, and yet they were afraid to receive you. Therefore they resorted to all sorts of artifices to throw obstacles in your way and discourage you. Neither the cloak that you sent me then nor your subsequent presents did I ever receive. They were declared bewitched, and were stopped on their way to me." [3] We may place beside these facts another of a very similar character, observed in India among the Miris. " On the arrival of the first

[1] Cavazzi : *Istoria descrizione de'tre regni di Congo, Matamba, ed Angolo,* p. 82.
[2] H. von Wissmann, *Wolf . . . Im Innern Afrikas,* p. 231.
[3] *Missions évangéliques,* lxiv. p. 447.

British officer ever seen in the hills, fowls were killed in every village, by the augurs, with the view of ascertaining from the appearance of their entrails if the visit boded them good or ill." [1] How does this case differ in any way from the preceding ones, except in the actual process employed ? And since the object of the divining methods is, as we have seen, the taking counsel with the unseen powers and the entreaty for their help and protection, and also the attempt to perceive in the test of the present, the success of the future which is already thought of as real, must we not give a similar meaning to the ordeal which fulfils the same office ?

We know, too, that the Dayaks of Borneo would never begin to clear a piece of ground for cultivation, if their chosen spot had not been authorized by favourable omens. But with the Wakonde people, " when a man wants to build a house anywhere, he makes a fowl and a dog take *mvai*. If they vomit the decoction, the site is considered propitious, and the man will set to work confidently." [2] Here the missionary Schumann makes use of the word oracle to designate an ordeal, which is, evidently, really a solicited omen.

Here, again, is a characteristic observation on the subject, an instance noted in India, among the Khonds. " The oath or ordeal of the hen is a minor oath to see whether a greater one will be necessary. For example, a person is to be forced to take the oath of the tiger or of iron. What is this person to do ? He will take a hen, and thrust its claws into boiling water three times over, saying : ' Bura from above, Bura from below, thou hast created the earth and made foliage, trees, cows, etc. . . . To-day I take an oath before thee ; if I am guilty, may the legs of this hen be burnt ! ' If the legs are injured, he will believe himself guilty, and restore the disputed object ; if not he will take the great oath of the tiger." [3] Thus we see that before undergoing an ordeal which may prove fatal

---

[1] Dalton : *Descriptive Ethnology of Bengal (Hill Miris)*, p. 31.
[2] Fülleborn : " Das deutsche Njassa und Ruwumagebiet," *Deutsch Ost Afrika*, ix. p. 310 (note).
[3] P. Rossillon : " Mœurs et coutumes du peuple Kui (Khonds), " *Anthropos*, vii. pp. 661-2.

(that of spending the night outside the village, exposed to the attack of the tiger) the native practises one of his own, upon which his decision is to depend; and this latter undoubtedly is a mere practice of divination by alternative. But is not "the great oath" in his eyes exactly the same thing as the "lesser oath," except for the element of danger? Otherwise why should the native unhesitatingly conjecture from the lesser operation what the result of the greater will be?

To conclude this part of our subject, in the dictionary of the Congo language drawn up by Bentley we read that the ordeal (by poison, the heated iron, the pearl placed in the corner of the eye, etc.) is called *nkasa*, and the consultation of the oracle by any process whatever, is also called *nkasa*, affixing to it the name of the means used in the consultation. *Nkasa za nianga* means, consulting the oracle by means of the *nianga* plant.[1] Thus the same word is used to express the idea of divination and also that of ordeal. The Congo native does not distinguish between the two, at any rate as to the essential quality of the operation. Its processes may differ in their material nature—this is, indeed, very varied in what is properly called divination—but the end aimed at remains the same. In any case it would be incorrect to say that divination is the genus of which the ordeal is a species. Such a mode of classification is ill-suited to the functionings of primitive mentality, which is but slightly conceptual. Divination and ordeal both belong to the same type of thought and action, one in which this mentality gets in touch with unseen powers from whom it entreats judgment as well as support.

If this be so, the ordeal will serve as a means of settling disputes of the most varied kind. For example, among the Dayaks of Borneo, "two young men were rival aspirants to the hand of a girl, and a challenge had in consequence been issued. The victor would be the one who managed to remain the longest under water. This singular kind of duel is not peculiar to the Kantu Dayaks, but is also

[1] Rev. W. H. Bentley: *Dictionary and Grammar of the Congo Language,* pp. 505–6.

practised by the Batong Lupar, Seribas, and other tribes in Sarawak. . . . At the first sign one of the two gives of becoming asphyxiated, the seconds, who are close by, take both from the water. Usually neither of the two would come to the surface of his own will, and would drown himself rather than acknowledge his defeat ; it being a point of honour with them not to be beaten in a proof of this kind." They resort to it in varied circumstances, and usually when there is no other way of settling a dispute. " Generally, before having recourse to this proof, a cock-fight is undertaken to settle the question ; but if no satisfactory result is obtained, then the severer test of the plunge is appealed to." [1]

This latter ordeal, then, in some way serves as a second court of appeal, the decision being first demanded by the cock-fight. Now the aim of this fight is to discover which side is favoured by the unseen powers. The cock does not obtain his victory except by the consent and support of these powers, and by virtue of their steady participation, each of the adversaries is identified with his cock. The test then is, in all points, comparable with divination by alternative ; the ordeal of the plunge, to which they finally appeal, is of the same type.

Here is another one, " by which . . . many disputed matters are settled very quietly. . . . Two small wax tapers are made, of equal length and size ; they are lighted together, one being held by the plaintiff, and the other by the defendant. . . . He whose taper is first extinguished is adjudged to be in the wrong, and as far as I have seen, he always implicitly accepts the decision. Sir Spenser St. John also quotes this form of ordeal." [2] We cannot help recalling Rabelais' Brid'oie who decides lawsuits by throwing the dice. His plan would appear far from ridiculous to primitives. In their eyes, on the contrary, it is the simplest and also the surest. The magic process by which they " consult Fate," whatever may be the chosen instrument, whether candle, dice, astragali, cocks, etc.,

---

[1] O. Beccari: *Wanderings in the Forests of Borneo,* pp. 177, 179 ; cf. Sir Spenser St. John: *Life in the Forests of the Far East,* i. p. 191.
[2] Rev. W. Chalmers in H. Ling Roth: *The Natives of Sarawak,* i. p. 25.

is as valid as the vision which they get in a dream, or the answer vouchsafed by the ancestors when they are conjured up. In the case of a struggle between two men, it declares in a word which will triumph, and which succumb. Chalmers expressly states that the sentence is always unhesitatingly accepted. The loser bows to the decision. He does not protest in the name of his sacred rights. The precise effect of the test is to make known on which side there are sacred rights. To refuse to accept its verdict would be to proclaim oneself rebellious to the unseen powers whose judgment it is. The native does not enter into any discussion about the matter, and he takes care not to persist, for that would only draw down worse evils upon him. To form some idea of a state of mind which appears so curious to us, let us remind ourselves that it is not unlike that of gamblers. They, too, solicit the verdict of dice or cards. If the play has been fair, the loser may be vexed, dejected, or furious, but he does not protest against the verdict. The only way he can reopen the question is to begin a new game if he can, and put his fate to the touch once more. Just in the same way, in certain cases, there is an appeal from a first ordeal to a second.

In the case of a dispute about money, or in other litigation of minor importance, one of the following tests is often resorted to at Sarawak in Borneo.

" 1. Two coins, both of the same size and covered with wax, but one of them scoured bright, are put into a vessel filled with water and ashes. Then each party takes one of the pieces out of the vessel and gives it to the *mandirs* (judges), who afterwards declare the words of that party to be true who succeeded in taking out the bright coin.

" 2. Both parties are plunged into the water by means of a bamboo cane put horizontally over their heads. The party emerging first is considered guilty.

" 3. Both parties are placed in boxes at a distance of seven fathoms, opposite one another, the boxes being made of nibong laths and so high as to reach the men's breasts. Then both receive a sharpened point of a lance's length to throw at each other at a given signal. The wounded person is supposed to be guilty.

"4. At a distance of two fathoms from one another two parallel roads are made, seventy feet long, at the extremity of which, in the middle of the intermediate space, a lance is stuck vertically in the ground. At a given signal, both begin to run upon the road. The person who first attains the goal, and touches the lance, is considered the innocent party.

"5. Two hens are chosen, of the same strength and colour, and each represents the cause of a party. These are so laid down that their necks are parallel, and the head of one touches the shoulder of the other. Then their heads are cut off simultaneously at one blow, and the cause of that party whose hen is dead first is declared to be lost." [1]

It would be easy to lengthen the list of these ordeals, but those cited doubtless suffice to show that, though apparently diverse, they are fundamentally identical. It is always a question of finding out which is "guilty," and which "innocent"—terms which are the equivalent of "loser" or "winner." Whatever the test may be, its mystic nature guarantees its infallibility, since, like the practices of divination, it reveals the decision of the unseen powers. For instance, if one of the adversaries wins the race, it is not because he is more agile and runs better than the other; it is because the unseen powers which favour him are stronger than those protecting his opponent. Here again, if we refer the effects produced to causes which *we* call "natural," we wander from the path pursued by primitive mentality, and then its reasoning seems absurd to us. But it is, on the contrary, quite consistent with itself, since it adheres exclusively to the consideration of mystic forces, disregarding secondary causes. The object of both ordeal and divination is to induce a manifestation of these forces.

We shall find then, in many of the primitive peoples, tests similar to those which have been noted in Borneo.

[1] C. A. L. M. Schwaner. Ethnographical notes in Ling Roth: *The Natives of Sarawak*, ii. p. clxxxviii.

In the Congo, for instance, "if two men go to law with each other, and both maintain their claim so emphatically that it is difficult to get at the truth, the judge orders them to appear before him. When they are present, he puts on the head of each a turtle-shell, which has been rubbed with certain powders, and he orders them to lower their heads simultaneously. He who has the misfortune to let his turtle-shell fall first, is considered to be the liar." [1]

III

If we now return to ordeals employed in criminal cases, they are so similar to the rest that we can scarcely explain them differently. Besides, the very idea of criminal cases is a vague and elusive one. These peoples are undoubtedly acquainted with contentions which we should call matters of civil law. Such are usually settled in " palavers," in which each of the interested parties defends his own cause, setting forth his pleas at great length, and calling his witnesses, etc., judgment being pronounced by the chief, frequently supported by some of the older men. But it may happen that these proceedings are cut short and referred to the ordeal for their conclusion, and the litigants can demand it in nearly every case. The constant confusing of the " guilty " person with the " loser " which I mentioned just now, sufficiently indicates that judicial distinctions which are quite simple in our eyes are unknown to primitive mentality.

" When a person is accused of a crime, and the accusations are not sufficiently defined, he is obliged to clear his character by oath (that is, by an ordeal) ; and this may be done in five different ways, the first four being used in civil cases of little importance, and the last in criminal matters, such as treason or lèse-majesté, and other transgressions of that sort. It is only important people who are allowed to make use of this last oath, and then only with the king's consent.

" 1. The accused is taken to the priest, who takes a hen's

---

[1] Merolla da Sorrento : *Relazione del viaggio nel regno di Congo*, pp. 100–1 (1692).

feather, and after greasing it, pierces the tongue of the accused; if it goes through the flesh easily it is a sign of innocence, and the hole formed by the feather heals up quickly and painlessly. But if the accused is guilty the feather cannot pass through, and he is at once condemned.

" 2. The priest takes a lump of earth into which he puts seven or eight hen's feathers, which the accused is obliged to pull out one after another; if they come out easily, it is a sign that he is innocent, but if this is difficult of accomplishment, his guilt is thereby proved.

" 3. The juice of certain herbs is put into the eyes of the accused; if it does him no harm, he is innocent, but if his eyes become red and inflamed, he is obliged to pay the fine imposed upon him.

" 4. The priest takes a copper bangle which has been made red-hot, and rubs it three times over the tongue of the accused; the result of this, showing whether the process has injured him or not, declares him either guilty or innocent.

" I saw all these four tests performed during the time that I was there, and in each case the accused persons were adjudged guilty . . . but I never saw the fifth and last test applied, for this scarcely happens once in twenty years; so I know nothing about it except from hearsay." [1]

In these ordeals, as in the preceding ones, we immediately recognize the type of divination by alternative. After having accomplished the initiatory rites which prepare the way to the realm of mystic powers, the " priest " puts the question in such a way that it can be answered by " yes " or " no." These ordeals, however, differ from those which we quoted recently, because they all (with the exception of the second) are practised upon the person of the accused. It will be his reaction—whether he is injured or not, whether the wound heals quickly or slowly, and so on—that shows whether he is innocent or guilty. It is by no means an indifferent matter whether the ordeal is practised on the accused himself, because we see that in certain cases it may take place by proxy, so that it is allowable for the

[1] W. Bosman: *Voyage de Guinée* (21e lettre), pp. 478–80 (Edition of 1704).

accused to be represented by some other person. In other cases, on the contrary, this is not allowed, and he is *obliged* to undergo the test personally. What are these cases ? Perhaps an examination of them may help us to penetrate a little further into the real nature of these ordeals.

"Most tribes have a milder concoction for trivial offences," says Macdonald. "The drug may be taken by proxy—it may be administered to a dog or a fowl or some animal representing the accused. In these cases the animal is tied by a string to the criminal "[1] (undoubtedly so that their physical participation in each other may be brought about).

The Wagogo, too, "in trivial cases allow the *muavi* to be tested, not on the accused himself, but on a hen which he is obliged to hold."[2] In the Upper Niger, "murder and theft are punishable by death, adultery by a heavy fine, confiscation of property, or slavery, whilst drinking of sassawood water is imposed on persons accused of lying or stealing. It is not uncommon, however, to allow substitutes to partake of this poisoned water, and persons are procurable who are acquainted with an antidote, and therefore take the poison with impunity. Dogs are even allowed to be used as substitutes, but, should they die, the owner has to pay a heavy fine, being deemed guilty."[3] Among the Bangala, of the Upper Congo, three young men accused of theft, indignantly deny the charge. "Three young plantains are cut—one to represent each boy— and the juice of the *mokungu* is pressed into the centre of each plantain stump left in the ground. Now when a plantain is cut it will, in a few hours, send up from this centre the beginning of a fresh growth, but if one of the three plantain stumps does not begin to sprout afresh by the next morning the lad represented by that plantain is the guilty one ; if two do not sprout then there are two thieves, and if neither sprouts then all three lads are regarded as guilty. On the other hand, if all three sprout

[1] Rev. Duff Macdonald : *Africana*, i. p. 204.
[2] H. Claus : *Die Wagogo*, Bässler Archiv, 1911, Beiheft ii. p. 56.
[3] A. F. Mockler-Ferryman : *Up the Niger*, pp. 46-7 (1892).

they are proved to be innocent of the accusation. . . .
The *mokungu* juice destroys the eye, so in mercy the ' eyes '
of the plantain are used as a substitute for the eyes of the
lad." [1] " In matters of theft among the Congo negroes
there is a proof by poison, and the poison is most frequently
administered to children or dogs. The disputants (the
plaintiff and the defendant and their friends) make their
appearance, and an impartial ' doctor ' gives an equal
dose of *m'bambu* to each of their representatives. The
interested parties divide into two camps, and the ' combatants ' advance to the middle, facing each other ; the
concoction is presented to them, and they are obliged to
take it, force being used if necessary. Then the two
camps begin to shout ' It is my dog living ; *yours* is dying ! '
or else ' Your child is dying, not mine ! ' These cries,
which create an intolerable uproar, last until the poison
begins to act. Should it not take effect, they renew the
dose once, or even twice. The first one to eject the poison
has won. If one of the combatants falls to the ground
in convulsions, he has lost. It is very seldom that a
corpse is left upon the field of combat, because the dose
of poison has been but a slight one." [1]

Many similar examples, collected from the same African
races, and elsewhere, might be quoted. Saving in exceptional circumstances (above all in the case of chiefs), sub-
stitution is allowed in trivial cases only—petty larceny,
slander, etc., or when it is a preliminary test to find out
whether one which may terminate fatally is to be undertaken. Among the Barotse, for example : " This is how
a wizard is discovered. Three weeks ago a man died in
a village here. Now in the way these people regard the
matter, a man can never die unless he is killed or has
been bewitched. The dead man's brother says to himself : ' I will find out who killed my brother ; I believe it
is my eldest brother.' He takes four or five hens, gives
them poison, saying : ' If you hens die, it will be because
my eldest brother has killed the next one. If the poison

[1] Rev. J. H. Weeks : " Anthropological Notes on the Bangala of the
Upper Congo River," *J.A.I.*, xl. p. 364.
[2] P. Pogge : *Im Reiche des Muata Jamwo*, pp. 36–7.

does you no harm, my brother is innocent, and my other brother just died of himself.' . . . Naturally all the fowls died, and the accused was brought before the chiefs." [1] They made him undergo an ordeal for which he was not allowed to find any substitute.

Nevertheless, the divining process of the ordeal, whether practised upon the accused himself, or upon a slave, child, dog, or fowl representing him, is equally valid, by virtue of the close relation existing between him and his substitute. Therefore in cases where proxy is not allowed, the ordeal must have yet another object in addition to its divining function, and this object cannot be attained unless the very person of the accused be put to the proof.

As a matter of fact, those to whom ordeal by proxy is forbidden, are almost exclusively those who are suspected of witchcraft. They must undergo the test personally. Now according to testimonies which are both numerous and explicit, the object of the ordeal in these cases is not simply to find out whether the accused person is guilty or not. It has yet another function, no less important ; it aims at combating and annihilating the malevolent principle harboured by the sorcerer, which is the true source of all his crimes. That is why it is necessary for the ordeal to take place, even when the magician is unmasked, confounded, condemned, nay, even when he has confessed. If it were designed merely to get assurance, and its operation were purely divinatory, it would henceforward be motiveless. However it is still considered indispensable, therefore it cannot be enough to get rid of the sorcerer. It must be just as necessary, if not more so, to reach and exterminate the noxious principle of which he is the instrument. Miss Kingsley perceived this necessity very clearly. She says : " It is the law that such trials should take place before execution ; but there is also involved in it another curious fact, and that is that the spirit of the ordeal is held to be able to manage and suppress the bad spirits trained by the witch to destruction. Human beings can collar the witch and destroy him in an exemplary manner, but spiritual aid is required to collar

[1] *Missions évangéliques*, lxiv. p. 179. (Louis Jalla.)

the witch's devil, or it would get adrift and carry on after its owner's death." [1]

This spiritual aid is furnished by the ordeal. It is possessed of a mystic quality which acts upon the malevolent power lodged within the witch and will render it incapable of working mischief. Nassau, who lived for a long time in the Congo district studied by Miss Kingsley, also writes: " The decoction itself is supposed to have almost sentience, an ability to feel, in the various organs of the body, like a policeman, and detect and destroy the witch spirit supposed to be lurking about." [2] The Italian missionaries of the seventeenth century had already remarked that everything took place just as if the poison had a mission expressly confided to it. " The priest, as if possessing supernatural authority over the potion, commands it not to remain in the stomach of the accused if he is a virtuous man, but to come out of him without doing him any harm ; but if he is guilty, it is to bring about the death he deserves." [3]

The presence of this evil principle within a person is a constant and terrible menace to his relatives, and also to the social group of which he forms a part. As soon as anyone is suspected of being its corporeal abode, he must drink the poison, whatever he may be, and however great the affection which has been felt for him hitherto. It is a question of the public welfare, which admits of no postponement. Hence tragic situations may sometimes arise. " A chief had lost one of his wives. . . . A little after, the son of one of the other wives, having gone out at midnight, a leopard came upon him and caught his foot fast at the door of the house as he was running in. The lad was badly bitten, and his mother induced Matope (the chief) to have resort to the usual methods of detecting witchcraft ; the result was that his own mother was pronounced a witch. We were very sorry for the poor woman. She lived in another village, over the stream from her son's hamlet. . . . She was fond of joking and fun, but this

[1] Mary Kingsley : *West African Studies*, p. 137.
[2] Rev. R. H. Nassau : *Fetichism in West Africa*, p. 244 (1904).
[3] Cavazzi : *Istoria descrizione de'tre regni Congo, Matamba, ed Angola* p. 91.

sentence made her an object of dread and aversion. Even the natives now shrunk from her, and her life became a burden. We tried to do everything for her; we gave her presents, invited her to come to see us, and cautioned her against drinking the poisoned cup. We made the village chief promise that it would not be administered. The result was that there was some delay in drinking the ordeal. We made every use of this respite by talking on the matter with Kapéui, the chief of the country, who was her brother, and who promised to use every influence on her behalf. Her son, the chief, was a very successful hunter. During the delay he could not go to hunt. The superstition was too strong for him. At the same time his mother was anxious to break the spell that bound him, she was so sure that she was innocent. She drank the dangerous cup and died, and however dearly the liberty was purchased, the hunter could now go forth to his usual pursuit." [1]

What likelihood was there, we might ask, that this chief's mother should have desired the death of her son's wife, or that she should have " delivered up " her own little grandson to a leopard? But the native does not imagine probabilities as we do. In his view the double misfortune which overwhelms the chief in so short an interval cannot be accidental. The death of the young wife was already a suspicious circumstance. The leopard which attacked the boy was assuredly not an ordinary animal; it was a leopard in the service of a witch, or inspired by such an one, or else a witch-leopard, i.e. united to the witch by a bond so close that it is no longer possible to differentiate between them. By demanding that the witch shall be sought for, the mother of the little fellow who was wounded only voiced the general feeling of the community. The matter is put to the proof, and the ordeal denounces the chief's own mother! The accusation does not seem so improbable as we should think. In these communities suspicions are often cast first of all upon the immediate circle or the nearest relatives of the person bewitched. (That was what took place in the case quoted

[1] Rev. Duff Macdonald : *Africana*, i. pp. 78–9 (1882).

by the missionary Jalla, related above, when the victim's brother was accused.) However improbable it might be, the charge would be credited. Partly because the ordeal is infallible, and also because the presence of the evil principle may be unknown to the person whose body it inhabits. From this moment the unhappy woman becomes plague-stricken, as it were. They shun her presence as if she were spreading an infectious disease. Her son dare no longer go out hunting, lest some misfortune perpetrated by his mother, befall him, as it has befallen his wife and his little son. It is essential, therefore, that the ordeal shall be tried, and in spite of the missionary's efforts, it takes place. If the accused had escaped with her life, they would look for the witch elsewhere. But she succumbs, and that is proof that the suspicions were well founded, and also the end of anxiety for the village. The ordeal has revealed and destroyed the evil principle, and if in doing so it killed the woman, how could that be avoided ?

Nevertheless we can imagine that there might be other means of dealing with this principle and making it incapable of doing further mischief without at the same time causing the one in whom it dwells to perish, especially when this person is its involuntary and even unconscious bearer. Weeks has encountered this idea in the Bangala people, who admit that the presence of the evil principle in a person does not necessarily make him guilty. They will then oblige him to undergo the ordeal, but in a way calculated to get rid of the evil principle, while sparing the life of the man. " Who benefits by the death of a father or a brother ? Why, the son or another brother. Consequently when a father is ill, the son is regarded with suspicion, and after trying all means to drive out the sickness the patient will, as a last resort, give his son the ordeal, but not enough to kill. If he vomits it, he is innocent ; that is proof beyond all doubt and no harm is done ; but if he does not vomit, but becomes dazed and stupid, well he is simply a medium by which the occult powers are working on his relative, and the ordeal dose will clear such powers out of him, and being no longer able to use him as a medium, the father or brother will recover. The

lad is carefully tended until the effects of the ordeal have
passed away, then he is warned not to let his body be used
for such purposes again, and he is set free, and is looked
upon by his playmates in the village with as much curiosity
as a schoolboy just out of hospital with a broken leg. The
boy's excuse is, and it is readily accepted by all, that he
was full of witchcraft and did not know it." [1]

Weeks goes so far as to say: " No stigma attaches to
a man who is found guilty, for ' one can have witchcraft
without knowing it.' " [2]

It is difficult, however, for the horror which this evil
inspires not to extend to the one who embodies it for the
time being. In the very rare cases in which there is no
actual infamy attached to this unfortunate person, he
nevertheless becomes an object of dread, and almost inevitably, of hatred. Even while sparing the youth in
the case noted above, a serious warning, which is almost
a menace, is given him. Should his father fall ill again
and remedies prove unavailing, the son will have to
submit to a fresh ordeal, and this time the dose of poison
will be final.

The Bangala believe, too, that witchcraft, when driven
out of one person, can enter another, by the will of the
former, and under the influence of the ordeal. " I knew
a case," says the same missionary, " of a cheeky urchin
who received a box on the ear from his uncle, and the
youngster turned round and said : ' I will bewitch you.'
Shortly afterwards the uncle fell sick, and in spite of remedies
and *nganga* (the doctor) he continued ill, but at last he
made the boy drink the ordeal, and not vomiting it he was
considered guilty of bewitching his uncle, who had the
boy thrashed (the dose had been too weak to endanger
his life) and demanded two hundred brass rods of the boy's
father to pay the *nganga* for administering the ordeal, and
to teach the boy to let other folk alone. . . . This uncle
married a new wife, who had a young brother who was
in my school. One day the uncle came asking for this

[1] Rev. J. H. Weeks : " Anthropological Notes on the Bangala of the
Upper Congo River," *J.A.I.*, xl. p. 396.
[2] Ibid., p. 364.

lad to give him the ordeal; I refused to give up the lad for such a purpose; 'and besides,' I said, ' he does not belong to your family.' (I had not heard of the marriage.) The man replied : ' Yes, he does ; I have married his sister, and he is bewitching me through his sister, who is my wife, and my nephew who took the ordeal some time ago says that he passed on the witchery to my brother-in-law.' It thus appears that a mischievous boy can say he has passed on his witchcraft to another lad and so get that youngster into trouble." [1]

In a neighbouring district, inhabited by the Balobo, they perform an autopsy to assure themselves of the presence of witchcraft in the sorcerer's body. The missionary, Grenfell, writes: " The man killed for witchcraft we knew very well. . . . There was a great outcry among his friends after his death, for the accuser failed to find the witch—some not uncommon growth in the intestines, which is deemed incontrovertible proof. In this case no trace of it could be found, and so by general consent the poor man was cleared of the charge of witchcraft." [2]

Bentley has even seen the natives about to dissect a corpse to look for the organ which, in their opinion, is infallible proof that the man, when alive, was a sorcerer. [3] This is a custom in many parts. Miss Kingsley had also drawn attention to it. " In many districts of the south-west coast and middle Congo it is customary when a person dies in an unexplainable way, namely without shedding blood, to hold a post-mortem. In some cases the post-mortem discloses the path of the witch through the victim—usually I am informed, the injected witch feeds on the victim's lungs—in other cases the post-mortem discloses the witch-power itself, demonstrating that the deceased was a keeper of witch-power, or, as we should say, a witch." [4]

Doubtless these are not cases of post-mortem following an ordeal. Death, however, has taken place under circumstances that are suspicious, and the post-mortem,

[1] Rev. J. H. Weeks : ibid., p. 396.
[2] Rev. W. H. Bentley : *Pioneering on the Congo*, ii. pp. 230-1 (Grenfell's letter).
[3] Ibid., ii. p. 233
[4] Mary Kingsley : *West African Studies*, p. 179 (1901).

in the cases last mentioned, reveals precisely what the natives observed by Bentley were looking for. Again, " the Pangwe," says Tessmann, " cannot imagine a principle except in bodily form, and even as a person ; the evil principle they call *ewu* takes the form of an animal. Hence they have a ' scientific ' method of proving whether a person has been a wizard or not ; if he has, the *ewu* is there ; if not, there is no trace of it. They obtain this proof by a regular post-mortem." [1] " The Bangala" (the very people among whom the Rev. Mr. Weeks lived), " find the word *ikoundou* difficult to define. It represents a sort of occult power which is at the command of a person, but curiously enough it is possible to find material traces of it after his death. Never having been present at any operation of this kind, I asked the natives to describe the material nature of the *ikoundou*, and it seemed to me that it must be represented by what the renal and biliary ducts yielded." [2]

Finally, in the Belgian Congo among the Ázande people, Hutereau discovered what may be called the theory of witchcraft and the physical sign which represents it, and from which it is very difficult to distinguish it.

" Every native who possesses a *mango* is an *elamango*. Any deformity in an organ is called a *mango*, and any malformation in the stomach is a very special sign of the existence of the *mango*. Therefore the natives use that term for the paunch, rennetbag and manyplies of the stomach of a ruminant. They say that the *mango* is usually found near the stomach, at the beginning of the intestine, and is a fleshy excrescence ; some persons possessing two of these. The *mango* gives its possessor the power of employing witchcraft, and therefore the *elamango* is regarded as a wizard. According to the Azande, he enjoys supernatural gifts ; he has the power of casting lots, causing death, creating accidents. . . . Such individuals can see clearly on the very darkest nights, they can enter the kraals silently, and cause their occupants to fall into the most profound slumber. . . . They also have the power of removing their witchcraft, and thus curing those whose death they have

[1] G. Tessmann : *Die Pangwe*, ii. pp. 128–9.
[2] C. Coquilhat : *Sur le Haut Congo*, p. 293.

desired. To oblige them to make use of this power, the *elamango* are threatened with execution as soon as their invalid victim shall have passed away." [1]　In a word, they are sorcerers. The powers which have just been enumerated are precisely those which are attributed to these people in the natives' collective representations of them.

" Every individual who is suspected of being an *elamango* must submit to the trial by *benget*. *Benget* is a poison extracted from the root of a toxic tree. . . . The solution thus obtained is an ingredient in a poison administered to fowls or to human beings. It is the oracle, the test without which the chief will not undertake anything in his own name, either for his family or for his people. We might say that the *benget* regulates all the public and private affairs of the Azande—the declaration of war, arrangement of expeditions, conclusion of peace, establishment of villages and plantations, the relations between villages, as well as voyages and removals. It is consulted alike for marriages, births, deaths, the sale and purchase of slaves, fishing, hunting, etc. The *benget* removes every obstacle, and all readily submit to its decisions, convinced of its infallibility as an oracle on all subjects."

Thus the *benget* can discover the invisible *mango* present in the body of the *elamango*, and it, too, has the power of subduing it. Hutereau continues : " In most cases it is considered enough to administer the test to fowls, but when a native is accused of being *elamango*, he is obliged to drink the poison himself to prove his innocence. The efficacy of the poison is first tried upon a fowl or a dog, and the animal is bound to succumb. Then the accused person must drink the dose that is decreed, and very often his accuser must prove the absolute veracity of his report by doing the same. The one of the two who dies is guilty, if it be the accused, of the crime of witchcraft ; if the accuser, of having slandered him.

" Should the native suspected of being *elamango* refuse to undergo the ordeal of the *benget*, he thereby confesses

---

[1] A. Hutereau : " Notes sur la vie familiale et juridique de quelques population du Congo belge," *Annales du Musée du Congo belge, Documents ethnographiques*, Série I. i. pp. 27–9.

himself guilty. The whole village will urge him to take the poison, reminding him of the infallibility of the oracle. Very often accused persons themselves offer to undergo the test if their accuser, in spite of their protestations, does not at once own that he is mistaken.

" The death of the person accused as the possessor of *mango* is not sufficient of itself ; the post-mortem must reveal its presence in his body. If it be not found there, the accuser must pay his relatives an indemnity—a woman slave and a certain number of spears." [1]

We might imagine that the accuser could shelter himself behind the fact that the accused has died from the poison. If the *benget* is infallible, how could it kill an innocent person ? His innocence must be a sham, for the absence of the *mango*, which is doubtless due to an unknown cause cannot cast doubt on the *benget*. Now the accuser does not defend himself thus, and he admits that he has been wrong. This proves, therefore, that the death of the accused is not of itself sufficient to prove his guilt, and that the Azande do not conceive of the witchcraft *without* the presence of *mango* in the body. Thus the *mango* is not only the sign of it, but its reality and very essence. [2]

Lastly, with the Azande, in certain cases the ordeal cannot be undergone by general proxy, but only by substituting a son for a father, or a daughter for a mother, and that is precisely because the object of the test is rather to get at the witchcraft than to kill the person who harbours it.

" A native accused of possessing the *mango* is not himself obliged to undergo the test by *benget*. He may be replaced by his son, as a mother may by her daughter, for the *mango* is hereditary by sex, that is to say, it is handed down from father to son, and from mother to daughter.

---

[1] Hutereau : ibid., p. 29.
[2] As a matter of fact, however, in tribes living near the Azande, the Medje and the Mangbetu, " it is not necessary to verify by autopsy the presence of the *notu* (which corresponds with the Azande *mango*). Every native who dies as the result of the test is inevitably considered guilty. If the *notu* is not found in him, it is because he must have had other witchcraft at his command. To get assurance on this point they consult the *mapingo* (divining method), and should this oracle reply in the negative, the accuser must pay the indemnity due for a murder."—Ibid., p. 76.

It may happen, too, that natives accused of being *elamango* do not wait to undergo the test ; carried away by anger at the accusation, they kill one of their children, so that its post-mortem may prove their innocence." [1]

Quite near them, in the Ababua tribe, " the *elimba* of the Ababua corresponds exactly with the *mango* of the Azande." [2] There are the same accusations, the same proofs, the same verification of the facts by means of the post-mortem, and the theory of heredity is similar.   " If the post-mortem does not reveal the presence of the *elimba* in the body of an accused person who has died as the result of the ordeal, his friends take up arms, but sometimes the accuser saves his life by paying the indemnity exacted for murder, as well as another for the false accusation of *elimba*." The Ababua go even further than their neighbours. With them, " the stomach of every dead person is opened with the view of proving to all that he does not possess the *elimba*, and that consequently neither his ancestors nor his descendants have it." [3] This precaution would make a certain number of ordeals useless and unnecessary, at least in cases where the post-mortem gives a negative result, but it does induce others, and possibly a great number of them, if the *elimba* is discovered in the body of the deceased.

In the Cameroons, Mansfeld witnessed similar ordeals. He expressly states that their object was both to unmask the wizard, and to destroy the witchcraft which actuated him.   With these natives, witchcraft is no longer an excrescence in the stomach or intestine ; it is a bird.   " The poison extracted from the Calabar bean is used in making the ordeal which is undoubtedly the most dangerous of all.   It is employed when public rumour credits anyone with possessing the ' evil spirit ' in his body, in the shape of a bird, and having in this form killed, or being about to kill, his neighbour.   This bird is the screech-owl which dwells, it appears, in the cardiac region, and which is able to leave the body during the night and go and suck a man's blood.   If, therefore, Odjonk is accused of harbouring in his body the witch-spirit, that is, the evil bird, and he is suspected of having caused Ajok's death, he must drink

---

[1] Hutereau : ibid., pp. 29–30.   [2] Ibid., p. 98.   [3] Ibid., p. 92.

the Calabar bean poison before the whole assembled village. If he ejects it, he is innocent ; if he does not eject it, he dies from the effect of the poison, which kills both the evil spirit and the one who possesses it at one blow." [1]

IV

From the facts collected here it is permissible to conclude that the ordeal by poison, practised in the trials for witch-craft which are so common among many African peoples, is a mystic process, similar to divination, the object of which is to discover the wizard, kill him, and at the same time destroy the witchcraft which imbues him. It has therefore nothing in common with a "judgment of God." Meinhof draws attention to this point. "Nowhere, as far as I know, does the African refer the result of the ordeal directly to God ; he attributes it to the magic powers of the charm employed, to which the guilty succumbs while the innocent escapes scot free." And in a note he adds : " The ordeal, like everything else, is undoubtedly the out-come of a Divine gift ; but it acts of itself in an independent (*selbstständig*) fashion, like a 'medicine,' without one's having to think of God's intervention." [2]   If it be permissible, I would add, to speak of " God " in this sense, when the tribes of the Upper Congo, or even most of the peoples of Central and South Africa, are in question.

Thus explained, the idea of the ordeal in its turn throws light on that of witchcraft, which holds so important a place in the collective representations of these tribes. It reveals the source of the evil-doing, which inspires so much dread and horror. The violence of the feelings it arouses is such that, at the least suspicion of witchcraft, the very tenderest bonds uniting intimate friends, husband and wife, brothers, parents and children, are ruptured suddenly and completely. Sometimes the person suspected is destroyed straight away by his own relatives, without

[1] A. Mansfeld : *Urwald Dokumente, Vier Jahre unter den Crossflussnegern Kameruns*, p. 178 ; cf. Staschewski : *Die Banjangi*, Bässler Archiv, vii. pp. 47–50 ; and Rev. Flickinger : *Thirty Years of Missionary Life in West Africa*, p. 70.
[2] C. Meinhof : *Afrikanische Religionen*, p. 53.

any judgment, and even without an appeal to the ordeal. Occurrences of this kind, reported by the missionaries, are almost incredible. To quote but one only : " A man and his wife residing in the immediate neighbourhood of Mount Coke (Kaffraria), were deliberately and in cold blood murdered by the man's brother, on a charge of witchcraft. Early in the morning one of the victims was called from his own residence by his brother, who, with a party of five others, was awaiting his arrival. The moment he entered the door a thong was cast round his neck ; he was dragged for some distance and beaten to death with sticks. The party then proceeded to the garden of the deceased, where his wife was found, who shared a similar fate. The house was then burnt, the only child of the deceased (a daughter) carried off, and the cattle driven to the kraal of the murderer." [1] Frequently the reputed witches are put to the rack and tortured in the hope of wringing an avowal from them. How can we account for the paroxysm of hatred which drives a brother or a friend to commit such deeds, and makes the social group sanction them ? Whence comes it that the terror which the " wizard " inspires has, as it were, absolutely no limits ?

" The word bewitcher (*msawi*)," says Macdonald, who is so careful an observer, " carries with it two ideas. The person so called (1) has power or knowledge sufficient for the practice of occult arts, and (2) is addicted to cannibalism. The second meaning is the more prominent. . . . Witches kill the victim for the purpose of eating him." [2] Junod says the same thing. " Witchcraft is one of the greatest crimes which a man can commit. It is equivalent to assassination, even worse than murder ; as a dim idea of anthropophagy is added to the simple accusation of killing. A wizard kills human beings to eat their flesh." [3]

The cannibalism in question here is in some sense a mystic action. The wizard's victims are devoured by him without their being aware of it. Once dead, they do not furnish him with food ; on the contrary, they die because he has

[1] *Wesleyan Missionary Notices*, iv. (1846). Letter from Rev. W. Impey, October 13, 1845.
[2] Rev. Duff Macdonald, *Africana*, i. p. 206.
[3] H. A. Junod : *The Life of a South African Tribe*, i. pp. 416–17.

already " eaten " them. Junod sets forth this belief of
theirs thus. " The wizard . . . gets into the kraal, tries
to penetrate into the hut by the door, finds it closed, . .
flies to the crown of the hut and descends through it into
the hut of the enemy, calmly sleeping on his mat. Then he
proceeds to the bewitching operation, and the poor bewitched
man is condemned to die. ' His shadow only remains.'
They say also : ' The corpse only has been left, his true self
has been stolen and eaten.' They have ravished him
(like a feather taken away by the wind). He will get up
in the morning, die some days later ; but what will die is
only his shadow. He himself has been killed during that
dreadful night. He has been eaten already. Here we find
again the idea of duality of human personality. How is
it possible that a man who has still to live some days or
months may be considered as already eaten up entirely I
do not pretend to explain. Such is the native idea, at any
rate. One of my informants tried to overcome the difficulty
by saying that what the sorcerer is taking in him to eat is
the inside, the bowels ; the external frame only remains,
and the man will die soon ! Most of the natives, when
you show them the absurdity of the idea, laugh, and that
is all." [1]

The idea is far from being absurd to them. They do
not know the physiological processes of the internal organs ;
they pay no attention to them. In their eyes, both life
and death depend, above all, upon mystic conditions. Do
we not know, too, that in their collective representations
the dead still live ? Why should it be impossible then
for these persons, who through the magic influence of the
cannibal wizard are already half dead, to preserve for
some time yet the external appearance of living beings ?

But this is what terrifies the natives most of all. These
wizards, against whom it is so difficult to defend themselves,
and who are, as Junod tells us, " numerous in every tribe,"
who can burden themselves with crime for many years
without being discovered, may be entirely ignorant of it
themselves. They are acting, then, as the unconscious agents
of the witch-principle within them. In fact, " they lead

[1] H. A. Junod : ibid., i. pp. 416–17.

a double existence—one by day, when they are men like the rest, and the other by night when they are carrying out their task as wizards. Do they know by day what they have done during the night ? This is a difficult question to answer, for it seems as if the natives were not very clear on this point. The really traditional idea, however, is that the wizard *does not know what he is doing* ; he does not even know that he is a wizard until he has been revealed as such. . . . He therefore acts unconsciously. When he has returned each day to his ordinary life, his nocturnal activities are unknown to him. For instance, my informants assure me that while a man is acting as a wizard, he may have sent a crocodile to kill a man, and yet be the first to show his sympathy for the poor victim, and to deplore the sad occurrence. And when the diviner points him out as the one whose witchcraft has caused the death, witchcraft of which he was entirely ignorant, he will be stupefied with astonishment. It does, however, seem that wizards who have carried on their horrible practices for a long period do know what they are doing, and may even be proud of it ; therefore they must be more or less conscious of the double life they lead in part. There are some who go still further ; they abandon their evil deeds, and become wonder-workers, in the good sense of the word, turning to account the knowledge they possess in order to thwart the enchantments of other wizards." [1] Similar ideas, as we have already seen, are well known in Central Africa. Thus, " the Bushongo share the belief, which is so common in Africa, that individuals may be possessed, even without being aware of it, of an evil spirit, and in this way cause the death of others. Persons who die without any apparent reason have succumbed, it is thought, to this malignant influence which seems, according to many accounts, to correspond with the ' evil eye.' Persons accused of witchcraft are subjected to ordeal by poison." [2]

This unconsciousness of their deeds, moreover, only makes the wizards still more dangerous. Torday and

[1] H. A. Junod : ibid. ii. pp. 464–5 ; cf. Junod : *Les Ba-Ronga*, p. 428.
[2] Torday and Joyce : "Les Bushungo," *Annales du Musée du Congo belge, Documents ethnographiques*, Série III, ii. p. 121 ; cf. ibid., p. 78.

Joyce just now compared them with the *jettatori*, and Junod repeatedly says " the *baloyi*, or people possessed of the evil eye." As a matter of fact, the evil principle lodged within them, the material existence of which is often established by the post-mortem, acts in exactly the same way as the evil eye. It spreads disaster on all around it, throughout the whole social group, and very often its first victims are the nearest relatives of the sorcerer, those who should be his most cherished and sacred care.

In these cases then, if we desire to do so, we may continue to use the words " accusation " and " judgment," from which the " accused " emerge either as " innocent " or " guilty," but only on condition that we ascribe to them a meaning widely different from the one they bear in Europe. Here it is not a question of justice in the slightest degree, and the ordeal is by no means designed to find out whether a penalty has been deserved or not. What engages the natives' attention is a problem of quite a different order. They are haunted, even terrorized, by the idea that among them there exist individuals, apparently just like other people, who possess the most formidable magic powers, and use them for committing the worst of crimes, without their being detected or taken red-handed, and even, sometimes, without their knowing it themselves. Against such a scourge the ordeal is the only effective defence.

Consequently, instead of ranging the " wizards " of primitive peoples beside the criminals prosecuted by our own penal code, we must place them in an altogether different category along with the *jettatori*. They are thus closely akin to those abnormal beings whom the social group gets rid of, as soon as their peculiarities are perceived, because they are " Jonahs " and bringers of evil. To this class belong children whose birth has presented unusual circumstances, those born with teeth, or those who cut the upper incisors first, and so on. The malevolent principle they embody makes them, like sorcerers, a menace to the social group ; they too, like sorcerers, must be exterminated, or at least rendered powerless to injure others. It is true that these *monstra* may only later become mischievous, while the evil power harboured by the wizard has already been the cause of many a disaster ; but primitive mentality scarcely perceives this difference. It has no difficulty in representing the future as already present, especially if it seems to be certain, and incites powerful emotion. Now it has not the slightest doubt about the malign influence which these abnormal children will exert. They are at this very moment " virtually " wizards. The natives actually admit this in so many words,[1] and that is the reason why they treat them as they do.

Undoubtedly, wizards are not all abnormal from birth; persons whose abnormality was unrevealed, and who have grown up without their real nature having been discovered. This is far from being the case. A man not of abnormal birth in any way may be trained to these diabolical practices, and become as formidable as his master. In certain districts of West Africa, especially in Gaboon, there exist secret societies whose members practise murder and cannibalism, and which are, in this sense, wizard-societies ; they draw their recruits from among adults. On the other hand, a certain number of tribes maintain that witchcraft is most frequently congenital and hereditary.

At any rate, while certain malformations of sinister omen are perceptible from birth or early infancy, others remain concealed and nothing permits of their discovery during the lifetime of those who have them. A mother, even if she had the courage to do it, could not conceal from her own circle that her baby had cut its upper incisors first, but how could one tell, except by opening a man's body, whether the fatal excrescence would be found on his intestines ? Here it is that the ordeal effectively intervenes. Someone is suspected of witchcraft, and the ordeal will solve the doubt. It has the double virtue of making known the presence of the malign influence and overcoming it ; it has power to subdue and destroy it. If the " accused " succumbs, everybody breathes freely ; the ravages of the plague have been arrested. If others remain, as is probably the case, the same method will get rid of them at the slightest suspicion.

[1] See chap. v. p. 156.

V

With reference to the natives of the Andaman Isles, Man writes : " They are in too primitive a state to possess any form of trial, or even to have any belief in the efficacy of the ordeal for discovering the guilty person, nor does it appear that any such practice existed in times past." [1]

In fact, in the most primitive peoples we know, in New Guinea, Australia, South America, ordeals such as we have recently been examining have scarcely been noted. Tests of this kind seem to be found especially in social groups which have reached a certain stage of political organization, in the Bantus, for instance, the negroes of West Africa, the Malays, etc.

Inasmuch as the ordeal is a species of divination, other divining practices may take its place. This is the case with the Australian aborigines, the natives of (German) New Guinea, etc., who do not, any more than the Congo negroes, admit death to be "natural," and who are no less anxious to discover the wizard who has "doomed" one of their relatives. We have already examined the very varied processes of divination which they practise in such circumstances ; but the ordeal is used to accomplish other ends—to exercise a mystic influence upon a malevolent power which it has to overcome, for example. Such a desire doubtless exists in peoples who are in a low state of development. Can we find among them nothing that permits them to gratify it ?

Of the natives of South Australia, Taplin writes : " An offender has to stand as a target for as many as like to throw a spear at him, and if he escapes them, he has expiated his crime." In a note, Taplin adds : " This is a true ordeal. According to aboriginal ideas, a man may be enabled by superior spirits to avoid spears ; or, if he be a guilty man, be rendered unable to avoid them by the power of some invisible spirit exerted upon him." [2] Taplin was right in thinking that to the native mind it is indeed an

---

[1] E. H. Man : " On the Aboriginal Inhabitants of the Andaman Islands," *J.A.I.*, xii. p. 160.

[2] Rev. G. Taplin : *Manners, Customs, etc., of the Aborigines of South Australia*, p. 57 (Adelaide, 1879).

ordeal, but possibly we must not explain it as he does. He sees in it a "judgment of God," as it were, of the same kind as those of Ancient Greece, or of Europe in the Middle Ages. Doubtless, to the mind of the Tatiara, the assistance of unseen powers alone will allow the man who undergoes the ordeal to elude the lances thrown at him. If these powers were unfavourable to him, all his skill could not save him. But it is not correct to say that the object of the ordeal is to demonstrate the innocence or the guilt of the man who is subjected to it, for such an ordeal is employed in many cases where there is no question about the guilt. Frequently the perpetrator of a murder or a rape is already known, for example. He does not deny his deed, and his relatives do not dispute this point in any way with the victim's next-of-kin. The ordeal is none the less demanded, and it is therefore different from a "judgment" designed to establish innocence or guilt.

In the documents relating to Australian tribes which I have been able to consult, I have, as a matter of fact, found nothing about ordeals instituted for this purpose. We do, however, find many like those among the Tatiara which Taplin has recorded, and it is always the known and avowedly guilty persons who have to undergo them. "If the murderer should escape," says Dawson," and should be known by the friends of the deceased, he gets notice to appear and undergo the ordeal of spear-throwing at the first great meeting of the tribes."[1] A little further on he describes this ordeal. "When a man has been charged with an offence, he goes to the meeting armed with two war spears, a flat light shield, and a boomerang. If he is found guilty of a private wrong he is painted white and— along with his brother or near male relative, who stands beside him as his second, with a heavy shield, a liangle, and a boomerang—he is placed opposite to the injured person and his friends, who sometimes number twenty warriors. These arrange themselves at a distance of about fifty yards from him and each individual throws four or five gneerin spears and two boomerangs at him simultaneously, 'like a shower.' If he succeeds in warding them off,

[1] J. Dawson : *Australian Aborigines*, p. 70 (Melbourne, 1881).

his second hands him his heavy shield, and he is attacked singly by his enemies, who deliver each one a blow with the liangle. As blood must be spilt to satisfy the injured party, the trial ends on his being hit. After the wound has been dressed all shake hands and are good friends. If the accused person refuses to submit to be tried, he is outlawed, and may be killed, and his brother or nearest male relative is held responsible, and must submit to be attacked with boomerangs. If it turns out that the man is innocent, the relatives have a right to retaliate on the family of the accuser on the first opportunity." [1]

Dawson expressly states that the ordeal takes place after the guilt has been established ; its object, therefore, cannot be to prove it. Nevertheless, it is indispensable, and so much so that in default of the guilty person, another member of his family, preferably his brother, must undergo it. Finally we may remark that, the trial once finished, the enemies who have faced each other and the friends on both sides are reconciled, and manifest the most amicable feelings towards one another. The same peculiarities have been noted by other observers. W. M. Thomas writes : " There is one particularly amiable trait in the aboriginal character, which is that no animosity remains in their breasts, nor does any shrink from punishment. At the close of a fight or punishment " (evidently an ordeal such as Dawson witnessed is in question here), " those who have inflicted the wounds may be seen sucking them and doing any other kind office required." [2]

The ordeal itself is described by Thomas in terms very similar to those used by Dawson. " Murder is punished by the whole of a tribe throwing a spear and a *wonguim* at the murderer ; if he escapes without any material injury, the male who is the nearest of kin to the murdered man may, with his bludgeon or *leonile*, strike at the man's head (no other part) till he is tired. During the punishment the murderer is not allowed to throw a single weapon, but may ward off the spears, etc., with his shield. I knew an

[1] J. Dawson : ibid., p. 76.
[2] W. M. Thomas : " A Brief Account of the Aborigines of *Australia Felix*," in *Letters from Victorian Pioneers*, p. 68 (1854).

instance of a man having a hundred spears thrown at him, who warded them every one off." [1]

Thomas speaks of " chastisement " and " punishment," therefore the object of the ordeal can in no sense be to discover whether the man be guilty or not. Like other investigators, he insists that what matters most is, not the result of the trial, but that it should take place. Whether the criminal succeeds in warding off all the spears or not is a secondary consideration. The essential thing is that he shall have been subjected to the ordeal according to rule. It is therefore not what we should properly call a punishment.

An ordeal similar to the preceding takes place in the same district in certain cases of adultery. " If the wife desert her husband for a more favoured lover, it is incumbent on her family to chastise the guilty pair ; the wife is usually speared to death by her father or brother, and if the punishment is not attended with fatal effects, she is returned to her lawful spouse. The man has either to submit to a certain number of spears being thrown at him, in which case he is allowed a small shield to protect himself, or to fight a single combat with one of her relatives, or with a selected member of the tribe." [2] Howitt says, too : " In cases of elopement with the wife of another man, it was the Wollaroi practice for the abductor to stand out before a number of the woman's kindred, who were armed with spears, he having merely a spear for his protection, to turn them aside." [3]

In Queensland, Roth observed the same custom, and he has described it with his customary exactitude. " The alleged culprit, notwithstanding the immense mental and physical strain, may thus, with the help of his two friends, succeed in escaping any serious effects from the thirty or forty spears which have been thrown during the good hour or more that he has exposed himself. Should he come through the ordeal successfully, and a lot depends upon

[1] W. M. Thomas : ibid., p. 67.
[2] W. E. Stanbridge : " On the Aborigines of Victoria," *Transactions of the Ethnological Society*, i. p. 288 (1861).
[3] A. W. Howitt : *The Native Tribes of South-East Australia*, p. 217, quoted by E. S. Hartland : *Primitive Paternity*, i. p. 295.

his previous conduct and the influence of powerful friends, his accusers will ultimately run up and cling round his neck, indulge in a certain amount of weeping, to make friends again, and finally fix the guilt a second time, generally upon the weakest tribe and its most friendless member. In this district someone *must* be killed for the death of every ' important ' male aboriginal." [1] According to the expressions used by Dr. Roth, it appears, indeed, to be a question of an ordeal here, but these same expressions also show that its aim is not the establishing the fact of a certain person's guilt. It is designed to satisfy a dead man whose wrath would be a matter of dread, and who must not be disappointed at any price. He demands a life, and if the ordeal does not end fatally, they must go elsewhere to find a victim who does not cost too much.

The same ceremony takes place in the tribes of Western Australia observed by Bishop Salvado. " If the parties are agreed that the delinquent is to be punished, then the chief of the aggrieved family sentences him to a penalty in proportion to his crime, and this sometimes consists of throwing *ghici* at his legs. He is made to stand some distance off as a target, and the injured man throws at him as many *ghicis* as he can command ; and it is all the better for the culprit if he is skilful enough to ward them all off. When the supply of *ghicis* is exhausted, vengeance is satisfied, there is no question of anything else. Peace has been made." [2] Sometimes the ordeal is a fight in which the accusers and accused are accompanied by their relatives and friends, but the contest ends when the first blood is drawn. This is particularly the case when several tribes are concerned. " The women begin to exchange abusive epithets and excite the men to such a point that, shouting in frenzy and quite beside themselves, they rush forward by leaps and bounds, making endless contortions and running hither and thither, their beards between their teeth, and their *ghici* couched, now advancing and now retreating, till the throwing of a *ghici* gives place to a veritable mêlée. On both sides the weapons are flying, and the

---

[1] W. E. Roth : *North Queensland Ethnography*, Bulletin 9, No. 6. p. 387.
[2] R. Salvado : *Mémoires historiques sur l'Australie*, p. 324.

women, running and shouting, encourage the men, providing them with the ' enemy's ' arms, which they pick
up and collect. In the midst of this tumult, as soon as
anyone falls to the ground, wounded or dead, the fighting
ceases instantly ; all ill-feeling is at an end, and all hasten
to succour the wounded." [1]

Such furious fighting is in reality only an ordeal, and
this last trait is a proof of it. If any other were needed, it
would be enough to recall that Australian aborigines,
like nearly all other primitives, are not familiar with pitched
battles, and always avoid fighting in the open. Real war
is made by surprise attacks and ambushes only, and most
frequently by assaults at daybreak against an unsuspecting
foe. The " veritable mêlée " which Bishop Salvado witnessed was a ritual ceremony, regarded as indispensable by
both the tribes who took part therein.

Grey, one of the first and keenest observers who ever
described the South Australian tribes, says, too : " Any crime
(except incest) may be compounded for by the criminal
appearing and submitting himself to the ordeal of having
spears thrown at him by all such persons as conceive themselves to have been aggrieved, or by permitting spears to
be thrust through certain parts of his body ; such as through
the thigh, or the calf of the leg, or in the arm. The part
which is to be pierced by the spear is fixed for all common
crimes, and a native who has incurred this penalty, sometimes quietly holds out his leg for the injured party to
thrust his spear through. . . . If the criminal is wounded
in the degree judged sufficient for the crime he has committed,
his guilt is wiped away ; or if none of the spears thrown
at him (for there is a regulated number which each may
throw) take effect, he is equally pardoned." [2]

Grey's expression is the absolutely correct one ; this
ordeal is of the value of a " composition." Properly speaking,
it is not a punishment, although as a matter of fact the one

---

[1] R. Salvado: *Mémoires historiques sur l'Australie,* p. 324; cf. W. M.
Thomas : " A Brief Account of the Aborigines of *Australia Felix,*" pp. 94-6,
and the description of a similar fight among the Botocudos, by Maximilien of
Wied-Neuwied : *Voyage au Brésil,* ii. pp. 186-90 of the French translation.
[2] George Grey : *Journal of Two Expeditions of Discovery in North-West
and Western Australia,* ii. pp. 243-4 (1841).

who undergoes it is most frequently punished for his crime thus. It is essentially a rite, a mystic performance, designed to prevent or put an end to the fatal consequences which the crime committed—whether murder, adultery, or the like—cannot fail to entail upon the social group. It is the application of a mystic remedy to a mystic malady ; an expiation, in the complete and etymological sense of the word. Eylmann, after describing in detail a similar trial in a case of adultery, of which he was a witness, adds : " The South Australian is not acquainted with the sort of duel which would help towards obtaining the verdict of a higher power in a lawsuit." [1] His ordeals are not " judgments of God."

The meaning of the Australian ordeal, in so far as it is, according to Grey, a " composition," is illustrated by the collective representations involved in the composition itself, among certain African peoples anyhow. A composition offered and accepted is not only the price of blood ; it has, too, a mystic effect which is no less important. " Although they " (the Bechuanas) " are revengeful to the last degree," says Dr. Moffat, " if an offender profit the injured party by a gift, at the same time confessing his error, or, as is common, put the blame on his heart, the most perfect unanimity and cordiality succeed." [2] With regard to the A-Kamba of British East Africa, Hobley has well described the mystic effect of the ceremony which re-establishes harmony between two families, after that of the criminal has satisfied the claims of that of the victim. " Until the ceremony has all been properly carried out, no member of the family of the murdered man can eat food out of the same dish or drink beer with any member of the family of the murderer, and in Ukamba, it is believed that unless the matter is properly adjusted according to the law, the members of the family of the murderer will continue to be involved in quarrels and be liable to be killed as their relative had been. If one tries to look at the matter from their point of view, it appears to be this—there is a bad spirit or *muimu* about, belonging to an ancestor ; it enters into a man and the result

[1] E. Eylmann : *Die Eingeborenen der Kolonie Süd Australien*, p. 177.
[2] Robert Moffat : *Missionary Labours and Scenes in South Africa*, p. 255.

17

of this is that the next time he quarrels with a neighbour he kills him. This spirit may continue to possess that person, or it may go on to another member of that family and the same result occurs. In the same way the *muimu* of the deceased, the murdered man, influences the *aiimu* (spirits) in the bodies of his family and makes them afraid. They know that this death-dealing spirit is abroad, and the members of the family are more likely to be killed if they become entangled in a broil. Thus both families are anxious that this state of affairs should cease, and that the troublesome spirit should be appeased and laid to rest." [1]

This view of the general ideas of the A-Kamba is very instructive. When one of them kills another in a quarrel, the one who commits the crime is not the real cause of it ; he is but the agent of a malign influence which has taken possession of him. Nothing is more in accordance with the orientation of primitive mentality, which at once traces every effect in the visible world back to a mystic cause in the invisible one. What is to be done, therefore, when a man has killed another who does not belong to his family ? Inflict a penalty on him ? As a matter of fact, he will have to pay a " composition," and perhaps he will be ruined or sold as a slave ; but the punishment which overtakes *him* is not enough to restore peace of mind to the two families, unless the " composition " has at the same time served to appease the spirit of the offended ancestor who was the cause of the crime, and who wanders about the group, to the terror of all concerned, for he is certain to induce other crimes if the rites necessary to secure his pacification and removal have not been performed. Hobley says again : " The payment of the cow, bull, or goat . . . is of ritual importance, and is called *etumo*. They are necessary to protect both the family of the murderer and the murdered one from the powers of the unappeased death-dealing spirit which is abroad. Even if the killing was accidental, the *etumo* payments and ritual must be observed, because it shows that there is some bad influence about or the accident would never have occurred." (As

---

[1] C. W. Hobley : " Further Researches into Kikuyu and Kamba Religious Beliefs and Customs," *J.A.I.*, lxi. pp. 422–3.

a matter of fact, we know that primitive mentality does not recognize such a thing as " accident.")

" In former times, when a man of one clan killed another in some inter-tribal fight, the custom was for a father or brother to waylay and kill a man of the clan who had killed his brother ; these two deaths cancelled each other, and there was no more question of compensation, but it was considered essential that the *etumo* fees should be paid and the proper ceremonial observed." [1]

Thus the satisfaction afforded to the dead man, even though fully carried out, does not suffice, and the survivors cannot feel at ease until a mystic operation has taken place to appease the spirit whose anger has been revealed through the occurrence of the disaster. The weapon which has struck the blow also remains deadly in its effect. " Among many tribes it is purified in some way ; among the Akikuyu it is blunted, and I believe some such observance is almost universal among African tribes. The performance of such acts originates in the idea that the weapon carries with it misfortune or fatality, and so it is with the Akamba. The weapon once used in murder continues to be a means of further destruction, but here there is no ceremony, no medicine or magic which can abate its fatal spirit. Since there is no way of ridding oneself of this curse, the Mkamba has recourse to craft and cunning ; he will lay the weapon on a path or place where a passer-by is likely to see it. Once the other has picked it up its bane falls on him and the the first owner is free from it. This belief is, I think, of special interest, because it speaks of the manner in which murder is regarded. We have seen how necessary to the murderer is the *etumo* ; it takes the curse of murder off the aggrieved party as well as off the murderer, but the last has still the fatality of the weapon upon him, a fatality which neither time nor art can erase." [2]

[1] C. W. Hobley : ibid., p. 426. In the same way, in the Solomon Isles (at Buin, Vellalavella, etc.) to re-establish the peace disturbed by the death of a man, there must be (1) an avenging, i.e. the death of a man belonging to the murderer's group ; (2) a compensation, or payment in cowrie-shells. Unless this payment is made, the murderer is still a danger.—R. Thurnwald : *Forschungen auf dem Bismarck Archipel und den Salomon Inseln*, iii. Tafel 29, note 18.

[2] Hon. Ch. Dundas : "History of Kitui (A-Kamba)," *J.A.I.*, xliii. pp. 526-7 ; cf. C. W. Hobley, loc. cit., pp. 426-7.

Australian natives know very little about property that can be transmitted, and they have no standard measure of value for the few objects which are interchangeable, therefore with them there could be no question of " compounding," in the ordinary sense of the word. The ordeal we have been examining takes the place of it. But like the A-Kamba composition, its object is not solely to pacify the injured party, the outraged husband, or the family who has lost a member. Murder and adultery have a mystic influence upon the entire social group ; they reveal a power which is being exerted to its detriment, a power which is a perpetual menace to it. It must be fought and conquered. That is the purpose of the A-Kamba *etumo*, and that, too, is an essential feature of the Australian ordeal. Thus its function, at least in part, is to exercise against certain forces of the unseen world a defensive action necessary to the well-being of the social group. In virtue of this feature then, it resembles the African ordeals directed against witchcraft, and we may therefore maintain, with Taplin and other investigators, but for different reasons, that it is indeed an ordeal.

This is not an isolated fact, for in many circumstances the Tlinkit argue in the same way. " Every abrogation of customary usages, everything out of the common" (we see at once how large an area this would embrace) "is known by the name of *chlakass* and considered the universal cause of whatever misfortune may arise—bad weather, sickness, defeat in war, unsuccessful hunting, and the like. . . . Thus bad weather will not be the result alone of the fact that a corpse has not been cremated ; it will also be caused by the natives having neglected to isolate a young girl during the period of puberty. Here are other causes which induced bad weather. A young girl had been combing her hair outside the hut ; the missionary had put on his snowboots before he left the house ; the school children in their play had imitated the cries of wild birds ; and we ourselves had cleaned the skin of a mountain goat with salt water ; moreover, we had dragged a dead hedgehog across the snow. This last is what one of our Indian companions, on another hunting expedition, resolutely refused to do, alleging that if he did so a violent wind would spring up. He preferred to carry the beast on his back, heavy as it was, all the way back to the camp." [1]

Every time that a traditional custom is thus infringed, especially if there is any prohibition attached to it, there will be some trouble or accident. As a rule, a certain misfortune corresponds with a certain infringement. For instance, among the Esquimaux " alternating prohibitions " are known. "They cannot go out to take walrus until they have done working upon *tuktoo* clothing ; and after beginning the walrus hunt, no one is allowed to work on reindeer skins. One day, in March, I wanted Tookoolito and Koodloo's wife to make me a sleeping-bag of tuktoo skin, but nothing could persuade them to do it, as it was the walrus season. ' They would both die, and no more walruses could be caught.'" [2] On the coast of Alaska, " where the observance of totemistic exogamy was no longer strictly practised, and where it was now permissible to take a wife from one's own clan, the older people used

[1] A. Krause : *Die Tlinkit-Indianer*, p. 300.
[2] C. F. Hall : *Life with the Esquimaux*, ii. p. 321.

to consider this promiscuity responsible for the great mortality of the Kenayer tribe." [1]

Even to-day, in the same districts, similar facts may be collected. Here is a characteristic one. "For a long time our hunting yielded very little result; the animals used to disappear before our eyes. Kridtlarssuark entreated the spirits to reveal the reason why we could get no game. When the invocation ceremony was over he said that his daughter-in-law Ivalork had had a miscarriage, and that she had concealed it in order to escape the punishment (for women in such cases are subjected to a certain number of deprivations). He then ordered his son to punish the guilty woman by shutting her up in a snow hut after having taken away her fur clothing. There she would die of cold or hunger, and only on this condition would the animals allow the hunters to trap them. They at once made a snow hut, and shut up Ivalork in it. That is how Kridtlarssuark treated his daughter-in-law, of whom he was very fond, and he did it so that innocent people should not suffer for her fault." [2]

[1] Von Wrangell: "Einige Bemerkungen über die Wilden an der N.W. Küste von Amerika." *Beiträge zur Kenntniss des russischen Reichs* (Von Baer und Helmersen), i. p. 104.

[2] Kn. Rasmüssen: *Neue Menschen*, pp. 35–6. Similar instances have been noted in South Africa. "Let me quote," says Junod (*The Life of a South African Tribe*, ii. p. 294), "the *ipsissima verba* of Mankhelu, the great medicine-man of the Nkuna court. I have never forgotten the earnest tone of his voice, his deep conviction when he was speaking to me in the following words, as a kind of revelation. ' When a woman has had a miscarriage, when she has let her blood flow secretly and has burnt the abortive child in an unknown place, it is enough to make the burning winds blow, and dry up all the land; the rain can no longer fall, because the country is no longer right. Rain fears that spot. It must stop at that very place and can go no further. This woman has been very guilty. She has spoilt the country of the chief, because she has hidden blood which had not yet properly united to make a human being. That blood is taboo. What she has done is taboo. It causes starvation.' " For the rain to reappear in that place, purifying rites are indispensable. In the same way with the Barotse, " as the moon was in her first quarter, the woman and her husband did not like the idea of such a long quarantine; they therefore concealed the occurrence (a miscarriage). Now this man . . . was one of the principal officers of the king's guard; a *sekomboa*, a man of between forty-five and fifty, a favourite with his master and generally respected. The miscarriage being noised abroad within less than twenty-four hours, his peers, the other *sekomboas*, fell upon him, dragged him, heavily bound, to the river, tearing out his hair with their long nails. . . . They kept him under the water until he was nearly dead, then beat him with rods till he came to himself, and finally left him on the bank in torrents of rain."—*Missions évangéliques*, lxvii. p. 380. (Coillard.)

In the east of Greenland, " if a tent is not provided with a new skin covering in spring, crested seals and Greenland seals must not be taken into it till after a lapse of some days. Early in the spring a man obtained a share of a crested seal. He took it into his tent to cut it up and remove the tendons. The tent covering was in good condition, but had been used the previous autumn. It happened that crested seals afterwards became very rare, and so this man was looked askance at by the others, because ' his conduct had made the seals angry, and caused them to leave the coast.' " [1]

" One day," says Boas, " a large whale to which we were fast went under a body of ice ; and after it had taken five hundred fathoms of line, we had to let it go, and lost the whale. That night, after we had gone ashore, my natives wanted to go to the tent of a woman who was reputed to be a great angakok. The woman, in her trance, said that I had offended the goddess in the sea by cutting up caribou-meat on the sea-ice, and by breaking the bones there." [2]

Among the Esquimaux nearer the north, whom Rasmussen visited, if a man witnesses the violation of a taboo, he immediately expects some misfortune. People who are in mourning, for instance, must refrain from doing many things. " One day, when he had to go and find ice to break, our companion, Jörgen Brönlund, a Greenlander, unknown to us, ordered a young fellow who had just lost his parents to fetch it. He thought he might just as well disregard the prohibition for once in a way, and so Agpalinguark (that was the young fellow's name) went to get the ice. But he was seen by two old women who were very much disturbed about this violation of custom. Something bad would be sure to happen ! And in fact, two days later, a fierce storm from the south-west broke over us. There was such a tremendous swell that the waves came sweeping up over the land and destroyed all the huts in the village. One of the chiefs then came to see us

[1] G. Holm : " Ethnological Sketch of the Angmagsalik Eskimo," pub. by W. Thalbitzer. *Meddelelser om Groenland*, xxix. p. 49.
[2] Franz Boas : " The Eskimo of Baffin Land and Hudson Bay," *Bulletin of the American Museum of Natural History*, xv. p. 478 (1870).

begging us in future not to allow such infringements of
their customary rules. ' We observe these regulations so
that the world may go on peaceably, for the powers must
not be offended. . . . In this country, when a rule has
been broken, men do penance, because the dead . . . have
unlimited power.' " [1]

These words are very characteristic. If we compare
what we have just learned from the reports of Junod and
Rasmussen, these expressions throw light upon one of the
aspects under which Nature appears to the primitive's mind.
By virtue of the mystic relation between the social group
(composed of both living and dead), the portion of land
it occupies, the beings, both visible and mythical, who live
and have lived there, the order of the universe (as we call
it), can only exist as long as the customary conditions are
maintained, and (in many peoples) if the personal influence
of the chief is exercised as it should be. Respect for prohibitions and taboos is one of the essential conditions.
One of the chief's duties is to see that they are not violated,
and if there should have been any infringement, to make
the offenders expiate their fault by appropriate rites. As
the " medicine-man " explained to Junod, a secret miscarriage which would allow the woman and her husband
to escape the expiatory rites, would entail danger of death
on the whole social group. The rain " *can* no longer fall."
The harvest will be dried up, the cattle will perish for
want of water, and the whole tribe will be reduced to a
state of despair. The woman is " very guilty," and nothing
can screen her from the punishment which alone can re-
establish normal conditions, and thus save the tribe. When
the social solidarity is such that by inducing a disorder
of this kind one member of the group can imperil the
lives of all the rest, no crime can be more serious than the
violation of taboos, for it ruptures the relations upon which
the welfare of all depends.

[1] Kn. Rasmussen : *Neue Menschen*, pp. 149-50.

II

We should be inclined to think that infringements are classed in order of importance, according to whether the consequences are near or far-reaching. That is to say, that from the collective representations of a social group, one might discover why the violation of such-and-such a custom reacts on the whole group, while another, on the contrary, only affects the individual who has committed it, or at most, his relatives. As a matter of fact we always meet with preconceived ideas such as the following : " If such a taboo is violated, such a consequence—more or less general, according to the case—is sure to ensue." Or again : " If such a thing happens, if that disaster occurs, it is because this rule has been infringed," or, in a more indefinite fashion, " an infringement (unspecified) must have taken place," (without the speaker's knowing which). How does the concealment of stillbirth involve the disappearance of the rain ? Arbitrary as connèctions of this kind appear to us, to primitive mentality they are so familiar that they seem quite natural. The native observes the traditional regulations just as he obeys the rules (pretty frequently complicated enough), of the language he speaks, without any difficulty, and without reflection. He does not imagine them to be other than they are. He will never ask himself why a certain infringement should bring about the ruin of the entire group, whilst another entails fatal consequences upon its author alone, or on a part of the group merely. If he is interrogated on this point, he will reply that his ancestors always thought thus, and he will wonder, not at the fact, but at the question.

We can, however, distinguish two principal forms of this connection in any given race. Sometimes a definite consequence is bound up with a definite infringement, and the one is directly inferred from the other—whether the consequence extends to one or more people, or even to the entire group, matters little. Hobley has given a great many instances of this kind in his " Further Researches into Kikuyu and Kamba Religious Beliefs and Customs." Here is a characteristic example reported by Junod. Among

the Ba-Thonga, a woman who is enceinte by any other
than her husband will have a difficult labour. There does
not seem to be any relation between these facts, but " for
the Thonga, . . . a protracted and difficult birth proves
that the child is not legitimate. This conviction is so
strong that when a woman knows that the child she is
going to bear is not her husband's, she will admit this secretly
to the principal midwife in order to spare herself the pains
of a difficult birth, as it is taboo to bear a ' child of adultery '
hiding the fact ; it would cause the mother untold suffering." [1]
This is the reason why the midwife, in the case of a very
prolonged labour, begins to have doubts about the legitimacy
of the child. Among the Washamba, another Bantu tribe,
" when the pains of labour are very protracted it is a proof
that the woman has had criminal relations with several
men." [2] That belief is fairly common. In Uganda, again,
" women may not eat salt during their pregnancy ; if they
do so, it is believed that the child will die. When, therefore, a newborn child falls ill, the husband blames his
wife for the fact, saying : ' This child is dying of an illness
caused by your having eaten salt.' " [3]

Preconceived ideas of this kind are very numerous,
and vary according to the community in which they are
noted. Sometimes they are so strong that those who violate
the taboo despair of escaping consequences which have
not yet shown themselves, and anticipate them. Here is
a remarkable case which was observed in the island of Nias.
A native who has been converted to Christianity is speaking.
" I was my parents' eldest son, and I had a little sister.
One day the priest (the medicine-man) came to our house.
He looked at my father, then cast a furtive glance at my
sister, and said : ' Do you know that your daughter must
die ? ' ' Why ? ' asked my father. The priest answered :
' Before her birth you knocked down pigs, you killed a
snake, you carried loads ; that is the reason why you will
lose your daughter. Why do you give yourself the trouble
of feeding her ? Nothing that you can do will help matters ;

[1] H. A. Junod : *The Life of a South African Tribe*, i. p. 39.
[2] A. Karasek-Eichhorn : *Beiträge zur Kenntniss der Waschamba*, Bässler
Archiv, iii. p. 188.
[3] Fr. M. A. Condon : " Contribution to the Ethnography of the Basoga-
Batamba (Uganda Protectorate)," *Anthropos*, v. p. 946.

she will have to die.' My father, in despair, went to my
mother, and told her what the priest had said. Both of
them were terribly dejected, but what was to be done ?
Finally my father said to his wife : ' Let us kill the child,
why should she eat our rice any longer ? ' and as I was
a strong lad, he made me get a sack and stuff my little sister
in and carry her away to the woods. . . ." [1] It does not
occur to the parents that the child may be saved. The
father's violation of certain taboos relating to the period
of gestation makes the child's death a necessity. The
language of the " priest " seems to us pitiless in its severity,
but possibly, if the infringement of rule were not expiated
by the death of the child, the entire social group might
have to suffer the consequences.

At other times the preconnection is simply between
the violation and a misfortune which will assuredly follow,
the nature of which is not determined beforehand. It
merely implies the certainty that the custom or taboo will
not be violated without " something happening." There
is a very strong feeling that the unseen powers, incensed
by the violation, will demand punishment ; primitive
mentality believes as firmly in the inevitability of this
as we do in the persistence of natural laws. What will
the sentence be ? The event alone will make it known,
unless indeed, as soon as the violation has become known,
the offender proceeds to undergo purification and expiatory
rites which afford satisfaction to the offended powers or,
in a general way, have the virtue of preventing misfortune.

When the preconnection is thus indefinite, it is most
frequently the appearance of the result which leads back
to the cause. " Something " has happened—persistent
bad weather, prolonged drought, a sudden death, a severe
illness, unsuccessful hunting or fishing, and so on. It is
clear that there has been some infringement of law, but
of what rule, what custom ? Is it even certain that the
misfortune proceeds from the violation of a custom or taboo ?
Sudden death, lack of success in hunting, etc., may be due
to other causes also ; to the evil practices of a witch, the
anger of an ancestor, for instance. How is the primitive

[1] *Berichte der rheinischen Missionsgesellschaft*, p. 61 (1909).

to find out what has actually been the cause ? He knows but one method of obtaining assurance, but it is an infallible one : he will ask the unseen powers, whose decrees must be ascertained and made favourable to him, above all, in circumstances of great difficulty.

Therefore if the accident in itself is not a sufficiently clear revelation, i.e. if the native does not know beforehand that when a certain accident happens a certain violation has been committed, he will have recourse, according to the circumstances, to dreams, ordeals, invocation of spirits —in short, to one form or other of divination, and he will be guided by what this teaches him. " Should someone meet with misfortune, or fall ill, or no longer trap any furred animals, he immediately thinks that he must have committed some sin. Then he repairs to the augur, or ' shaman,' and makes him continue his operations until the cause of the disaster has been revealed, and finally does what he can to expiate his fault." [1] (He carves a little wooden image of a man and hangs it on a tree in the wood.) " The Indian . . . without knowing why, believes that bad luck or misfortune, such as accident and loss of property, sickness or death, is inflicted upon him as a punishment by the Evil Power, because of his violation of one of the ' medicines.' . . . It is impossible for the Christian races to understand, or estimate the powerful influence which the ' medicine ' beliefs have for ages exerted upon the Indian character and tribal life. . . . ' Supernatural power ' is probably the nearest equivalent to the word ' medicine ' in its common Indian use." [2]

This belief is to be met with in many races. To give but one more example, taken from the Fân people of French Congo : " Every time that our negro has any accident, misfortune, disaster, nay, even a simple failure, he will attribute it to his totem who has been angered by some *nsem* or ritual defilement, by the violation of an *eki*, or something of that sort. Therefore it is essential to appease him. The greater the disaster, the greater must have been the cause or fault which induced it, and the more necessary

[1] G. W. Steller : *Beschreibung von dem Lande Kamtschatka*, p. 276.
[2] W. McClintock : *The Old North Trail*, p. 181. (Blackfeet, 1910.)

it is to expiate it (even though it may have been quite involuntary), by considerable sacrifice." [1]

The man who has been overtaken by misfortune or sustained a defeat will therefore nearly always ask himself (unless he thinks that an enemy's hand has dealt the blow) : " What have I done ? Wherein am I guilty ? What rule have I infringed ?" His conscience, or a scrupulous self-examination will reveal that he has failed to fulfil such-and-such an obligation, and he will repair his fault. It may happen that a man, knowing he has violated some taboo, and seeing that a disaster is spreading throughout his social group, feels himself responsible for it, and makes up his mind to confess, so that by expiation he may appease the offended powers. Wangemann, the missionary, tells the story of a scruple of this kind in a Koranna native who had become a Christian. " Drought and famine having supervened, Richard Miles felt his conscience reproach him so that he looked upon this disaster as a punishment for the sin that he had committed. One night he and his wife rose from their beds, and he fell on his knees, entreating the Lord not to punish the whole Mission for his sin. That very night rain fell, and the next morning Richard Miles went to the missionary and confessed that he had been guilty of adultery." [2] An absolutely similar need of expiation will make itself felt in a pagan's conscience when misfortune suggests to him that his relatives are undergoing punishment inflicted by the unseen powers because of his having violated some taboo. " A canoe with half a dozen men on board, sailed from Aitutaki to Manuae (Hervey's Island), a distance of fifty-five miles, in order to collect red parrakeets' feathers. Having succeeded in their object, . . . they started on their return voyage, but were driven out of their course by strong contrary winds. After a few days, food and water began to fail, and a miserable death stared them in the face. Routu, the commander of the canoe, now addressed his companions : ' I see why we are thus driven about over the ocean by unfavourable winds. We have sinned in taking away the sacred red

[1] P. H. Trilles : *Le totémisme des Fân*, p. 507.
[2] Dr. Wangemann : *Die Berliner Mission im Koranna Lande*, p. 156.

parrakeets' feathers. A costly sacrifice is demanded by the angry gods. Throw me into the sea, and you will yet safely reach home.' . . . The voyagers . . . complied with this request." [1]

Whether the violation has been involuntary, and its author did not even know that he was committing it, matters nothing ; the wrong has been done, and its consequences cannot fail to appear. It is these same consequences which awaken a suspicion of it, and divination then makes the fault known, and at the same time reveals a way of repairing it if possible.

In Dahomey, " the cleansing of the ' doctor ' (*féticheur*), followed by his visit to the market, is a real purification ceremony both for him and for the people, a purification which is entirely a religious rite, for it only concerns faults committed voluntarily or involuntarily against fetish-worship. It is to be noted, too, that the natives never tell us of any cases but those of involuntary errors. One may, without knowing it, have eaten a food which is forbidden to his family, or have bought in the market flour-balls cooked in utensils or wrapped in leaves which he may not use. It may even happen that a prince has taken his usual bath when he should not have done, one of his dead brothers not having received burial rites. In all these things, an individual is guilty through ignorance only ; but is not this ignorance due to some evil genius which thus involves the people of Dahomey for the purpose of exciting the anger of their own fetishes against them ? " [2] Observations of this sort have been frequently made in both hemispheres. To give but one more only : "When a person falls sick (in New Zealand) and cannot remember that he has broken any law of *tapu* himself, he endeavours to discover who has got him into the scrape, for it is not an uncommon practice to make a person offend against some law of *tapu*, without his being aware of it, with the express object of causing the anger of Atua to fall upon him. This practice is a secret art called *makutu*. And it has often happened that an innocent person has been sacrificed to the rage of the relatives of a sick man,

[1] W. W. Gill : *Savage Life in Polynesia*, p. 172.
[2] A. Le Hérissé : *L'ancien royaume de Dahomey*, pp. 125–6.

under the belief that he had caused the disease by such unlawful means." [1]

According to our view of the matter, if it appears that a man has infringed some rule without knowing it, and above all without any means of knowing it, his unavoidable ignorance is nearly always accepted as an excuse. The rule has not been broken in reality, because it did not rest with the man whether it should be observed or not. The attitude taken by primitive mentality with regard to this same fact is widely different. First of all, infringement of the rule brings about the consequences independently of the doer's intentions, and as it were automatically. The rain can no longer fall, a tempest rages, the game disappears, not because a woman who was enceinte desired to be rid of her offspring, but because she did not observe the necessary rites when the miscarriage had taken place. It matters little whether her action was intentional or not. If the miscarriage were accidental, matters would have turned out just the same. But there is more in it than that. The absence of intention, in anyone who has been guilty of infringing a regulation, rather aggravates than excuses the fault. As a matter of fact, nothing happens by chance. How then can a man have been induced to commit a crime without wishing to do so, or knowing that he was doing it? He must already be the victim of an occult power, or the object of anger which must be appeased—at least (and this is a still more serious supposition), unless he has within himself, unknown to him, some power for evil. Instead, therefore, of feeling reassured by the fact that he could not know his wrongdoing when committing it, and that it was consequently inevitable, his anxiety is all the greater. It becomes henceforth indispensable to find out (by divination, as a rule), how it happens that he has been placed in so parlous a state.

Even when it is simply a question of what we call a " crime passionnel," which, strictly speaking, is neither involuntary nor unknown to him who commits it, primitive mentality interprets it in a fashion which proves baffling to us. The motives for the crime are obvious—the man

    [1] Ed. Shortland : *Traditions and Superstitions of the New Zealanders*, p. 116 (1856).

has yielded to hunger, rage, jealousy, love, etc. . .
Primitives see this, for they are very frequently shrewd
observers of human nature, as their stories and their proverbs
prove. In the case of people they know well, the motives
determining their actions hardly ever escape them. But
these motives are secondary causes, and in their eyes, such
causes are never the true explanation of anything. The
tree which falls on the passer-by knocks him down and kills
him, but to their minds his fall is not the real cause of his
death. The tree crushed him because a wizard had " doomed "
him ; it was but the agent, and the one who carried out
the sentence, so to speak. So, too, a man who slays his
rival yields to his passion, but that is not the true reason
for his deed. *That* must be sought elsewhere ; whence
comes it that he has been inflamed by the passion to which
he yields ? Another, in a brawl, kills one of his neighbours.
He struck him in a moment of anger. But who instigated
the dispute in which the criminal engaged ? and how does
it happen that *his* spear should be close at hand at that
very moment ?

The real cause of occurrences, therefore, is always connected with the unseen world. If it comes from without,
the man is both the guilty person and the victim (these two
conditions are not clearly distinct to the primitive's mind,
as they are to our own). If it be due to a principle which
imbues him, he is a *porte-malheur*, a wizard, and it will
not be long before the fatal accusation is formulated.

III

The same collective representations and their preconnections afford an explanation of facts which seem at
first sight even more mysterious than the preceding. In
many communities, those who have come to an end in
certain ways—as a rule, have suffered violent deaths—
are treated in a special manner. They do not receive the
same funeral honours as others. Their friends hasten to
get rid of the corpse, and the dead man seems to be excluded
from the social group to which he ought (in the form
suited to his present state) still to belong. They behave

18

towards him as they do towards those who are a reproach
and a danger to the group; they cast him out, as they do
abnormal children, those who possess, unknown to themselves, a power for evil, and wizards. He has, in fact, come
to his end by a " bad death," that is, not merely a death
which is unnatural—for no death, or hardly any, is natural,
in the sense in which we use the term—but a death which
reveals the wrath of the unseen powers. He has been
struck down by them; and for fear of having to share his
fate, he must be avoided, and all relations between him
and the social group must be severed.

In Borneo, for instance, " these tribes show no sign of
the ancestor-worship which is founded only upon fear.
The natives, however, are afraid of the cemeteries and the
corpses of those whose sudden death has terrified them;
of those who have died of suicide, accident, or suffered a
violent death, and of women dead in childbirth. They
declare such deaths to be a punishment inflicted by the
spirits upon those who have perished for some crime they
have committed. No religious ceremony is held over them;
their corpses are simply buried in a special way." [1] " Those
who violate divine or human regulations (*adat*) meet with
misfortune or sickness; if the spirits are really incensed
against them, they cause these guilty ones to be killed in
combat, or by accident, or to commit suicide; in the case
of women, they die in childbed. All those who perish
thus have died ' a bad death.' They do not receive funeral
honours." [2] The circumstances of their death reveal what
Dr. Nieuwenhuis calls their guilt, and in any case they
show the anger of the unseen powers with them. This
anger pursues them beyond the tomb. " All who die from
any other cause than illness lose the privilege of honourable
burial, and also, according to the belief of the survivors,
are deprived of enjoying the future life in the *Apu Kesio*.
The souls of the dead who have been assassinated, or
accidentally killed, or have committed suicide, or fallen
on the field of battle, women dead in childbed, stillborn
children, all arrive by two different routes at two other

[1] A. W. Nieuwenhuis: *Quer durch Borneo*, ii. pp. 69–70.
[2] Ibid., i. p. 102.

places where they must henceforth live with other poor wretches who have shared the same fate. The corpses of such people inspire the Kayans with special horror ; that is why they are simply rolled up in a mat and put into the ground." [1]

Such feelings with regard to " bad death " are not met with in Borneo alone. They are common in uncivilized communities. At Bougainville, " when a man dies by falling from a tree, they think he has been killed by Oromrui " (he is the spirit most dreaded). "In the Gazelle peninsula the natives are forbidden to bury a man who has died thus, and they leave the body lying where it fell. At Bougainville, they carry it to the funeral pyre in exactly the same attitude as that in which it was found." [2]

As the Borneo Kayans hold, " those who die of violent deaths at Bougainville have to live apart even in the other world. This kind of death (i.e. on the battlefield or by accident) is considered highly ignominious." [3]

In Australia, says Dawson, " the deaths of adults caused by epidemic are not avenged, nor are the natural deaths of boys before having beards, or of girls before entering womanhood, or of those who have lost their lives by accident, such as drowning, falling from trees, snake-bite, etc." [4] In other words, " bad death " deprives them of funeral honours. In German New Guinea, " the souls of those who have suffered a violent death, by assassination or by accident, remain in the neighbourhood of the place where the disaster took place, dwelling on large trees, and thence bringing trouble upon the survivors. You see," adds the missionary, " what confusion reigns in the natives' ideas of morals ; it is not the man's murderer who has acquired defilement, but the soul of his victim. I am speaking of the Bongu people only. According to them, the victim, that is to say, the soul of the victim, is not admitted to the village of the dead. Such souls are not allowed to rest ;

[1] A. W. Nieuwenhuis : ibid., p. 91.
[2] R. Thurnwald : " Im Bismarck Archipel und auf den Salomon Inseln," *Zeitschrift für Ethnologie*, xlii. p. 134.
[3] E. Frizzi : *Ein Beitrag zur Ethnologie von Bougainville und Buka,* Bässler-Archiv, Beiheft vi. pp. 11–12.
[4] J. Dawson : *Australian Aborigines*, p. 70.

they live on certain trees, and feed upon the most unpleasant fruits, those which even the pigs reject." [1]

In South Africa the Basutos consider that those who die of hunger or have been struck by lightning have succumbed to a "bad death," and treat them accordingly. "The victims of famine are left unburied," [2] and in another publication Casalis says : " It is painful to me to have to confess that the Basutos never bury persons who have died of hunger. This is a result of their religious system. Since every interment must be carried out with sacrifices to the *barimo* (ancestors), it does not seem possible to hold an interment when the deceased has left no cattle, or has no friend to provide any for the sacrifice. Therefore in times of famine and destitution, children may often be seen dragging the corpse of their father to a gully and leaving it there." [3] Other motives must undoubtedly be noted in addition to the one which Casalis gives. If the Basutos, not content with depriving these dead of the customary sacrifices and ceremonial, even refuse to bury them, it is because the horror which the "bad death" inspires is too great. They dare not touch the bodies, and besides, if they did consign them to the ground, they would offend the members of the social group whose influence is impressed upon it, making it fertile or barren (these are the ancestors), therefore it is better to break off all relations with them, and that is why they are left in the gully.

The victims of a thunderbolt have the same treatment meted out to them. Not to exclude them, as quickly as possible, from the social group would be to expose the survivors to the same fate. A man has been killed by lightning, and it is asked : " ' Where is he ? ' ' Down there in the place where he fell. We do not bring a man like that back to the village.' I go down to the high road. Some men are collected in a hollow. Two of them are digging a trench. . . . They show me an old blanket, soaked with rain and covered with mud, and when a corner of it is raised, I see Tsai's body still warm ; he is going to be buried

[1] *Berichte der rheinischen Missionsgesellschaft*, p. 239 (1899), p. 135 (1907).

[2] E. Casalis : *Les Bassoutos*, p. 213.

[3] *Missions évangéliques*, xvi. pp. 5-6 (note).

immediately, without his grandmother having seen him again, or his parents, who live but two hours' ride from here, having been informed, so that they might look their last on him.' 'Why are you burying him so quickly, even before his body is cold, and without letting his parents know?' 'We cannot bring a man like that back to the village.' 'Why not?' 'Because if we did, the lightning would come back again, and kill other people in the village.' " [1]

This dread goes so deep that the Basutos hardly venture to give any help to those who are struck by lightning. " These poor creatures think that if they approach the place where the lightning has struck, without having previously undergone the customary purification they would draw down upon their own homes a similar catastrophe." [2] In 1912 a house, in which there were six children and two young men, was set on fire by lightning. " They did not succeed in opening the door. They appealed for help, and their cries of agony were heard a long way off, and lasted for some time, but nobody made the least effort to go to their aid. These poor children knew that their parents were there, only a few steps away from them. . . . Suddenly the roof of the house fell in. A few more cries of agony and all was over. Nobody dared go near houses that had been burnt down. . . . The people, even the parents of the children, dared not come to the cemetery." [3] The Bechuanas consider that a tree, when struck by lightning, has also succumbed to the " bad death," and it is destroyed. " When lightning strikes a tree in the neighbourhood of a town, or in the plantations, the chief takes his attendants there, and they begin to destroy the tree by fire and steel. It is no easy task to exterminate the trunk and branches of an ancient mimosa which was rooted there about the time of the Flood, and is nearly as hard as marble, but they put so much energy and perseverance into the task that very soon not the least trace of it remains." [4] For the

[1] *Missions évangéliques*, lxxiv. 2. pp. 172–3 (Dieterlen) ; cf. Colonel Maclean : *A Compendium of Kafir Laws and Customs*, p. 85.
[2] Ibid., xxviii. p. 304. (Maitin.)
[3] Ibid., lxxxvii. 1. pp. 105–6. (P. Ramseyer.)
[4] Ibid. xix. p. 406. (Lemue.)

negroes to undertake such a laborious job shows that their reasons for it are imperative.

Similar practices, inspired by similar beliefs, are to be found in West Africa. In Dahomey, "the death of the canoeist who is drowned in passing the bar is considered to be a punishment inflicted by Hou (the fetish of the undercurrent there). Therefore the body of the victim is buried in the sand, or, as others tell us, thrown into the sea." [1] Among the Mossi, "suicides are buried as dogs would be at home (for here all dogs are eaten); lepers suffer the same fate, and are buried at night, without ceremonies of any kind. Death from accident, whether occasioned by a fall, snake-bite, or anything else, is held to be the work of an evil genius who must not be offended by the rendering of funeral honours to his victim, or he would return and slay another member of the family. That is why those who have died an accidental death are interred without ceremony, not even the grave-diggers being present; their heads are not shaved, for (say the Mossi) God has called them to him with their hair on. The grave is dug and they are put in it, and that is all." [2] With the Waniaturu, "if a man has been killed by lightning, they say that he has met with his punishment because he was a sorcerer." [3]

Lastly, in the case of the Fân of the French Congo, Father Trilles has very carefully collected the general ideas and customs relating to the "bad death." "No one admits that the man who is struck by lightning has met his death by accident. In no case—and in this least of all—is an accident really considered such. . . . The violation of an *eki* is nearly always the cause of the calamity, according to the natives. Before the body of the man so killed can be buried or serve as a fetish, therefore, the medicine-man must examine into the cause of the death, and find out which *eki* has been violated and brought about this man's fall. This having been done, two sentences will be pronounced, one on the individual, and the other on the tribe, clan, and family of the dead man particularly. . . . The

---

[1] A. Le Hérissé : *L'ancien royaume du Dahomey*, p. 109.
[2] P. Eugène Mangin, P.B. : "Les Mossi," *Anthropos*, ix. p. 732.
[3] Eberhard von Sick : *Die Waniaturu*, Bässler-Archiv, v. Heft. 1–2, p. 55.

family, as a whole, all equally concerned, and represented
by its chief, will pay ; and the tribe, all equally concerned,
and represented by the tribal chief, will pay too.

"The second penalty is imposed on the dead man.
Since he has violated an *eki*, he must be punished. The
spirit has already visited him with the direst penalty that
can be inflicted on the living ; it has required his death.
The tribe in its turn, responsible as a whole, will inflict
the heaviest punishment that the dead can suffer ; it will
deprive him first of the funeral sacrifices, and then of the
posthumous rites. There shall be no dance, no song for
this man ; nothing but the wailings of the women within
the hut. His body will be carried into the wood without
any funeral ceremony whatever, then it will be buried
beneath an ant-heap, so that the ants may destroy it as
soon as possible. . . . His skull will not be preserved with
those of his ancestors, and consequently his memory will
gradually fade away. All those who die from accident,
whose skulls cannot be found, have usually suffered the
same fate." [1] In short, "bad death," when laying a man
low, at the same time obliges his social group to excommu-
nicate him. It hastens to remove him from their midst,
lest it draw down upon itself the anger of the unseen powers
who have struck at him. This explains why the funeral
ceremonies, which usually bring the dead again into relation
with his group, are omitted, and doubtless, too, is the reason
why the Fân bury him beneath an ant-heap. The more
quickly his flesh is separated from his bones, the faster
will the deceased arrive at his destined state.[2]

IV

If this be so, what will be the feeling regarding those
who have been quite close to "bad death," who have nearly
succumbed, and yet, by a stroke of luck or supreme effort,
seem to be escaping with their lives ? Will they be aided,
will there be a helping hand stretched out, will the by-

---

[1] R. P. H. Trilles : *Le totémisme des Fân*, pp. 338–40.
[2] Cf. R. Hertz : " La représentation collective de la mort," *Année sociologique*, x. pp. 66–7.

standers strive to accomplish the impossible to snatch them from a death which appears so imminent ? It would seem as if an irresistible instinct of human sympathy would move them to it. Primitives, however, are nearly always driven by an irresistible instinct of fear and horror to do exactly the opposite.

Thus it is that in Kamschatka, " if anyone fell into the water accidentally, it used to be considered a great sin (*Sünde*) to help him out. Since he was destined to drown it would have been wrong, in their opinion, to save him from his fate. That is why, if he escaped, nobody would allow him to enter his house, nobody would speak to him again, they would not give him the smallest scrap of food ; henceforward he would be unable to find a wife ; they regarded him as virtually dead. He was condemned either to seek his fortunes some way off, or to remain in his own district and die of hunger. If a man fell into the water in the presence of others, they would not allow him to get out again ; on the contrary, they used force to make him drown, to make sure of his death." [1]

Can one imagine conduct more atrocious and inhuman ? Nevertheless, just a moment before the poor wretch's life was in danger, his companions were ready to share everything with him, food, weapons, shelter, etc. ; they would defend him if he needed defence, avenge him if a member of a hostile group did him a wrong—in short, they would fulfil, towards him as towards all the rest, all the manifold obligations that the absolute solidarity of these communities demands. He falls into the water accidentally and is in danger of drowning, and immediately he becomes an object of dread and repulsion. Not only do they refrain from hastening to his aid, but if he appears to be saving himself, they prevent him ; should he come to the surface, they drive him under the water again. If, in spite of all this, he does succeed in surviving his immersion, the social group refuses to admit that he has escaped death. They no longer know him ; his membership is rescinded. The feelings he inspires and the treatment meted out to him recall the excommunications of the Middle Ages.

[1] G. W. Steller : *Beschreibung von dem Lande Kamtschatka*, p. 295.

All this is because cases of this kind are exactly like " bad death." It is not the death itself, nor the actual circumstances accompanying it, that terrifies the primitive mind ; it is the revelation of the wrath of the unseen powers and of the sin for which these angry powers require expiation. Now when a man runs the risk of accidental death, the revelation is as clear and conclusive as if he were already dead. He has been " doomed," and it matters little that the sentence has not been carried out. To help him to escape would be to become a party to his wrongdoing, and draw down upon one's own head a like misfortune. The primitive dare not do it. We remember the unfortunate children burnt to death in a house that had been struck by lightning ; the parents, who are close at hand, do not venture to intervene. For the doomed man to wish to escape death is to exasperate the unseen powers yet further, and this rage may react on his relatives ; he *must* therefore die. The accident—which was no accident, since nothing happens by chance—is a kind of spontaneous ordeal. Just as the ordeal reveals to many of the African peoples the evil spirit imbuing such-and-such an individual, so does the accident betray the misdeed which has led to the culprit's being doomed by the unseen powers. In both cases, this terrible revelation instantly brings about the same revulsion of feeling. In one moment the man who was a companion, friend, and relative has become a stranger and an enemy, an object alike of horror and hatred.

Steller is not the only one who has observed this ; others have borne witness to the same fact. For example, Nansen says : " They (the Esquimaux) shrink from assisting one who has met with an accident at sea, if he seems to be already in the pinch of death, fearing lest they should happen to lay hands upon him after life has departed." [1]

Nansen accounts for their inhuman conduct by the fear which they have, as a rule, of coming in contact with dead bodies. This explanation may seem likely because it most nearly approaches our own way of thinking and feeling. It is, however, not the correct one, and I merely record the fact, which confirms Steller's testimony. G. Holm,

[1] Fr. Nansen : *Eskimo Life*, p. 137 ; cf. ibid., p. 245.

speaking of the Greenlanders on the eastern coast says too : " So great is their dread of touching a corpse, that in the case of an accident there is no question of handling or assisting the injured person from the moment they conclude hope is over. Suiarkak capsized one day at the beginning of April, when he was about to land on the ice-foot. He scrambled out of his kayak, but sank almost immediately. His father and several friends who were present on the ice-foot, and had immediately hastened in their kayaks to his assistance, made no attempt to rescue him when he sank, although he could be easily seen, and an oar might easily have reached him." [1]

The very details of this incident prove that what paralyses the father of the victim and the other spectators of the drowning is not the fear of touching a corpse, but the mystic revelation of which the accident is a sign, for the help of an oar would suffice to save the man who is in the water, and then there would be no question of a corpse. But how dare they resist the punishment inflicted by the unseen powers ? " When a man who had been driving in a sledge fell through the ice and we helped him out of the water, we were received at his home as if we had done something heroic." [2] It *may* possibly be done by the travellers who do not rely on the same invisible powers as the Esquimaux, but for the latter the sentence admits of no appeal. Even to save his son, a father would never dare to brave the doom which the accident reveals, and thus endanger the safety and possibly the very existence of the entire social group.

Similar circumstances have been reported by those investigators who first noted South African manners and customs. Among the Kafirs, for instance, according to what Van der Kemp tells us, " a dying man is sometimes abandoned by all, and it may even happen that he reappears, and undergoes the same treatment a second time. To account for such cruel conduct, they allege that they believe that an illness or other misfortune causes its victims to be

[1] G. Holm : "An Ethnological Sketch of the Angmagsalik Eskimo," edit. by W. Thalbitzer, *Meddelelser om Groenland*, xxxix. p. 75.
[2] Ibid., p. 137.

multiplied, if they do not get rid of the first one attainted. For the same reason they never help a man who is drowning, or is otherwise in danger of death, and if he utters cries of distress they flee from the spot as fast as they can, unless indeed they throw stones at him so that he may sink. Even women in travail must not cry out, lest they should see everyone fly from them, and be forced to remain abandoned and unaided." [1] This last feature has been observed in a very different place, in the Tlinkit of British Columbia, although the explorer interprets it in a slightly different sense. " I often used to hear piteous groans in several directions, proceeding from the hill near our house. I asked the Tlinkits what the reason was, and they told me that several women about to be confined were in the wood. They added, by way of excuse, that nobody *could* help them then, because in that condition they were ' unclean.' Thus they lay there in the bitter winter weather, in the cold and rain, without their lamentable cries moving a single soul to pity." [2] Finally, in the Solomon Isles, "if a sacred shark has attempted to seize a man, but he has escaped, they are so much afraid of his anger that they will throw him back into the sea to be devoured." [3] There is no need to suppose that the shark must have been a " sacred " one to account for their terror. It was quite enough for them, as for the Esquimaux and the Kafirs, that the man in danger of his life had been irrevocably doomed by the unseen powers.

V

Among the "accidents" and "misfortunes" which, on overtaking a man, at the same time forbid any help for him, and even ordain his complete ruin, shipwreck holds the first place with certain peoples, like the Fijians, for instance. The rule used to be that those who were "salvaged" should be killed and eaten. "Those who escape from shipwreck are supposed to be saved that they

---

[1] Lichtenstein : *Reisen im südlichen Afrika*, i. p. 421 (note).
[2] Holmberg : " Ueber die Völker des russischen Amerika," *Acta societatis scientiarum fennicæ*, iv. pp. 317–18.
[3] Quoted by R. H. Codrington : " Religious Beliefs and Practices in Melanesia," *J.A.I.*, x. p. 302.

may be eaten, and very rarely are they allowed to live. Recently at Wakaya, fourteen or sixteen persons who lost their canoe at sea were cooked and eaten." [1] A chief and his followers were fishing on a reef near the coast when a canoe was shipwrecked quite close to them. " 'Now we shall have something good to eat,' said the fishermen, approaching the wreck. 'You shall not touch a single one of these men,' said the chief (who had been converted), 'I mean to save their lives.' 'That is impossible,' said they; 'they *must* die, they have been shipwrecked.' " [2] " A canoe belonging to Ovalau set sail for Gau, but was capsized on the voyage. The crew continued to keep hold of the vessel, which drifted towards the island of their destination. They even arrived there in safety; but unhappily, to use the nautical phrase, 'they had salt water in their faces.' They landed at a spot where they would have been welcomed, had not the sad accident happened to them. As soon as they reached the beach, they were all clubbed, cooked, and eaten." [3]

Missionaries who have borne witness to so cruel and seemingly inexplicable a method of procedure, have not failed to inquire into the reason and origin of it. " The murder of those who are wrecked," says Waterhouse, " is a recognized institution, not originating in simple cruelty; it is rather the result of education. On the discovery of anyone 'swimming for life,' the oven in which they are to be cooked is forthwith prepared. It would appear from research that the victims of this savage custom are usually natives of the Fiji Islands, to whose misfortunes only is this severe penalty attached. Such are looked upon as abandoned by the gods, and the slaughter of them is considered acceptable to the deities, and indeed necessary. . . [On the other hand] there are many small clans now living in various parts of the group, who are the offspring of Friendly Islanders who were cast away on these Islands." [4] Father Joseph Chevron also writes : " People well acquainted

[1] Th. Williams : *Fiji and the Fijians*, i. p. 210 (1858).
[2] *Wesleyan Missionary Notices*, March 1852. (Letter from Rev. J. Waterhouse.)
[3] Rev. J. Waterhouse : *The King and People of Fiji*, p. 201 (1853).
[4] Ibid., pp. 334–5.

with the matter have assured me that in their opinion it is more than a right, it is indeed a religious duty to devour the shipwrecked wretches who are cast on their shores by tempest, were it even their own father or mother ; if possible, in the case of Europeans they do not wait till the ship has foundered before they carry out this monstrous obligation." [1]

The Fijian who fell into the sea was not ignorant of the fate which awaited him if he succeeded in swimming ashore. The Rev. R. B. Lyth relates the story of a shipwrecked man who managed to conceal himself after reaching the shore. He was at length discovered by a Fijian man. He went boldly up to him, and would follow him into the town, though the other very much wanted him to remain in the path until the chief was informed of his arrival. . . . When they came to the town the people soon gathered round their victim, touched his eyes with their hands, and began to say to him: " Oh yes, it is salt water," meaning, " You have been wrecked ; we must kill you." [2]

The slaughter of shipwrecked persons, therefore, as the missionaries have realized, was a sacred obligation which no one would venture to contravene. By virtue of the same theory, objects which were in a canoe lost at sea could no longer be the property of their shipwrecked owner if by some extraordinary chance he should survive. " A native priest of Lomaloma set sail in company with some canoes manned by Christians, and his canoe was shipwrecked. Those on board escaped by clinging to the outrigger, which had become detached. The Christians heard of the disaster, and going down to the shore saw that the priest's canoe had drifted in with the tide. They took out the mats and other things they found, and returned them to the owner. For some time, however, he refused to receive them, saying that it was contrary to the Fijian custom." [3] Possibly he esteemed himself fortunate in having to deal with Christians in the matter, and escaping from shipwreck without expiating his disaster by death. In any case, how-

[1] *Annales de la Propagation de la foi*, xiv. p. 192 (1842).
[2] *Wesleyan Missionary Notices*, vii. p. 150. (Letter from Rev. R. B. Lyth. December 1848.)
[3] Rev. J. Calvert: *Missionary Labours among the Cannibals*, p. 300 (1858).

ever, he was afraid that by accepting the things he had lost with the canoe he might aggravate his misdeed, and draw upon himself a fresh calamity.

Similar customs, as we know, are met with in many islanders and maritime peoples. " A very barbarous custom exists on this coast (Borneo) . . . wrecks and their crews belong to the chief of the district, where they may suffer severe misfortune." [1] The mystic nature of this custom is specially marked in New Zealand. " A wreck of any kind, or even a canoe of friends and relatives upsetting off the village, and drifting on shore where the village was, became the property of the people of that village ; although it might be that the people in the canoe had all got safely to land or were coming by special invitation to visit that very village ; perhaps to lament for their dead ! Strangest of all, the unfortunate people in the upset canoe would be the very first to resent—even to fighting—any kind alleviation of this strange law ! " [2]

Colenso cannot sufficiently express his astonishment at this custom which, he says, consorts neither with reason nor humanity ; but in the light of the circumstances which precede it, it becomes intelligible. The accident has revealed that the shipwrecked persons are victims of the anger of unseen powers, who are evidently punishing them for some misdeed. It is not the villagers' duty to screen them from its consequences ; to do so would be dangerous, both for the rash folk who risked it and also for the shipwrecked people themselves, for they would thus be in danger of a (possibly graver) misfortune, since the one that had already befallen them had been checked and hindered. Therefore they simply *must* be despoiled of their possessions. Any helpful intervention, however well-intentioned, would prove fatal to them, and they would reject it by force, if need were. The only acceptable interference is that which secures the accomplishment of the decree that has been made against them—a case similar to the one in which the Esquimaux thrust back into the water the poor half-drowned wretch who is trying to save himself.

[1] Sir Spenser St. John : *Life in the Forests of the Far East*, i. p. 295.
[2] W. Colenso : " On the Maori Races of New Zealand," *Transactions of the New Zealand Institute*, i. p. 25 (1868).

We are reminded of the Indian of New France who, having seen himself in a dream at the mercy of an enemy tribe, next day begged his friends to fasten him to the stake and make him undergo the tortures which are inflicted on prisoners. " His friends did not hesitate to perform this service for him, and he was so severely burned that it took him six months to recover. But in a dream he had seen himself visited by calamity, and since the dream may be believed, he considered himself doomed by the unseen powers, and his friends helped him to undergo his sentence. Well then, being shipwrecked is a revelation of the anger of invisible forces, just as being taken prisoner by the enemy is ; hence it is both the duty and the just concern of the shipwrecked man to suffer the loss of his possessions. Those who are his friends must help him in this. In spite of appearances, their conduct does " consort both with reason and humanity."

It is not only in the case of shipwreck, however, that this custom is enjoined. Every serious accident, and a death in particular, may give occasion for it. For example, with the Maoris of New Zealand: " At the death of a chief, a *taua*, or stripping party, came and stripped the family of all eatables and other movables, digging up root crops, and seizing and spearing tame pigs, and devouring and carrying them off ; and if by any chance the family were not so stripped, they would be sure deeply to resent the neglect ; as much on account of their being lowered (that is, not taken notice of) as for the violation of the *tapu*, in failing to carry it out. Again, in case of any infringement of the *tapu*, or in any error or wrong, real or supposed, the *taua* would be sure to pay its visit ; such *taua* was not unfrequently a friendly one ! at once quickly made up of the closest relatives and neighbours to the offender ; for, as he must be stripped and mulcted, they might as well do it as others, and so keep his goods from wholly going to strangers." [1]

[1] W. Colenso: ibid., p. 41. Note a similar custom prevailing in the Fiji Islands. " On Vanua Levu death is a signal for plunder, the nearest relatives rushing to the house to appropriate all they could seize belonging to those who lived there with the deceased. Valuables are therefore removed and hidden in time."—*Fiji and the Fijians*, i. p. 187. (Thos. Williams.)

This is a most valuable piece of evidence. It not only confirms the preceding one, but it makes its meaning clear. From the expressions used by Colenso, does it not appear that the *taua* is considered equally necessary, that the family which has to undergo it has been visited by misfortune or death, and that a violation of taboo must have taken place ? The reason for the custom is the same in both cases, because both involve the same collective representations. Misfortune reveals a wrongdoing ; it is equivalent to wrongdoing, and it, too, must be expiated.

In the early days of colonization, this custom of *taua* had been applied to white men as well as to the natives, and they naturally could not understand it at all. " This calamity " (a fire), wrote Earle in 1827, " had made us acquainted with another of their barbarous customs ; which is, whenever a misfortune happens to a community, or an individual, every person, even the friends of his own tribe, fall upon him and strip him of all he has remaining. As an unfortunate fish, when struck by a harpoon, is instantly surrounded and devoured by his companions, so in New Zealand, when a chief is killed his former friends plunder his widow and children ; and they, in revenge, ill-use and even murder their slaves ; thus one misfortune gives birth to various cruelties. During the fire, our allies proved themselves the most adroit and active thieves imaginable ; though previously to that event we had never lost an article, although everything we possessed was open to them." [1] It is abundantly clear that it is not a case of robbery here, any more than it was a case of pillage when the shipwrecked persons were despoiled of their all. The New Zealand natives are fulfilling a sacred duty towards their allies, and should they fail therein they would believe they had deserved reproaches, or possibly something worse, from them. The disaster showed that the Europeans were in the dangerous situation of persons attacked by the invisible powers on account of some violation of taboo, and in order to extricate them from the difficulty, the sentence must be rigorously carried out, and their friends could not be too zealous in despoiling them.

[1] A. Earle : *A Narrative of a Nine Months' Residence in New Zealand,* p. 96. (Christchurch, N.Z., 1909.)

Elsdon Best was also a witness of similar occurrences. " The old custom of *muru*," says he, " is rapidly passing away, but in former times it was strictly carried out. It was applied in many ways. For example, should a person meet with some accident or other trouble, a party of the tribe would proceed to despoil him and his family of their portable personal property. This was also done sometimes at the death of a person ; his family would thus lose their food, etc., which would be seized and taken by the plundering party, who often acted in a very rough manner." [1]

" At this forest hamlet we were treated to an illustration of the ancient custom of *muru* or *kai taionga*, i.e. the taking forcibly or demanding payment for some injury or loss sustained by the person or persons from whom such payment is demanded. A girl of this place had been assaulted some time previously, hence our party demanded compensation. Why people should pay for the privilege of being afflicted by some trouble is a somewhat difficult problem for the European mind to solve, though it appears to be simple enough to the Maoris." [2] It is not an insoluble difficulty however. Elsdon Best's *muru* is evidently nothing but the *taua* described in more precise terms by Earle and Colenso, for the custom was evidently flourishing vigorously in their time. There is so little mystery about it that Colenso fully recognized its significance, and himself compared it, and quite rightly too, with the penalties connected with the violation of a taboo.

Falling into the enemy's hands and being made prisoner is a misfortune, the results of which are comparable with being shipwrecked, struck by lightning, etc. Like these, it reveals the anger of the unseen powers, doubtless offended by some misdeed of the victim's. It therefore inspires the same feelings. Thus, in New Zealand, " the slave . . . if skilled, or if active and industrious, and willing to serve his new masters, . . . was sure to rise and have some influence ; which, however great his rank might have been in his own tribe, he would never again have there

---

even if he could return. . . . This . . . is easily understood,
when it is considered that his own tribe attributed his being
enslaved to the anger of the *atua* (evil demon) and that
by his becoming so he had lost his ***tapu*** ; and if they were
to compassionate and restore, they, too, would incur the
anger of the ***atua***, which they dreaded above all things." [1]
Earle had already remarked: " If a slave effect his escape
to his own part of the country, he is there treated with
contempt." [2] In North America, too: " If a man of any
nation, even a warrior, who is made prisoner and happens
to have been adopted or enslaved, should eventually succeed
in escaping to return to his own relatives, they will not
receive him, nor recognize him as belonging to them any
more." [3] " If any of the tribe " (the Tshimshian Indians
of British Columbia) " are captured and made slaves, they
lose the confidence of the nation " (should they ever return),
" neither will these use any influence they may have with
an adjoining tribe, to regain the liberty of their relatives." [4]
We can easily see the reason of this. Colenso discerned
it in New Zealand, and it is enjoined on primitive mentality
everywhere.

In the primitive's eyes misfortune is a disqualification,
and he who has been attacked by it has at the same time
suffered moral degeneration. As an object of the wrath
of the unseen powers he becomes a danger to his friends
and to the social group, and they avoid his presence. Thus,
in the New Hebrides, missionaries had at first been made
welcome, but later on several misfortunes occurred. " The
natives had pitied them in their illness, but they were wholly
indisposed to give any further heed to their instructions,
or have anything more to do with the new religion. They
attributed the fact of the teachers having been ill, and of
two of them having died, to the displeasure of Alema, their
principal god ; and thence inferred that their god must

---

[1] W. Colenso : " On the Maori Races of New Zealand," *Transactions o
the New Zealand Institute*, i. p. 22.

[2] A. Earle : *A Narrative of a Nine Months' Residence in New Zealand*,
p. 124.

[3] J. Carver : *Voyage dans l'Amérique septentrionale*, p. 258.

[4] H. Beaver: *Original Information respecting the Natives of the North-
West Coast of America*. Extracts from the Papers and Proceedings of the
Aborigines Protection Society, ii. v. p. 135 (1841).

be more powerful than the god of the teachers. The consequence was, that for several months the teachers were entirely deserted, and were often in great straits." [1]

" Res est sacra miser." These words express exactly what the primitive thinks and feels at the sight of an unfortunate person, that is, if we give the word " sacra " its *full* meaning—not " worthy of respect and consideration," but " placed in a special condition which does not allow of its being approached or touched." The missionary, Casalis, has found a very happy way of expressing this. " In the native tongue," says he, " ' happiness ' and ' purity ' are synonymous terms. When a Basuto says that his heart is ' black ' or ' dirty,' it may equally mean that his heart is ' impure ' or ' unhappy ' ; and when he says his heart is ' white ' or ' clean,' it is only from his explanation that one can find out whether he means that he is innocent or joyous. Our earliest converts could not be persuaded that there would be no profanation in approaching the Holy Table when they were in trouble. . . . They consider the sufferings and accidents of all kinds which may befall humanity as an impurity, a stain, and give that name to them." [2]

VI

Among primitive peoples almost everywhere illness, when serious or prolonged, is regarded as a defilement and a condemnation. He who is attacked by it is looked upon as " res sacra " therefore. The others stop attending to his wants; they manifest towards him an indifference which seems positively inhuman to us (but which in reality is nothing but fear), and finally, they leave him to his fate. Father Gumilla, for instance, expresses his perplexity on this point thus : " I have never been able to understand how the Indians (and I am speaking here of all the races in question) can reconcile the great love which parents manifest for their children, and the affection, whether much or little, that married pairs feel for each other, with the

[1] Rev. A. W. Murray : *Missions in Western Polynesia*, p. 140.
[2] Casalis : *Les Bassoutos*, p. 269.

indifference, amounting almost to total disregard, shown for these same beings when they are ill. Yet more, how is one to reconcile the savage and inhuman indifference one has witnessed, with the tears, groans, and noisy demonstrations of grief one hears from these people during the funeral and its attendant ceremonies ? "

" This indifference is carried so far that even when the sick or dying man is the master of the house and the father of a large family which is dependent entirely on him, nobody troubles about him. Nobody cares whether he eats or drinks. From the attitude of these people, one would imagine either that they have no feelings, or else that they are anxious for his death. Yet neither of these is really the case. When the hour for the repast has arrived, they place by the hammock where the invalid is lying the same food that they give to everybody else. If he eats it, it is well ; but if he does not even taste it, that is also all right. Throughout the course of his illness he never hears a word of comfort nor is he ever encouraged to swallow a mouthful. . . . You will think that I am exaggerating, but whatever terms I may use, they can never express the unfeeling and pitiless severity of this attitude." [1]

Father Gumilla himself, however, realizes that this indifference is only an apparent one. If from one particular moment then, the Indians cease troubling in any way about their sick, it must either be because it appears as if their care were henceforward useless, or else there is something stronger than their sympathy which is opposed to their giving these attentions. That is exactly what happens in a great many tribes. In Paraguay, " whether the sick man belongs to the lowest class, or whether he is a cacique (chief), respected and feared, the doctor can do no more, and others take no more trouble. Whether he is able to sleep or not, whether he takes nourishment or goes without, matters little. They bring him a little of what the others are having. If he puts it aside for lack of appetite, saying, ' I am not hungry,' they do not insist. . . . The very utmost which natural compassion leads the people of the house

---

[1] P. Gumilla : *El Orinoco illustrado*, pp. 235–6 ; cf. Maximilien de Wied Neuwied : *Voyage au Brésil*, iii. pp. 170–1 of the French translation.

to do is to drive away the flies which settle on his face. If he complains, uttering the usual interjection ' Ay ! ' they answer him by a word of affection. . . ." [1] According to this testimony there is a total absence of all solicitude, as in the case of the Indians of the Orinoco, but it does not proceed from indifference, since the affection of those around is manifested in a slight degree towards the invalid. Spix and Martius merely remark that they do not trouble about nourishing food for the sick. " The most energetic measure they employ in many illnesses is a starvation diet ; they carry it to its extreme, often advantageously in fever cases, but on the other hand almost to the point of death for those who are suffering from chronic maladies." [2] In another volume, however, Von Martius, after having spoken of the " diabolical method " of treating illness, draws attention to the native attitude to sick people, and gives the reason of it. " If the cause of the sickness is not at once evident, the person attacked by it is henceforth considered to be quite another being, one who no longer has the same relations with his family as hitherto ; he is possessed, having succumbed to the power of hostile influences. He suffers from a malady from which his own power alone can save him (possibly with the help of some of the forces of Nature). His very touch has in it something disturbing and dangerous ; therefore he is left as much as possible to himself ; others shrink from him in fear." [3]

Mr. Grubb, a recent investigator, was a witness of this apparent indifference and this abandonment in the Lenguas of Grand Chaco. " As long as there is hope of recovery, the wizard and the friends show great kindness to the sufferer, and do all that they can for him, and I have frequently noticed instances of very careful and tender nursing as far as their limited knowledge went. But when once the hope of life has been extinguished, both sick, wizard, and family give up the struggle. The patient is then, to a great extent, regarded as already dead, and little further attention is paid to him. When death seems

[1] P. José Sanchez, Labrador : *El Paraguay católico*, ii. pp. 38–9.
[2] Spix und Martius : *Reise in Brasilien*, iii. p. 1281). (Rio Yapura.)
[3] C. F. Ph. von Martius : *Das Naturell, die Krankheiten, das Arzttum und die Heilmittel der Urbewohner Brasiliens*, pp. 132–33.

imminent, the dying person is removed from the village and laid outside, with a mat thrown over him, although he may be quite conscious. They think nothing of his discomfort at this time. The hot noontide sun may be pouring down upon him, . . . or tropical rain may be falling, or perhaps the cold south winds of winter may be chilling him. . . . Quite close to him preparations are being made for a hasty departure (for his interment). . . . No kindly word is spoken to him, no friendly hand holds his. . . . Oftentimes he suffers the agonies of thirst, but no one attends to his needs. And yet these Indians are not unkindly ; they grieve for their dying friend ; they will miss him and mourn his loss, but their cruel belief overcomes all natural feelings." [1]

The cruel belief to which Grubb refers is the idea that the most awful misfortunes will follow if a dead man should remain unburied when the sun goes down. His presence among them during the night inspires them with abject terror, and they therefore are always in a hurry to be rid of him. It often happens that in their eyes a dying man is regarded as already dead. (By many primitives, life is considered to have ceased *before* the respiration has quite stopped and the heart no longer beats.) At such a moment the Lenguas think only of getting rid of the dead, and their fear leaves room for no other feeling. But during the period, which is often a long one, which elapses between the time when all hope is given up, and the period of his death agony, if the sick man is abandoned, and all appear indifferent to his needs and his distress, it is clear that it is a different "cruel belief" which causes such treatment. However much they may pity him, they dare not approach him because it entails too much danger, since, like the Kamschatkan who has fallen into the water, and the woman about to die in childbirth among the Tlinkit people, like the man struck by lightning in South Africa, and the shipwrecked native of the Fiji Isles, he is henceforth " res sacra." In all these cases, the apparently unfeeling attitude of the immediate circle is accounted for in the same way.

[1] W. B. Grubb : *An Unknown People in an Unknown Land*, pp. 161–2 (1911).

That in the opinion of certain of the South American natives, serious and incurable illness is thus one of the forms of that "accident," that "misfortune," which reveals the wrath of the unseen powers against the one attainted, we may conclude from the attitude they maintain with regard to the care of their sick. But with respect to other races which have progressed further, and whose ideas of the unseen powers have assumed more or less of an anthropomorphic view, such as certain Polynesian races, for instance, the testimony on this point is more explicit. Here are some of the most characteristic features. "As soon as an individual was afflicted with any disorder," says Ellis, "he was considered as under the ban of the gods; by some crime or the influence of some enemy, he was supposed to have become obnoxious to their anger, of which his malady was the result. These ideas relative to the origin of diseases, had a powerful tendency to stifle every feeling of sympathy and compassion, and to restrain all from the exercise of those acts of kindness that are so acceptable to the afflicted, and afford such alleviation to their sufferings. The attention of the relatives and friends was directed to the gods, and their greatest efforts were made to appease their anger by offerings, and to remove the continuance of these effects by prayers and incantations. The simple medicine administered was considered more as the vehicle or medium by which the god would act, than as possessing any power itself to arrest the progress of disease. If their prayers, offerings, and remedies were found unavailing, the gods were considered implacable, and the offending person was doomed to perish. Some heinous crime was supposed to have been committed."[1] In another passage he says: "Every disease was supposed to be the effect of direct supernatural agency, and to be inflicted by the gods for some crime against the taboo, of which the sufferers had been guilty, or in consequence of some offering made by an enemy to procure their destruction. Hence, it is probable, in a great measure, arises their neglect and cruel treatment of their sick. . . . The natives acknowledged that they possessed articles of poison which, when taken in the food,

[1] Rev. W. Ellis: *Polynesian Researches*, iii. pp. 46–8 (1829).

would produce convulsions and death, but those e ects they considered more the result of the god's displeasure, operating by means of these substitutes, than the effects of the poisons themselves. Those who died of eating fish, of which several kinds found on their coast are at certain seasons unsuitable for food, were supposed to die by the influence of the gods, who, they imagined, had entered the fish, or rendered it offensive. . . . Those who were killed in battle were also supposed to die from the influence of the gods, who, they fancied, had actually entered the weapons of their murderers. Hence those who died suddenly were said to be seized by the god." [1]

These expressions are perfectly clear. If nothing is done for these sick people, it is because the natives believe that their trouble would be absolutely useless. The sick man has been smitten by the " gods " ; the only way to save him is to persuade the gods to be appeased and pardon him. If they tried a direct means of attacking the evil (which they would not anyhow be able to do, seeing what their ideas of health and disease are), by thwarting the will of the gods, they would only exasperate them still further, increase the sufferings of the sick man, and draw down the divine anger upon fresh victims. Prayers, offerings, supplications, incantations, and sacrifices can be of use, but they are the only therapeutics possible in such a case. Moreover, the wrath of the gods is attributable either to the influence of an enemy who has gained them over to his side, or else to transgression of some sort. The gravity of the crime is commensurable with that of the illness. If the latter proves to be mortal, it shows that the crime was unpardonable, and in that case it is the more necessary that fear should stifle pity.

Ellis's testimony is confirmed by that of many others. In the Wallis Islands, for example, " these people believe that all illness comes from the offended gods, and therefore they hasten to placate them by offerings of *cava*. Some of them take their sick to a chief, so that his authority may render the intercession more acceptable to the divinity." [2]

---

[1] Rev. W. Ellis: *Polynesian Researches*, i. pp. 395–6.
[2] *Annales de la Propagation de la foi*, xiii. p. 12 (1841). (P. Bataillon.)

At Futuna : " Our islanders view disease and infirmity as the result of divine wrath alone. As soon as anyone falls ill, they hasten to the temple of the god who *wants to eat him*. They carry to these temples, fruit, cloth, sometimes the most cherished of all their possessions, so that they may appease the evil genius by these offerings." [1]   On the other hand, Turner speaks highly of the humanity of the natives in Samoa.   " The treatment of the sick, was as it is now, invariably humane, and all that could be expected. They wanted for no kind of food which they might desire, night or day, if it was at all in the power of their friends to procure it.   In the event of the disease assuming a dangerous form, messengers were despatched to friends at a distance, that they might have an opportunity of being in time to see, and say farewell to the departing relatives." [2]   If it were so, the Samoans undoubtedly were exceptional, for missionaries and travellers nearly always testify to the contrary.   In Savage Island (Niué) for instance, " the treatment of the sick was very barbarous. They were removed into the bush and placed in a temporary hut, where they were left until they might recover or die. Their relatives took food to them, but no one remained with them ; this practice was owing to the great horror they had of disease." [3]

It is perhaps among the Maoris of New Zealand that one can best see how the abandonment of the sick and the apparent lack of feeling in their relatives arose out of the mystic idea of illness.   " No remedy is known," says Fr. Servant, " for internal maladies.   A person who is attacked by one stretches himself on the ground in despair, and sends to consult a Maori priest to find out whether he can reckon on any chance of recovery. . . . If the auguries are unfavourable, the priest declares that the sick man will die.   From that moment they refuse him all food, even his family abandons him, leaving him a prey to the god who, they believe, is devouring his flesh and intestines.   Thus the prediction of the superstitious priest never fails to be

---

[1] *Annales de la Propagation de la foi*, xiii. p. 378.
[2] Rev. G. Turner : *Nineteen Years in Polynesia*, p. 225.
[3] A. W. Murray : *Missions in Western Polynesia*, p. 367.

fulfilled, because the patient always dies, if not of disease, at any rate of hunger." [1] They no longer dare offer him food, because the atua (god) has taken up his abode in his stomach, and on this account, both the stomach and the patient have become tapu (taboo). "The youngest and favourite wife of Tipi, the principal chief of the place, fell ill to-day. According to the universal native custom on such occurrences, she was removed from his house to an open shed near it, and became tapu, so that she might eat no food." [2]

The most exact description of these customs is probably that given by J. L. Nicholas. "No sooner does a person arrive at a certain stage of illness among them, than they believe the unhappy creature under the wrath of the etua ; and, incapable of accounting for the disease with which he is afflicted, as of applying a remedy to it, they can only consider it as a preternatural visitation of retributive justice, which it would be impious to resist by any human expedient. Many a poor sufferer who, with a little ordinary attention, might soon be restored to health and vigour, is devoted by this horrid superstition to perish in the very midst of his kindred, without a single effort being made for his recovery." [3] Whilst the indisposition is of a nature that admits of more or less alleviation, it is allowable to relieve the patient by any means at command, and to help on his recovery. But should the illness be persistent and increase in intensity, the wrath of the unseen powers can no longer be ignored, and the sick man becomes tapu. Nicholas was a witness of the long-drawn-out suffering of a Maori chief who was dying for weeks. "They insisted that no human being should administer to his wants while he yet survived. The reason of their laying the poor fellow under this horrible interdict was because they now believed that the etua was fully determined to destroy him ; and for this purpose had made a firm lodgment in his stomach, whence no mortal power durst venture to expel him, nor would he once quit his position, but remain there, increasing the agonies of the

[1] "Société de Marie," Annales des missions d'Océanie, i. pp. 93-4 (1841).
[2] E. J. Wakefield : Adventure in New Zealand, i. p. 49 (1839-44).
[3] J. L. Nicholas : Narrative of a Voyage to New Zealand, ii. p. 303 (1817).

sufferer till he thought proper to put an end to his existence.
. . . Though the immediate family of Duaterra still continued
to evince the same deep and tender affection as before,
still they agreed with his other dependants in excluding
him from any further assistance . . . and leaving him now
entirely at the disposal of the *etua*, they were studious
only about providing for his interment." [1]

The traveller asks for news of the sick man. They tell
him " the *etua* was then preying upon his entrails, and that
the chief would be killed as soon as they were all devoured.
This notion, much more than the complication under which
they labour, accelerates the death of sick people in New
Zealand. So strongly is it impressed upon men and their
friends, that when the symptoms appear at all dangerous,
they think any sort of remedy would be impious ; and however afflicted they may be at the loss of them, they never
once murmur against the mysterious vulture which gnaws
them away according to his appetite." [2] A Roman Catholic
priest says, too: " If it seems certain that a sick native cannot hope to recover from the disease that has attacked him,
his relatives often refuse him all food whatever ; after
having arranged his bed as comfortably as they can, they
go off and leave him, pretending that ' their god is eating
him.' This expression is so common among the Polynesians
that they are constantly heard to say : ' So-and-so died in
battle ; his brother *was eaten by the god*,' i.e. died of illness.
In spite of this apparent hard-heartedness towards the
sick, do not imagine that our Islanders do not feel the loss
of their relatives and friends ; the old custom of lamenting
a death by tearing one's limbs and face, is by no means
given up yet." [3]

What causes the *etua* thus to decide on the death of
a poor wretch ? We have found that the reasons for this
" dooming " may be very varied, but the violation of a
taboo holds the first place. Here is another instance
(again noted in New Zealand), which demonstrates very
clearly the preconnection between this violation and a

[1] J. H. Nicholas : ibid. ii. pp. 165–7.
[2] Ibid., ii. p. 170.
[3] *Annales de la Propagation de la foi*, xiv. p. 210. (R. P. Petitjean, Wan-
garoa, N.Z.)

mortal illness. "Rangitatau, a girl of Rotorua, who for some time lived at the Mission station of Otawhao married and had a female child. One cold night, when on a visit to Taramatakitaki, a great chief, she borrowed a garment from him to wrap herself in; during the night the insects annoyed her so much that, according to the native custom, she caught and ate them. Next day, the infant was taken ill; this she attributed to her having eaten the sacred insects upon the *tapu* garment of the chief, for which the *atuas* were angry, and had punished her by afflicting her child with disease. The child grew worse, and she thereupon strangled it, thinking it was bewitched." [1] Such an action seems at first absolutely incredible, but the mother knew that her child was doomed. As the malady became worse, the wrath of the *atua* was revealed as implacable; what was the use of struggling against it, and what means could the mother employ? Was it even allowable to go on suckling the child? We recall the confession of the Nias native who killed his little sister at his despairing parents' order, because the "priest" had told them that she could not live, on account of her father's violation of taboo before she was born.

As long as the malady has not assumed a deadly character, the relatives hope that the unseen powers will not prove inexorable, and they do all that they can to persuade them to relent. Just as a European family is ready to devote its last penny to physicians, surgeons, and druggists, in its desire to obtain relief for its sick relative, so do the primitives despoil themselves of all their possessions in order to consult the augurs, and to make sacrifices and offerings. "Should they see their father or mother in danger of death, they (the Fijians) would not hesitate to cut off the first joint of the ring finger in the hope of appeasing the wrath of their deities, and should the invalid not recover after this first offering has been made, they will mutilate themselves afresh, cutting off another joint at each crisis, and amputating in turn all their fingers and even their wrist, convinced that this final sacrifice will satisfy the vengeance of the gods and

---

[1] G. F. Angas: *Savage Life and Scenes in Australia and New Zealand*, ii. pp. 143-4 (1847).

recovery will be certain. . . . Nearly all the natives I saw at Vita Levu were one or two fingers short."[1]

In South Africa, the same collective representations give rise to a similar procedure. " When the natives (the Basutos) are seriously ill, they are to be found lying on the ground, barely covered with a worn-out kaross, and deprived of all capable and affectionate ministrations. Their nearest relatives seem to be afraid of them, or rather, I suspect that laziness makes them afraid of the trouble the care of the invalid may prove, and so they keep away from them." [2] The truth is that these natives, like other primitives, are afraid of touching the sick whom they consider " doomed." Casalis clearly recognized that the Basutos place sick people in the vast category of " res sacræ." " Death and everything that directly precedes or follows it is the greatest of all impurities. Therefore sick people, those who have touched or buried a corpse, or dug a grave for it, the persons who inadvertently walk over a tomb, or seat themselves on it, the nearest relatives of a dead man, murderers, and warriors who have slain their adversaries in combat, are all considered unclean. Cattle taken from the enemy, the town where an epidemic is raging, the tribes who have fallen a prey to warfare or disaster, corn which has been blighted or ravaged by locusts, huts or people struck by lightning, are also all considered unclean, and treated as such."[3] The last of these categories includes the objects of the wrath of unseen powers, and sick people who do not appear likely to recover are in similar case.

Persons smitten with blindness are not, as a rule, abandoned, but since misfortune is held to disqualify them, they sink to a very low level. Among the Bechuana tribes, " as soon as a man has the misfortune to become blind, even if he be one of the great chiefs, he is no longer numbered with the living, so to speak. They say of him *oshule*, he is dead.

" Nevertheless, they look after their blind, that is to say, they give them something to eat and drink, but they

[1] *Annales de la Propagation de la foi*, xvi. p. 192. (P. Joseph Chevron.
[2] *Missions évangéliques*, xxxii. p. 322. (M. Schrumpf.)
[3] E. Casalis : *Les Bassoutos*, p. 270.

do not accord them the honour and respect they formerly showed them. Not long ago a Mochuana said: ' With us, it is all up with a blind man ; we make him sit with the women ; he never takes part in our councils again. Nevertheless, we do not refuse blind people food, and in this we behave better than the Korannas, who, when they are going to leave a place, never let the blind follow them ; they leave them in some enclosed place, with a small supply of milk, which will hardly last more than a meal or two.' " [1]

The wounded are treated like the sick, and for the same mystic reasons. Natives wounded by wild beasts (which in such a case are not ordinary animals, but the agents of a wizard, or of the unseen powers), specially inspire fear, and their friends shun them. " A custom prevails among all the Bechuanas whom I have visited of removing to a distance from the towns and villages, persons who have been wounded. Two young men, who had been wounded by the poisoned arrows of the Bushmen, were thus removed from the Kuruman. Having visited them . . . I made inquiries but could learn no reason, except that it was a custom. This unnatural practice exposed the often helpless individual to great danger ; for, if not well attended during the night, his paltry little hut, or rather shelter from the sun and wind, would be assailed by the hyena or lion. A catastrophe of this kind occurred a short time before my arrival among the Baralong. The son of one of the principal chiefs, a fine young man, had been wounded by a buffalo ; he was, according to custom, placed on the outside of the village till he should recover ; a portion of food was daily sent, and a person appointed to make his fire for the evening. The fire went out ; and the helpless man, notwithstanding his piteous cries, was carried off by a lion, and devoured. Some might think that this practice originated in the treatment of infectious diseases, such as leprosy, but the only individual I ever saw thus affected was not separated." [2]

Can one imagine that this chief light-heartedly exposed his son to such a risk ? Why was he obliged to conform with this custom ? Dr. Moffat, without knowing it perhaps,

---

[1] *Missions évangéliques*, xxi. p. 105. (M. Lauga.)
[2] Robert Moffat : *Missionary Labours and Scenes in South Africa*, p. 465.

gave the solution of the puzzle, when he spoke of infection For the Bechuanas, it is indeed a case of avoiding infection ; but it is infection of a mystic character. The accident is a revelation. If the chief's son was wounded by the buffalo, it was in consequence of his having been " doomed," either by a wizard or by the unseen powers—by incensed ancestors, for instance. Perhaps, although Moffat does not say so, and possibly may not have known it, they had had recourse to divination to find out what the cause might be, and had learnt that the wounded man had brought upon himself the anger of the unseen powers by the violation of a taboo or some other departure from established custom. In such a case he is not only attacked by misfortune, but he becomes " res sacra," and, as such, he is a bringer of woe. He must therefore be isolated until his recovery shall have proved that the wrath of the gods is appeased.

A similar case occurred among the Kafirs. " A wolf entered the hut and carried off a fine girl who was sleeping just within the doorway. Her cries speedily brought the men to her help, and the wolf was compelled to abandon his prey. The child's cheek was, however, so torn by the teeth of the animal, and it was thought that she must be abandoned, according to their custom, as not likely to recover." [1]

In the case of the Sakalaves of Madagascar, " if an accident happens (if a man is wounded by a crocodile), he is taken prisoner and accused, for he must certainly have committed some crime against the ancestors, or disregarded some *fady* (taboo). It is a terrible thing to be bitten by a crocodile. Up to now, I have seen two such instances. . . . The unhappy wretch runs the risk of dying on the spot, for he is considered accursed. He is obliged to hide himself ; nobody can have anything to do with him, and once recovered, he must never speak of his accident. The spirits had pointed him out, and if he recalls the occurrence it will cost him dear." [2] On account of his having been wounded, he has been excommunicated, like the man who fell into the water in Kamschatka. Again, in French Guinea, " if by chance

---

[1] W. Shaw : *The Story of my Mission to South Africa*, p. 503 (1860).
[2] *Missions évangéliques*, lxxxv. 2. pp. 227-8. (M. Rusillon.)

a leopard or a crocodile should have killed anyone in a village here," says Madrolle, "the whole village must be entirely evacuated and destroyed, and a heavy penalty is demanded from the family to which the victim belonged" (here we recall the *taua* and the *muru* of New Zealand), "'for,' say the chiefs: 'your family must be notorious villains, and have committed many crimes, for God to send leopards and crocodiles to punish you.'"[1] A traveller of the seventeenth century, in a very confused report, does, however, manage to show both the fear that wounded or very sick people inspire in the natives of the west coast of Africa, and the affection they feel for them. "They have no compassion for one another, hardly even giving water to the wounded, whom they leave to die like dogs, most frequently abandoned even by their wives and children. At Frederickton we saw a sick man forsaken by all, and the Moors wondered how we dared approach him. Our surgeon cured him, for his malady was an overloaded stomach. Returning to land, we saw him drinking with all the rest, who were caressing him fondly, yet a week before that his wife and children had abandoned him, because they did not know what he was suffering from."[2]

Everything, in fact, depends upon the course taken by the malady, and the feelings change according to the prognosis. If, contrary to all expectation, the sick man recovers, he is no longer a "doomed" person to be shunned, and left to suffer alone; he is a friend welcomed back with transports of joy, received without fear of incurring the wrath of the unseen powers. Hence it is that there are so many practices of divination among all these peoples as soon as the state of a sick man appears to be serious. They are desirous of finding out whether he will recover and so it is that the divination, as often as not, is at the same time a prayer, and that, moreover, what is predicted as certain appears to primitive mentality to be actually existent.

Should the reply obtained from the augur be definitely

[1] Arcin: *La Guinée française,* p. 431.
[2] Villault-Bellefond: *Relation des côtes d'Afrique appelées Guinée,* pp. 363-4 (1669).

unfavourable, therefore, all hope is at an end. The prayer has not been granted, the sick person will die, and his death is already a reality ; accordingly he will be abandoned. " I once saw," says Rowley, speaking of British Central Africa, " a woman anxiously watching her sick child ; greater kindness no one could have shown. Two men came into the village for the night, one of whom was a medicine-man His skill was quickly sought by the mother. He looked at the child, gravely throwing up his dice, in order to see what hope there was for it. The mother watched the result with painful eagerness, and it was not favourable to her hopes. She entreated the man to try again, promising him a large reward if the prognostication was favourable. The man complied with her wishes, and this time the poor woman saw nothing but death for her offspring. But she had not lost hope ; she redoubled her entreaties for a favourable cast of the dice, promising additional reward, all of her possessions, everything she had, but the result was the same—death. She crouched down in despair ; her little one would die ; she lost hope ; her child was henceforth dead to her ; and a low death-wail proceeded from her lips. I tried to give the poor woman encouragement ; told her that the medicine-man knew nothing about it, that her child might live if she still cared for it, but my words were as idle tales, her faith in the test was implicit. I was travelling, and left the village immediately after, yet I have no doubt of the result ; the child would be taken outside the village ; the mother would leave it in agony ; and there it would die untended and apparently uncared for. And yet the mother had an affection for her little one, and would feel and mourn its loss as much as mothers, in like circumstances, would in England." [1]

How could she have paid heed to the missionary who counselled her to look after her child ? For her, the only thing was to find out whether her baby was " doomed," and if its fate admitted of no appeal. Three times the answer to her prayer had been a negative one, and from that moment her child was dead, in her eyes. She does not strangle it, like the young Maori woman whose daughter

[1] Rev. H. Rowley : *The Universities' Mission to Central Africa*, pp. 212–13.

CHAPTER X

THE MYSTIC MEANING OF THE CAUSES OF SUCCESS

I

BETWEEN the white men's activities and their own, and between the things they make themselves and those which the white men bring with them, primitives certainly do draw a line of demarcation. Everything proceeding from white people participates in their mysterious and superhuman character, and is consequently *ipso facto* sufficiently explained. For instance, there is no need to examine the way in which firearms are made, since primitives know beforehand why they have such a powerful effect. If, on the contrary, it is a question of their own workmanship, their hunting or fishing tackle, their weapons, the natives know how they adapt the means at command to their destined end, and they possess a clear and often very remarkable knowledge of their technique. Actual, and sometimes secret, instruction in these matters passes the knowledge on from generation to generation. A careful and detailed study of these methods, their evolution, progress, and decay in a given race or a certain geographical area, is at this very time engrossing a large number of ethnographers, especially in North America. It will afford a valuable contribution to our knowledge of primitive mentality.

Up to the present, the facts that are known permit of our saying that the part played by technique in the making of tools is quite a subordinate one in the primitive's eyes, however. That instruments shall be well made is not the most important thing, but that they shall be successful. The influence of secondary causes never appears to him efficient enough ; the result depends, above all things, on the assistance of the unseen powers. No human activity, whether of native or white man, ever succeeds without their concurrence. According to the words used by an American investigator: " Success is never obtained by natural means." The primitive who has a successful hunting expedition, or reaps an abundant harvest, or triumphs over his enemy in war, debits this favourable result not (as the European in a similar case would do) to the excellence of his instruments or weapons, nor to his own ingenuity and efforts, but to the indispensable assistance of the unseen powers. Undoubtedly he has more than one reason for believing that white men are powerful magicians, but he would not be so quickly and completely convinced of it if he did not conceive of their activity by his own.

He himself undertakes nothing without having a " medicine " to ensure success. In New France, for instance, " the greatest opposition to the understanding of the Faith, which we encounter in this country, is that all their remedies for sickness and disease, their chief recreations when they are in health, their fishing, hunting, and their trading, are imbued, as it were, with diabolical rites" [1] (that is, rites designed to obtain the favourable intervention of the spiritual powers). Italian missionaries on the Congo in the seventeenth century, say the same thing. " In addition to the ceremonies already described, every negro invents others, according to his fancy, for all domestic circumstances whatsoever ; and these he strictly observes, his fear that he will not succeed without them being insurmountable ; it seems as if these ceremonies were the efficient causes of the result he desires to obtain." [2] These last words are very striking, for they could not express more clearly the fact that the collective representations of the negro, differently orientated from our own, refer all real causation to the unseen world.

German missionaries in New Guinea have been witnesses of the same circumstances and express the same views. " Nothing," say they, " is undertaken without having

[1] *Relations des Jésuites*, xxvii. p. 52 (1645–6).
[2] Cavazzi : *Istoria descrizione de'tre regni Congo, Matamba, ed Angola*, p. 115.

recourse to enchantments (*Zauber*). There are charms for hunting, warfare, birds, fish, pigs, barter, the ground, thunder, lightning, rain, earthquake ; charms for wives, for dancing, remedies, diagnosis, charms for use as counter-charms, and so on." The list would be an endless one. I shall give a few specimens merely.

"Dogs which are intended for hunting the wild boar are made eager by magic formulæ pronounced over them alone, and in the most diversified methods. Over a certain onion the following incantation is uttered : ' A sea-eagle was holding a fish in his claws. The east wind was roaring, and the sea tempestuous, but the eagle held his fish fast and did not relax his hold.' They then burst the onion with their teeth and make the dogs inhale its acrid juice through their nostrils. The effect of this will be to make the dog hold fast to the boar which he seizes." [1] Again : " If they want to entrap animals in pits, it is necessary to pronounce a magic formula over each of these. They carry this to such a degree that until quite recently the people living to the north of the Sattelberg never dug pits for wild boars because they did not know the formulæ to use ! Without them—to the Papuan mind this is quite evident—there was no hope of catching any. They use the greatest care in uttering these formulæ over the pits ; they fumigate them with a flaming magic staff, and they spread a magic powder (flour of brimstone) all about. Finally they put into the snare thus prepared a ' pit-stone,' the ' soul ' of which is able to attract the game, and henceforward it cannot fail to appear." [2]

The traffic in pigs is a considerable one, and every native tries to secure a good bargain at the market. The seller makes use of a charm, so that he may get the highest possible price ; the buyer does the same, in order to make a good impression with the things he offers in exchange, and to get the fattest pig that he can. " Certain stones are supposed to ensure success in barter, and these are called *parnaga*. . . . These *parnaga* contain within them the vital principle of pigs. In preserving these stones from noxious influences

[1] R. Neuhauss : *Deutsch Neu Guinea*, i. pp. 400–12.
[2] Ibid., iii. p. 330. (Jabim.)

by means of a certain liquid, the pig is preserved at the same time. . . ." Is it a question of out-rivalling others at dancing? "It not infrequently happens that the Papuans undertake long journeys for the purpose of learning dances from a tribe celebrated for them. . . . Moreover, in the ceremonial dances all possible charms are employed in order to make the limbs supple." [1]

The concurrence of the unseen powers is no less essential in agricultural pursuits. "When the Bakaua cultivates his land there are many things which he must do, and others which he must not do, if he is to make sure of success. Dangers threaten him on every side, and these proceed from the unseen powers with whom he must be on good terms, so that they may remain favourable to him. . . . While engaged in planting, he calls upon the dead by name, begging them to protect his field, so that their children, the living of the present day, may have something to eat, and may be prosperous. . . . Then the owner of the field buries his magic stones within it. These, inherited from his ancestors, are imitations of taro tubers. . . . When the harvest is over they are unearthed and taken to the new field." [2]

The Jabim tribe, bordering on the Bakaua, proceed in the same way. "The natives believe themselves to be dependent in a very special way upon the spirits of the dead (*balum*) in their agricultural pursuits. Nothing is done without the most meticulous care and the greatest possible precautions. . . . Before planting the first taros in the field they have just burned and cleared, they first invoke the dead. . . . Afterwards, when planting, they invoke the spirits. To purchase their favour, they bring them some of their treasures (wild boar's tusks, dogs' teeth, etc.) so that they may adorn themselves with the soul of these objects. . . . Later on, the fields resound with the 'bull-roarers,' people calling on the ancestors by name, and thus they hope to secure a specially fine crop of the fruits of the field." [3] A little later still, "between the first-fruits and the beginning of the harvest, dances are inaugurated,

---

[1] R. Neuhauss: *Deutsch Neu Guinea*, i. p. 161.
[2] Ibid., iii. p. 434.   [3] Ibid., iii. pp. 332-3.

and these generally last the whole night. For the most part they bear the closest possible relation to the harvest, and they are intended to make the vegetation become as dense as may be." [1]

These forms of agrarian magic are well known, and fairly common. Here are some others, which show how much diversity there is in the mystic conditions upon which a good harvest depends. " In the natives' opinion, the prosperity of the vegetation in the fields is largely dependent upon certain games which, as a consequence, may only be played during the period following on the sowing season. Thus swinging, practised by means of a Malacca cane fixed to the branch of a tree, has, they believe, a good effect on yams that have just been planted. At such a time, then, young and old, men and women, are on their swings, and as they go and come they sing their swing songs. These are frequently no more than the names of yams dug up, and a harvesters' joyous call repeated with varying refrains— ' I have found a splendid root ! ' . . . By thus calling out the names of the various varieties of yam, they make their shoots show themselves. . . . So that the leafy parts of the yam may be luxuriant, grow green, and develop in size, the Kai play at cat's cradle. Playing at tops with the big kernels the country produces, or even with a kind of wild fig will, they believe, accelerate the growth of taro which has been recently planted (for the latter will turn round, too, and enlarge). Accordingly they must play this game at the sowing season only. It is the same with the game which consists in piercing the stalks of taro leaves with the ribs of sago leaves, thus making miniature lances. . . . There is a yet more remarkable feature than this limiting of certain games to the special agricultural period, and that is that the Kai do not allow any of the ' tales of long ago,' or the popular legends to be related except when the newly planted seed germinates and buds." [2] The missionary adds, a little further on : " The final upshot of the Kai legends is that they are related only to serve a definite end—namely, to further the growth of the yams

[1] R. Neuhauss : *Deutsch Neu Guinea* (Neighbourhood of King William Cape), iii. p. 253.
[2] Ibid., iii. pp. 125-6. (Kai).

planted in the fields. By recalling the memory of the early primitives, whom they connect with the origin of the fruits of the field, they believe that their growth will be favourably affected. Once the sowing season has passed, and especially when the young plants have begun to send out their tendrils, they stop relating these legends." [1]

The Papuans undoubtedly know how to give the plants they cultivate the necessary care. They clearly distinguish the different genera, species, and varieties, each of which has been given a name. But to bring these yams to maturity is an undertaking the success of which depends, first and foremost, upon mystic causes. From the moment when the Papuans select a piece of ground and clear it by burning, to the time when they gather in their harvest, if they have been able to protect it from wild boars, birds, and other depredators, they have had to prepare, induce, and hasten the growth of the vegetables by an infinite number of magical practices. Their games, for instance, are a serious religious performance, obligatory at one time, and forbidden on all other occasions. So, too, the recital of legends is not simply an evening's amusement, but it secures the presence of those " early primitives " to whom they owe the yam, and it will make the influence of these more direct and effective.

Among the Papuans of British New Guinea, at Kiwai, on the mouth of the Fly River, they frequently amuse themselves with the game of cat's cradle, which everybody knows. But, " in certain cases, a more particular interest attaches to it. The game is most often played when the stalks of the newly planted yams begin to shoot up from the earth. Sticks are put in the ground to support the winding tendrils, and the first few stems are tied to them by means of pieces of strings which have been used for making cat's cradles. It is sufficient, however, to hang pieces of these strings on top of the first few sticks, without actually tying the stalks to them, and some people merely throw a few pieces of cat's cradle strings here and there on the ground in their gardens. In each case the purpose is to ' help ' the stalks of the yams to grow well and wind in the right way. Several other games of the Kiwai people

[1] R. Neuhauss: *Deutsch Neu Guinea*, iii. p. 161.

have an analogous reference to their gardens, or to other occupations." [1]

The game of cat's cradle, which is extensively used, often possesses the same magic virtue in places outside New Guinea. To quote but a few instances only : in the Gazelle Peninsula of New Pomerania it is especially played when the bread-fruit trees begin to form their fruit.[2] With the Dayaks of Borneo, " certain festivals demand certain games ; for instance, the feast of the sowing season requires different games from the lesser and the greater harvest ones, from that which opens the harvest season, or begins the new year. At the sowing festival they spin tops and wear masks ; when they begin to gather in the rice, they bombard each other with pea-shooters, etc. It is noteworthy that these games, which are performed by priests on ceremonial occasions, at other times simply form the amusement of the rest of the tribe." [3] They are games, but their significance still exists, and is undoubtedly known to them all. Among the Kayans, " men often amuse themselves by spinning tops. These tops are oval, smooth, and glossy, and weigh between four and five pounds. Each man tries to get rid of his predecessor's top with his own, in such a way that the latter will continue to revolve until it, too, in its turn is superseded by the next one. . . . In this way each succeeding operation on the rice plantation is inaugurated by religious and culinary ceremonies, during which taboos lasting for some nights, and certain games are enjoined on the whole community, as are wrestling matches, contests in high and long jumps, races, and so forth. . . ." [4]

In South America, " what surprised me most with respect to the game of *chuke* [5] was that with the Choroti of

---

[1] G. Landtman : "Cat's Cradles of the Kiwai Papuans, British New Guinea," *Anthropos*, ix. p. 221.

[2] P. Georg. Bögershausen M.S.C. : "Fadenspiele in Matupit, Neu Pommern, Gazelle Halbinsel," *Anthropos*, x-xi. p. 908.

[3] A. W. Nieuwenhuis : *Quer durch Borneo*, ii. pp. 130-1.

[4] Ibid., i. pp. 167-70 ; cf. i. p. 329.

[5] A game, somewhat resembling the French *jeu de l'oie*, played with wooden blocks or dice, flat on one side and rounded on the other. The scoring is decided by the position taken by these in falling, and their direction with regard to the " houses " toward which they are thrown.—TRANSLATOR'S NOTE.

Grand Chaco, at any rate, it was only played at a certain time of the year, in the month of March, when the rainy season ends in Chaco and the winter begins. Then they used to start it, and in every village they would carve the blocks for the *chuke* and they would play it all day for hours together, sometimes from early morning till late at night. That very fact seemed to indicate that there were some mystic ideas connected with the game. Moreover, they played it with a feverish haste, and the result of each stroke was announced in a loud voice so that it might be heard a long way off. The Choroti expressly declared that they only play *chuke* at the beginning of winter when the *algarobe* and other edible fruits are beginning to fail. That is to the Chaco Indians the beginning of a period when they often have a great struggle for existence. Thus the game is then played that it may have the effect *of increasing the number of their fruits and adding to the general prosperity of the Indians.* This result is attained by the circumstance that there are always one or more players who win, and this, in some mystic way, is an advantage to them all." [1]

A similar influence which is exercised by the recital of stories has been well described by Perham. " In Dayak life," he says, " the sense of the invisible is constantly present and active. Spirits and goblins are to them as real as themselves. . . . In the head feast it is Singalang Burong who is invoked to be present. He may be described as the Mars of Sea Dayak mythology, and is put far away above the skies. But the invocation is not made by the human performer in the manner of a prayer directed to this great being ; it takes the form of a story, setting forth how the mythical hero, Kling or Klieng, made a head feast and fetched Singalang Burong to it. This Kling, about whom there are many fables, is a spirit, and is supposed to live somewhere or other not far from mankind, and to be able to confer benefits upon them. The Dayaks perform their prayers then, as they walk up and down the long veranda of the house . . . describe Kling's *gawé pala* (great feast) and how Singalang Burong was invited and came. In

[1] R. Karsten : *Beiträge zur Sittengeschichte der südamerikanischen Indianer,* p. 102.

thought, the Dayaks identify themselves with Kling and the resultant signification is that the recitation of this story is an invocation to Singalang Burong, who is supposed to come, not into Kling's house only, but to the actual Dayak house where the feast is celebrated ; and he is received by a particular ceremony, and is offered food or sacrifice." [1] By some mystic virtue in the story related, the Dayak *becomes* the hero, the host of the god, and as a consequence the god himself has actually come among the Dayaks, and is really received by them. The story has proved much more effective than an invocation or even a prayer would be. It brings about a participation in which, as Perham expresses it, the story-teller and the hero are identified with one another. He very rightly accounts for this fact by the mystic nature of Dayak mentality. The New Guinea Papuans manifest the same characteristic. When at a certain season of the year they recall the benefits conferred by their heroes, in order to expedite the growth of the taro, they, too, feel the actual presence of those whose story they are telling, and identify themselves with them.

In the central regions of the Celebes, " it is practically only at the time of the rice harvest, i.e. from about August to October, that tales are told. This rule is generally observed, and the recital of legends at any other time is considered to be a violation which may affect the harvest, ordinarily a very scanty one, unfavourably. In these tales (known as ' Tales of the Ancestors '), the ancestors are yet living in the form of spirits. . . . At this time of year, more than at any other, the natives do homage to their ancestors, either in presenting them with offerings or in extolling their deeds." [2] Although this author does not say so, it is hardly rash to conclude that the To Radja, like the Papuans, attribute mystic virtue to the recital of these tales.

II

In South America, among the Bantus and the people of West Africa, in most of the Oceanic islands, and in yet

[1] Rev. J. Perham, in H. Ling Roth : *The Natives of Sarawak*, ii. pp. 174–5.
[2] Dr. N. Adriani : " Étude sur la littérature des To Raja," *Tijdschrift voor indische taal-land-en volkenkunde*, xl. p. 341.

other places, the very unequal division of agricultural labour between the sexes has been noted. The work of the gardens, plantations, and fields falls, nearly everywhere, mainly upon women, without prejudice to their other tasks, such as the care of the children and the preparation of food, etc. Even where the men are not entirely free from field labour they only share in it, as a rule, for certain preliminary or final operations. It is their task, for instance, to cut down the trees on the land which is to be cultivated, to remove the stumps, and clear the ground, but the real work of agriculture, properly so called, is done by women only.

This has been considered an abuse of strength, and a special instance of that more than debatable rule according to which the more debased the community the more miserable is the condition of its women, or else it has been thought to be a necessary consequence of the circumstance that the men are often employed elsewhere, in warfare, hunting, travelling, at their assemblies, and so on. These diverse explanations are possibly not entirely incorrect, but the true reason of it lies elsewhere. Beyond the fact that the man himself often has occupations quite as laborious as the cultivation of the soil, he would not, if he could, change this division of labour, the origin of which is a mystical one. If women are almost exclusively burdened with all that pertains to the cultivation of plants and trees, it is because, in the social group, they represent the principle of fertility. In order that the fields and the trees under culture may be productive, there must be a close relation or participation established between them and the social group which attends to them ; the principle of fertility must pass over to them, and consequently the members of the group must have it within themselves. It would be useless for men to take as much trouble in the fields as women, useless even if they took more trouble and expended more energy upon the ground, and sowed and transplanted with as much or even greater care. It would all be labour lost ! The earth's yield would be but a reluctant and meagre one. The bananas and coco-nut palms would be almost sterile. The work of women alone makes fields and gardens fertile, for it is to their sex that this power is due. Such being the reason for this division of labour, its mystic character makes it unassailable. Even if the men desired to take upon themselves this hard task, they would not be able to accomplish it successfully. Moreover, the women would not consent to give it up, for fear of famine.

This is not a *merely probable* hypothesis. Not infrequently writers, in noting the fact, have at the same time indicated the reason for it which the natives themselves give, but without drawing any inference from it. In Borneo, "women play the principal part in the rites and active operations of the padi (*rice*) culture; the men only being called in to clear the ground and to assist in some of the later stages. The women select and keep the seed grain, and they are the repositories of most of the lore connected with it. It seems to be felt that they have a natural affinity to the fruitful ground, which they speak of as becoming pregnant. Women sometimes sleep out in the padi field while the crop is growing, probably for the purpose of increasing their own fertility or that of the padi, but they are very reticent on this matter."[1] In New Caledonia, "the teeth of old women are taken to the yam plantations as a charm for a good crop, and their skulls are also erected over the paths for the same purpose."[2] Among the Bantu tribes it often happens that a man repudiates his wife because she does not bear children, and he fears that the plantation she cultivates may become sterile also. In Togoland, "a woman who is enceinte always wears a little bag on her head. . . . In it are to be found little pieces of yam, cassava, maize, pisang, etc. . . . and also a tiny fragment of the stone women use in grinding maize. . . . All these field products are to remind her that, just as the woman brings forth the fruit of her body, so that which she has cultivated in her field must also produce its own. In Togoland, in fact, the principal part of the labour in the plantations falls upon the women."[3]

In South America, evidence with regard to this matter

[1] Hose and McDougall : *The Pagan Tribes of Borneo*, i. p. 111.
[2] G. Turner : *Nineteen Years in Polynesia*, p. 425.
[3] G. Spiess : *Zum Kultus und Zauberelauben der Evheer* (*Togo*), Bässler-Archiv, i. p. 225.

is very explicit. Fr. Gumilla tells us of a discussion which he had with some Indians about it. " Sowing, tilling, reaping, and storing the field products is all done by the women. I would say to the men : ' My brothers, why do you not help your poor wives in the labour of sowing the fields, for they work hard in the heat of the sun, with their infants at their breasts ? Do you not realize that they may fall ill, and your children likewise ? Come now, come and help them ! ' ' Father,' they would answer, ' you do not understand these things, and that is why you are troubled about it. You must remember that our women know how to bring forth, and we do not. If they sow the seed, the maize stalk yields two or three corn-cobs ; the yacca stem bears a triple yield, and thus every-thing is increased. Why is this ? Because women are able to bring forth, and are able to command the seed they sow to be productive. Let them do the work of sowing then, for we do not know so much about it.' " [1] The expressions put into the mouth of the Indian by the missionary show clearly the idea of " participation " between the woman and the seed.

A recent observer, Dr. R. Karsten, has been investigating similar beliefs on the part of the Jibaros. " The female plants," says he, " must be essentially cultivated by the women, and the male plants by the men. At any kind of agriculture, however, the rough work, that is, the felling of the trees and the clearing of the ground, when new plantations are made in the forest, is done by the men. On the other hand, although for instance the plantain is always planted by the men, yet the women later on take part in attending the tree and sing incantations to promote its growth. Just as the earth-deity of the Jibaros itself is regarded as a woman, so the women are always supposed to exert a special, mysterious influence upon the growth of the crops.

All agricultural practices of the Jibaros centre round the particular deity of the women, the great Earth-Mother Nungüi. She has not only taught the women agriculture, but also all kinds of housework . . . especially how to

---

[1] P. Gumilla : *El Orinoco illustrado* (2nd edit.), ii. pp. 274–75.

feed and attend the principal domestic animals—the swine and chickens, and the hunting dogs." [1] Further on he says : " There is supposed to exist an intrinsic connection between the woman and the field-fruits which she cultivates, just as she is believed to exert a particular influence upon the domestic animals that are confided to her care. This first of all holds true of the married woman. When a Jibaro marries and has to found a new household, to make new plantations and breed domestic animals—swine, chickens, and hunting dogs—his first business is to make a special feast for his young wife, through which power and ability is in a mysterious way imparted to her for her coming obligations. This feast—next to the head feast the greatest feast of the Jibaros—is called *noa tsangu*, that is, the ' tobacco feast of the women.' Without knowing the general significance of this feast it is impossible fully to understand the ideas the Jibaros connect with agriculture." [2]

" The most important of the domestic plants is the manioc, and when new manioc fields are made . . . the rough work is done by the men, who fell the trees and clear and level the ground on the spot selected for the new plantation. After this the work of the women begins, who further prepare the ground for planting." [3]

It is true that Nordenskiöld noted the contrary custom in Chaco, among the Ashluslays and the Chorotis. " It is the men alone," he says, " who cultivate the fields. The sowing and the reaping is done by men and women conjointly. On the other hand, it is always the women and children who bring home the sheaves, unless they are put on horses or asses." [4] But, apart from the fact that the observation is very brief, it does, nevertheless, grant that a share of the labour is left to the women, especially in the sowing season, and in any case, were this exception well founded, and even confirmed in yet other tribes, the conclusions drawn from the facts already related would not be invalidated thereby. It is still true that the collective representations of many primitive peoples connect, in some

[1] Rafael Karsten : " Contributions to the Sociology of the Indian Tribes of Ecuador," i. p. 7, *Acta Academiæ Aboensis*. (Finland, 1921.)
[2] Ibid., p. 11.   [3] Ibid., p. 14.
[4] E. Nordenskiöld : *La vie des Indiens dans le Chaco*, p. 48.

mystic fashion, the fertility of the fields with the fruitfulness of women. Consequently, cultivation itself, accomplished by women, has the sense of participation. We must not say merely that agricultural labour is attended by magical practices; the work itself is a magic operation, since it is women who perform it.

III

It is not the mystic influence of women alone that will secure an abundant harvest. For that it is necessary, as we have already found, to reckon also upon the kindly offices of the ancestors, whose favour is sought by all kinds of means—prayers, invocations, offerings, sacrifices, fasts, dances, the recital of legends. With many tribes, too, the personal influence of the chief is also requisite. There is a sort of " contact action," as it were, comparable with that of a catalytic agent. The chief is the necessary intermediary between the social group and the unseen powers upon whom the fertility of the soil and of plant life depend. Should he fail to fulfil that office, these powers, among whom the ancestors must be reckoned, become hostile, or even simply indifferent, and the tribe is threatened with death by famine.

This explains, at least in part, the almost unconquerable aversion felt by certain chiefs to the idea of conversion. "Mafa" (a Mosuto chief), "was held back mainly by his chieftainship. In these lands the office carries with it many public functions which ill consort with the laws and principles of the Word of God. In a place where the majority of the people are still heathen, for a chief to declare himself a Christian is almost equivalent to abdication." [1] "Wait until I am dead," said one of the chiefs of the Wallis Islands. " and you can labour unopposed at the conversion of the island. Besides, it is our gods who make the kawa and the coco-nut palm and the banana grow, for there are none of these in the white man's country; and if I renounced my faith, I should be afraid of bringing famine upon my land." [2] " ' Your God,' said the king of Uvea, in the same

---

[1] *Missions évangéliques*, li. p. 124. (Mabille.)

[2] " Société de Marie," *Annales des missions de l'Océanie*, i. p. 422. (Fr. Bataillon.)

archipelago, to a missionary, ' your God was able to make the trees of your land, but it was not He who made the kawa ! ' And not only did this king thus limit the power of God, but he concluded that the diversity of plants was due to a plurality of gods. Every plant, according to him, had its own special creator, who had no power over the other plants." [1] Primitive mentality is, above all, inclined to the concrete, and has little that is conceptual about it. Nothing astonishes it more than the idea of one universal God. The primitive mind proceeds by means of participations and exclusions. The natives of the Wallis Islands have their land, which in some way makes a part of their social group, with the plants growing and the animals living there, and the ancestors and the unseen powers upon whom the prosperity of the group depends. The white people's community, which they represent to themselves as formed on the same model, has nothing in common with theirs ; therefore neither the white man's chiefs nor the unseen powers which he calls God can do anything to benefit the vegetation of the Wallis Islands. It is the native chief alone who can secure its growth, both during his life and after his death.

At Kiriwana, in the Trobriand Archipelago, " our big chief, Bulitara, was asking me one day if I had these occult powers. When I told him that I made no such claim, he said : ' Who makes the wind and the rain and the harvest in your land ? ' I answered, ' God.' ' Ah,' said he, ' that's it. God does this work for your people, and I do it for our people. God and I are equal.' He delivered this dictum very quietly, and with the air of a man who had given a most satisfactory explanation." [2] " A ruling chief," says Brown a little later, " was always supposed to exercise priestly functions, i.e. he professed to be in constant communication with the *tebarans* (spirits) and through their influence he was enabled to bring rain or sickness, fair winds or foul winds, sickness or health, success or disaster in war, and generally to procure any blessing or curse for which

[1] Rev. Fr. Mangaret : *Mgr. Bataillon et les missions de l'Océanie centrale,* i. pp. 172–3.
[2] Rev. —. Fellows in Rev. George Brown, D.D. : *Melanesians and Polynesians,* p. 236.

the applicant was willing to pay a sufficient price." [1] In short, he directly participates in the unseen world. This inestimable privilege accounts for the undisputed authority he enjoys, the scrupulous respect shown him, the super human powers recognized in him and to which he himself lays claim. As Sir James Frazer has clearly shown, he is a kind of " living god."

This personal *mana* of the chief is often communicated to everything that comes in contact with him, and to make sure of the favourable influence emanating from him, he will be requested to materialize it, as it were, in such a way that it can be transferred. Rajah Brooke, who enjoyed unparalleled prestige among the Dayaks, has himself told of the solicitations addressed to him.

" When I seat myself on the mat, one by one they come forward and tie little bells on my arm ; a young coco-nut is brought, into which I am requested to spit. The white fowl is presented. I rise and wave it, and say : ' May good luck attend the Dayaks ; may their crops be plentiful, may their fruits ripen in due season ; may male children be born ; may rice be stored in their houses.' . . . This exhortation over, the dance begins . . . they wash my hands and my feet, and afterwards with the water sprinkle their houses and gardens. Then the gold dust and the white cloth which accompanies it, both of which have been presented by me, is planted in the field." [2]

A contemporary witness tells us of the same customs, and explains why the Dayaks thought so much of them. " When Mr. Brooke visits their residences, instead of supplicating him, they each bring a portion of the padi seed they intend to sow next season, and with it the necklaces of the women, which are given to him for that purpose, and which, having been dipped into a mixture previously prepared, are by him shaken over the little basins, which contain the seed, by which process he is supposed to render them very productive." (It is interesting to note that the mystic influence of the women is here combined with

---

[1] Rev. George Brown : *Melanesians and Polynesians*, p. 429.
[2] *Narrative of Events in Borneo and Celebes*, ii. pp. 42–3. (Sir Jas. Brooke's Journal, 1848.)

that of the great chief.) "Other tribes, whom from their distance he cannot visit, send down to him for a small piece of white cloth, and a little gold or silver, which they bury in the earth on their farms, to attain the same result. On his entering a village, the women also wash and bathe his feet, first with water, and then with the milk of a young coco-nut, and then once with water again ; all this water which has touched his person, is preserved for the purpose of being distributed on their farms, being sure to render an abundant harvest certain. On one occasion, having remarked that the crops of rice of the Samban tribe were thin, the chief immediately observed that it could not be otherwise, as they had never been visited by the Rajah, and he begged me to try and induce Mr. Brooke to visit them, to remove the cause which had rendered their crop a small one." [1]

Near Lake Toba, in Sumatra, " the winds receive the name of the quarter of the sky whence they come, or rather, they are named after the chief of that region, which proves that the Battak sees in his chief, not only the absolute lord of people and things, but he is in a way divine, or at any rate a representative of divinity. The people could not understand our saying that we most certainly had no power over the wind." [2]

Collective representations of the same kind lead to similar customs in South African tribes. " If the king (of the Matabeles), for example, who is regarded as the master of the heavens as well as of the earth, does not shower upon the latter, as regularly as the people want it, the blessing of a fertilizing rain, they are immediately disturbed. It is, they say, because the king's heart is ' offended ' or ' ill,' or even ' black ' (they make use indifferently of all these terms).[3] He will not give any rain until he is feeling better-disposed. . . . The first thing to do is to find out the cause of this, and nearly always it is discovered that in some town or district a crime of some sort has been committed, i.e. something has been done which

---

[1] Hugh Low : *Sarawak*, pp. 259–60.
[2] *Berichte der rheinischen Missionsgesellschaft*, p. 10 (1904).
[3] See chap. ix, p. 291.

is displeasing to the king.   Then reparation must be made ;
in most cases that will take the form of the massacre of
chiefs, the destruction of the town or towns, the captivity
or the dispersal of the women and children. . . . The king's
wrath must be appeased ; it is the only way to put an end
to the scourge of drought." [1]   This remark shows that the
beneficent influence of the chief upon surrounding Nature
(in the present case, upon the rain), apparently does not
depend entirely upon his will, but on the state of his " heart."
Perhaps it is " black," because somewhere in his vicinity
or further off, an important taboo will have been violated
without his being aware of it, and this has offended the
unseen powers.   It is a case, therefore, of the mystic influence
emanating from the chief, the personal *mana* which irradiates
those around, and is his by virtue of his participation in the
unseen world.

IV

Instead of a peaceful occupation like agriculture let
us consider warfare, which is a very common form of
activity in many primitive peoples ; we shall find that
primitive mentality interprets the facts in the same way,
and success in it is seen to be dependent upon a similar
participation.

" They (the Indians of New France) seem to recognize
that there is a destiny for war.   They do not attribute
the victory to the strength or courage of their soldiers,
nor the good leadership of their captains, but to Fate
or the manitou who allows one nation to overcome
another when he pleases.   That is why they fast, hoping
that this manitou will manifest himself to them during the
night, and will say : ' I am delivering your enemies to you
that you may devour them ; go and find them." [2]   Among
the Creek Indians, " war parties leaving the town were
always headed by a man of proved physical prowess and
cunning. . . . Another individual, called *hobaya* (prophet),
accompanied such forays.   He was versed in songs and
rituals with which he could weaken the enemy and blind

[1] *Missions évangéliques*, xxxix. pp. 461–2.   (Thomas.)
[2] *Relations des Jésuites*, lviii. p. 54.   (Outagamis.)

the eyes of their warriors. He could also foretell events and determine whether raids or hunting excursions would be successful." [1] The following story illustrates the blind confidence of these same Indians in the unseen powers who are to lead them to victory. " The Creeks were meditating the infliction of a mortal blow on the Blackfeet, and for this purpose they had collected all the forces at their disposal, amounting to more than eight hundred men. Before setting out to find the enemy, they resorted to all kinds of magic and witchcraft in order to make sure of success in their expedition. It was decided that a young girl should be blindfolded and placed at the head of the troops to serve as guide to the army throughout the expedition. Should they be successful, this young heroine was to become the wife of the most valiant of the warriors. . . . This arranged, they started on their march full of confidence and boldness, following their strange guide across hills and valleys, ravines, and morasses. One day she would take a northerly direction, the next she might go to the south or east, but this diversity of direction mattered little, for the war-manitou was reputed to be guiding her steps, and the infatuated Creeks were content to follow their blinded girl-leader day after day." [2]

" The man who is desirous of commanding," says Charlevoix, speaking of the Canadian Indians, " never thinks of levying troops unless he has previously fasted for some days, during which he is daubed with black, holds no conversation with anybody, invokes his tutelary genius day and night, and above all, notes his dreams very carefully. . . . Then they make some water hot, clean the chief's face, dress his hair, and grease or paint it. They put different colours on his face, and dress him in his finest robes. Thus adorned, he chants his death song in a muffled voice ; his soldiers, that is, those who have offered to accompany him (for no one is constrained to do so) then intone one after another their war chant (for each has his own, which no other is allowed to use, and there

[1] F. G. Speck : "The Creek Indians of Taskigitown," *Memoirs of the American Anthropological Association*, ii. p. 114.
[2] Fr. J. de Smet, S.J. : *Voyages dans l'Amérique septentrionale*, pp. 150-2.

are some, too, that are appropriated by each family). . . .
Then they deliberate awhile. . . . The chants are followed
by dances . . . fairly quick, figurative movements, representing the different operations in the campaign, yet
always measured and harmonious. A feast terminates
the ceremony." [1]

All these preparations, which are continued on the
following days, and right up to the departure of the warriors,
are of a mystic nature, their object being to secure for the
troops the support of the unseen powers. Once started
on the campaign, they continue the same proceedings.
" They deduce omens from everything, and the wizards
whose business it is to explain these, advance or retard
their marches as they please. . . . They encamp long
before the sun goes down, and they usually leave a large
space surrounded by a palisade in front of the camp, or
they may enclose it by a kind of trellis work upon which they
place their manitous, turned to the side they wish to go
to. They invoke these for an hour, and in the morning,
before breaking camp, they do the same thing. After that
they think they have nothing to fear : they imagine that
the spirits have taken upon themselves the duties of sentinels,
and the whole army sleeps in tranquillity under their protection. . . . In an enemy country they must not make
a camp fire ; there must be no sound, no hunting ; they
must not speak to each other except by signs." [2] (The
North American Indians were accustomed to converse
by means of gesture.)

In South Africa, among the Kafirs, the social structure
and economic conditions were different from those of the
Iroquois and the Hurons ; nevertheless, taking these dis-
similarities into account, we find that with them, too, warfare
is conceived and carried on in like fashion. " A chief among
the Amazulu practises magic on another chief before fighting
with him. Something belonging to the chief is taken, and
the other washes himself with *intelezi* (water in which various
plants have been infused) in order that he may overcome
the other when they begin to fight. And, forsooth, the one was

[1] Fr. F. X. de Charlevoix : *Journal d'un voyage dans l'Amérique septentrionale*, iii. pp. 216–18.
[2] Ibid., iii. pp. 236–3. (Iroquois and Hurons.)

conquered long ago by having his things taken and practised on by magic. And if the cattle fly from an enemy, their dung and the earth which retains the marks of their foot-prints are taken to the chief that he may churn them and sit upon them. And the men say: ' The chief is now sitting upon them ; he has already eaten them up ; we shall find them.' And when they have found them they say: ' The doctor of the chief is a doctor indeed.' " [1]

Here we recognize the disposition of the primitive mind to regard, as actual and already accomplished, a future event which, for mystic reasons, seems to be certain. Since magic operations which are infallible have been performed, the enemy chief is conquered at this very moment, his cattle are already captured. Victory has not only been prepared and prefigured, it has literally been gained. The fortune of war is not decided on the battlefield where the armies encounter each other; the decision has already been arrived at in the realm of the invisible. This accounts for that " curious consecration of the cattle," spoken of by Lichtenstein, as practised by the priests when a war is in prospect. " Its aim is to protect these animals, the possession of which is often the sole cause of the war, from the risk of being forcibly carried off by the enemy." [2] The chief prepares the way beforehand by opposing his magic to the magic he deems his adversary to possess. " Sekukuni set his magicians to work, and Mapoch did the same on his side. Each hoped to be able to destroy his enemy's power by supernatural means. One day, to the great terror of the Matabeles, they found at their city gate a basket containing an enormous rhinoceros gazing at them with a threatening air. The wizards were imme-diately obliged to put this formidable visitor out of action and unable to injure their cause. . . . In many African tribes truly horrible magic practices, destined to annihilate the enemy, may be noted. A prisoner may be burnt to death, and his skin, when tanned, used in ceremonies intended to fortify and brace the warriors." [3]

[1] Rev. C. H. Callaway : *The Religious System of the Amazulu*, p. 345.
[2] H. Lichtenstein : *Reisen im südlichen Afrika*, ii. p. 542.
[3] A. Merensky: *Erinnerungen aus dem Missionsleben in Süd Ost Afrika*, pp. 163–4.

In the Barotse tribe, Coillard noticed a circumstance curiously like that of the Creek Indians which we related recently, the direction of the march being confided to a young girl supposed to be inspired by the unseen powers. "The young girl . . . is not the *vivandière* of the regiment, she is its prophetess. Selected by the diviner's astragali, she is the interpreter of the gods, and nothing is done without her direction. It is she who gives the signal for the departure and the halt. She bears the horn which contains the war medicines and charms. She is always at the head of the vanguard, and nobody, even when the troops are resting, is allowed to pass in front of her. Should she get tired, or fall ill, the younger warriors must carry her. When they encounter the enemy, she must fire the first shot, and however long the engagement may last, she is not allowed to sleep, or even sit down, or to eat or drink. . . . In return for her services, the young prophetess will be made a *maori*, one of the wives of the king." [1]

In the wars in the Congo, diviners play the same part as they do in North America and in South Africa. "They are the referees in all decisions, especially when the uncertainty of the event leads to hesitation. They bless, they curse, they call down disaster upon the enemy, and knowing that in his camp are other magicians, their rivals, they try to kill these by means of their incantations. . . . They vaunt themselves on knowing, from the special revelations made to them, victories and defeats beforehand; they claim that they can penetrate the heart, and have complete knowledge of all that is going on, even in the unseen world." [2] "An approaching war between two villages is the signal for great activity among the medicine-men. They must find out by their insight into the future how the coming fight will terminate. Charms to protect the warriors against gunshot, spear, and arrow must be prepared." [3] The Bangala consider that the insignia worn by white officers

[1] *Missions évangéliques*, lxiii. pp. 377–8.
[2] Cavazzi: *Istoria descrizione de'tre regni Congo, Matamba, ed Angola,* p. 226.
[3] E. J. Glave: *Six Years of Adventure in Congoland*, pp. 104–5.

on their uniform are for the purpose of protecting them from wounds ; these too, are charms.[1]

Even courage is not to be accounted for without a mystic cause. " How is it that a white man has no fear, for all his being so weak and not nearly a match for us ? He must possess a charm that makes him invulnerable." [2] The following conversation clearly shows what the opinion of natives is upon this point. " They thought that we possessed a medicine which made us invincible, if not invulnerable. To illustrate this ; some time after we had been in the land I was sitting by the side of Mankokwe ; Mr. Dickinson, our doctor, was with me. The chief became, all at once, very affectionate ; he put his arm round my neck and I knew then that he was going to ask me for something. Said he at last : ' Is that your medicine-man ? ' I assented. ' Ask him to give me your war medicine.' I laughed heartily, and told him we had no such medicine. He disbelieved me and said : ' That is not true, you have, you *must* have, and you do not like to give it me. But do ask him for it.' ' I speak the truth,' said I ; ' we English have no other war medicine than a brave heart.'

" He would not believe, and thus resumed : ' No, that is not true, it cannot be. I have a brave heart too ; but what is the good of a brave heart ; a brave heart alone is no good Listen. The Manganja have brave hearts ; the Ajawa came into their country ; they could not fight the Ajawa, but directly they saw them they ran away. Why ? Not because they had not brave hearts ; but because the Ajawa have stronger war medicine than they. Now you have stronger war medicine than the Ajawa ' (the English had recently put their tribe to rout), ' so strong that if only one Englishman went against the whole of the Ajawa, *they* would all run away. Do give me your war medicine.' " [3]

In the chief's eyes, there could be but one possible explanation of the British victory. He would be incredulous

[1] Rev. J. H. Weeks : "Anthropological Notes on the Bangala of the Upper Congo River," *J.A.I.*, xl. p. 392–3.
[2] H. von Wissmann : *My Second Journey through Equatorial Africa* (English version), p. 47.
[3] Rev. J. Rowley : *The Universities' Mission to Central Africa*, p. 148–9 (1867).

of any other. The gallantry of the British does not account
for their superiority, nor would their guns, or their greater
experience of military tactics. War is a struggle between
wizard and wizard, between one magic spell and another ;
the victory will rest with the combatant whose " war-
medicine " is the more powerful. The event had proved
that in this case it was the British who possessed it. Mr.
Rowley had certainly denied that this was so, but it was
denying the evidence. It is natural, after all, that the British
should not want to share this wonderful medicine with anybody else, and the native hears their decision without any
surprise.

From these ideas, which are met with almost everywhere, it follows that a war that has been well prepared
is virtually won. The conqueror (we must call him such,
since victory is already assured to him) will not encounter
any resistance. The enemy's weapons will misfire, their
eyes will be blinded, their limbs will fail them, their cattle
will be captured, and so on. As a rule, the attack is a
surprise, and takes place at dawn. That is the ordinary
method of fighting among uncivilized races ; there are
very few exceptions to it. A set battle is unknown to
primitives, and the idea of it would seem absurd to them.
" I remember one of the chiefs questioning me about our
mode of warfare, and his look of amazement when I described
the rows of men placed opposite each other and firing at
one another with guns. He eagerly inquired whether the
men were within range, and when I replied in the affirmative
he exclaimed: ' Then you are great fools.' . . . Then he
asked where the chief stood. ' Oh,' said I, ' he remains
at home and sends his men to fight.' At which there was
a burst of laughter." [1]

Their method of fighting is altogether different. " The
Bechuanas, for example, stealthily approach the village
which they wish to take, surround it on all sides, and about
two o'clock in the morning, when all within it are wrapped
in a most profound slumber, they hurl themselves upon
it, uttering fierce yells ; they massacre every man or
beast they encounter, and gain an easy victory over the

[1] Rev. S. Macfarlane : *Among the Cannibals of New Guinea*, p. 115 (1888).

poor unhappy wretches who have started up out of their sleep, petrified with fear, and having no alternative but to be burnt alive in their huts, or feel the enemy's assegai at their throats." [1] Very often the assailants wait until the night is at an end. With the Bangala tribes, " the attack commences at cockcrow, between five and half-past five in the morning. Men hurl themselves in masses on the quarters occupied by the sleeping enemy, each hut being surrounded by from ten to thirty warriors, its single low door being closely guarded. There is a heavy burst of firing, and the huts are set on fire. The unfortunate creatures thus taken unawares hasten to the outlet from the kraal, where death awaits them. The women alone are spared, and these are led away into captivity." [2] In other parts, the fighting men will be fewer in number, will be armed, not with guns, but with spears and bows, and they will massacre the women instead of making them captives. But the time and the arrangement of the attack will vary but little, whether it be in Borneo, Polynesia, North or South America, or elsewhere.

The primitives have undoubtedly taken into account the fact that this kind of attack is the safest, and that the enemy who is surprised in sleep will be able to offer but a feeble resistance. Nevertheless, this utilitarian motive cannot be the only, nor indeed the principal, reason for a custom which is so common. It must be a surprise attack, therefore it cannot take place in the daylight. The people would not be within their huts, possibly not even in the village. They would have time to seize their weapons, and it would be difficult, perhaps impossible, to surround them. But neither can a surprise attack take place in the darkness of night. Natives do not like to be out of doors in the shadows, even on moonlight nights. They are afraid of unlucky encounters, of meeting spirits wandering abroad, especially the spirits of the dead. There remains, therefore, only the dawn, the break of day. " The Kai (of German New Guinea) always accomplishes his warlike exploits early in the morning. In that way, he has the whole long day

---

[1] *Missions évangéliques*, xi. pp. 21–2. (Casalis.)
[2] C. Coquilhat : *Sur le Haut Congo*, p. 297.

before him, for the satisfaction of his vengeance, and it gives him time enough to get home again in safety before nightfall. In the dark he is afraid of the spirits of those who have been killed; in the daytime, these can do him no harm." [1] Similarly, in a region widely removed from this (in Central Chaco) the same reason obtains. " Warfare consists of surprise attacks. But as the people have a great dread of evil spirits, the attacks never take place by night; they are timed for a short time before sunrise. Even if the Indians are in the enemy's vicinity, they will always await that hour." [2] In the equatorial regions and in the tropics, where there is an extremely brief period of dusk, the assailants take a very short time only, and the attack must be carried out with lightning speed.

We should be inclined to believe that such an attack will always succeed, since it is in reality, not a fight, but a massacre of people taken unawares in sleep. However, it does sometimes fail. " It may happen," says Coquilhat, " that the tribe attacked awakens in time, and is able to inflict a crushing defeat on the assailant." Possibly one of the natives was awake, and gave the alarm. Besides— and on this point the witnesses are precise and fully agreed— in spite of the advantage which the attack secures by being unexpected, it is never completely carried through. If it does not succeed immediately and entirely, if the assailants suffer the slightest loss, they do not persevere, but at once sound the retreat. Neuhauss has very plainly shown the reason for this. " The consciousness of not having the luck on their side robs them of all their confidence. Their war medicine is not operating, therefore all their efforts will be in vain." [3]

At the moment of their rush upon the sleeping village they are certain of victory. Not only so because the enemy is defenceless, and cannot leave his huts without being struck down, but also and above all because their " medicine " is acting. The enemy is in their power, he is " doomed," just as the man who has been bewitched is " doomed "

[1] R. Neuhauss: *Deutsch Neu Guinea,* (*Kai*) iii. p. 62.
[2] Vojtech Fric: " Eine Pilcomayo Reise in dem Chaco central," *Globus,* lxxxix. p. 233.
[3] R. Neuhauss: *Deutsch Neu Guinea,* iii. p. 65.

to be the prey of tiger or crocodile. He is unable to defend himself. It most frequently happens that the event confirms the attempt and the massacre is carried through without let or hindrance. But if there should be unexpected resistance, if several of the assailants, indeed if only one of them is killed or seriously wounded, the attack ceases immediately and the enemy retires, for it has been proved that the " medicines " are not operating as they should be. Perhaps their effect is paralysed by other and stronger measures which the enemy has brought to bear. Persistence would then be folly.

Dr. Nieuwenhuis has noted this characteristic in Borneo. " The fact that the death or even wounding of a single man, in the fights which these tribes undertake, is sufficient to put the whole tribe to flight is also a very significant one. They see in it, in fact, a sure sign of the wrath of the spirits, and at the same time it proves what a powerful impression such a circumstance makes upon them." [1] But this powerful impression is caused mainly by their fear that the unseen powers are hostile. As soon as there is a sign of such disfavour, the native bows before it, just as he accepts without cavilling the result of a trial by ordeal. In the Fiji Isles, " if intended mischief is once frustrated, he (the native) will cease to entertain the idea of repeating the attempt. A house is set on fire ; but the flames are extinguished in time. The incendiary submits to his defeat, and makes no further effort of that description. A murder is prevented ; the agents consider it to have been so decreed. An unfortunate captive is taken ; he makes no attempt to save himself. His only wish is to secure a speedy termination of his sufferings." [2]

Waterhouse says again : " A most striking feature in the arrangements for attack is the primary preparation for defeat. Many days are sometimes spent in preparing the *orna* (bypaths by which to run away easily in case of defeat) while the subsequent attack may not last very many hours." [3] The Fijians were not wanting in courage, but they could

[1] A. W. Nieuwenhuis : *Quer durch Borneo*, ii. p. 167. (Bahau.)
[2] J. Waterhouse : *The King and People of Fiji*, p. 307.
[3] Ibid., p. 317.

not contravene the decisions of the unseen powers, and they judged it wise to provide for their being hostile.

In Central Africa, " when two chiefs meet in war, for instance, victory does not depend merely on strength and courage, as we might suppose, but on fetish medicines. If some men on the side of the more powerful chief fall, they at once retire and acknowledge that their ' medicines ' have failed, and they cannot be induced to renew the conflict on any consideration." [1] Lastly, the same conviction accounts for a similar action on the part of the Creek Indians who were confidently following the leadership of a young girl whom they had taken as their guide. They ended by encountering a detachment of the enemy and they massacred them. " This first engagement " says Fr. de Smet, " struck dismay into the conquerors, for they, too, had seven men killed and fifteen wounded. They uncovered the young heroine's eyes, and the manitous whom they had considered so propitious to them being now reported unfavourable to their designs, the combatants dispersed in haste, taking the very shortest route to their homes." [2]

V

The weapons used in warfare are manufactured with all the care the natives can bestow on them ; they often bear witness to an ingenuity which renders them dangerous and deadly. But their efficacy does not depend entirely, or even chiefly, upon their visible and material qualities. It depends essentially upon the mystic virtue which the " medicines " or the magic operations have conferred upon them. A warrior's weapons are therefore sacred, and often no one but himself must touch them. In peace time, they are surrounded by infinite safeguards, to concentrate and maintain within them the magic influence which will assure their success.

Thus in New Pomerania (the Gazelle Peninsula), " they used at one time to keep all the clubs in the *malira* house. This was a hut expressly built to keep the ' medicines '

---

[1] Rev. F. S. Arnot: *Garenganze*, p. 237 (2nd edit. 1889).
[2] Fr. J. de Smet, S.J.: *Voyages dans l'Amérique septentrionale*, pp. 150-2.

and all the objects relating to them. . . . In time of war they would bring these clubs out, after having pronounced magic incantations over them in the hut. They had previously been rubbed with *malira* (this is the leaf of a tree endowed with magic virtues), or some of it was attached to each of them . . . each kind of club having its own special *malira*. . . . All these enchantments were designed to make the clubs so deadly that a single blow would be enough to kill the enemy on the spot. They state that these operations, like the clubs themselves, have come to them from afar." [1] Quite near there, at Bougainville, similar methods are in use. " In order that the spears may not fail to hit their mark, they are consecrated—particularly during a certain dance in honour of the dead—by being struck against the ground, which breaks their point. Or again, they may be consecrated by being aimed at a target made of the corpse of a man who has died a violent death (while constructing a chief's house, for example.) They then collect the spears which have hit the mark, sharpen the points afresh, and provide them with hooks." [2] The natives are not content, therefore, with subjecting their weapons to a magical process ; they desire to discover in which of them the desired effect has been produced, and they will make use of these only. Before they are employed, they must have undergone some test. We do the same with our guns. But with the Melanesians, the test is a mystic one, even as is the efficacy of the weapons tested.

Codrington has clearly shown that theirs are poisoned arrows, though not in the sense in which Europeans would use the term. " What is sought " (by the Melanesians) " and as they firmly believe obtained, is an arrow which shall have supernatural power (*mana*) to hurt, in the material of which it is made, and in the qualities added by charms and magical preparations. . . . The point is of a dead man's bone, and has therefore *mana* ; it has been tied on with powerful magic charms, and has been smeared with stuff hot and burning, as the wound is meant to be, prepared

---

[1] R. Parkinson : *Dreissig Jahre in der Südsee*, p. 131–2.
[2] R. Thurnwald : " Im Bismarck Archipel und auf den Salomon Inseln," *Zeitschrift für Ethnologie*, xlii. p. 128.

and applied with charms ; that is what they mean by what we, not they, call poisoned arrows. And when the wound has been given, its fatal effect is to be aided and carried on by the same magic which has given superior power to the weapon." . . . As a means of combating this influence on the part of the victim's friends, " if the arrow, or a part of it, has been retained, or has been extracted with leaf poultices, it is kept in a damp place or in cool leaves ; then the influence will be little and will soon subside. . . . In the same way, the man who has influenced the wound . . . and his friends will bring hot and burning juices and chew irritating leaves ; pungent and bitter herbs will be burnt to make an irritating smoke . . . the bow will be kept near the fire to make the wound it has inflicted hot, or as in Lepers' Island, will be put into a cave haunted by a ghost ; the bowstring will be kept taut and occasionally pulled, to bring on tension of the nerves and the spasms of tetanus to the wounded man." [1] Thus everything happens in the region of the mystic ; both the friends and the enemies of the wounded man operate therein. What we call the physical effects are, to the Melanesians, supernatural ones, or rather, we distinguish between the two, which they do not. According to our view of it, if the arrow is a poisoned one, it is because its head has been smeared over with some toxic product, but according to the natives, it is only charged with *mana*, the influence of which is such that it continues to operate upon the wounded man at a distance.

I shall not lay stress upon these customs, which are almost universally practised. Natives feel confidence in weapons which have undergone a magic preparation only. In South Africa, for instance, among the Makololo, they make use of a " gun medicine," without which, according to the popular belief, they could not aim correctly.[2]

What is true of weapons used in warfare applies equally to those which serve for hunting and fishing, and in a general way, to tools and instruments. Their effectiveness depends above all on their *mana*, and most frequently it is the result

[1] R. H. Codrington : *The Melanesians*, pp. 308–10.
[2] D. Livingstone : *Missionary Travels and Researches in South Africa*, p. 175.

alone which reveals whether a certain implement is sufficiently endowed with it, or exceptionally so. " For instance, the Déné mind sees mystery everywhere, irrespective of its intrinsic value or peculiar make ; the native attaches more or less unaccountable qualities to some mechanical device, weapon of the chase, or fishing implement on its proving successful (probably accidentally). ' Post hoc, ergo propter hoc ' seems to be the basis of all his judgments. An old net, for instance, which by a stroke of good luck has been set for a shoal of fish, will be infinitely more esteemed, even though it may be in locks (*sic*) than a new one which has been used but once, probably in the wrong place. Here it is a question of personal supernatural powers extended to things inanimate." [1] This last remark of Fr. Morice's is a very true one. At the same time, it would probably be better not to say that the Déné reasons according to the ' post hoc, ergo propter hoc' theory. To the primitive there is no such thing as chance. If an old and worn-out fishing-net obtains an abundant catch, it is because the fish were ready to enter it. If they thus obeyed the influence which drew them thither, it was because the net possessed a mysterious and profound virtue which they found irresistible. Therefore other nets, even in good condition, if they have caught but few fishes, will be set aside in favour of this one, since its power has been proved. Hearne had already remarked, speaking of the Indians in the same district : " They frequently sell new nets, which have not been wet more than once or twice, because they have not been successful." [2] It is useless for these snares to be new and well made ; what good is there in keeping them if they lack the essential thing, the magic power of influencing the fish ?

In Borneo, too, among the Kayans, weapons of the chase are esteemed according to the success they attain. " A hunter who has shot down a pig or a doe with a single bullet will cut out the ball to melt it down with other lead, and will make a fresh batch of bullets or slugs from the mixture, believing that the lucky bullet will leaven the

[1] Fr. A. G. Morice : "The Great Déné Race," *Anthropos*, v. p. 141 (1910).
[2] S. Hearne : *A Journey from the Prince of Wales's Fort in Hudson Bay to the Northern Ocean*, p. 239 (note) (1795).

whole lump, and impart to all of it something of that to which its success was due. Compare also a similar practice in regard to the seed grain." [1] On the other hand, " if a house has been partially destroyed by fire, nothing of what is left will be used in the building of the new one. They have an indefinable feeling that the use of material taken from a house which has been burnt down would expose the new building to the same fate, as if this material might infect it with its own misfortune."

In Samoa, " qualities of good or bad fortune were constantly attributed to neuter objects. Fish-hooks, for instance, were considered to be lucky or unlucky. Some canoes or boats were considered to be much more fortunate in attracting sharks or other fish than other canoes were. Weapons were also considered as being courageous or cowardly." [2]

Primitive African races afford many examples of the same kind. Here are some of them. " Bushmen despise the arrow which has failed of its mark, were it but once only. The one which has struck home, on the contrary, is of two-fold value in their eyes. Consequently, however much time and trouble it entails, they would rather make new ones altogether than pick up and use again those which have been unsuccessful." [3] Should it happen that a weapon which is usually lucky fails to bring down the quarry, it is because a more powerful charm than its own is acting upon it and paralysing its effort. Its want of success *can* have no other cause. " As a rule, after a day's hunting among the buffaloes or hippopotami, I returned home with at least one of these animals. But during one season it happened that for two consecutive days I failed to kill anything, although I saw plenty of game. . . . The men who accompanied me were thoroughly disheartened at my want of success, and were convinced of the interference of some spirit who had bewitched my gun, and would earnestly ask my permission to expel the objectionable evil-doer. ' Let us have your rifle and we will remove the Moloki,'

---

[1] Hose and MacDougall : *The Pagan Tribes of Borneo*, i. p. 204 (note).
[2] Rev. George Brown : *Melanesians and Polynesians*, p. 249.
[3] H. Lichtenstein : *Reisen im südlichen Afrika*, ii. p. 442.

said they ; and upon my inquiring the mode of ejectment they proposed trying, they answered : ' Simply put the barrel in the fire till it is red hot, and burn out the evil spirit.' " [1]

In Loango, " the natives often venture out fishing, even when the bar is dangerous, if there is promise of a rich haul. In such a case the *banganga* (sorcerers) hasten to arrange sticks, rags, fragments of cloth, bundles of linen, all forming a most curious chain, upon the shore. These are charms designed to promote the capture of the fish and to prevent the nets from breaking and the boats from upsetting with their human freight. When they have been used for any occasion, once the fishing is over, they are usually left to the mercy of the wind and waves, but if in spite of unfavourable circumstances, there should have been a good haul without any untoward incident, then the second-hand fetishes acquire extraordinary value from the fact that they have been unusually lucky. They are picked up and carefully arranged so that they may be used another time." [2] As a matter of fact, to primitive mentality any experience ever so little out of the common, whether for good or evil, has the value of revelation, like the revelations obtained by means of omens and divination. It therefore requires just as much consideration, and the native must be guided by what he has thus learnt with regard to the views of the unseen powers. In the present case, it is worth knowing that he may fish without danger, even when the bar is rough, if protected by these charms

We may compare with these facts Thalbitzer's acute observations respecting certain amulets in use among the Esquimaux.

" The amulet does more than merely represent the animal or human being which it imitates or by which it is made. The amulet is alive, because it has been made during the recitation of a charm or spell, when the dominating qualities of the animal or the part of the body have been invoked ; the power of these qualities is at any rate potentially present in the animal. It evidently makes no great difference whether it is the thing (animal) itself or an imitation

---

[1] E. J. Glave : *Six Years of Adventure in Congoland*, pp. 117–18.
[2] Dr. Pechuël-Loesche : *Die Loango Expedition*, iii. 2. p. 402.

which is used as an amulet ; it has the same power. But
there may be a shade of difference in the conception of the
inherited amulets, which consist of discarded implements
or utensils—often only the fragmentary remnants. Here
it is not the original qualities of the things which are of
importance ; as was the case of the animal amulets . . . but
rather its inherited qualities, good luck in hunting, for
example, which once followed the weapon when used by
the original owner, and which is now the dominating power
of the amulet." [1]

Finally, since the material and visible qualities of an
implement or trap of any kind, are subordinate to its value
in respect of its invisible and mystic qualities, which use
alone reveals, the most valuable assistance may be given
by any object whatever (even if apparently irrelevant to
the end in view), provided that experience has once shown
it to be powerful. Among the Maidu people of North
America, therefore, "any strangely shaped or coloured
stone or object found was picked up, and its powers tested.
If on finding and carrying it a man had good luck in anything,
the stone or object would then be preserved carefully as
a charm for that purpose." [2] This charm, as we see, closely
resembles what gamblers call a " mascot." When the
Maidu sets out to hunt, this stone will be as necessary to
him as his weapons.

Sometimes the unfamiliar object met with gives its
possessors valuable influence over certain beings, and natives
are therefore very desirous of securing it for themselves.
Fr. de Smet relates a very characteristic story with regard
to this. "They (the Cœurs-d'Alène) told me that the first
white man they ever saw was wearing a cotton shirt, with
a black and white pattern all over it, which seemed like
small-pox to them ; and he was also carrying a white wrapper.
The natives imagined that the spotted shirt was the Great
Manitou which possesses mastery over the terrible disease
called small-pox, and that the white wrapper was the Great
Manitou of snow. They thought therefore that if they

[1] W. Thalbitzer : " Ethnographical Collections from East Greenland,"
Meddelelser om Groenland, xxxix. p. 630.
[2] R. B. Dixon : " The Northern Maidu." *Bulletin of the American Museum
of Natural History*, xvii. p. 267.

could obtain possession of these divinities their nation would be for ever freed from the deadly scourge, and their winter hunting expeditions would be facilitated by the vast amount of snow which would fall. In exchange for these two articles, then, they offered several of their finest horses. The bargain was readily agreed to by the white man, and from that time onward, for many years, the spotted shirt and the white wrapper were the objects of the most profound veneration. On solemn occasions they were carried in procession and placed on a very high elevation, which was the consecrated place devoted to their superstitious rites. There they were solemnly spread on the ground, and the great ' pipe of peace ' offered them with as much veneration as they used in offering it to the sun, fire, earth, or water. Then the whole company of magicians and medicine-men intoned canticles in their honour." [1] To be able to account satisfactorily for the powers attributed by these natives to the two strange objects, and the intense respect they showed them, we must not forget that the man of whom they had purchased them was the first white man they had ever seen. He must undoubtedly have appeared an extra-ordinary being to them, and a very powerful magician at any rate, and therefore the strange things he brought with him must be endowed with marvellous virtue, and exercise absolute sway over both small-pox and snow (which they resembled), and these objects would bring good luck to their tribe if they became possessed of them.

VI

Without proceeding further in our inquiry with regard to the primitive's mystic orientation of the causes of success, I shall dwell upon a final point, which supports the conclusions already reached. Whatever the instru-ments, weapons, tools, or processes employed, primitives, as we have seen, never consider success certain or even possible if these alone are used, without the concurrence of the unseen powers having been secured. Material aids, although indispensable, play but a subordinate part. It

[1] Fr. J. de Smet, S.J. : *Voyages dans l'Amérique septentrionale*, pp. 223–4.

is in accordance with this conviction that primitives act, both in war and in peace. In certain cases which I shall rapidly indicate, they even go beyond this. Material means are no longer necessary, and the primitive, without using any instrument whatever, can attain his end simply by the mystic virtue of his desire.

In North Queensland, on the Tully River, " a black will earnestly yearn for some particular fruit, etc., to come into season, and will send one of the larger species of spiders to bring it—and it will come. The coastal aboriginals especially and firmly believe in this method of satisfying any particular craving." [1] " If the members of one tribe wished to work harm on one of another tribe, the men would leave their camp, and select a secluded sandy spot ; they would then make a depression in the sand in the centre of which a rude figure of a man is moulded. By concentrating their thoughts on the one they desire to harm, and by singing a weird song, the mischief is wrought. The subject of their animosity will develop a high fever and will probably die within a day or two." [2]

This is a case of witchcraft by effigy. The man " doomed " is undoubtedly represented by a rudimentary type of human figure, but no physical influence or actual violence of any kind is exercised upon the symbol. Their thoughts firmly fixed upon the victim to his undoing will suffice, and their own inherent desire to kill him must bring about his death. Sometimes, when the wish is uttered, its effect is believed to be deadly. " A certain white settler, being very much annoyed with a native, told him in as powerful language as he could muster, that he wished he might die, and that he had no doubt he would die within a twelvemonth. The native professed to treat this prognostication with derision ; nevertheless, on calling about a year afterwards, the settler was informed that the native had fretted so much about it that he died." [3] Evidently this native believed that he had been " doomed." The wish expressed by the white

[1] W. E. Roth : " Superstition, Magic, and Medicine," *North Queensland Ethnography*, Bulletin 5, No. 107.
[2] W. H. Bird : " Ethnographical Notes about the Buccaneer Islanders, N.W. Australia," *Anthropos*, vi. p. 177.
[3] B. Seemann : *A Mission to Viti*, p. 190 (1862).

man was equal to casting a spell upon him, as he thought, and the same fatal effect was bound to follow.

Campbell has borne witness to the same belief in South Africa. " Pelangye, on the death of his father, inherited all his cattle, which were very numerous. When Mateebe's brother was murdered by Bushmen, Mateebe accused Pelangye of ' wishing ' that the murder might take place ; on which ground he seized all his cattle, and ordered his houses to be burnt. . . . The fact was that from the large, round, and singular eyes of Pelangye, Mateebe either believed, or pretended to believe, that he possessed the power of witchcraft, and that through the exertion of this power his brother had been murdered by the Bushmen." [1] In this example we have no difficulty in recognizing a likeness, already previously noted,[2] to the evil eye, and the malevolent principle informing the wizard, and we observe, too, that the latter is accused of having exercised his influence merely by wishing that something should happen. The same idea is common in the Congo district, and in West Africa. " The Warega search for the supernatural in everything. They believe that everybody has the power of affecting Fate and making a wish come true. They do not explain exactly how it can be done, but they clearly attach an idea of witchcraft by effigy to this belief." [3] In other words, they think that anybody can cast a spell on another and bewitch him merely by virtue of wishing to do it. On the Niger, " yesterday there was a procession of the wives of the late son of the king . . . whose death I have already alluded to. The women came down to the waterside to wash. . . . They proceeded to drink poison, from a belief that they had wished their husband's death. . . . Out of sixty of these poor, infatuated wretches, thirty-one of them died ; while others, who vomited immediately, escaped death. . . ." [4]

In Calabar, again, " I heard some mournful cries in the bush . . . and approached the place from whence the cries proceeded, which was about twenty yards from the

[1] Rev. J. Campbell : *Travels in South Africa ; Second Journey*, ii. p. 184.
[2] See chap. viii. p. 249.
[3] Commandant Delhaise : *Les Warega*, p. 213.
[4] M. Laird and R. A. K. Oldfield : *An Expedition into the Interior of Africa*, ii. pp. 277–8 (1837).

waterside, on the coast, and I saw there a woman lying chained by a leg to wood, with the arms and legs pinioned, awaiting the period of high water, to be launched into the sea, there to become the unhappy prey of voracious sharks. On inquiring . . . I found that she was one of the wives of a chief who had died a few days before, and the brother had selected her to suffer for having wished his deceased brother's death ! " [1]

These facts would be incomprehensible if we were ignorant of the collective representations which cause primitives to act thus. In the first place, the desire in question is not necessarily a conscious wish, definitely formulated. In a moment of anger and impatience when tortured by jealousy, the wife may have wished that her husband were dead, without even owning the wish to herself, or taking it into account. She may deny this in all good faith—but the poison, in killing her, will prove the contrary. If the desire did exist, were it but for an instant, its fatal effect was made possible, especially in a case where a woman revealed within herself the evil principle of which sorcerers are made. It is this which the ordeal by poison can ascertain. But even the existence of this principle is not necessary ; desire alone has the power to kill, just as witchcraft may. The natives in this part of Africa are fully persuaded of this, and hence arise the complications of which Dr. Pechuël-Loesche gives us some idea. " We can scarcely question the fact that there really are persons who consider themselves wizards in the worst sense of the word, and even avow this publicly. Is not a spiteful feeling with regard to another sufficient to injure, even to kill him ? Ill will has the same effect as ill doing. Its influence acts like that of the sun in warming, and the cool wind in refreshing, us. Its poison is like the poison of noxious plants, or the venom of the asp. This idea endues chance with very great force. Evil thoughts may meet with a successful issue, and then the consequence is a guilty conscience. He who has indulged in them accuses himself, or at any rate he acts in such a way as to awaken suspicions in others, and incites them to accuse him, all

[1] M. Laird and R. A. K. Oldfield : *An Expedition into the Interior of Africa*, i. pp. 349–50.

the more so because natives are extremely clearsighted in everything which concerns personal relations." [1] If, then, the desire for a person's death is actually equivalent to killing him, it is because, like the evil eye, and the bad spirit imbuing abnormal persons and sorcerers, its mystic power alone suffices to attain its end.

In New France, " they " (the Indians) " imagine that anyone who wishes or desires the death of another, especially if he be a sorcerer, often obtains the realization of his desire ; but the sorcerer who has felt the wish will himself die after his victim." [2] Among the Ten'a " the wishes of the shaman, when proffered with a special intense act of the will, all have this efficacy, through, of course, the intervention of his familiar demon. An instance of this kind may be seen in the Ten'a version of the Flood, where, to cause the reappearance of the land, the raven wishes with such energy that he faints from the effort." [3]

With the Shasta tribe, " in cases of murder, the friends and relatives of the murdered man went about praying that the murderer might die, or be injured in some accident ; if this happened to him, or to any of his family (who were generally included in these prayers), it was regarded as due to the latter that the accident or death took place, and the relatives of the murdered man were then held just as much responsible for the blood money as if they had killed or injured the individual by bodily violence." [4]

Sapir, too, tells us : " A powerful shaman might also reach his victim by merely ' wishing ' him or (mentally) ' poisoning ' him, as my informant put it ; this method was frequently employed by mythological characters such as Coyote, and was indicated in the language by a special verb. . . . It not infrequently happened that when someone fell ill, that a particular shaman was accused by another of being the responsible party ; in such cases the accused shaman was compelled to cure the sick person or else suffer death as

---

[1] Dr. Pechuël-Loesche : *Die Loango Expedition*, iii. 2. pp. 335–6.
[2] *Relations des Jésuites*, xii. p. 12. (Fr. Le Jeune.)
[3] Fr. Jul. Jetté : "On the Superstitions of the Ten'a Indians," *Anthropos*, vi. p. 250.
[4] R. C. Dixon : " The Shasta," *Bulletin of the American Museum of Natural History*, xvii. p. 453.

a penalty." [1] This last feature is another proof that the desire to injure is akin to enchantment. Nearly everywhere, in fact, the wizard convicted of having caused the illness of a person is himself obliged to undo the evil he has brought about ; that is an invariable consequence, and the wizard's punishment is not inflicted until afterwards. Should he refuse to revoke the enchantment, he is put to the torture and then killed. Thus it very frequently happens that the man accused of such a crime, even though he knows himself to be innocent, has no other chance of safety than to confess, and to pretend to revoke the magic spell cast upon his reputed victim.

In a story related by an Indian Hidatsa there appears a medicine-man who has lived with bears. They taught him, and it was from them that he obtained his magic power. "He helped his people in many ways. When they were hungry, he thought in his mind thus : ' There should be buffaloes near the village ' ; and when he would thus think it, it was so."[2] In British Columbia " if one Indian is vexed with another, the most effectual way of showing his displeasure, next to killing him, is to say to him : ' By-and-by you will be dead.' Not infrequently the poor victim thus marked becomes so terrified that the prediction is verified. When this is the case the friends of the deceased say that they have no doubt about the cause, and therefore (if they are not able to meet the contest which may ensue) the prognosticator, on the first opportunity, is shot for his passionate language."[3]

Quite recently, too, Preuss noted similar facts in the Indians among whom he lived. " They attribute quite extraordinary power to words and thoughts. . . . Everything that is done is referred not merely to external activity, but considered as the result of reflection also. The very fact of the action is quite insignificant in comparison, and in a sense it is not differentiated from reflection. . . . Words

[1] E. Sapir : " The Religious Ideas of the Takelma Indians of South-West Oregon," *Journal of American Folk Lore*, xx. p. 41 (1907).

[2] Pepper and Wilson : " An Hidatsa Shrine and the Beliefs respecting it," *Memoirs of the American Anthropological Association*, ii. pp, 309–10.

[3] R. C. Mayne : *Four Years in British Columbia*, p. 292. (Letter from Duncan, the missionary.)

are not regarded merely as a means of expression, but as a method of influencing the gods, i.e. Nature, just like entreaties and music. . . . What the words mean is already realized from the mere fact of their being uttered, supposing, of course, that the necessary magic force resides in the person speaking. . . . In various ways we may see that when man acts, thoughts take first rank as a means of action, and that they can even produce their effect independent of the words or the material act." [1] What Preuss calls reflection (*Nachdenken*) or thought (*Gedanke*) does not in fact differ from what English and American investigators designate " wish." With these primitives it is scarcely a question of theoretical conceptions, but of complex psychological states in which the emotional element most frequently predominates.

In South America, among the Lenguas of Grand Chaco, " when a man expresses a desire for rain or for a cool south wind, his neighbours, if they do not share the desire, protest strongly and implore him not to persist in his wish. They always considered that I had particular power in influencing the south wind, and believed that by whistling or hissing I could bring it up at will. This probably was owing to the fact that Europeans welcome this wind as a pleasant change from the exhausting heat." [2] This may be quite possible, but we must also take into account the virtue inherent in the desire, especially in the case of a magician as powerful as these natives believed Mr. Grubb to be. With the Araucans, " the concerted lamentations of women around the body are more than a mere funeral custom ; they are a series of curses pronounced upon his murderer, and in certain cases they are of magic efficacy. In default of any more positive form of vengeance, this is a way of exercising it." [3]

Lastly, with respect to the Todas of India, Rivers says : " I was told by two men that they believed that a sorcerer, by merely thinking of the effect he wished to produce, could produce the effect, and that it was not necessary for him

[1] K. Th. Preuss : *Die Nayarit-Expedition*, i. pp. xcvi-xcvii.
[2] W. B. Grubb : *An Unknown People in an Unknown Land*, p. 138.
[3] T. Guevara : *Psicologia del pueblo Araucano*, pp. 271-2.

to use any magical formula or practise any special rites." [1]

This very common belief helps to explain other beliefs founded on it, and the customs referring to it. In many places, for example—in South Africa, India, and elsewhere—when after a prolonged drought rain does fall, working in the fields is forbidden, even if the rain be but a slight shower, and apparently about to stop. " If it has rained throughout the night, no one may go to cultivate the fields next day, for fear of worrying the rain and causing it to stop." [2] As a matter of fact, the man or woman who wanted to work out of doors could not help wishing the rain to stop, and that desire would influence it. In Northern India, " when rain is wanted, if anyone runs out of a house bareheaded while it is raining, he is ordered in at once, or he is told to put on his cap or turban, for a bareheaded man is apt to wish involuntarily that the rain might cease, and thus injure his neighbour." [3] It sometimes happens that this same power is attributed to the wishes of animals. In the Malay Peninsula, " it is supposed to be lucky to keep cats because they long for a soft cushion to lie upon, and so (indirectly) wish for the prosperity of their masters . . . but it is considered unlucky to keep dogs. . . . The dog longs for the death of his master, an event which would involve the slaying of animals at the funeral feast, when the bones would fall to the dogs." [4] Involuntary wishes these, but none the less productive of effect.

From this belief of theirs, we can more readily understand the special nature of the terror inspired by the magician in certain social groups, the exasperation which finds its expression in the tortures inflicted on him, and the suddenness of the aggression when, after long hesitation, the natives finally decide to get rid of him. He can work so much evil, and at such a trifling cost ! For him, more than for any other, it is enough to think intensely and desire earnestly that something shall happen, and the wish meets

---

[1] W. H. R. Rivers : *The Todas*, p. 255.
[2] E. Holub: *Sieben Jahre in Süd Afrika*, i. p. 431.
[3] W. Crooke : *The Popular Religion and Folk-lore of Northern India*, i. p. 78 (1896). [4] W. W. Skeat: *Malay Magic*, pp. 182–3, 190–1.

with fatal fulfilment. Therefore, when he pleases, without doing anything to attract attention, without even lifting his little finger, he can bring ruin, disease, and death upon his neighbour. There are but two courses open to one in dealing with such a man—either to purchase his goodwill or to destroy him. Hence, on the one hand, the privileges he enjoys, the advantages of all kinds which he procures for himself, and which no other can either refuse or dispute, and on the other, only too frequently his most tragic end.

This power to injure by the intensity of the thought alone is very closely connected with what is commonly called the evil eye or *jettatura*. Hobley gives the reason for this. He says : " A few people here and there throughout the country are believed to possess this gift, women as well as men possess it . . . the possessor is born with it. It will gradually dawn upon the people that So-and-so possesses the power, owing to the fact that if that person audibly admires a beast belonging to a neighbour, the animal shortly after that becomes sick. . . . It would therefore seem that the idea is not based on an evil chance, but upon an envious thought. . . . If a cattle owner hears that a man who has this power . . . has been admiring one of his cows, he will send for him and insist on his removing the evil ; this is done by the man wetting his finger with saliva, and touching the beast on the mouth, or on various parts of the body with his wetted finger ; this is believed to neutralize the enchantment." [1] The proprietor of the sick animal, therefore, thinks that his beast is the victim of enchantment, worked on it by the man who, in looking at and praising it, has felt a desire for it. This desire, whether expressed or not, acts upon it, and there is but one remedy—the one which is always used in cases of witchcraft. The one who has worked the spell must himself destroy its power. The man whose desire is productive of harm is regarded as a wizard.

" Presently a small herd of fine animals came into view. As we were intently observing them, and someone pointed in the direction in which they were, Aba Ganda said : ' Be

[1] C. W. Hobley : " Further Researches into Kikuyu and Kamba Religious Beliefs and Customs," *J.A.I.*, xli. p. 433.

sure not to do that before the Gallas. Don't look much at their cattle, and certainly avoid praising them. The Gallas are very jealous of their livestock ; a stranger's admiration of it would be attributed by them to a covetous heart and would instantly excite their ire. Take no notice of their cattle, and if you say anything let your remarks be of a depreciatory character rather than otherwise.'" [1] In Arabia Petræa, " if anyone looks upon an animal with a covetous eye, as if he desired to possess it, the country-folk believe that his soul enters into direct relationship with the animal, and that the latter will die if his owner keeps him. In the same way, if a man covets a woman, child, article of clothing, or anything else, his soul has the power to injure the object coveted, and it will suffer thereby. If the author of the evil is known, he will be robbed of a piece of his clothing, and this will be used in fumigating the sick man's quarters. That occasionally succeeds, but it is not invariably the case. If the offender is not known, recourse must be had to a ' seer,' who will find out who it is that has affected So-and-so's animal, or So-and-so himself thus." [2]

Covetousness, then, is of itself not merely a feeling or desire, but a positive and effectual action of the soul of him who covets upon the thing coveted. According to Preuss' expression thought, in this case, really has the same effect as action. Casalis had noted this too. He says : " Covetousness has its own proper meaning. These people realize only too well its dread power, and seem to regard it as an axiom that it is impossible to impose silence on the un-governed desires of the heart. I remember how, shortly after my arrival in Lessuto, a chief trying to repeat the ten commandments, could find but nine. We reminded him of the tenth—' Thou shalt not covet.' ' But that is not a separate commandment,' he replied ; ' I have said that already, when I said " Thou shalt not steal," " Thou shalt not commit adultery." ' Thus the conscience of a heathen revealed to him what Our Lord was obliged to explain to those who had received the law." [3]

---

[1] Ch. New : *Life, Wanderings, and Labours in Eastern Africa*, p. 249 (1874).
[2] A. Musil : *Arabia Petræa*, iii. p. 314.
[3] Casalis : *Les Bassoutos*, pp. 322–3.

This remark leaves us no doubt about the matter. In the collective representations of the Basutos, coveting is an act of the same kind as stealing. (Among the Bantus, adultery is of the nature of an attack upon property.) What we call a provision of morality is to them the working of a mystic force exerted upon the object coveted to its detriment. Casalis and Musil attribute this force to the "soul." The term is. a convenient one, yet it corresponds but ill with that which primitives have in mind. The close relation established by them between desire, covetousness, the evil eye, and the malignant principle which constitutes witchcraft would lead us to think that there is no question here of the "soul," such as we understand it. Perhaps we should rather see in it the manifestation of the *mana* emanating from all things, animate or inanimate, every living being, an influence which is particularly strong in the case of persons who are chiefs, ancestors, sorcerers, and so on. In certain of its properties this *mana* participates in the spiritual principle called the "soul," but in others it is widely different.

Whatever it may be, it is at least certain that according to the collective representations of primitives, desire of itself possesses the mystic virtue of influencing its object, without any magic formula or definite rite. In this there is nothing strange to a mentality which is accustomed to consider secondary causes and means of every kind as negligible, and to fix its attention on the unseen causes which it regards as the only effective ones

CHAPTER XI

THE MYSTIC MEANING OF THE WHITE MAN'S APPEARANCE AND OF THE THINGS HE BRINGS WITH HIM

I

THE sudden appearance of white people among primitives who had previously never seen any, and in some cases had not even imagined them to exist, and the establishment of the early relations between the two peoples, are events of a kind likely to throw light upon important characteristics peculiar to the mentality of undeveloped races. How does such a mentality react when first brought into contact with white people, and all the strange and extraordinary things they bring with them? If we were in possession of accurate and detailed information about this first meeting, it would be a kind of natural experiment in which primitive mentality, brought suddenly face to face with unforeseen circumstances, is thrown entirely out of gear with its customs and traditions.

Unfortunately the witnesses of events so interesting to the science of anthropology, explorers, missionaries, and naturalists—are not always careful to observe them with the necessary caution. Surprised at what they see, and unable to make a study of people whose language is unknown to them, and who moreover are both distrustful and timid, they merely pay attention to whatever seems unusual, strange, and improbable in the external appearance of the " savages " and their ways, or else they confine themselves to describing how relations with them, friendly or otherwise, have been brought about. On the other hand, it is self-evident that it is but very rarely that the natives themselves offer any testimony of the impression made upon them by their first experience of white men.

The shock of the encounter must have been all the more violent since, as a rule, they were living in a " closed world," without any idea that its walls might be scaled. Their cosmography, as far as we know anything about it, was practically of one type up till the time of the white man's arrival upon the scene. That of the Borneo Dayaks may furnish us with some idea of it. " They . . . consider the earth to be a flat surface, whilst the heavens are a dome, a kind of glass shade which covers the earth, and comes in contact with it at the horizon. They therefore believe that, travelling straight on, always in the same direction, one comes at last, without any metaphor, to touch the sky with one's fingers. Now, as they know that Europeans come from far away over the sea, the supposition that we are nearer heaven comes naturally to them. It seems to them, therefore, clearly impossible that I have not been in the moon, and they wanted to know if in my country we had one or several moons, and if we also had only one sun. It was most amusing to see the signs of incredulity which my negative answers elicited amongst my audience. . . . It was with real sorrow that they heard me assert that in Europe the sky was quite as far from the earth as in Borneo." [1] The Polynesians, too, " imagined that the sea which surrounds their islands was a level plain, and that at the visible horizon, or some distance beyond it, the sky or *rai* joined the ocean, enclosing as with an arch, or hollow cone, the islands in the immediate vicinity. They were acquainted with other islands, as Nuuhiva, or the Marquesas, Vaihi, or the Sandwich Islands, Tongataboo, or the Friendly Isles. The names of these occurred in their traditions or songs. Subsequently, too, they had heard of Beritani or Britain, and Paniola or Spain, but they imagined that each of these had a distinct atmosphere, and was enclosed in the same manner as they thought the heavens surrounded their own islands. Hence they spoke of foreigners as those who came from behind the sky, or from the other side

[1] Od. Beccari : *Wanderings in the Forests of Borneo*, pp. 337–8 (edit. of 1904).

of what they considered the sky of their part of the world." [1]

It is the same thing in the Mortlock Islands. " The natives drew with chalk actual maps of the whole of the Caroline Archipelago, and also of the neighbouring Mariana Islands. . . . One of them told us all sorts of things about the Palaos Islands, to the west of the Caroline Isles, and it seemed that, according to their geography, these islands were regarded as the *ultima Thule*, for in reply to our question as to what land lay beyond these isles, the native drew a line to the west of them and explained in a very clear and simple way that yonder, beyond the Palaos Islands, the dome of the sky was too close to the earth to permit of navigation ; the utmost that could be done was to crawl along the ground or swim in the sea." [2] In the Gambier Islands, " we were asked many questions about our country ; and when we said that it was very far away, they asked whether it touched the sky." [3] In Samoa, " of old, the Samoans thought the heavens ended at the horizon and hence the name which they gave, it is said, to the white men, viz. *papalangi* or ' heaven-bursters.' " [4] Among the Melanesians of the Loyalty Group, " to the mind of the Lifuan, the horizon was a tangible object at no great distance. Many of the natives thought that if they could only reach it they would be able to climb up to the sky." [5]

Such an impression is not peculiar to the races of the Southern Pacific. It is to be met with in South Africa. " Heaven is for them (the Thonga) an immense solid vault which rests upon the earth. The point where heaven touches the earth is called *bugimamusi*, a curious word of the *bu-ma* class, the prefix *bu* meaning ' place,' viz. the place where the women can lean their pestles against the vault (whilst everywhere else pestles must be leant against a wall or tree)." [6] In North America, " in Indian belief, the earth

[1] Rev. W. Ellis : *Polynesian Researches*, iii. pp. 168–9 (1829).
[2] Von Kittlitz : *Denkwürdigkeiten einer Reise nach dem russischen Amerika, Mikronesien, and durch Kamtschatka*, ii. pp. 87–8.
[3] *Annales de la Propagation de la foi*, ix. p. 50. (Lettre du missionnaire Caret.)
[4] G. Turner : *Nineteen Years in Polynesia*, p. 103 (1861).
[5] E. Hadfield : *Among the Natives of the Loyalty Group*, p. 106 (edit. 1920).
[6] H. A. Junod : *The Life of a South African Tribe*, ii. pp. 280–1 (1912).

is a circular disk, usually surrounded on all sides by water, and the sky is a solid concave hemisphere coming down at the horizon to the level of the earth.   In Cherokee and other Indian myths the sky is continually lifting up and coming down again to the earth like the upper blade of a pair of scissors." [1]   The sun, which lives outside this hemisphere, slips between the earth and the sky-line in the morning when there is a momentary slit, and it returns from the western side in the evening in the same fashion. [2]

In a world thus enclosed on all sides, and in which each tribe knows but itself and its nearest neighbours—above all in the case of island dwellers—what will be the effect produced by the sudden appearance of beings such as they never yet have seen, beings like men, and yet differing from them in colour, using unknown weapons, speaking in a strange language, and manifesting many other peculiarities ? The natives will be excited and terrified, rather than merely astonished.   That such beings may exist, their legends and myths have already prepared them to admit.   The unseen world, which is but one with the visible world, is peopled by beings more or less clearly defined, more or less like men, and more particularly is it peopled by the ghosts and ancestors who still remain men, though now in a different state.   What is really unheard-of is that the beings belonging to the unseen world should show themselves in the full light of day, should arrive on strange vessels, disembark, talk, and so forth. Everything they do, and everything they bring with them gives rise to a kind of religious dread such as travellers have frequently described.

I should like to relate the story told by an aged native of British Columbia.   It is somewhat long, but it gives a

---

[1] J. Mooney : " The Ghost-dance Religion," *Reports of the Bureau of American Ethnology, Smithsonian Institute*, xiv. p. 971 (1881).

[2] This idea of the heavens resting on the earth at the horizon makes primitives, as a rule, interpret quite literally what the missionaries tell them about heaven, and they manifest no surprise thereat.   The missionaries are bound to know all that is going on in heaven, for does not their country lie quite close to it ?   " Not long ago, during Divine service (at Bongu, (German) New Guinea), a native said to us : ' Of course you white men know all about heaven and about God, for you are quite close to it.   See how near the sky is to the earth there, where you come from, and look what a long way off it is here, where we are.   We have our gods, and you have yours.' "—*Berichte der rheinischen Missionsgesellschaft*, p. 120 (1903)

vivid impression of the natives' first encounter with white men. " A large canoe of Indians were busy catching halibut in one of these channels. A thick mist enveloped them. Suddenly they heard a sound as if a large animal was striking through the water. Immediately they concluded a monster from the deep was in pursuit of them. With all speed they hauled up their fishing lines, seized the paddles, and strained every nerve to reach the shore. Still the plunging noise came nearer. Every minute they expected to be engulfed within the jaws of some huge creature. However, they reached the land, jumped on shore, and turned round in breathless anxiety to watch the approach of the monster. Soon a boat, filled with striking-looking men, emerged from the mist. Though somewhat relieved of fear, the Indians stood spell-bound with astonishment. The strangers landed, and beckoned the Indians to come to them and bring them some fish. One of them had over his shoulder what was supposed to be only a stick ; presently he pointed it at a bird that was flying past ; a violent ' poo ' went forth ; down came the bird to the ground. The Indians ' died.' As they revived again, they questioned each other as to their state, whether any were dead, and what each had felt. The whites then made signs for a fire to be lighted. The Indians proceeded at once, according to their usual tedious fashion of rubbing two sticks together. The strangers laughed, and one of them snatching up a handful of dried grass, struck a spark into a little powder placed in it. Instantly flashed another ' poo ' and a blaze. The Indians ' died.' After this, the newcomers wanted some fish boiled. The Indians therefore put a fish and water into one of their square wooden buckets, and set some stones on the fire, intending, when they were hot, to cast them into the vessel, and thus boil the fish. The whites were not satisfied with this way. One of them fetched a tin kettle out of the boat, put the fish and the water into it, and then strange to say, set it on the fire. The Indians looked on with astonishment. However, the kettle did not consume ; the water did not run into the fire. Then again the Indians ' died.' When the fish was done, the strangers put on a kettle of rice on the fire. The Indians looked at each other and whispered *akshahn, akshahn* (maggots, maggots). The rice being cooked, some molasses were produced and mixed with it. The Indians stared and said : ' The grease of dead people.' The whites then tendered the rice and molasses to the Indians, but they only shrank away in disgust. Seeing this, to prove their integrity, they sat down and enjoyed it themselves. The sight stunned the Indians, and again they all ' died ' . . . . The Indians' turn had now come to make the white strangers die. They dressed their heads and painted their faces. A *nok-nok*, or wonder-working spirit, possessed them. They came slowly and solemnly, seated themselves before the whites, then suddenly lifted up their heads and stared. Their reddened eyes had the desired effect. The whites ' died.' " [1]

The Indians had " saved their face," and the successive " deaths " occasioned by the display of the weapons, utensils, and food of the white men, did not last long. All these new experiences, all these astonishing persons and things are almost immediately classified in their minds, accustomed as they are to imagine the occult powers. The gun at the sound of which the bird is killed, the pot which rests on the fire without being burnt up, etc., are so many unheard-of marvels ; but then there is no necessity to look for an explanation of them, because those who accomplish these wonders come from the world of occult powers, or else they are very closely connected with it. The Indian is taking part in a dream with his eyes open. But he knows that what he sees in the dream is at any rate quite as real as anything he perceives in his waking state.

The Esquimaux of the eastern coast of Greenland were not unaware that white men existed, but they had never seen any. " Our first meeting with the people of Angmagsalik," says Holm, writing in 1884, " was most curious. . . . They had imagined us as supernatural beings like the ' inland-dwellers' and the ' dog-men,' which are pure products of the imagination." [2]

The people just referred to had heard of Europeans, but

[1] *Metlahkatlah ; Ten Years' Work among the Tsimsheean Indians*, pp. 67–8 (C.M.S., 1869).
[2] G. Holm : " Ethnological Sketch of the Angmagsalik Eskimo," edit. by Thalbitzer, *Meddelelser om Groenland*, xxxix. pp. 7–8.

in the Pacific, for instance, they came absolutely as a surprise. Nearly everywhere the white people who disembarked were taken for ghosts. In the Wallis Islands, " several natives still have a vivid recollection of that event, and an old man whom I always enjoy questioning tells me that at the first appearance of the European vessel, they did not doubt but that it was a dominion of the gods floating on the waves. The people were confirmed in this impression on seeing the masts, which they took for coco-nut palms." [1] (Missionaries very frequently use the term " gods " for the word which means ghosts or ancestors.) In New Caledonia, " they think white men are the spirits of the dead, and bring sickness ; —this is the reason why they want to kill white men." [2] In the Gambier Islands, " they asked us if we were born of men, and without waiting for our reply the old man added : ' Are you gods ' ? (that is, ghosts)." [3] In the same archipelago " the first appearance of Europeans on their shores," writes another missionary, " threw the natives into a state of extreme astonishment, immediately succeeded by fear and terror. At first, when distance prevented them from distinguishing the people on the strange ship clearly, our good natives, in their simplicity, took the small vessels which left the ship for coco-nuts floating on the sea, but when the ship's boats came nearer and seemed to be full of unknown beings whose very existence they had never imagined, their consternation was extreme. The clothing with which they perceived the Europeans to be covered made them first of all believe that their visitors were a tattooed race. Those whose garments covered them almost entirely passed for *marapé* (men tattooed right up to the face, of whom our islanders stand in considerable awe). Finally they decided that they were malevolent gods, come to work their ruin." [4] In Australia this same belief is found in many tribes which live at a great distance from each other. " They (the natives) gave me the name of a chief who had fallen in battle, and affirmed that I had again come among

---

[1] *Annales de la Propagation de la foi*, xiii. p. 21.   (Fr. Bataillon.)
[2] Rev. Geo. Turner : *Nineteen Years in Polynesia*, p. 424.
[3] *Annales de la Propagation de la foi*, ix. p. 50.   (Lettre du missionnaire Caret.)
[4] Ibid., x. p. 202 (1837).   (Lettre du P. Laval.)

them as a white fellow." [1] " At Darnley Island, the Prince of Wales Islands, and Cape York, the word used at each place to signify a white man also means a ghost. Frequently when the children were teasing Gi'om " (a white woman who lived for several years with the natives) " they would be gravely reproved by some elderly person telling them to leave her, as ' poor thing ! she is nothing, only a ghost.' The Cape York people even went so far as to recognize in several of our officers and others on shore, the ghosts of departed friends to whom they might have borne some fancied resemblance, and in consequence, under the new names of Tamu, Tarka, etc., they were claimed as relatives, and entitled to all the privileges of such." [2] I do not lay any stress upon these well-known facts.

It is not the colour of Europeans alone which gives rise to the idea that they are ghosts. In the Andaman Isles, previous to any acquaintance with white races, which is a comparatively recent occurrence, " the natives had not the faintest knowledge of even the neighbouring coast of Burmah, much less of the world at large. . . . The few voyagers who from time to time ventured near their shores were regarded as deceased ancestors who, by some dispensation, had been permitted to revisit the earth. . . . In confirmation of this may be cited the name by which the natives of India are to this day called, viz. *chàwgala* (literally, departed spirits)." [3] Now the natives of India are coloured men.

In the Congo territory, when white men came to a district where none had ever been seen before, " the people were much afraid that the presence of the white men would stop the rain and bring on a drought. When they passed people on the road, even, they were heard to say : ' O mother, there will be no more rain !' They had constantly to tell the people that the rain was in God's hands, not theirs." [4] In a general way, the presence of white men was a cause of anxiety. The natives nearly everywhere seemed to be

[1] E. P. S. Sturt : *Letters from Victorian Pioneers*, p. 248 (1853).
[2] J. Macgillivray : *Narrative of the Voyage of H.M.S. " Rattlesnake,"* (1852).
[3] E. H. Man : " On the Aboriginal Inhabitants of the Andaman Islands," *J.A.I.*, xii. p. 100.
[4] Rev. W. H. Bentley : *Pioneering on the Congo*, i. p. 166. (R.T.S., 1900.)

somewhat afraid that it would be followed by catastrophe and death. Bentley says: " There was much anxiety as to the effect of our presence in the country. There was a pretty general fear that disease and death would follow. . . . In the country round, wise men shook their heads, and were sure that the San Salvador people would die very fast ; there would be no rain ; pest and disease of all kinds would surely follow. Everyone was on the alert and anxious and apprehensive, even in San Salvador." [1]

In many places in the same district, white men were first of all taken for black people who had risen from the dead. " During the earlier part of my residence at Lukolela, I had heard the word *barimu* mentioned several times in connection with myself. I afterwards discovered that it meant a ghost ; it was suggested that I was originally an African, and had died and returned to earth with a white skin." [2] " He (the chief) sat down very near us at the invitation, and even shook hands with us, examining curiously the hand he had just taken." (He was convinced that they were spirits, not human beings.) " We suggested that we were very warm, substantial ones, and that we were in the habit of sleeping and eating as other mortals ; indeed, we had just accepted a goat for our dinner from our friend beside him : did spirits eat and sleep ? ' But you are spirits, not men,' he insisted. I showed him my wife and baby on the steamer. Had spirits wives and babies ? The chief laughed at the idea, but then thinking, perhaps: ' Why should not spirits have wives and babies ? ' he continued. ' No, you are spirits, you are not good ; why do you always bring trouble ? Our people die, our farms do not produce as they should, our goats and fowls die, sickness and trouble comes, and you are the cause. Why do you not let us alone ? ' " [3]

Whether they be ghosts or spirits, white men belong to the world of unseen powers, or at least are in very close relations with it. The mere appearance of them, as we have just seen, may be a portent—and consequently a cause—of misfortune. Therefore when accidents, above all sudden

---

[1] Rev. W. H. Bentley: *Pioneering on the Congo*, i. p. 137.
[2] E. J. Glave : *Six Years of Adventure in Congoland*, p. 95 (1893).
[3] Mrs. H. M. Bentley: *The Life and Labours of a Congo Pioneer* , p. 212,

deaths or epidemics, have occurred shortly after their arrival, the natives have held them responsible. In Polynesia, for instance, missionaries have very often had to suffer on account of this coincidence. As a matter of fact their first intercourse with Europeans was nearly always fatal to natives, and later experience proved a strange confirmation of their fears. " Most of the diseases which have raged in our islands during my sojourn there," writes Williams, " have been introduced by ships. . . . First intercourse between Europeans and natives is, I think, invariably attended with the intro- duction of fever, dysentery, or some other disease which carries off numbers of people. At the island of Rapa, nearly half the whole population were thus swept away." [1] At Tanna, in the New Hebrides, " the priests wanted to kill us . . . because our presence there was certain to make their coughs worse. . . . There was a firm belief among all, that of late years, since they had visits from white men, their influenza epidemics were far more frequent and more fatal than they used to be. This impression is not confined to Tanna ; it is, if I mistake not, universal throughout the Pacific." [2]

The natives' dread of disease (that is, of the fatal and mystic influence exercised by disease) was so great that if one of them left the island and returned after a period of ab- sence, they considered him quite as dangerous as a foreigner. Murray once saw one who had made a stay in Samoa dis- embark at Savage Island (Niué). Here is his account of it. " The first day crowds assembled—armed, and wishing to kill him. The Samoan canoe given to him, together with his chest and property, they wanted to send back to the vessel as soon as they were landed, saying that the foreign wood would cause disease among them. He reasoned with them, told them to examine the wood ; it was the very same as grew in their own island. And as to himself, he said : ' You know it is my country ; I am not a god ' " (that is, a dead man or a ghost), " ' I am just like yourselves, I have no control over disease.' . . . Night came on and he had no place

[1] Rev. J. Williams : *A Narrative of Missionary Enterprise in the South Sea Islands*, pp. 281–2 (1837).
[2] Rev. G. Turner ; *Nineteen Years in Polynesia*, p. 28 (1861).

to lay his head. The people, fearing pollution, were afraid
to let him sleep in their houses." [1] "For years, too, after they
began to venture out on ships, they would not immediately
use anything they obtained, but hung it up in the bush in
quarantine for weeks." [2] "The dysentery which ravaged
in 1842 in other parts of the group . . . raged fearfully in
Eromanga. They (the natives) traced it to some hatchets
taken on shore from a sandal-wooding vessel, and threw
them all away. It is supposed that a third of the population of the island died at this time." [3]

Thus not only white men themselves, but everything
which comes from them or with them, everything that they
have touched, has the power of causing infection and death.
Not on account of actual contagion in the way familiar to
us—for the primitive has no idea of anything of that sort—
but because white people, whether they will or no, exercise
a fatal influence due to their relationship with the unseen
world. "The most marvellous powers have been attributed
to me," says Grubb. (He was the first white man to dwell
among the Lenguas of Grand Chaco.) "I have been supposed to be able to hypnotize men and animals, to bring up
the storms and the south winds at will, to drive off sickness
when I felt so inclined. . . . They believed that I had the
power of the evil eye, and knowledge of the future, that I
was able to discover all secrets and to know the movements
of people in different parts of the country . . . to drive off
the game from any particular part of the country, and to
speak with the dead." [4] In short, the people feared Mr.
Grubb as a wizard, with the added circumstance that as
he came from so far off his witchcraft would be all the
more dangerous.

Long after the first shock of surprise ceased to be felt,
after the native had seen white men living in his vicinity,
eating, drinking, sleeping, and even dying as he did, he yet
retained the impression that the European enjoyed some
indefinite and mysterious power. In South Africa the
early missionaries were invariably taken for wizards. "The

[1] A. W. Murray : *Missions in Western Polynesia,* pp. 360–3 (1863).
[2] Ibid., p. 388.
[3] Ibid., p. 178.
[4] W. B. Grubb : *An Unknown People in an Unknown Land,* p. 47 (1911).

missionaries who have come among them (i.e. the Kafirs of Xosa) have up to now been unable to avoid being regarded as wizards, and that is the chief reason why Van der Kemp was obliged to leave the country. In fact, on one occasion when there was a prolonged drought, the queen-mother sent a messenger to him, ordering him to make rain. . . . If at the end of three days there was still no rain, he would be treated as an enemy and a traitor. . . .It chanced that rain happened to fall during the specified period, and Van der Kemp was saved for the time being. But they were only the more insistent on requiring the same service of him again, and since on two successive occasions his prayers were unsuccessful he was obliged to leave the country for the sake of his own personal safety." [1] Among the Zulus also, who lived near the Xosa, " in former years, when the real object and character of the missionary were not understood as well as now, the people used to apply to him to bring on a shower in time of special need ; and even now they seem to think, oft-times, that he has some peculiar, magical kind of control over the clouds. . . . Moreover, as the missionary was naturally wont to put on dark-coloured thick clothes when a raw, rainy wind began to blow, many of the natives used to conclude there was some mysterious connection between the black coats and a plentiful shower." [2]

Moselekatze did not fail to ask Moffat if he " could make rain." [3] Among the Bechuanas, during a prolonged drought, the missionaries were frequently accused of having been the cause of it. " Some weeks after my return from a visit to Griqua Town," says Moffat, " a great discovery was made, that the rain had been prevented by my bringing a bag of salt from that place in my waggon. . . . The people at last became impatient, and poured forth their curses against Brother Hamilton and myself, as the cause of all their sorrow. Our bell, which was rung for public worship, they said, frightened the clouds ; our prayers came in also for a share of the blame. ' Don't you,' said the chief rather fiercely to me, ' bow down in your houses and pray and

[1] H. Lichtenstein : *Reisen im südlichen Afrika*, i. pp. 410–11.
[2] Rev. L. Grout : *Zululand*, pp. 132–3.
[3] R. Moffat : *Missionary Labours and Scenes in South Africa*, p. 550 (1842).

talk to something bad in the ground ? ' . . . and then the rain-maker proclaimed that he had discovered the cause of the drought. . . ' Do you not see, when clouds come over, that Hamilton and Moffat look at them ? ' This question, receiving a hearty and unanimous affirmation, he added, that our white faces frightened away the clouds, and they need not expect rain so long as we were in the country." [1]

The same circumstances have been noted elsewhere— in Sumatra, Borneo, South America, etc. The first missionaries everywhere were looked upon as mighty wizards, not in their character of missionaries, for that was not understood at all, but merely because they were white men and, as such, endowed with redoubtable magic powers. " When we began to talk about the removal of the station " (on account of the lack of water in the place), Faku said : ' Why don't you make rain ? I know the Dangwana (the Mission station) is a dry place, and I put you there thinking you would make rain for yourselves, and then we would get some at the same time.' It was in vain to contend. He said further : ' Why do you talk to me about God ? You yourself are God : do give us rain.' " [2] The same request may be made to another white man who happens to reside in the district. In the Bangala country, for example, the European administrator finds himself the object of their solicitations. " Last night a deputation waited upon me to try and get me to exercise my magic powers to stop the rain. My confession of incompetence not being taken seriously by them, I set myself up for a meteorological expert at their service." [3]

II

If white men are wizards and can dispose at will of the forces of the unseen world, their weapons and instruments also must possess magic properties. Instead of noting their construction and mechanism, primitives attribute the effects they produce to these same magic properties. Here

[1] R. Moffat : *Missionary Labours and Scenes in South Africa*, pp. 319–25.
[2] A. Steedman : *Wanderings and Adventure in the Interior of South Africa*, ii. p. 282 (1835).
[3] C. Coquilhat : *Sur le Haut Congo*, pp. 214–15.

we have an opportunity, which occurs but rarely, of seeing primitive mentality brought face to face with objects that are altogether new to it. We can get a life-like picture of the attitude it at once adopts. Suppose it is a question of the effect of firearms, for instance, Dalton says : " The most sensible of the Dayaks have a superstitious dread of firearms ; each man, on hearing the report, fancies the ball is making directly towards himself, he therefore runs, never finding himself safe unless he hears the explosion of gunpowder ; thus a man hearing the report of a swivel five miles off, still continues at full speed, with the same trepidation as at first, having not the least conception of the range of gunbarrels. I have frequently been out with Selgie and other chiefs, shooting monkeys, birds, etc., and offended them in refusing to fire on large birds at a distance of a mile or more ; they invariably put such refusal down to ill-nature on my part. Again, firing at an object, they cannot credit it is missed, although they see the bird fly away, but consider that the shot is still pursuing, and it must fall at last " [1] (on account of the magic power possessed by the weapon).

These Dayaks, therefore, when they see Europeans using their guns, do not think of noticing what really happens, nor what the conditions are. The deadly effect of the bullet, in their opinion, is entirely due to the mystic power with which the whites have endowed their weapons. The projectile *must* therefore reach its goal, however distant this may be. Should it fail to do so, it must be because the European was not in earnest about it, or else that a yet more powerful influence has intervened. The native never analyses anything. He does not reason about what he sees, since he finds no subject for reasoned thought in it. There is no new problem facing him, and therefore there is nothing which requires explanation. " My Kayans," says Beccari, " had great faith in my rifle, believing that the bullet, once fired, will follow the person aimed at until it has overtaken and killed him." [2] " This barbarian," says Andersson, speaking of an Ovambo chief, " not only believed that white men's guns were invincible, but also entertained the notion

---

[1] E. T. Dalton in H. Ling Roth : *The Natives of Sarawak*, ii. p. 127.
[2] Od. Beccari : *Wanderings in the Forests of Borneo*, p. 297.

that, without any weapons, by merely looking at a person, a white man could cause his death. ' If not,' the brave chief was heard to exclaim, ' how was it that Nongoro was killed by the mere report of firearms ? ' The Ovambo never seemed thoroughly to understand the dreadful efficiency of these weapons, until their disastrous defeat by Green and his party. It would appear that their previous fearlessness arose in a great measure from merely seeing, when fired, the flash of the discharge, and *not the missile*. ' When we throw an assegai, or shoot an arrow we see it going through the air,' said they, ' but with your rifles nothing but a harmless fire is perceived.' From a supreme contempt of our arms, they had now, however, gone to the other extreme, and had the most exaggerated notion of their fearful destructiveness." [1]

Like the Dayaks and the Kayans they doubtless believed that the missile pursued the victim in flight, and thus it was the detonation which killed. The idea of the Indians of Queen Charlotte Island (British Columbia) with regard to this, is very characteristic. " What most of all puzzled the Indians was to see how on earth ' the same gun could fire two shots at once,' by which they meant the report on the shell being discharged, and the bursting of the shell a few moments after on the ground." [2] In this two-fold act—the detonation at the start, which kills and the explosion afterwards, which also kills—there was a magical process which astounded the Indians.

Finally, it frequently happens that natives when first making use of a gun, do not think of taking aim, and this naturally accords with their idea of firearms. " With practice and instruction the Papuan policeman can be trained to be a fairly good shot, more especially as he has naturally very keen sight . . . but considerable difficulty is always experienced with the native police in drilling into him the necessity of ' sighting,' his natural impulse being to point his rifle at the target and blaze away, without ever a thought of sighting." [3] . . . It is reported that the Papuans are ex-

[1] C. J. Andersson : *The Okawango River*, p. 140.
[2] F. Poole : *Queen Charlotte Islands*, p. 154 (1872).
[3] "Papua," *Annual Report*, p. 85 (1908).

ceedingly keen on shooting . . . but though there are good shots among them, most of them seem to be quite as satisfied with the sound of the detonation as if they had hit the mark." [1] " It is really a miracle that there are neither dead nor wounded ! " (The writer is referring to a fight between two parties of Battaks in Sumatra.) " It is really a piece of good luck, too, that the Battaks do not know enough to take aim ! For their success they rely entirely on *Debatta* (a higher power). If anyone is hit, everybody thinks it is because this power has directed the blow." [2] In this, they imagine the efficiency of European weapons to be exactly like their own. In Ruanda, in East Africa, " the natives have no hesitation in saying that arrows, spears, swords have no power but that received from the *bazimu* (the ancestors and the forces of the unseen world), and that these same *bazimu* can make even the finest weapons ineffectual." [3]

However formidable the white man's weapons may be, the effect of them may be contraverted, and even nullified, if a power of magic charm superior to their own be brought to bear upon them. The Kafir, with a blind confidence in the power possessed by the wizard of his tribe, will fearlessly expose himself to the white man's bombs and bullets. Even the most disastrous experience fails to convince him of his error. The sole conclusion he draws from it is that the white man's magic has once more proved stronger than that of the Kafir sorcerer, but when the latter has once discovered the charm which ensures victory, the white man's rifles and guns in their turn will prove ineffectual. " After this " (a certain magical operation) " every warrior was fully persuaded that he was invulnerable, that the bullets would be deflected on either side of him, that, even should they hit him, they would flatten against his body and fall harmless to the ground." [4]

[1] " Papua," *Annual Report*, p. 100.
[2] *Berichte der rheinischen Missionsgesellschaft*, p. 137 (1900) ; cf. Brenner : *Besuch bei den Kannibalen Sumatras*, p. 338.
[3] Fr. A. Arnoux : " Le culte de la société secrète des Imandwa au Ruanda," *Anthropos*, vii. p. 288.
[4] H. A. Junod : *The Life of a South African Tribe*, i. pp. 439-40.

III

Printed books and writing are no less astonishing to primitives than are firearms, but they find no hesitation in accounting for them. They immediately perceive them to be divining instruments. " My books puzzled them," says Moffat, in reference to certain Bechuanas ; " they asked me if they were my *bola* (prognosticating dice)." [1] Livingstone, too, says : " The idea that enters their minds is that books are our instruments of divination." [2] We remember the reply made by a Transvaal native to the missionary who was reproving him for consulting the dice : " That is *our* book ; you read your Bible every day, and you believe it, and we read ours." [3] The book, like the astragali, predicts the future, reveals what is hidden, is both guide and counsellor ; in short, it is a mystic power. Of the Barotse Arnot says : " The only difference, they think, between our *lequalo* and theirs is that ours is a confused mass of little black marks on paper, and theirs is surely much more sensible, as it consists of substantial things ! " [4] Livingstone says again : " To all who have not acquired it, a knowledge of letters is quite unfathomable ; there is nought like it within the compass of their observation ; and we have no comparison with anything except pictures to aid them in comprehending the idea of signs of words. It seems to them supernatural that we see in a book things taking place, or having occurred at a distance. No amount of explanation conveys the idea unless they learn to read." [5] " Sekhome . . . asked me one day whether Mr. Price had started on his return journey to the Mission. I told him I did not know. ' Well then,' he said, ' ask your books ; they will tell you.' " " In the Matebele country ' the books ' were regarded at the time of my visit, and by almost all with whom I came in contact, as the ' sacred things ' or the ' divining things ' of the white man's religion. ' To learn the books ' was therefore regarded

[1] Robert Moffat : *Missionary Labours and Scenes in South Africa*, p. 384.
[2] David Livingstone : *The Zambesi and its Tributaries*, p. 557 (1865).
[3] Vide supra, chap. vii. p. 194.
[4] F. S. Arnot : *Garenganze*, p. 75.
[5] D. Livingstone : *Missionary Travels and Researches in South Africa*, p. 189.

as a formal entrance upon the practice of the white man's mode of worship. It occupied an initial position in their minds similar to that our baptism really occupies. They had no idea that a man might learn to read and yet choose to remain a heathen." [1]

This last remark throws a strong light upon the idea which reading presents to the primitive mind. It is a magic process designed to secure for the white man all that negroes ask of their dreams, their visions, and their astragali. We should say that he who is converted to Christianity learns to read (so that he may follow the service and become acquainted with the Scriptures). The native, on the other hand, says: He who learns to read is being converted. As a matter of fact, when he abandons his astragali for books, he no longer addresses himself to those unseen powers, those ancestors, to whom he has been accustomed to pray, and whom he has consulted up to now. But he reckons that reading will provide him with the same kind of revelation, proceeding from yet higher powers, and that the protection afforded him will therefore be all the more effective. " He was learning to read, absolutely convinced that such marvellous knowledge was a panacea for all ills and a sure road to good fortune ; but one fine day, after an accident had occurred to him, he began to have doubts about the efficacy of the acquirement, and he threw his primer into the waste-paper basket." [2] Learning to read, therefore, in the native's eyes is equivalent to changing his religion.

How can these printed characters reveal so much to the one who deciphers them ? The primitive no more tries to explain this than he does to find out why the rifle and cannon carry death to so great a distance. Books are mirrors. " When the Xosa Kafirs first saw Europeans reading, they called the book *nadi*, adding *ot heeta* (a mirror for speaking). Ever since then, they called a mirror *nadi ok hangeela* (a mirror for looking into)." [3] In the Congo, too, " my reading a book puzzled them greatly," says Glave ; " they thought it an instrument of magic with which I could see far into the

---

[1] Rev. J. Mackenzie : *Ten Years North of the Orange River*, p. 336.
[2] *Missions évangéliques*, xl. p. 170 (1865).
[3] H. Lichtenstein : *Reisen im südlichen Afrika*, i. p. 165.

future, and even asked me to look in my *talla talla* (mirror)
to inform them whether a sick child would recover." [1] But
as a rule, natives prefer to say that the book " speaks." " A
Bechuana one day asked what the square objects on the
table were, and was told that they were books, and
that the books gave information. He immediately put
one to his ear, but hearing no sound, said : ' This book
tells me nothing.' He then shook it and tried it again
and finally laid it down, saying, ' Perhaps it is asleep ' ?
Another time a native brought me a parcel which my
wife had sent me. I took a letter from this parcel
and read it aloud to a chief who was with me, a man
who knew what writing was, whereupon the messenger who
had brought the parcel said, in a very frightened voice :
' I shan't carry any more letters. If that one had spoken
to me on the way, I *should* have been afraid ! ' Another
messenger refused to carry a letter until he had put his
spear through it, so that it might not speak to him on the
way." [2] " Recently, our young brethren were in a village
proclaiming the Gospel, and one of them, taking the New
Testament in his hand, said that he was only repeating
what the Word of God said, when Sechachi seized the book,
put it to his ear, and exclaimed : ' It is a lie ; I am listening
carefully, and the book is not saying anything at all,' and
then there were roars of laughter and mocking gibes." [3]

Since reading is a purely magical process which consists
in seeing or hearing, it ought not to have to be learnt, but
should be acquired, and that not in a series of laborious
efforts, but all at once. " They (the Bechuanas) thought
that it would be a fine thing indeed to be able to read books
in common with myself, and supposing that there was some
royal road to learning, they very simply imagined the art
could be acquired by a single exertion of the mental energies,

[1] E. J. Glave : *Six Years of Adventure in Congoland*, p. 74.

[2] R. Moffat in *Missions évangéliques*, xvi. p. 207 ; cf. D. Crantz : *History
of Greenland.* " In the beginning of their acquaintance with the Europeans,
they were so frightened at the speaking paper that they did not dare to carry
a letter from one to another, or to touch a book, because they believed it
must be conjuration, that one man could tell the thoughts of another, by
a few black scrawls on a white paper. They also seriously thought that
when a minister read God's commandments to them he surely must have
heard the voice first out of the book."

[3] *Missions évangéliques*, xxxvi. p. 96 (1856). (Maitin.)

or by some secret charm that they thought I might possess. I had administered medicine to some few sick, and one who was seriously ill had derived much benefit from having a quantity of blood taken from his arm ; and as the doctors among the Bechuanas generally unite physic and charms, they very naturally thought that I might be able to charm a knowledge of reading into their heads." [1] " It was the same thing with the Ashantis.   Among other things Opoku said to us : ' Give me some of your medicine so that I may rub my eyes and be able to read what is printed.'   We told him he was too old, but we would teach his children to read. Whereupon he began to laugh, and went off." [2]

In default of a charm which would instantaneously furnish them with the power to read, however, some negroes decided to acquire the art by the ordinary methods, but without any great faith in them.   " At first these good people set to work very reluctantly, protesting that it was absurd to expect a negro to be clever enough *to make paper speak*.   But our persuasions having prevailed, they decided to try.   In spite of all their forebodings some slight progress was made, and at each lesson the chances of ultimate success seemed to be on the increase.   Finally the great problem was really solved ; one fine morning about ten or twelve of our pupils discovered that they were able to find, unaided, the actual meaning of several sentences they had never yet attempted. World-wide publicity was accorded to this fact, and the wise men of the district declared that we must have *changed the hearts* of their compatriots by means of some very powerful charm." [3]

This last is a very significant circumstance.   To the minds of the Basuto " soothsayers," the natives who have learned to read have been converted, that is, they have renounced what we may call ancestor-worship.   Now the missionaries, powerful magicians as they undoubtedly were, would never have obtained such a result if they had not made use of magic weapons.   " The notion that external and material methods can act upon the soul and change its nature, is so

[1] R. Moffat : *Missionary Labours and Scenes in South Africa*, p. 599.
[2] Ramseyer und Kühne : *Vier Jahre in Asanti*, p. 123.
[3] E. Casalis : *Les Bassoutos*, pp. 86–7.

deeply rooted in them that the first conversions to Christianity which they witnessed were all attributed to the effect of some mysterious specific which the missionaries had made their pupils take, unknown to themselves." [1] By virtue of a similar belief, " Faku will not listen when the subject of his children's learning to read is introduced ; he is pained at knowing it is possible to express the sound of his name upon paper, being probably influenced by a superstitious idea of our having it in our power, by this means, to bewitch him." [2] With the Bangala of the Upper Congo, " what endless exclamations and discussions there were when they came to be paid ! I had previously taken down the names of those who had been engaged, and they were immensely astonished at hearing me repeat them some hours later. It was the first time that they clearly understood the object of writing, although I had often told them that writing was the custodian of words. They nevertheless continued to attribute extraordinary powers to it, such as my instantaneous communication, when separated by an immense distance from them, with N'sassi (Captain Hanssens) and Boula Matari (Stanley), the arrival of materials, etc." [3]

Even when the native has apparently understood what writing is, even when he can read and write himself, he never entirely loses his feeling that there is some mystic power connected with it. Dr. Pechuël-Loesche noticed this fact in Loango. " Whilst the astonishment produced by this wonderful accomplishment is slightly lessened, because some of them have learnt to read and write, their respect for it remains. . . . To see a negro very gravely powdering with sand or dust what he has just written in pencil, is very comical. But this action is not merely an amusing imitation of the white man. It has a more profound significance ; for earth strengthens and sanctifies." [4]

As to the practical utility of reading and writing, that is only appreciated after a long time. " When Moshesh the chief wants to send orders to subjects at a distance, he

[1] E. Cassalis : Les Bassoutos, pp. 86–7
[2] A. Steedman : Wanderings and Adventures in the Interior of South Africd, ii. p. 273 (1835).
[3] C. Coquilhat : Sur le Haut Congo, p. 216.
[4] Dr. Pechuël-Loesche : Die Loango Expedition, iii. 2. pp. 58–9.

calls one of his special messengers and tells him all that he wants them to know, down to the very smallest detail. The messenger retains all his master's words very faithfully in his memory, and repeats them exactly as they were given. Experience has shown that this method of communication is a better one than letters for natives, because in writing one sums up a long argument in a very few words, while the Mosuto, in order to understand thoroughly what he is being told, must have it set out at length and in all its details." [1]

The foregoing instances have nearly all been taken from Bantu tribes. A few examples will doubtless suffice to show that primitive mentality everywhere visualizes reading and writing in much the same way as in Africa. Thus, in speaking of Western Australia, Bishop Salvado says : " I am naturally led to refer to the kind of veneration felt by savages for the books and written papers which they call ' talking papers.' They attribute magic power to them, believing they are able to reveal secret things, and they are so persuaded of this that when they want to clear themselves of some charge made against them, they say : ' Here is the talking book or the paper ; now you can see who is right.' " [2]

In North Australia, " the natives have also, as it were, extended this feeling of sacredness of the persons of their own messengers to those of aboriginals who are carrying messages for white men. A letter is always . . . carried in a cleft stick so that it can be seen easily . . . the cleft stick acting as a special passport. They look upon the *paper yabber* (letter) as a mysterious thing which is endowed with the capacity of seeing. . . . An aboriginal who abstracted a stalk of tobacco from a parcel he was carrying . . . was highly indignant with the *paper yabber* for telling the white man what he had done, because he had hidden it in a hollow log while committing the theft, so that it should not be able to see what he was doing." [3]

On Easter Island, " one day," says a missionary, " while

---

[1] *Missions évangéliques*, xxxi. p. 210 (1856). (Maeder.)
[2] Bishop Salvado : *Mémoires historiques sur l'Australie*, p. 182.
[3] B. Spencer : *Native Tribes of the Northern Territory of Australia*, p. 36. (C.M.S., 1914.)

I was taking my class, I perceived a ship. Hoping it might possibly touch our coast, I went to my hut to write a few lines. From a distance my pupils watched me very carefully ; they imagined I was endowed with the faculty of speaking to those who were absent, and that I was now making use of this power. As soon as I returned to them they asked me what I had been saying to the ship." [1] These little Polynesians were themselves learning to write, but that did not prevent their believing that their master, the white man, was able, by means of signs which he traced on paper, to communicate from a distance with people whom he could not see; and to hear their words in reply. At Rarotonga the natives, when they saw the missionary reading, said that he and his God were talking to each other. " They thought that the paper which has been written upon talked, and they were surprised at hearing no sound." [2] In New Caledonia, " we have already said more than once," writes Pastor Leenhardt, " that ' receiving the Gospel ' means, in the Caledonian tongue, ' learning to write.' " [3] In the school at Nias, " when we had ordered some coco-nuts to be brought, and were resting in the shade near the house, a man called out, ' Don't let the children go near ! These foreigners have books ! ' The poor fellow took us for magicians." [4] " In Borneo, the Kayans begged Dr. Nieuwenhuis to protect their hut by hanging up some pieces of newspaper, which always makes a great impression on the people of the interior, on account of its mysterious signs. . . . The Dayaks' idea that if men can read it is because the printed letters whisper something to them, accounts for the respect they show for everything written or printed." [5] Lastly, not to make our list too long, the Bannars of Laos have the very same notions about writing. " ' What ! ' they say to the missionary, ' how is it that you hear it speaking, while we cannot hear a single sound of its voice ! ' Then they ask us about the future, convinced that nothing is

[1] *Annales de la Propagation de la foi*, xxxviii. p. 125. (Fr. Eugène Eyraud.)

[2] Rev. J. Williams : *A Narrative of Missionary Enterprises in the South Sea Islands*, p. 175 (1837) ; cf. pp. 118–20.

[3] *Missions évangéliques*, lxxxii. i. p. 276.

[4] *Berichte der rheinischen Missionsgesellschaft*, p. 210 (1891).

[5] A. W. Nieuwenhuis : *Quer durch Borneo*, ii. p. 337.

hidden from those who possess a knowledge of *laboor* (paper).
. . . Some wanted to know how a war would turn out ; others
desired to hear how long they might expect to live. We could
have made a livelihood by telling fortunes ; it was no use
our telling them that the paper could not make known
things of that kind, we always heard our questioners saying
to each other : ' They know it very well, but they don't want
to tell us.' " [1]

IV

Other things introduced by Europeans, and the results
of their work, however surprising these may be, are nevertheless at once accounted for, just as weapons, writing, and
books have been, in the primitive's mind. White people
are certainly mighty wizards ; and if they obtain the results
they aim at, is there anything surprising in it ? These
results, as far as the primitive judges of them, do not depend
upon what we should call their essential and adequate
conditions, or, at any rate, to a very secondary degree only.
Their really " efficient cause " always is the magic power
possessed by the white man. Even when they do not understand anything at all about the matter in question, they
nevertheless account for it in this way. Thus " the Angmagsalik attached supernatural power to our anthropological
measurements, although I myself did nothing which could
give occasion to such a belief. Those who were most addicted
to this superstition were old people or people suffering from
some bodily defect. One man, when I had finished measur-
ing him, exclaimed : ' Well now, let us hope the hand will
get better ! ' His hand had been stiff for a very long time
and he was suffering from pain in its joints." [2]

They give the same explanation, and with better reason,
when it is a case of results which the natives desire for
themselves. " The goats belonging to the Mission seemed
to get on very well, and Mr. Buchanan was beset with many
entreaties for a medicine to increase the goats of the neigh-

[1] *Annales de la Propagation de la foi*, xxvii. pp. 412–13. (Lettre du
missionnaire Combes.)
[2] G. Holm : " An Ethnological Sketch of the Anmagsalik Eskimo," edit.
by W. Thalbitzer, *Meddelelser om Groenland*, xxxix. p. 86.

bouring chiefs." [1] Not far away, in another district of Central Africa, " I was more than once asked for medicine to make dogs fierce. It was obvious that European dogs were more powerful and better barkers than the miserable curs which haunt native villages." [2] These people do not notice that the European dogs are better fed, or at any rate if they do see it, which is quite possible, they do not think of connecting this fact, as the cause, with the vigour of the dogs, as the effect. They are already persuaded that the good health of the dogs is due to a " charm " which the white man possesses. " In Teso," says the same missionary, " we were also credited with the possession of medicine for making babies white. This came out when one day the chief's wife expressed great astonishment at our little son having a white skin at so youthful a period of his existence as six months old. She had always thought that Europeans were born black like all the babies she had ever seen, and turned white later by the assiduous application of some potent medicine."

This quaint idea is not unique. In Togoland, " when a European child is born, most of the people cannot understand how it is he is not a negro, seeing he was born in Africa. They admit *a priori* that the influence of locality is stronger than that of heredity." [3] Of the Basutos Casalis writes : " I took the first little white boy ever born in the country to the chief town. . . . The mothers were eager to bring their own babies to compare with ours, and to ask us how we managed to keep him as healthy as he appeared." [4] How they " managed " meant, " what charm was used," for undoubtedly there would be some magic charm or process involved. As a rule, the lowest grades of natives, seeing that the white men themselves are not like other men, do not know what to think their children are likely to be ; indeed, they hardly expect them to have any. In Nias Island, " up to that time they had never conceived it possible that the children of a *tuan* (white lord) could die. . . . They thought that the *tuan's* children at any rate would escape

[1] Rev. Duff Macdonald : *Africana*, i. p. 46 (1882).
[2] Rev. A. L. Kitching : *On the Backwaters of the Nile*, p. 266 (1912).
[3] C. Meinhof : *Afrikanische Religionen*, pp. 67–8.
[4] E. Casalis : *Les Bassoutos*, p. 84.

death, because he had so many 'charms' he could use to prevent it." [1] In (German) New Guinea, " of all the many things which the native has become acquainted with through his intercourse with white people, up to now nothing has astonished him so much as the little white babies. Possibly the reason is because for a long time the Papuan believed that the white strangers were not really men, but some kind of spirits who had fallen from the sky behind the horizon yonder, or had come out of the earth, without being born." [2]

According to the Bangala of the Upper Congo, white men come out of the water, and that is where they get their materials from. " Some of the natives assert that I get cowries, pearls, and *mitakou* from the depths of the earth. Others say that these fine things come from the bottom of the sea ; to them the white man is an aquatic being, and I myself sleep beneath the waves. But they are all agreed in considering me related to *Ibanza*, a god or a devil of whom they often talk. The more I deny my supernatural ancestry, the more firmly do they believe in it." [3]   Here we can readily recognize the traces of a belief which is widespread throughout the Bantu districts of Africa and even beyond, and that is that the Europeans come from the depths of the sea. " When the Landrost asked Gika (a Kafir chief) why the people had murdered those who were driven ashore upon his coast, he said they had no business in his country, but should have kept in their own, meaning the sea, for the Kafirs thought they had risen up from the bottom of the sea, having seen the top mast first, then gradually more and more till they beheld the hull, which made them conclude they were natives of the water." [4]   " He (a Barotse chief) often asked me why, since we come from the north, we should have appeared in the south, and how we travelled here. Textile materials are a source of great astonishment to them, they cannot believe that they are made by human beings ; no, say they, these materials come from the bottom of the sea, and the people who travel in ships go there to get them

[1] *Berichte der rheinischen Missionsgesellschaft*, p. 38 (1906).
[2] Ibid., p. 74 (1902).
[3] C. Coquilhat : *Sur le Haut Congo*, p. 215.
[4] Rev. J. Campbell : *Travels in South Africa*, p. 526.

Everything which seems strange to them is done by the men in the water. I believe that to their way of thinking there are some kinds of magicians or deities who inhabit the depths of the sea." [1] " It seems," says Junod, too, " that in former times the Thonga believed that the white people, not only Portuguese, dwelt in water." [2]

It is possibly in the Lower Congo that this belief is most fully developed. " Nearer the coast, the people believe that the dead are bought by the white men, and that the spirits go to work for the white men under the sea ; there they weave cloth, and make the various things sold for native produce.[3] . . . Matiko and several others accompanied a missionary to Banana ; they prosecuted an awed search for their dead relatives among the population there, expecting to find some. On their return to San Salvador, the people asked after their dead friends, and were disappointed that none of them had been seen at Banana ! And this at San Salvador, four hundred years after the first white men went to live there ! The natives also believed . . . that tinned meat . . . was human flesh. They had always heard that white men bought the spirits of men, and now the mystery was solved, as to what they did with them. The home of the white men, they were sure, was under the sea, for on the coast they saw the ships slowly rise far out from the land ; first the mast, then the hull." [4]

One can readily imagine that things like the compass, telescope, opera-glasses, mirrors, etc., when seen for the first

[1] *Missions évangéliques*, lxi. p. 480.
[2] H. A. Junod : *The Life of a South African Tribe*, ii. p. 332.
[3] A curiously similar belief prevails in New Guinea. The white men, it is believed, have not themselves manufactured the things they possess, steamers, tomahawks, calico, etc, . . . but have obtained them from the spirits of the dead. This is evident from the fact that if, for instance, a tomahawk is broken, a white man cannot make it intact. The spirits bring the various things from their land on steamers, and when they arrive the white men go out to meet them and seize all the things, steamers and all, carrying them off. The natives at first connected my constant inquiries as to their ideas about the dead with this belief. They thought that I wanted, through their help, to get into contact with the spirits in order to obtain some boatload or other of beautiful things. . . . The first white men who arrived in the country were thought to be returning spirits of the dead. The word used for a white man is *manakai* or *markai*, which, like *oboro*, means " spirit of a dead person." Clothes are called *oboro-tama*, or skin of a spirit.—Landtman : " The Folk-tales of the Kiwai Papuans," *Acta societatis scientiarum fennicæ*, xlvii. p. 181.
[4] Rev. W. H. Bentley : *Pioneering on the Congo*, i. pp. 252–3.

time, surprise and terrify the natives. Seeing that they
have already concluded without further thought that
white men are very powerful magicians, they naturally
think that the most ordinary things they use must possess
magical properties. " Soap," says Macdonald, " was a
great novelty to the natives ; they were much amused with
the peculiar ' feel ' it gave to clothes. They thought it
was a kind of clothes ' medicine,' and trusted more to its
magic than to their own rubbing." [1]

As we have already seen, the native doctor's remedies,
and still more those of the white man, produce their effect,
not by virtue of their natural properties, but because of the
mystic influence they exercise. According to native ideas,
the conversions which a missionary is able to effect are
due to a similar influence. " Many of them," says Moffat,
" alarmed at the progress made by the ' medicine of God's
word ' as they term it, were loud in their complaints of the
new order of things which was introduced, and some were
so determinately opposed to this new order or doctrine,
that they removed to districts beyond the reach of the
Christian atmosphere. Some were concerned lest the water
in the river which passed our houses might receive an infusion,
and being drunk, transform them too." [2] The following
circumstance clearly shows how natives represent to their
own minds the magic operations which can bring about
conversion. " In 1856 a young man was being instructed,
with a view to baptism. . . . His relatives were terrified,
and believed they were about to lose him. On the pretext
that his father was ill and wanted to see him, they took
him away from the Mission station and back to his birth-
place, where they first of all endeavoured by all kinds of
arguments and entreaties to convert him to paganism
once more. As his absence was prolonged, some of the
missionaries came to inquire after him. They were told
that he was dead and buried, but as a matter of fact his
relatives had imprisoned and concealed him. Finally they
had made him swallow a remedy calculated to cure his
abominable ' conversion-disease,' and they had washed all

[1] Rev. D. Macdonald : *Africana*, ii. p. 96.
[2] R. Moffat : *Missionary Labours and Scenes in South Africa*, p. 576.

his clothing so that the poison of the new faith might be completely expelled." [1]

In East Africa, " the Baluba . . . at once pronounce the things they have never seen before, and which they fear will bring trouble upon them, to be ' witchcraft ' (*Zaubermittel*). . . . In their eyes I, with everything belonging to me, was considered a most mighty wizard, whose presence in their country could portend no good. Whenever I looked at my watch, or consulted the compass, there was a general panic." [2] These unknown objects might indeed be possessed of extraordinarily harmful qualities, and they could not escape from them too quickly. Almost everywhere, a photographic apparatus seemed a peculiarly dangerous object.

" Ignorant natives," says Junod, " instinctively object to being photographed. They say : ' These white people want to steal us and take us with them, far away into the lands which we do not know, and we shall remain only an incomplete being.' When shown a magic lantern, you hear them pitying the men shown on the pictures, and saying : ' This is the way they are ill-treating us when they take our photographs ! ' Before the 1894 war broke out, I had gone to show the magic lantern in remote heathen villages, and people accused me of having caused the disturbance through having brought to life again men who had died long ago." [3]

Even when natives have had years of intercourse with white people, the slightest change in what they are accustomed to see is quite enough to excite their fears afresh. For instance, a four-masted schooner appeared in Ambriz. " Such a thing as a ' ship with four sticks ' had never been seen before, and without waiting to inquire, every black ran away from Ambriz ; and the same thing happened on her return from Loanda. It was only after repeated voyages that the natives lost their fear of her ; they could give no other reason than that it had never been seen before and that therefore it must be a signal for the white men to do something which they could not understand." [4]

[1] Dr. Wangemann : *Die Berliner Mission in Zululande*, p. 197. (Lettre du missionnaire Posselt.)
[2] H. von Wissmann, *Wolf . . . Im Innern Afrikas*, p. 229.
[3] H. A. Junod : *The Life of a South African Tribe*, ii. p. 340.
[4] J. J. Monteiro : *Angola and the River Congo*, i. p. 125.

Occurrences of this sort have constantly been noted. I shall quote but a few such cases, taken from the primitive peoples of the South Pacific, and these show clearly how the feeling of fear excited by the appearance of something hitherto unknown predominates over every other, and at first excludes all else. For example, with the Narrinyeri, Taplin says : " I remember well the first time some of the women heard our clock strike. They listened with astonishment ; then inquired hurriedly in a whisper : ' What him say ? ' and rushed out of the house in terror without waiting for an answer." [1]

Until the Europeans came, Australian aborigines had never seen boiling water. " When Pamphlet arrived among them, they had no more idea that water could be made hot than that it could be made solid ; and on his heating some in a tin pot which he had saved from the wreck, the whole tribe gathered round us and watched the pot till it began to boil, when they all took to their heels, shouting and screaming ; nor could they be persuaded to return till they saw him pour the water out and clean the pot, when they slowly ventured back, and carefully covered the place where the water had been spilt, with sand. During the whole of our countrymen's stay among them, they were never reconciled to this operation of boiling." [2]

Their first experience of steel (about which they afterwards became so eager) seems to have been very similar to that of the boiling water. Macgillivray relates : " While getting words from a very intelligent native whose attention I secured by giving him various little presents from time to time, I had occasion to point to a bamboo scoop lying in the canoe in order to get its name. The man, to my surprise . . . taking up a bit of stick, showed me that this scoop was used as a knife. Not to be outdone, I took one of our common knives and cut away vigorously at a piece of wood, to show the superiority of our knives over this one ; he appeared suddenly to become terrified, talked vehemently to the others, drew their attention to me, and repeated my motions of

[1] Rev. G. Taplin : *The Narrinyeri Tribe*, p. 68.
[2] Narrative of M. Oxley's expedition to survey Port Curtis and Moreton Bay, in Field's *Geographical Memoirs on New South Wales*, pp. 59–60 (1825) ; cf. G. Taplin : *The Narrinyeri Tribe*, p. 42.

cutting the wood, after which his canoe pushed off from the steamer's side. My friend refused to accept of the knife—as I afterwards found the natives had also done to other people when iron implements were offered them—nor would he pay any further attention to my attempts to effect a reconciliation." [1]

At Ualan, in the Caroline Islands, to natives who are already somewhat accustomed to the presence of white men, a knife is the object of unbounded admiration, and many of them want to try it. "I did not wish to appear disobliging, although I was afraid they might not be able to use it unaided without danger. As a matter of fact, one of them did cut his finger. The wound was a trifling one ; nevertheless, the whole party betrayed immense terror. The injured man fell into a condition of stupor, and sat there motionless, with his eyes closed, just like a man expecting an immediate death." [2] It was only with difficulty that Von Kittlitz could reassure him by showing him the scars of old cuts on his own fingers. This incident shows that the natives looked upon the knife with very different eyes from those of Europeans. To them the fragment of refined steel was endowed with wonderful occult power, and consequently the very slightest wound it inflicted might prove fatal.

Similarly " the most astonishing thing was the small box, explained by a Port Moresby native to those around, as containing things that told roads, heights, and weather. I opened it and showed them my barometer, thermometer, and compass, and tried to explain to them their uses. ' Shut it, shut it, put it away, now put it away ; we shall be all sick.' " [3]

In short, under whatever form the white man's activity attracts the attention of the native, until custom has rendered it familiar it is at once and unhesitatingly interpreted in the same sort of way. The doctor who treats their maladies,

[1] J. Macgillivray : Narrative of the Voyage of H.M.S. " Rattlesnake," ii. pp. 29–30 (1852).
[2] Von Kittlitz : Denkwürdigkeiten einer Reise nach dem russischen Amerika, Mikronesien, and durch Kamtschatka, ii. pp. 27–8.
[3] J. Chalmers and W. W. Gill : Work and Adventure in New Guinea (Kabadi District), p. 159. (R.T.S., 1885.)

the explorer or trader who crosses their territory, the missionary who establishes himself among them and explains the Gospel to them—if these succeed in their undertakings, they do so only by virtue of the magic power of which their " medicines " are the vehicle. It is therefore according to their success that these same " medicines " are estimated, and upon their worth that the white man's prestige in its turn depends.

It therefore seems incorrect to state, as has so frequently been done, that primitives fear and respect nothing but force. On the contrary, what Europeans understand by this term is not even known to them, and they consequently appear quite indifferent to it. If they do yield to brute force, it is without having understood its nature. That which inspires fear and respect in them is mystic force, that of the unseen powers whose co-operation the white man knows how to secure, and this alone it is which makes his implements and weapons effective and irresistible.

CHAPTER XII

THE PRIMITIVE'S DISLIKE OF THE UNKNOWN

AFTER having attempted to analyse primitive mentality, at least as far as the essential characteristics of its being and its functioning are concerned, it will be interesting to see how it develops and the laws which govern this development. Unfortunately, the preliminaries necessary to a study of this kind are still unavailable. With very few exceptions, primitive peoples have no history. Their myths, which in other respects prove so instructive, do not take its place. The little that we do know with any certainty about their institutions and their languages allows only of hypotheses that are but arbitrary.

Up to the present, however, it is possible to formulate one general law, founded upon the testimony of many investigators. Primitive peoples, as a rule, show themselves hostile to everything coming from without, at least unless it be from neighbouring tribes like their own, people of the same race, customs, and institutions, with whom they could live on friendly terms. From the real "stranger" they neither borrow nor accept anything. Any changes, even if they are undoubted improvements, must be forced upon them. If they are free to accept or to reject them, their choice is not a matter of doubt. They form, as it were, sealed systems in which every entrant runs the risk of setting up a process of decomposition. They are like organisms capable of living for a very long time whilst the general environment changes but slightly, but which very rapidly degenerate and die when invaded by new elements.

From the physiological point of view, as we know, intercourse with white people nearly everywhere (North and South America, Polynesia, Melanesia, etc.) has proved fatal to native races. Most of them, decimated by the diseases the whites bring with them, have disappeared, and many of those now remaining are becoming extinct. From the social point of view we note just the same phenomena. The primitives' institutions, like their languages, quickly disappear, as soon as they have to submit to the presence and influence of white races.

That primitive societies should be unable to withstand the shock of this encounter, might have been foreseen from their constitution, which makes their communities so different from those in which we live, and so easily vulnerable. Their ancestors, both recent and remote, the unseen spirits and forces of all kinds, the species which people the air, water and soil, the very earth, and even its rocks and incidental configurations, everything within the limits of the locality occupied by the social group " belongs " to it, as we have seen, in the mystic sense of the word. It is reciprocally bound, by a complex network of participations, to the place itself and the unseen powers which people it and make their influence felt in it. Hence relations that appear to us perfectly natural and harmless, run the risk of exposing the group to dangers which are ill-defined and therefore all the more to be dreaded. The slightest intercourse with foreigners, the simple fact of receiving food or implements from them, may lead to catastrophe. Who knows how this may affect such-and-such an occult power, and what may be the result ? Hence arise those signs of dread and distrust among primitives which the white races often interpret as expressing hostility ; then there is bloodshed, reprisals follow, and sometimes the extermination of the group is the result. If, on the other hand, friendly relations are established, if a regular trading takes place between the white men and the natives, especially if several of them come to live and work among the white people, as a consequence of a more or less voluntary " engagement," the consequences are often no less disastrous. In a very short time the native, abruptly exposed to fresh influences, comes to despise and forget his own traditions. His own code of morality tends to disappear. He begins

25

to speak a kind of *patois* or pidgin-English, the sense of solidarity of the group is weakened and with it its desire to exist.

In any case, as long as it lasts, as long as the social group feels itself a living force and does not abandon the struggle, it repels instinctively, as it were, the new elements imported by the foreigner. It is in this way, as we shall presently see, that we must understand what is generally called the misoneism of primitive peoples. Left to themselves they are naturally conservative, but it is by no means sure that they would be more hostile than any others to certain innovations. Their institutions do change, though very slowly, and it seems as if they accept the changes when they are proposed by an authority which they respect, and in a form which does not make them uneasy. Spencer and Gillen state this explicitly with regard to the Arunta tribe.[1] In all other cases, resolute and insurmountable mistrust is awakened and remains persistent.

I

In the first place, primitives will hardly ever accept without hesitation food, even if of a known variety, offered by foreigners. In British New Guinea, for example, where the Administrators frequently come in contact with natives who have not yet seen Europeans, " while the many tribes of natives we met on our expedition showed no suspicion and absolute confidence in us, after we had succeeded in establishing friendly relations, frequently coming to our camp and sitting round the fire at night, and bringing their women and children to see the ' pale-faces ' during the day-time, they all, without exception, refused even to taste any food we offered them, although they would wrap it up in leaves, probably as a curiosity." [2] " The Arabi River natives are now friendly. . . . They were given presents by the manager of the store, and were also given food, but they would not touch it." [3]

---

[1] Spencer and Gillen : *The Native Tribes of Central Australia*, p. 324 (1899).
[2] " Papua," *Annual Report*, p. 170 (1911).
[3] Ibid., p. 89 (1914).

The fact that the food is not prepared in the usual way is quite sufficient to account for this repugnance. " The Managulasi natives are unacquainted with the use of the earthenware pot, and do all their cooking with stones ; in fact, they refuse to eat food cooked otherwise. I saw two natives from very close to the district nearly starve, because they had not the necessary stones to prepare their food." [1]

In the myths collected by Landtman among the Kiwai Papuans of New Guinea, we see expressed in various forms the fear which foods they are not acquainted with inspires in the natives. " Sêpuse left a ripe banana close to Sido who, after eating it, ' fell down dead ' (which means ' fainted ') not being used to that kind of food." [2] " Bidja was the first man to touch fish, for up to that time the Mawata people only collected shell-fish. They called ordinary fish *ebihare* (mysterious beings) and ran away from them. Bidja (who had been instructed to do so by a spirit in his dream), shot a stingray, cooked . . . and ate it. . . Contrary to their expectation the people found in the morning that Bidja was no worse for eating . . . *ebihare*. . . . Thenceforward the people discontinued their work in the gardens and went fishing." [3] In another legend a mythical person saw a coco-nut for the first time. " He husked one of the nuts, broke it open, and by way of trial gave a piece of the kernel to one dog, which he did not care about. But the good dogs all sprang up, bit the other and snatched away the coco-nut which they devoured. They licked their lips and whined for more. The man waited a little, but as nothing happened, he thought, ' Oh, that good *kaikai*,' and . . . tasted it himself." [4] He believed that the dogs would fall victims to their imprudence.

This distrust and these precautions can be accounted for in many ways, and especially in the two following. Everything yet unknown is suspicious ; who knows what fatal power may possibly be concealed in the apparently

[1] " Papua," *Annual Report*, p. 128 (1912).
[2] G. Landtman : " The Folk-tales of the Kiwai Papuans." *Acta societatis scientiarum fennicæ*, xlvii. p. 95.
[3] Ibid., p. 212.
[4] Ibid., p. 318.

harmless food offered to the native ?   On seeing fruit with
which he is unacquainted in a country he has not explored,
a white man will avoid tasting it until he has ascertained
that it is not poisonous.   In the same way, new food
inspires the primitive with a fear that it may be the vehicle
of a deadly witchcraft, and nothing will persuade him to
taste it.   In the second place, eating, to him, is not merely
the satisfaction of an elemental need.   It is an act the
significance and mystic effects of which may be of paramount importance.   The food-substance is incorporated with
the very being of the man who eats it, the participation
between them is so close that the two form but one, and
what the primitive eats becomes a part of his ego.   Among
many uncivilized races, as we know, everyone religiously
gathers up the tiniest fragment of food remaining, and
carries it away to throw it into the water, or burn it, or
destroy it in some other way, for if these fragments fell
into the hands of an enemy, he would henceforth control
the existence of this careless person.   Still stronger would
be the reasons, therefore, for not taking into one's own
body and assimilating an unknown substance which might
prove fatal.   Hence primitives will only eat food which
past experience has shown to be harmless, the beneficial
effect of which is accounted for by the mystic relations
established between the social group and certain animal
and vegetable substances.   Very frequently special ceremonies at certain times of the year dramatically express,
renew, and strengthen these relations, upon which the
very life of the social group depends.

   A superstitious belief related by Spencer clearly shows
what, according to the natives, the consequence of partaking
of a food unknown to their dietary may be.

   In many tribes of Northern Australia, " the existence
of half-castes, given unwillingly by their mothers, speaking
in pidgin-English is ' Too much me been eat em white
man's flour.'   The chief difference that they acknowledge
between their life before and after they came into contact
with white men was, not the fact that they had intercourse
with white men, instead of, or side by side with, blacks,
but that they ate white flour and that this naturally affected

the colour of their offspring." [1] The negroes were not long in finding this explanation insufficient, but at first they accepted it as their wives did, and it was the first that occurred to their minds.

In the same way, if the white man's cooking inspires the native with invincible repugnance, it is, too, on account of the malign influences which their utensils might engender. In the eyes of the New Zealand Maoris, no impurity could exceed that of the cooking utensils. In the case of the Tarahumares of Mexico, "some of them, after eating from my plates and cups, went to the river to rinse their mouths and wash their hands carefully, to get rid of any evil that might lurk in the white man's vessels." [2]

For the same reason, similar suspicions extend to all the objects from which a malign influence is to be feared, because their origin is doubtful. Thus it has been noted that the natives of the New Hebrides refused to accept things brought by one of their own race who had lived among white people ; they watched these closely, or rather they put them in quarantine. When once thoroughly at home with the missionaries, the Bechuanas of South Africa owned that the presents they had sent to the king on their first arrival in the country, had not been delivered to him, lest the acceptance of them might be followed by some disaster. There are innumerable instances of this kind. Without laying any further stress upon them, I shall merely remark that the term " misoneism " but ill describes them. It is not solely, nor indeed actually because they are new that these things are rejected ; it is also, and even more, because they are potential bearers of fatal influences.

II

When it is a case of discontinuing a traditional custom or deliberately adopting a practice hitherto unknown, resistance is as energetic as it is obstinate. Investigators, especially missionaries, have clearly realized the reason

---

[1] B. Spencer : *The Native Tribes of the Northern Territory of Australia*, pp. 25–6.

[2] Carl Lumholtz : *Unknown Mexico*, i. p. 224. (Macmillans, 1903.)

for this. " The New Guinea man is intensely conservative, and he does what his father and grandfather and great-grandfather did ; what was good enough for them was quite good enough for him, as the man who was building a canoe in Wadau said when he rejected with scorn the suggestion to build a big, comfortable platform in the canoe as the Boianai people do, instead of the little skimpy ones at each end the Wadau people affect. ' No, it is not our way ' (and perhaps the Boianai people might object to the infringement of their patent rights)." [1]

The same missionary relates that at a certain great festival the natives sacrificed pigs by the most deliberate and cruel methods, and that they had been ordered hence-forth to despatch their victims as quickly and humanely as possible. " Very early in the morning the killing of the pigs began, and towards the end some of the old people got anxious at the awful breach of custom in the way the butchering was being done, and a deputation came to tell us that they must kill one pig in their own way so that the mango trees might hear the squeals, otherwise they would not bear fruit." [2]

In (German) New Guinea " the natives burn the fine tortoise-shell with the rest of the tortoise. It is their custom and they do not depart from it. We have often pointed out that this tortoise-shell is very valuable and they could get a good deal of money for it, but up to now our sug-gestions have been in vain. They always used to promise to change their custom ' next time ' in order to satisfy us, but when the next occasion occurred they did just the same as before. They have not courage enough to abandon old customs . . . they lack the necessary energy." [3]

In New Pomerania, " when a boat is under way, the outrigger is on the left. If the waves come from this side, it serves effectually to break their force. As these boats are alike fore and aft, you would think that when the waves are on the right the natives would navigate in

---

[1] Rev. H. Newton : *In Far New Guinea*, pp. 125–6.
[2] Ibid., p. 154.
[3] P. Fritz Vorman, S.V.D. : " Das tägliche Leben der Papua (unter besonderer Berücksichtigung des Valman Stammes auf Deutsch Neue Guinea)." *Anthropos*, xii–xiii. p. 901 (1907).

such a way that the outrigger can be on the right.
Nothing of the sort. The Kanuck has so great a dislike of
any innovation that he persists in going on with this to
larboard even when the waves are on the starboard side
and filling his bark with water. When I argued with them
on this point, the natives granted that a change in their
customs would only be advantageous, and I always wondered
whether it was from lack of ability to make up their minds
that they were unable to adopt a change which they yet
recognized as an improvement." [1]

In short, as the Nias missionaries state, " the natives
do not know and will not have anything different from
what they already have, and it satisfies them entirely.
They want nothing better." [2] This is a fact ; and we can
easily perceive the reason of it, which is almost the same
everywhere. By abandoning or in any way modifying
their traditional customs and adopting new ways, they
would expose themselves to incalculable risks, and above
all, to the anger of their ancestors, those powerful members
of the social group, and this for some advantage which,
even if certain, is in any case not indispensable. Such
a fear is openly expressed by the natives of Kiwai in New
Guinea. " My friends had been describing to me certain
ceremonies they employ for the purpose of making the
crops grow, and they were really anxious about the wisdom
of adopting the new religion, which they fully realized
would require them to give up these practices, for if they
did not do as their fathers had done, how could the yams
and sago grow ? ' It's all very fine,' they urged, ' for
Tamate (Chalmers, the missionary), as everything he eats
comes out of tins, which he gets from the store on Thursday
Island, but how about us ? ' " [3]

In South Africa, a European was endeavouring to
domesticate the Bushmen. " He tried to persuade them
to purchase goats with ostrich feathers, or skins of game
procured in the chase. At this proposal they laughed
inordinately, asking him if their forefathers ever kept cattle ;

[1] Pfeil (Graf J.) : *Studien und Beobachtungen aus der Südsee*, p. 92.
[2] *Berichte der rheinischen Missionsgesellschaft*, p. 217 (1895).
[3] A. C. Haddon : *Head-hunters, Black, White, and Brown*, p. 98.

intimating, that they were not intended to *keep*, but to eat, as their progenitors had always done." [1] A similar suggestion, made by a German missionary, was received in exactly the same way. " I entreated them," says he, " to remain here, to make gardens and plant corn. I offered to give them the seeds ; but they burst out laughing, and said it would kill them to do so." [2]

In the Bantu tribes, whose organization is already fairly complicated, the conservative spirit is no less strong. For instance, it was hopeless to try and dissuade Kafirs from their horrible methods of dealing with sorcerers. It was the custom, and against this magic word no argument can avail. " What would the spirits of our ancestors say if we were to change our customs ? To punish us they would make our wives and our fields barren, and at length the white man would ' eat up our land.' " [3] " Formerly," says the Rev. John Philip, " it was against their practice to deviate from the customs of their ancestors. When urged to plant corn, etc., they used to reply that their fathers were wiser than themselves, and yet were content to do as they did ; they also regarded every innovation as an insult to the memory of their ancestors." [4] The first French missionaries in this district bore witness to the same fact. " According to native ideas," says Casalis, " there could be no more direct provocation of the anger of the ancestors they worshipped than by departing from the precepts and examples they left behind them." [5] " Ask the Basutos the reason for these customs, and they will not be able to tell you. They do not reflect, and they have neither guiding principles nor doctrines. The only thing that is of importance in their eyes is the accomplishment of certain traditional acts, and the preservation of the connection with the past and those who lived in it." [6]

The supreme conduct of life, therefore, is to do what ancestors have done, and to do that only. The earliest

[1] R. Moffat : *Missionary Labours and Scenes in South Africa*, p. 63.
[2] *Berichte der rheinischen Missionsgesellschaft*, p. 49 (1897).
[3] Fr. Ægidius Müller : "Wahrsagerei bei den Kaffern," *Anthropos*, ii. pp. 48–9.
[4] Rev. J. Philip : *Researches in South Africa*, ii. p. 118 (1828).
[5] *Missions évangéliques*, xv. p. 122 (1840).
[6] Ibid., lxxxii. 2. p. 336 (1907). (Dieterlen.)

investigators quoted several examples of this. " The Mat-chappees," says Campbell, " though very fond of potatoes, have never been prevailed upon to plant any, because they resemble nothing which has been handed down to them from their forefathers." [1] With reference to the same tribe, a contemporary of Campbell's writes as follows : " That their horticulture does not include the tobacco plant, is a circumstance to be wondered at, when it is considered how excessively fond they are of smoking, and that the nations beyond them, as well as the Hottentots at Klaar-water, cultivate it with success ; and where they have therefore seen, and become well acquainted with the plant. But this is again proof of the force of custom, and of the slowness with which uncivilized men admit improvement, when it contradicts ancient habits or prejudices ; for on being asked why they did not themselves grow tobacco instead of begging it from every stranger, who visited them, they replied that they did not know the reason, but believed it was because it had never been their practice to plant it. Yet the cultivation of this, and of various other vegetables which I mentioned to them, was confessed to be a desirable object ; and it appeared from this acknowledgment that they were not absolutely averse to making the attempt." [2] It may be so, but this latter point remains doubtful. The natives' assent apparently signifies, first and foremost, that they do not want to contradict the white man. It says nothing about what they will really do.

" The chiefs who have died," says Junod, " become the country's gods. What they have done is what must yet be done, the way in which they lived is the supreme model ; the traditions bequeathed by ancestors to their descendants most clearly demonstrate the religion and moral code of these people. Custom, handed down from pre-historic times, makes their law. Nobody dreams of evading it. To do differently from others, *psa yila*, it is forbidden. It would be an attack on the divine authority of the an-cestors, and an act of sacrilege. The more free of foreign

[1] Rev. J. Campbell : *Travels in South Africa (Second Journey)*, i. p. 191. (1822).
[2] Rev. Wm. J. Burchell ; *Travels in the Interior of Southern Africa*, ii. p. 588.

elements the tribe is, and the less it is subjected to extraneous influences, the more firmly is this principle maintained." [1]

This feature of inviolability extends to every sort of custom, to the division of labour between the sexes, for instance, which besides depends sometimes upon reasons of a mystic nature.[2] One day Moffat saw among the Bechuanas the wife of an exalted personage who, helped by others, was building a hut, preparing to climb on to its roof by the aid of a branch of a tree. He remarked that women ought to leave that sort of work to their husbands. There was a general outburst of laughter. " Mahuto, the queen, and several of the men drawing near to ascertain the cause of the merriment, the women repeated my strange and, to them, ludicrous proposal, when another peal of mirth ensued. Mahuto, who was a sensible and shrewd woman, stated that the plan, though hopeless, was a good one, as they often thought our custom was much better than theirs." [3] A polite, and possibly sincere, remark ; yet this queen would never deliberately have changed any custom respected from time immemorial. Since they know the missionary well, and he speaks their language, they do not hide from him what they think. Let women's work be done by men ! Such a ridiculous idea could only occur to a white man !

The regulations thus imposed by tradition form a very complicated system, yet everyone thinks it quite natural to conform to them in all points and at all times. " Superstition," says Mauch, " plays an enormous part in the life and conduct of the Makalolo, and their most trifling actions are regulated by it. Such for instance, as the way in which wood is put on the fire, the method of seating oneself in a hut, of holding the broom or the spoon, of satisfying the demands of nature, etc. The bellows will have no power unless they are made of the skin of a goat which has been skinned while still alive ; the furnace will not burn properly unless a certain charm has been mixed with the clay, and

---

[1] H. A. Junod : *Les Ba-Ronga*, pp. 226–7.
[2] Cf. supra, chap. x. pp. 316–20.
[3] R. Moffat : *Missionary Labours and Scenes in South Africa*, pp. 252–3.

during its making it has received a present of beef, tea and beer, etc." [1]

Even when once established, an innovation for a long time remains doubtful. It is a well-known fact that the old custom, for mystic reasons, is always ready to regain the supremacy, and in certain circumstances it actually does so. I shall quote but one example. " To the Bushongo, raffia cloth, introduced more than three hundred years ago, is still considered an innovation. On all ceremonial occasions, the high dignitaries dress themselves in dried skins, as their ancestors did. Or again, when a woman goes into mourning she puts on a garment made of skin ; she abstains from eating cassava, which was introduced but fairly recently, as if by obeying ancient customs she could appease the powers which are the source of her grief." [2]

However great may be the force of habit, however apparently instinctive the respect it inspires, some clever and inventive persons, in these communities as in our own, are always attracted by novelty. What will happen if a man tries to modify any existing habit ? Unless he acts with extreme caution, and takes pains to secure the consent, I might almost say the complicity, of the influential persons of the group, the consequences may prove very disastrous to him. In most primitive communities, and especially in those of South or Central Africa of which we have been speaking, he runs a risk of losing his life. " The whole existence of the native," says Fr. Ægidius Müller," is a system of customs to which he must conform ; if he discards them he falls under a suspicion of witchcraft." [3] There are abundant examples of this ; here are a few of them. In the Congo region " the most progressive men," says Bentley, " are the first to be destroyed. When the india-rubber trade commenced, the first to sell it were killed as witches ; so, too, with every innovation." [4] There is nothing more dangerous than not to do as others do,

---

[1] Carl Mauch : " Reisen im Innern von Süd Afrika (1865–72)." Petermann's Mitteilungen. *Ergänzungsheft*, n. 87, p. 43.

[2] Torday and Joyce : " Les Bushongo," *Annales du Musée du Congo belge*, Série III, t. ii. p. 13.

[3] Fr. Ægidius Müller : " Wahrsagerei bei den Kaffern," *Anthropos*, ii. p. 55.

[4] Rev. W. H. Bentley : *Pioneering on the Congo*, i. p. 278 (1900).

to do better, or above all, to do something which has never been done before. "Some twenty-five years ago," writes Weeks, " I knew a blacksmith who made a very good imitation, from old hoop-iron, of a trade knife, and when the king heard of it he thought it was too clever and threatened him with a charge of witchcraft if he made any more like it. . . . Some years ago I knew a native medicine-woman who was successful in treating certain native diseases, and as she became wealthy, the natives accused her of giving the sickness by witchcraft in order to cure and to be paid for it ; for they said : ' How can she cure it so easily unless she first gave it ? ' She had to abandon her practice or she would have been killed as a witch. The introduction of a new article of trade has always brought to the introducer a charge of witchcraft, and there is a legend that the man who discovered the way to tap palm trees for palm wine was charged as a witch and paid the penalty with his life." [1]

Why should the idea of sorcery immediately present itself to the native in these cases, and many like them ? It doubtless arises out of the constant orientation of primitive mentality which immediately refers all it sees or ascertains to a mystic cause, without paying the slightest attention to what we call the series of objective and visible causes and effects. The Congoland smith succeeds in making a European knife out of a piece of iron which is part of a barrel-hoop, and we admire his initiative, and the skill and perseverance of the artisan who has been able to do so much with such poor material and such inferior tools. Primitive mentality remains quite indifferent to these good qualities ; it does not even notice them. What strikes the primitive mind, and the point it alone fastens upon, is the disquieting novelty of the result obtained. How could a knife like the white man's have been produced in the smithy, if the maker had not had a magic influence to aid him ? He therefore becomes a suspicious character. Anyone who, like him, obtains a success nobody had imagined before, will expose himself to the same accusation. It matters little if he makes no mystery of the operations he

[1] Rev. J. H. Weeks : " Anthropological Notes on the Bangala of the Upper Congo River," *J.A I.*, xxxix. p. 108.

has thought out or carried into effect. According to native ideas, his success is not due to them, but to an occult power which alone has made the means employed effective. Immediately the troublesome question arises : how was he able to secure the co-operation of this occult power ? Is he not a wizard ?

By virtue of this same decree, " no man can be richer than his neighbour, nor must he acquire his riches by any other than the usual or established means of barter or trade of the native products of the country, or his plantations. Should a native return to his town, after no matter how long an absence, with more than a moderate amount of cloth, beads, etc. . . . he is immediately accused of witchcraft . . . and his property distributed among all, and he is often fined as well." [1] To the primitive mind, to succeed too well and obtain an unusually happy result is equivalent to being the only one to escape from a danger which has overwhelmed all the rest, and this they think is invariably due to witchcraft, since there is no such thing as chance. We have already had examples of this,[2] and here are a few more. A Kafir who was the sole member of his social group to recover from smallpox, was killed during the night by other members of the tribe, and to justify this act of murder they alleged that it was he who by his witchcraft had brought the plague into the kraal.[3] " During an epidemic which raged here (Fiji Isles) for some months, as we alone were exempt from the malady, our islanders imagined us to be the cause of the scourge, and invented a story to this effect. I had, they said, a mysterious box, and when I opened it, fevers spread about the country." [4] Thus, even when a native knows the way to avoid approaching disaster, he would rather suffer with the rest than be the only one to escape, and he will make no effort to withdraw. As regards the Waschamba, " a native knows

[1] J. J. Monteiro : *Angola and the River Congo*, i. pp. 280–1.
[2] Cf. supra, chap. i. pp. 47–50.
[3] *The South African Commercial Advertiser* (April 17, 1841). Extract from the Papers and Proceedings of the Aborigines Protection Society, ii. 5, pp. 158–9.
[4] *Annales de la Propagation de la foi*, xxviii. p. 38⁷ (1856). (Lettre du R. P. Mathieu.)

quite well that he could drive away a swarm of locusts by shouts, beating of drums, the smoke of a fire if he made one, but he does not make use of any of these methods, for if his land were thus to be the only part spared, his less fortunate neighbours might accuse him of witchcraft, the very fact of his plantation not having suffered being brought forward as proof. More certainly still would they impute to him the sending of the swarm of locusts on to their land. That is why, as a defence against this pest, they make use of magic means only." [1] Why should locusts come and devour the Waschamba crops ? It is assuredly some malign influence which has attracted them hither, and the fact that one individual's land alone escapes will indicate him as the guilty person. To the primitive mind, such an evidence is actual proof.

The man, too, who lives to a great age and is the sole survivor of his generation, is equally suspect. How did he contrive to lengthen out his life thus, while all his contemporaries have disappeared ? Should some misfortune occur, suspicion will immediately fall on him. " Kiala, the chief of the town," says Bentley, " had relatives in Mpete, a town two hours distant ; one of them died, and the accusation of the cause of the death by witchcraft was fastened on an old man of Mpete. Kiala and his party urged that he should take *nkasa*. There had been no intervention of a witch-doctor, but the old man had outlived all his generation and the people said that he survived because he was the cause of the death of all of them ; he was the witch, so of course he survived. We cautioned Kiala, and he was afraid to let things take their usual course for fear of the State ; he therefore determined to put him to death without actually killing him ! He took a party up to Mpete one moonlight night, caught the old man in his house, and bound him. They dug a hole in front of the house, put the old man in, and buried him alive. If he died it was his business ; nobody had killed him ! " [2]

[1] A. Karasek-Eichhorn : *Beiträge zur Kenntniss der Waschamba,* Bässler Archiv. i. p. 182 (1911).
[2] Rev. W. H. Bentley : *Pioneering on the Congo,* ii. pp. 335–6.

The " misoneism " which we find among these peoples,
then, is the direct consequence of the conformity which,
for reasons peculiar to primitive mentality, is strictly
binding on all individuals. To be singular in any way
whatever, is to lay oneself open to suspicion. Among
certain Bantus, for instance, "the son must not aspire to
anything better than his father has had before him. If
a man desires to improve the style of his hut, to make a
larger dwelling than is customary ; if he should wear a
fine or different style of dress to that of his fellows, he is
instantly fined ; and he becomes, too, the object of such
scathing ridicule, that he were a bold man indeed who would
venture to excite it against himself." [1] Among the Kafirs,
" the rites and ceremonies . . . are not matters of indifference, which may be performed or neglected at the will of
the native, but they are the *trust* and *confidence* of the Kafir ;
and in his estimation, his life and well-being depend on
their due performance, and were he to despise and neglect
them, he would . . . lose caste, and be avoided by his
friends and neighbours as a suspicious character, who must
be trusting to the arts and powers of witchcraft or he would
never be guilty of such a heinous crime. And should any
misfortune befall the kraal, and a priest be applied to, to
perform the *umhlahlo*, or ' smelling out,' such suspicious
person would, no doubt, be pointed out by the priest as
the cause thereof, and punished as a wizard. Another
thing, which effectually prevents them from committing
any infractions of these rites and ceremonies, is the superstitious fear which they themselves have of incurring the
displeasure of the *umshologu* (ancestors) by so doing, and consequently, that some supernatural evils should befall them." [2]
This arbitrary conformity does not weigh on individuals as much as one might think. They are accustomed to it from infancy, and as a rule they do not
imagine that things could be different. The relations of
the individual to the social group (the family, clan, and
tribe) make it easy to bear. In short, in these communities

---

[1] Ch. New : *Life, Wanderings, and Labours in Eastern Africa*, p. 110.
[2] Col. C. S. Maclean, C.B. : *A Compendium of Kafir Laws and Customs*.
p. 106.

the individual is far less distinct from his group than in our own. The social solidarity may not be closer, it assuredly is not so complex, but its nature is more like that of a living body. The individual is more completely a member of the group, in the strict sense of the term. The claims of the vendetta, for instance, are equally satisfied, whether it be the murderer himself or any other individual belonging to his group who suffers death at the hands of one of the victim's relatives. All the members of a family are equally responsible for the debt of any one of them, etc. " As a rule, among the Basutos, the important acts of life are not left to individual caprice, but regulated and arranged by the entire family. In short, the individual never really attains his majority, he must be more or less in the tutelage of his family, clan, and tribe. He has no individuality, he is but a member of the familial or national community." [1]

This attitude gives rise to one of the most frequent and persistent misunderstandings between missionaries and natives. The missionaries want to save souls. They use every effort to try and induce each member of their flock, male or female, to abandon heathen practices and become adherents of the true faith. But natives, as a rule, have no idea of *individual* salvation. They think, as the missionaries do, that death is but the portal to another existence, but they have no idea that each one of them may be saved or damned on his own account. Their profound and perpetual sentiment of solidarity with the group and with their chiefs (when the community comprises any), makes it impossible for them to understand what the missionary so ardently desires for them, and even what he really wants to accomplish. There is too great a gulf between the primitive mind and the missionary's aim. How could the native imagine his personal destiny as dependent alone upon his faith and his actions—to say nothing of Divine grace—when he has never even contemplated such individual independence in the community to which he belongs?

Consequently, conversions to Christianity, when they do occur, are general in their nature, especially where the

---

[1] E. Jacottet: "Mœurs, coutumes et superstitions des Bassoutos," *Bulletin de la Société de Géographie de Neuchâtel,* ix. p. 123, note 2 (1897).

chief's authority is already established, or where the collective existence of the group is personified in him. " The need of support is second nature to them (the Basutos), and we might say that from birth they bear the mark of the collar. Their attachment to their chiefs is something instinctive, such as that of the bees for their queen. It would never occur to them that they might combine to break their yoke ; at most, if it becomes too oppressive they may try to avoid it personally by a change of masters." [1] Let us suppose that these masters, as so often happens, remain deaf to the persuasions of the missionaries. " If, setting aside these lesser chiefs, hardened in their absurd pride, we turn to their subjects, what will *they* say to us ? ' We are only our masters' dogs, children without understanding. How can we accept what our masters reject ? ' " [2]

It is the same with the Barotse. " Everything must originate with the head of the tribe ; if Lewanika orders us to learn what you tell us, we shall learn ; if he rejects your teaching, who will dare to act differently ? " " The nation has but one mind, one will. The individual is annihilated, we have here the centralization principle pushed to its extreme limit, or to put it in another way, the death of all for the sake of one." [3] If the chief does not go to church, the building remains empty. " What we noticed at Seshaké was that even if the village were overflowing with people, if the chiefs did not come to our services, no one else was present." [4] More than once, moreover, the missionary realizes and deplores the fact that individual conversion is, as it were, impossible for the native ; it is asking too much of him. " For the poor Mosuto to receive the Gospel, means a refusal to share in a ceremonial which is ordered by the chief and regarded as essential to the prosperity of the tribe ; it means refusing to use his assegai against neighbouring tribes. In a word, it means renouncing the name and status of Mosuto, and thus exposing himself to having the few cows he possesses carried off, and these are the sole means of subsistence for him and his family." [5]

---

[1] *Missions évangéliques*, lxi. p. 447 (1886). (Duvoisin.)
[2] Ibid., xxiii. p. 85 (1848). (Schrumpf.)
[3] Ibid., lxii. p. 217 (1887). (Jeanmairet.)
[4] Ibid., lxiii. p. 105 (1888). (Jeanmairet.) [5] Ibid., xiii. p. 5 (1838).

These, however, are but the material results of the rupture of a social bond, whose nature we are very far from understanding. According to the words of Father Trilles: " In the Bantu conception of the cosmos, the individual does not exist ; organized collectivity on the other hand is, properly speaking, the only *being* which has a real existence. This is actual, the former accidental ; this persists, while the other is transient." [1]

Facts like this are constantly met with in other than Bantu tribes. To take but one instance only, the German missionaries at Nias have frequently proved, and many times described, the impossibility of effecting individual conversions. " Nobody wants to make up his mind on his own account. The counsels of the old men must decide in cases of a change of religion, for to our Nias native such matters are State affairs. It will be all or none. . . . The strictness of the social bond relieves the individual of all responsibility, but at the same time it deprives him of his personal liberty. From his rigid social solidarity, and the slight value accorded to individual personality in consequence, there arise situations requiring much time and experience before they can be estimated aright." [2]

III

To these reasons, both positive and mystic, which bind primitive peoples so closely to their customs and make innovations unwelcome, we must add another not yet stated and by no means the least important. Primitive mentality, intensely mystic as it is, is but very slightly conceptual. It feels very strongly, but it hardly ever analyses, nor does it think in abstract terms. Consequently, when it forms its judgment of values, in which its likes and dislikes, its feelings in general and its passions are expressed, it must at the same time represent to itself in concrete fashion what the object of these is. In other words, it does not formulate general judgments of values, founded upon a positive comparison of things apparently

[1] R. P. H. Trilles : *Le totémisme des Fân*, p. 369.
[2] *Berichte der rheinischen Missionsgesellschaft*, p. 274 (1907).

very dissimilar, any more than it constructs general concepts of an abstract nature. Judgments of this sort would involve intellectual processes which are quite simple and familiar to us, but for which the primitive has neither taste nor aptitude. He instinctively shuns them, as it were.

Moreover, he does not estimate the value of a process, method, tool, utensil, in short of any means whatever of acting so as to attain a result, as we are accustomed to do, that is, by observing the yield of the method, instrument, etc., and comparing it objectively with others, regarding each feature of it in the abstract and apart from any other consideration. He can doubtless perceive the greater or lesser efficiency of the methods and instruments he employs, but he does not make this the exclusive object of a special scrutiny ; he does not judge it by itself. The mystic elements upon which the success of an enterprise or action of any sort whatever depends, must always enter into the reckoning. Consequently, the primitive's judgment of values will remain concrete and comparatively specialized, and often this proves disconcerting to European investigators. They do not understand how the natives, seeing before them two examples of the same thing, the one native-made, clumsy, and ill-contrived, the other of European make, of improved pattern and easy to handle, can continue to prefer their own as they so often do, at any rate in the early days.

" These " (the missionaries' houses), " the natives say, are very excellent houses ; but ' why cannot they live in houses such as their fathers lived in ? ' Their canoes are the same ; our vessels and boats are here, and are better than their own ; but still they will be contented with what they have. Their mode of dress . . . will also do for them . . . To all this they will generally yield their assent, but make no effort to improve. They praise our superior habits, but continue to practise their own." [1]

The Fijians' assent is a matter of pure politeness, it is rarely that the native does not try to please his inter-locutor by assenting to what he says. Moreover, the primi-

[1] *Wesleyan Missionary Notices*, vi., p. 199 (December 1848). (Journal of the Rev. Walter Lawry.)

tives' attitude is explained by the nature of their judgment
of values. The European houses and ships are quite the
right thing for Europeans, and the Fijian houses and ships
are equally convenient for themselves. It matters very
little to find out which buildings in themselves it would
be pleasanter to live in, or which vessels would prove more
seaworthy. Such a question does not occur to the primitive
mind. If their boats allow of their going from one island
to another, and of making fairly long voyages, it is not
only nor indeed chiefly on account of their nautical
qualities, it is primarily because the occult powers favourable
to the Fijians and attentive to the prayers of their chiefs,
give these boats the power of traversing space, protect
them from storms and contrary winds, triumph victoriously
over other occult powers which are hostile, and so on. In
short, the successful use of these canoes presumes nothing
short of a complex ensemble of definite participations
shared by the Fijian group and the invisible powers upon
which it depends. Who cannot see that it is exactly
the same with the white man's ships ? The use of these
splendid vessels, too, must be subordinated to the sum-
total of the mystic life of his social group, and everything
seems to prove that Europeans stand in relation to occult
powers of an uncommon kind. These are unknown and
hence probably hostile to the Fijians, therefore what use
could they make of such vessels ? Who knows whether
these powers, aroused to anger by seeing " *their* " vessels
adopted, might not cause the Fijians to perish ? The
most ordinary prudence therefore requires them to remain
faithful to traditional customs in this as in other respects.
If, to suppose an impossibility, the Fijians should become
white men, that is, if their social group should be fused
with that of the whites, and their respective ancestors
mingled together, if their guardian spirits were to fraternize
—then, and then only, could the Fijians, without risk and
with possible advantage, accept and adopt the white man's
implements and his way of life. Until that should happen,
they can but remain faithful to their own customs, the
only ones which guarantee any security. When they agree
with Europeans that their way of doing things is better,

they say to themselves, " better for you ! " The idea of its being " better in itself " has no meaning for them.

These same Fijians, " in taking English medicine during their illness, . . . frequently renounce heathenism, in the idea that this is necessary to secure the efficacy of the physic." [1] We see how they reason the matter out. The idea of any physiological effect the medicine may have is altogether foreign to them. Its mystic influence is the only one they conceive of. From this standpoint, the Christians' remedies could have no virtue in themselves, or of an universal kind ; they are good for the Christians. Let us therefore become Christians, and then these wonderful remedies will cure us as if we were English. " One of King Tanoo's wives," says Waterhouse, " having embraced Christianity ' to give efficiency to the English medicine ' she was then taking, was compelled by Tanoo to return to heathenism as soon as she recovered. ' You are only a Christian to save your neck from strangling when my father dies,' was the remark of the chief when he ordered her to apostasize." [2]

In other primitive communities, whether inferior or superior to the Fijians of a generation ago, we should find the same specializing of the judgment of values, the same difficulty, not to say impossibility, of imagining that what is good and useful to the white man may, for the same reason, be good and useful to the native ; that he may be cured by the same medicaments, use the same methods, have the same education and the same religion, and find the same destiny in the next life. " ' You are right,' say the Papuans to the missionary. But—they add—' the other has always been our custom. To us the *rotoi* (spirit, deity), has given the *Ai* ; to you, God's word and the teachings of Christ. We are black men, and you white.' These are arguments which are constantly advanced." [3]

In British New Guinea, " I knew of an instance where the daughter of a native missionary had died. He accused

[1] Rev. J. Waterhouse : *The King and People of Fiji*, p. 420 (1866).
[2] Ibid., p. 108.
[3] *Berichte der rheinischen Missionsgesellschaft*, pp. 115-16 (1899). (German) New Guinea.

the local sorcerer of causing her death. He was remonstrated with for believing in *puri-puri* (witchcraft). His reply was to the effect that ' you are white men, and do not understand the New Guinea medicine. I am a New Guinea native, and I know it.' " [1] His apparent conversion to the white man's faith was in vain ; his solidarity with his social group was stronger still. In the island of Nias, " the native is extraordinarily and inveterately attached to his immemorial customs, and he does not desire any progress, even in external conditions, although the new things he sees and hears may appear finer and in every way superior. That is the reason why schools do not get on well here ; to the Nias idea, reading and writing, and all intellectual knowledge as a rule, is as superfluous and useless as anything well can be." [2] In other words, it may be good for the white man, because it is part of the sum-total of his activity, and he has the guarantee of his past experience to go upon. The Nias man has none of this, and if he were to adopt it, he would doubtless repent it.

The Jibaros of Ecuador smoke for pleasure, but they have learnt to do so from white men. " That this is so we may conclude from the fact that for such a purpose they do not smoke any tobacco but that received from white men, never using their own. The tobacco the Jibaros have grown themselves is used exclusively for ceremonial purposes. On the other hand, the white man's tobacco is never used in Jibaro ceremonial. They do not seem to believe in it sufficiently for that." [3]

IV

After prolonged intercourse with white men, native ideas and sentiments about the whites and what they bring with them, gradually become modified. The change comes about in many ways, and is affected by the question whether the white men are fairly numerous, whether they occupy the country or merely visit it, recruit labourers among the

[1] " Papua," *Annual Report*, p. 163 (1912).
[2] *Berichte der rheinischen Missionsgesellschaft*, p. 236 (1890).
[3] Rafael Karsten : *Beiträge zur Sittengeschichte der südamerikanischen Indianer*, p. 56 (1920).

natives or not, proceed with a greater or lesser show of force, and so on. It happens only too often that the native community does not survive this irruption ; the maladies brought in the train of the whites, and the demoralizing that often follows their arrival, sometimes cause the blacks to disappear in a very short time. When they do adapt themselves to the new conditions, we find that at first it is but slowly, though later their progress is accelerated. In what we may call the first period, it is not the natives who adapt themselves to the European way of life ; rather do they adapt to their own civilization what they borrow from the whites. " It is surprising to note," says Eylmann, " how little the native has been influenced by his relations with white people, as regards his weapons. As far as I am able to judge, natives have everywhere preserved the traditional forms of these weapons, and even manifest extreme conservatism about the materials of which they are made. The tribes between Lake Eyre and Tennant's Creek still make their weapons of wood and stone, as they did when they were undisputed masters of their territory. The natives more to the north of Tennant's Creek, however, use steel and glass for the points of their long lances." [1]

Steensby, in the course of a sojourn among the " Polar " Esquimaux, paid particular attention to finding out how the social group which had just begun to enter into permanent relations with white men, received the " advance " these brought with them in the way of technical knowledge. The conclusions he arrived at are interesting. " It must not be believed that any and every kind of European implement finds a welcome in the eyes of the Polar Eskimos. They have had a remarkably good understanding of how to choose out the kinds and forms which were best suited to their requirements. The most useful European instrument the Polar Eskimos can obtain is still a file. . . . We see very clearly among the Polar Eskimos, that they have chosen the apparatus, which for them meant a reduction of labour in their old modes of procedure. But they have still held fast to their old methods and the old forms, in so far as

[1] E. Eylmann : *Die Eingeborenen der Kolonie Süd Australien*, p. 363.

they were not obliged to modify them in using the new apparatus. The Polar Eskimos are thus to a certain extent still people of the Stone Age, who are employing the help yielded by the modern mechanical methods, without adopting the mental accompaniments. For them, iron is a material of similar kind to bone, and they deal with bone and metal in quite the same manner as with the file. I found an interesting example of this in a harpoon-point of the Polar Eskimo Manigssok ; every part of it had been filed out of a massive piece of iron." [1]

As long as the essential institutions of the group persist, its mentality also remains the same, however great the external changes in the manner of life may be. Clear-sighted missionaries have often noticed this. When converted, natives are still unable to conceive the idea of personal salvation clearly. Their feeling of systematized solidarity with their group and their chief has not given way to a more definite consciousness of their own personality, and to them the missionary simply takes the place formerly held by the chief. " When, after having spoken of the destruction of the world by fire predicted by St. Peter, I appealed to my hearers, crying, ' Where will you then fly from the wrath of God ? ' several voices replied at once, ' To you, *moruti* (missionary), our father.' " [2] To secure God's favour for the group, and procure the benefits assured thereby for each member of it, is now the missionary's business, just as before their conversion took place, it was the work of the tribal chief to guarantee the group the support of ancestors and spirits by means of ceremonies and traditional sacrifices. In the very moment of changing his customs the native finds the means of keeping his respect for custom inviolable ; he behaves with regard to the new just as he did to the old. " Our native Christians are very conservative. Tradition, which in civil matters is the law accepted by all, becomes, in religious matters, the law of God. To change anything is to act contrary to God's law." [3]

[1] H. P. Steensby : " Contributions to the Ethnology and Anthropology of the Polar Eskimos, *Meddelelser om Groenland*, xxxiv. pp. 348–9 (1910).
[2] *Missions évangéliques*, lxiii. p. 19 (1888). (Coillard.)
[3] Ibid., lxxvii. 2. p. 187 (1902). (Christeller.)

The difference between the mystic and prelogical mind of the primitive and the white man's way of thinking is so far-reaching that any abrupt transition from the one to the other is inconceivable. A gradual and progressive transformation of the first into the second, if it were possible to note it, would be of extraordinary interest to anthropology. Unfortunately, circumstances have nowhere permitted of this hitherto, and it is to be feared that the future will be no more favourable in this respect. The few primitive races which do exist to-day will doubtless share the fate of those which are already extinct. It is therefore all the more necessary to collect as carefully as possible all that we can yet learn of the way in which primitive mentality reacts at the time when its customary course is suddenly disturbed by the irruption of new elements.

CHAPTER XIII

THE PRIMITIVE'S ATTITUDE TO EUROPEAN REMEDIES

I

It almost invariably happens that one of the earliest relations established between the primitive and the European is that of patient to doctor. It is rarely that the explorer, naturalist, missionary, and even the Government official, has not at some time or other to act as doctor. How will such ministrations be accepted and understood? Upon this point we have a fairly large and unvarying amount of evidence. In examining it more minutely we shall probably find a confirmation of the analysis of primitive mentality we have already attempted.

" Some three hours every morning," says Bentley, " are spent in dressing large and loathsome ulcers, which, under the stimulating and healing influence of our lotions, rapidly assume a healthy appearance. One would think that the healing of these sores of five years' standing or more, in as many weeks, would elicit some sign of surprise or wonderment from onlookers. One would almost think that this medical attention, carefully, kindly, and constantly bestowed and combined, as it generally is, with board and lodging and constant genial efforts to win confidence and attachment would inspire here or there a little gratitude. But neither astonishment nor gratitude are visible, although the temperament of the people is by no means phlegmatic. One begins to question very seriously whether gratitude is, with these people, a natural instinct, exercised very occasionally." [1]

In the following case the missionary's disappointment

---

[1] Rev. W. H. Bentley : *Pioneering on the Congo*, i. pp. 444-5.

is still more acute. " A day or two after we reached Vana we found one of the natives very ill with pneumonia. Comber treated him and kept him alive on strong fowl-soup ; a great deal of careful nursing and attention was visited on him, for his house was beside the camp. When we were ready to go on our way again, the man was well. To our astonishment he came and asked us for a present, and was as astonished and disgusted as he had made us to be, when we declined giving it. We suggested that it was his place to bring us a present and to show some grati-tude. He said to us, ' Well indeed ! you white men have no shame ! I took your medicine and drank your soup, and did everything you told me, and now you object to giving me a fine cloth to wear ! You have no shame.' In spite of his protests he got nothing more out of us." [1]

We might be inclined to think that the missionaries were the victims of a sorry jest, but facts of a similar kind are by no means rare. For instance, " Nlemwo " (a native who was accompanying Bentley), "tells us that one day they came to a village where someone was very sick ; and the doctor gave this man a dose of medicine. On returning the same way and asking the man if he felt better, he replied that he was quite well, and also requested the doctor to pay him for having taken the medicine ! " [2] " The rapid recovery of the Chief is the wonder and talk of the country," says Bentley, in another place. " I am better known as the white man who cured Don Daniel than as ' Bentele.' When I went to see him, he was not in a grateful mood, although he owned I had cured him. ' What a fuss you made ! I had to eat a fowl, and feed well ; what strange things you white men are ! Why did you not give me a present when you left ? What a mean fellow you are ! ' " [3]

Is such an attitude peculiar to the natives of the Congo district ? Far from it ; we shall find the same thing in other regions of Africa, and even in other parts of the world. For instance, Mackenzie had cared for and cured a native whose face, which had been lacerated by a tiger, bore traces

[1] Rev. W. H. Bentley : *Pioneering on the Congo*, i. p. 414.
[2] Mrs. H. M. Bentley : *The Life and Labours of a Congo Pioneer*, p. 123.
[3] Ibid., p. 317.

of a terrible wound. This native visited him one day. He came, thought Mackenzie, " to exhibit the cure and to make at least a touching speech expressing his indebtedness to me. He sat down and narrated the whole thing over again, mentioning the various medicines which had been given, etc. He then said : ' My mouth is not exactly where it used to be . . . but the wound is quite whole. Everybody said I should die, but your herbs cured me. You are now my white man. Please to give me a knife.' I could not believe my own ears, and asked, ' What do you say ? ' ' I haven't got a knife ; please to give me a knife. You see,' he added, as I wondered what reply I could make, ' you are now my own white man and I shall always come to beg of you ! ' This seemed to me a most wonderful transposition of relationship ; and I began to think the man's mouth was not the only oblique thing about him. I mildly suggested that he might at least thank me for my medicines. He interrupted me, ' Why, am I not doing so ? Have I not said that you are now my white man and do I not now beg a knife from you ? ' I gave the man up as a very wonderful specimen of jumbled ideas." [1]

It does sometimes happen that the European receives some manifestation of gratitude, but he is always careful to note that it is exceptional. " On the 30th I received a present, the first token of gratitude ever offered me for my medical care (after many years of practice). Gratitude is a very rare plant." [2] " Most people, after having been attended to, would go away without even saying thank-you if I did not insist upon it. On one occasion only did I receive a dish of food as a token of gratitude, and that, of course, was offered by a woman. On the other hand, it is by no means a rare thing for a patient to ask for a present, a curious way of beginning a friendship." [3] " In a little more time," said another missionary from the same district, " I shall become so accustomed to the habit of begging which is so prevalent here, that I shall esteem it quite a normal thing not only to have no acknowledg-

---

[1] Rev. J. Mackenzie : *Ten Years North of the Orange River*, pp. 44–5.
[2] A. et E. Jalla : *Pionniers parmi les Marotse*, p. 167.
[3] *Missions évangéliques*, lxxxvi. 1. p. 22 (1911). (Prosch.)

ment made me, but to be asked for a piece of cloth, or some other present, by the people who have been the object of my care. I do exact, but not without some difficulty, a certain formality in coming in and going out, but many seem to ask for medicine as if it were their just due. Happily there are exceptions, and now and then I am cheered by some sign of gratitude. Yesterday, for instance, a girl who had been cured, brought our baby a fine mealie-cob, and thanked me heartily." [1]

In New Guinea the same circumstances prevail. " In the early days," says Newton, " a man with awful sores on his legs asked me to pay him for allowing me to give him relief. It sounds a bit Gilbertian for the patient to ask a fee from the ' doctor.' " [2] "At all our Mission stations people have told me stories of patients who have been nursed and treated and discharged cured, and then have asked if the missionaries were going to give them (that is, in the way of tobacco) any return for their having taken all that foreign medicine or come such a long way to the missionary's house for so many days." [3]

German missionaries in Sumatra had the same experience. " The Bataks receive medical attention . . . without showing the slightest trace of gratitude or expressing any thanks whatever. Max Bruch, the missionary, relates a truly classical example of the kind. His wife had come to the assistance of a Batak woman who was in great danger, and had saved her life. Her relatives refused to take the missionary's wife back home again, and when they finally did so, they demanded tobacco from Mr. Bruch because they were tired out." [4] In other passages the same missionaries report that " many of them are grateful for medical attention, but others are naïve enough to imagine that they should receive a present from the missionary for having given him the pleasure of treating them." [5] " I was treating a young man who had been badly wounded by a fall from a tree. . . . When he was able to ride again, I made him

[1] *Missions évangéliques*, lxxix. i. p. 404 (1904). (Reutter.)
[2] Rev. H. Newton : *In Far New Guinea*, p. 272.
[3] Rev. A. K. Chignell : *An Outpost in Papua*, p. 206 (1911).
[4] *Berichte der rheinischen Missionsgesellschaft*, p. 294 (1900).
[5] Ibid., p. 225 (1902).

come to the Mission station to have the wound dressed.
' You must come again the day after to-morrow,' I said.
He replied that he would prefer my coming to him. ' But
you have much more time to spare than I have.' He
answered naïvely, ' But then, Tuan (master), you must
remember, I don't get the horse for nothing ! ' The journey
cost him five cents (a few halfpence). ' And so that you,
who are by no means poor, may save your five cents, you
expect me to go on coming to you ! ' I was vexed at per-
ceiving that my services were rated so low, and that this
young man seemed to hold them in no esteem whatever." [1]

In Borneo, " in passing through this village (on the
river Limbang), I had given a man afflicted with sore eyes
a little sulphate of zinc ; he already had found, or fancied
he found, some benefit from the medicine, and in remem-
brance brought me a jar of arrack . . . which he insisted
I must drink. . . . I mention the circumstance of the poor
fellow bringing the arrack, as however grateful soever they
may be in their hearts for such kindness, they seldom show
it. I have not known half a dozen instances during my
whole residence in the East." [2]

Williams, too, tells us : " Four years' experience among
the natives of Somosomo taught me that if one of them,
when sick, obtained medicine from me, he thought me bound
to give him food. The reception of food he considered
as giving him a claim on me for covering ; and, that being
secured, he deemed himself at liberty to beg anything he
wanted, and abuse me if I refused his unreasonable request.
I treated the old king of Somosomo, Tuitkatau II, for a
severe attack of sickness, which his native doctors failed
to relieve. During the two or three days on which he was
under my care, he had at his own request tea and arrowroot
from our house ; and when recovered, his daughter waited
on me to say that he could now eat well, and had sent her
to beg an iron pot in which to cook his food ! One more
example. The master of a biche-de-mar vessel took a
native under his care whose hand was shattered by the
bursting of a musket. The armourer amputated the injured

[1] *Berichte der rheinischen Missionsgesellschaft*, p. 225 (1909).
[2] Sir Spenser St. John : *Life in the Forests of the Far East*, ii. pp. 132–3.

part, and the man was provided for on board the vessel for nearly two months. On his recovery, he told the master he was going on shore, but that a musket must be given him, in consideration of his having been on board so long. Such a request was, of course, refused ; and, after having been reminded of the kindness shown him, to which he probably owed his life, the unreasonable fellow was sent ashore, where he showed his sense of obligation by burning down one of the captain's drying-houses, containing fish of the value of three hundred dollars." [1]

II

In the cases we have just quoted, the list of which might be indefinitely prolonged, the behaviour of the natives who have received medical attention from Europeans appears unreasonable and even inexplicable. The latter feel more or less surprised, angry, discouraged, or both amused and indignant, according to their temperament. Some are seriously annoyed, others shrug their shoulders, but it seems as if not one of them ever asks himself whether there may not be some psychological problem to solve here, and whether the lack of understanding between the white doctor and his patient may not arise from a misconception on both sides. The doctor has his own ideas about illness and about therapeutics, and these seem so natural to him that he imagines the native to possess them also. As a matter of fact, the latter's ideas on the subject are widely different. If the white doctor took the trouble to examine minutely the way in which the native interprets the attentions he receives, he would be less astonished at finding them so little understood and appreciated, and even at hearing an indemnity demanded for them.

In the first place, in the native's eyes, as we know, the curing of a malady is the defeat of the charm which has caused it by means of a more powerful one. " In doctoring the simplest case, the *lingaka* (native doctors) inculcate the belief that although they choose to give medicines, they, and not the medicines, effect the cure. They

[1] Th. Williams : *Fiji and the Fijians*, i. pp. 128–9.

' charm ' the sickness by the power in them, and do not
' cure ' it by the mere action of the drugs." [1]   It is essentially,
as Miss Kingsley puts it, the influence of spirit upon spirit.
If the natives attribute any virtue to the remedies themselves, these possess it solely because they are the vehicle
of the occult power.

How, then, can their idea of the remedies which Europeans prescribe for them be in any way different ?   Their
illness is due to the presence of a noxious influence in the
body ; and the cure is effected when the " doctor " has
succeeded in dislodging it.   When the white doctor is
treating an ulcer, for instance, it is a matter of course to
him that his patient grasps the very evident relation between
the dressings and remedies on the one hand, and the wound
to be cleansed, brought together, and cauterized on the
other.   As a matter of fact, however, this relation between
them escapes the native mind altogether, at any rate until
it has been to some extent modified by its owner's prolonged
association with white men.   Indifferent as the primitive
is to the connection between secondary causes and their
effects, even when but a slight effort would suffice to establish
it, he does not see this, or at any rate he does not stop to
notice it ; his attention is fixed on an entirely different
point.   To him, secondary causes are not really causes ;
they are but instruments, which might be anything else.

Consequently, the natives may be quite willing to submit
to a lengthy and complicated treatment, but they will
not ask themselves why it is demanded of them.   They
will not understand anything about the matter, and often
through their negligence in complying with the most necessary directions they are the despair of the doctors.   To
their minds, these regulations are of no importance, and
the cure ought to be effected instantaneously, even without
them.   As a rule, they employ European remedies willingly
when they have confidence in those who offer them, partly
because it diverts them and they believe these medicines
to be endowed with beneficial, mystic qualities.   But that
does not imply that they grasp the necessity for them,
nor even the useful end they serve.   " What really is

[1] Rev. J Mackenzie : *Ten Years North of the Orange River*, p. 389.

rather discouraging," writes a Barotse missionary, " is the impossibility of getting the natives to continue a regular and fairly prolonged treatment, whether it be medical or surgical. Several who have been operated on disappear the very day after the operation, and do not return until four or five days later, the dressings removed and the wound exposed. Happily their robust constitution allows of cures which would never be effected in Europe." [1]   " I arrested the hemorrhage (it was the carotid artery which was cut) and I insisted that his relatives should bring the patient to the Mission station, but they would not consent. I looked after the case for several days in succession. The swelling and inflammation gradually diminished until he was able to talk and to eat without too much difficulty. But what must they do but take off the dressing one fine day ! (The Zambesi believe that our remedies ought to act like charms, instantaneously.) When I arrived, the man was about to bleed to death." [2]   " The natives will swallow anything you like to give them," says Germond, " but the effect of the medicine must be immediate. If you talk to them about diet and treatment and hygienic precautions they will not listen to you." [3]

" The natives (Bechuanas) are passionately fond of medicine," says Moffat. . . . " No matter how nauseous the draught may be, they will lick their lips even if it is asafœtida. On one occasion I requested a man at a distance to send someone for medicine. He sent his wife. Having prepared a bitter dose, I gave it into her hand, directing her to give it in two portions, one at sunset, the other at midnight. She made a long face, and begged hard that he might take it all at once, lest they should fall asleep. I consented, when down went the potion into her stomach, when I exclaimed, ' It is not for you ! ' Licking her lips, she asked, with perfect composure of countenance, if her drinking it would not cure her husband." [4]

Stories of this kind, incredible as they appear, are by

---

[1] *Missions évangéliques*, lxxix. 1. p. 404 (1904). (Reutter.)
[2] A. et E. Jalla : *Pionniers parmi les Marotse*, p. 139.
[3] *Missions évangéliques*, lxxi. p. 19 (1896). (Paul Germond.)
[4] R. Moffat : *Missionary Labours and Scenes in South Africa*, pp. 591-2 (note).

no means rare. " The doctor . . . found great difficulty
in making them keep quiet until the ulcers healed. A
medical man, fond of his practice, is greatly discouraged by
negro patients. They will take any quantity of his ' little
bullets,' as they term pills, but they will pay no attention
to his other instructions. A native girl was once taking
down a revolver, which went off, when the bullet passed
through one leg, and lodged in the thigh of the other.
Fortunately Dr. Laws of Livingstonia was on the spot. He
dressed her wounds and told her that she must not move.
Most of us were afraid she was killed. Judge his surprise
when, on coming to her in the evening, he found her meeting
him at the door ! " [1] In the Ovambo territory " people
often travel some distance to ask the missionary for medicine,
and he asks them : ' What does the sick man complain of ? '
The reply invariably is ' I don't know. They simply sent
me to get some medicine.' The natives seem to think that
the missionary possesses some sort of panacea which will
suit every case." [2] Among the Fân, " one of the things
that sick people find most astonishing is that the white
doctor simply administers the medicine without having
recourse to any incantation or exorcism of any kind. ' It
is not to be wondered at that such a medicine does no good,'
said a worthy negro, who knew a little French, to me one
day. ' The doctor did not say a word, either before he
gave it or after. No, I am wrong,' he added, he did
say " Drink it up, nigger ! " ' Thus you see it could not
have any effect.' . . . Among the people we were friendly
with was a worthy doctor who always sang some lively
refrain while he was being consulted, or during an operation.
' It amuses the negroes,' he used to say. They had an
enormous amount of confidence in him. ' That doctor
at any rate,' said one of them to me one day, ' is not like
the rest ! He sings as our own medicine-men do ! ' If
the doctor in question had only known the reason for the
popularity he enjoyed, a popularity *he* attributed to his
skill ! " [3]

Other primitive peoples, widely removed from those

[1] Rev. Duff Macdonald : *Africana*, ii. p. 217.
[2] *Berichte der rheinischen Missionsgesellschaft*, p. 189 (1905).
[3] R. P. Trilles : *Le totémisme des Fân*, p 412 (note).

we have instanced, are no better able to understand what
the medical or surgical treatment of Europeans consists of.
If they agree to undergo it, it is for sundry reasons which
the doctors by no means suspect. The native has no idea
what purpose the remedies used really serve, and he does
not trouble about the matter. In the Friendly Isles, "a
man called on Mr. Thomas to mend a pair of spectacles,
supplied from the Mission store some time ago, and which,
he said, did not answer very well, though he had taken great
care of them, *covering* them all over with *coco-nut oil*"[1]
(as a sign of respect and veneration, no doubt).

"On the Mimika River (in Dutch New Guinea) the natives
often used to cut themselves severely with our axes and
knives before they realized their sharpness, and their wounds
healed astonishingly quickly with ordinary clean methods.
The only trouble was that they liked to take off their bandages
and use them for personal adornment."[2] Speaking of the
Papuans, Chignell says : " It is hard—I sometimes find it
quite impossible—to make these people understand. A
man will come to you with a bad ulcer, and you dress and
bandage it, and tell him to be sure to come again to-morrow,
and he forgets all about it, or turns up at the end of a week
to say that he does not fancy the *fio* is doing much good.
. . . Perhaps they think the medicine is a sort of charm,
and ought to work instantaneously."[3]

That is certainly their idea, and other investigators
have no hesitation in saying so. " The poor sufferers were
much astonished and disappointed that Mr. Patteson did
not heal them by miracle." [4] In Borneo (at Kwala Kapuas)
" the medicines used must relieve the sufferers immediately.
If they do, all is well, and they offer thanks to God ; but
if the cure is not instantaneous, they begin to doubt His
goodness."[5] In Sumatra, among the Bataks, " no sooner
did the missionary Schrey open his little medicine-chest,
than everyone declared himself ill, and wanted a remedy.
One coughed noisily, another had fever, and a third com-

[1] *Wesleyan Missionary Notices*, vi. 1848. (Journal of Rev. W. Lawry.)
[2] A. R. Wollaston : *Pygmies and Papuans*, p. 167.
[3] A. K. Chignell : *An Outpost in Papua*, p. 205.
[4] E. G. Armstrong : *The History of the Melanesian Mission*, p. 4.
[5] *Berichte der rheinischen Missionsgesellschaft*, p. 141 (1888).

plained of pains in his limbs, etc. Every one of them received some medicine, and went away satisfied, but they were very much surprised if the trouble did not disappear at once." [1]

Lastly, not to prolong this list of instances unduly, facts of this kind were noted by Nordenskiöld in Grand Chaco, in South America. "I myself," he says, "have sometimes had occasion during my stay among the Indians to practise the profession of medicine. It is impossible to compel an Indian to take any care of himself for a prolonged period. They must be cured at once, and if not they will not use the medicine any more. Morphia, cocaine, and opium are the only remedies they care about." [2]

When Bentley expected to find the Congolese astonished at his having cured ulcers of long standing in five weeks, he was a long way out in his reckoning. If he had cured them in five minutes, the natives would not have been at all surprised. The disappearance of the ulcer is due to the influence of a charm ; why should it not take place in the twinkling of an eye, if the charm is strong enough ? The white man is a mighty wizard. If he desired it the native would be free of his trouble in a moment. What is the good of so many medicines and prescriptions and regulations and all the dieting, and so on ?

This goes a long way towards accounting for the reluctance shown by the natives in allowing themselves to be taken to the white men to be looked after, and the difficulty there is in keeping them in hospital, when they have finally decided to go there. They do not understand that time is necessary to treatment. They have no clear idea of the efficacy of the means prescribed for them ; moreover, they feel dread and mistrust. On this subject, Dr. Bellamy has aptly described the state of mind of the Papuans of British New Guinea. He says : " The natives are somewhat reluctant to come to the hospital for treatment and till now have not been got to understand that the hospital is there for their good." [3] In the Trobriand Islands, " the prospect

---

[1] *Berichte der rheinischen Missionsgesellschaft*, p. 174 (1906).
[2] Er. Nordenskiöld : *La vie des Indiens dans le Chaco*, p. 95.
[3] " Papua," *Annual Report*, p. 35 (1906).

of any systematic treatment which took a man or a woman out of his or her village away from their garden and all their friends was by no means a pleasant one. Besides, the Trobriand medicine-men, the *tomegani*, had treated the cases, and folks went on dying. Was it likely the white man's medicine would cure a Papuan ailment ? So at least they argued. The first half-year's history of the hospital is a story of an uphill fight against native prejudice, native superstition, and native stupidity. . . . Their lack of faith in the *Guhanuma* (European) medicines was itself a disadvantageous circumstance. Many of the first cases were the worst that could be found, viz. the cases of longest standing (venereal disease). The patients were inclined to give a trial of three days, and if not better then, what was the good of going on ? Their gardens, their fishing, their canoes called them. And so they slipped away, under cover of darkness, by ones and twos." [1] As time went on matters improved, and the natives learned to appreciate what the hospital could do for them.

In South Africa there was the same mistrust to be overcome. " An old man, the chief of several villages, had been struck blind, and from what he had heard of me, he thought I might be able to restore his sight. . . . He consented to be operated on. . . But as soon as I told him that it was essential for him to spend some days in Thabu Bossiou, in some Christian household or other, it put a different complexion on the matter. It was in vain that I tried to explain the reason for this. . . . ' I am afraid to go and live with the Christians; I fear they will practise some witchcraft upon me.' He gave up the idea of being operated on." [2] " They have their own medicines, the *ngaké* . . . and they hold that these drugs should cure black people, while our medicines are good for *us*. This belief is not peculiar to the Zambesi people, but perhaps they are more prejudiced against scientific treatment than other tribes. In any case, they have an instinctive dread of amputation." Dr. Prosch added : " Hospital life is not appreciated by our negroes. Abundant and regular meals,

---

[1] " Papua," *Annual Report*, pp. 109–10 (1907) ; cf. ibid., p. 150 (1910).
[2] *Missions évangéliques*, xxii. pp. 406–7 (1847). (Dr. Lautré.)

a clean dwelling, and the most unremitting care are not sufficient to counterbalance the mistrust of us still felt by all who do not know us intimately. . . . Then, too, they cannot make up their minds to leave their pagan comfort, if I may apply such a term to the unsavoury conditions which are the usual surroundings of our poor. We do not suspect the difficulty they find in accommodating themselves to our ways. I could tell of cases where sick people who were dangerously ill, to whom every sort of indulgence has been granted, whose relatives have been received with a present of *maas* (curds), have effected an escape unknown to us, and gone to hide themselves to avoid the shelter offered by Christian charity." [1]

In the same way, even long familiarity with Europeans can scarcely succeed in reconciling natives already somewhat civilized, like the Basutos, with the white man's remedies and his hospitals. " The Lesuto Government has established doctors in the administrative centres, making it a rule that every consultation and every remedy is to be paid for by a fee of sixpence, a fee which permits even the very poorest negroes to avail themselves of the doctors' care. And it has also founded two hospitals. . . . Here is the Basuto view of the matter: " The medicines of the Government doctors are no good at all ; they are nothing but water, for what could they give for sixpence except water ? One might go to a white doctor once, or even twice, but not a third time, for then he would tell you you were wasting his medicine, and he would make up a bottle with poison in it, to get rid of you. In the hospital they take your clothes away, and you won't see them again. They will not give you any food, and when anybody dies, they put his body into a special house to cut it up in pieces.' And so on, and so on." [2]

According to Dieterlen, these evil prognostications are due to the fact that " the blacks think the whites wish to injure them, or wish them no good. They do not believe in their disinterestedness. They are distrustful, for fear of being deceived, despoiled, injured, and led into misfortune.

[1] *Missions évangéliques*, lxxxvi. 1. pp. 20-1 (1911).
[2] Ibid., lxxxiii. 1. p. 308 (1908). (Dieterlen.)

These feelings are innate and quite natural to them ; they are irresistible and ineradicable. . . ." This may be so, and bitter experience may be thus expressed by a missionary who is saddened but not daunted. In any case, as we have already seen, the natives' repugnance to entering and staying in the hospital is not due to a general and incurable feeling of distrust alone, but also to the fact that they do not understand anything about the care exercised upon them, especially when they are asked to devote days, weeks, sometimes even months, to obtain a result which they consider ought to be instantaneous. It is just this lengthy sojourn which awakens their worst suspicions. What can be the intention of the white doctor, the mighty wizard, in keeping them thus ? What magic is he going to practise upon them ?

The conditions of the misunderstanding we have noted as existing between the sick native and his European doctor are thus defined. The more trouble the doctor takes over his patient, the more difficult and complicated the treatment, especially if he is obliged to have the sick man under his own eye, to feed and look after him and see that he follows the regulations, the more does he consider that he has a claim on his gratitude, and the more will he expect his thanks, at least. Now the native doubtless would be ready to thank him if he had been cured instantly, if, as he expected, the medicines had had the effect of a touch of the magic wand. But all the circumstances which the doctor considers meritorious do but alienate his patient, and render him uneasy. The days pass by, one drug succeeds another, and a new dressing is substituted for the old one ; the patient submits to it all more or less readily, but he thinks that the white man ought to be grateful to him, and that he, the patient, is the one who is deserving of thanks. The more prolonged the cure, the more does the doctor owe to the sick man who lends himself to the treatment. Father Trilles, in the passage we have already quoted, perceives this clearly when he says : " Europeans are often both astonished and indignant at finding that natives whom they had thus carefully nursed, instead of being grateful to them, should on the contrary demand to be paid. Both patient and doctor are in the right each according to his view of the matter : the doctor, imbued with our European and Christian ideas, is justly annoyed at seeing his disinterested care thus ignored ; while the sick man, on his side, is also right, for he thinks that in the circumstances he has been merely the subject of experiment."

III

We have still, it appears, to account for the persistence with which the native who has been looked after by the European doctor comes to demand a present from him, frequently, too, announcing his intention of coming to ask for others. If he meets with a refusal, he becomes rude and abusive, and if he dares do so, he takes his revenge. He adopts the attitude, and expresses the surprise and indignation, of a man deprived of that which is his due. The strength and reality of these feelings are unquestionable.

To understand how they arise, we must note that such feelings are manifested, not only when a native has been, for a longer or shorter period, the object of the white man's medical care. They are shown in connection with other services rendered, and especially when a white man has saved the life of a native about to succumb to an accident. In the Congo territory " a canoe was upset in the cauldron off Underhill Point ; two men were drowned, but the canoe which Crudgington sent there at once, managed to reach the third man, and brought him ashore alive. Before he was starting home next day, he asked Crudgington to ' dress ' him. When he declined, the man began to pour out his disgust at the white man's meanness, and became too abusive whereupon Crudgington locked him up in the store, and would not release him until his friends brought us a couple of goats—one for the rescuer, and one for Crudgington, as the owner of the canoe by means of which the rescue was effected. The goats were paid, and it is to be hoped the man learnt a lesson." [1]

Nothing is less likely to have been the case, and neither Crudgington nor Bentley seems to have grasped what was passing in the native's mind. Here is another and very

[1] Rev. W. H. Bentley : *Pioneering on the Congo*, i. p. 476.

similar circumstance, again related by Bentley : " The paramount chief in the Ndandanga township was a certain Tawanlongo. A secondary chief named Matuza Mbongo had of late been rising in influence. Matuza's wife died in childbed, and a report was current that before she died she saw Tawanlongo in her dream. Matuza seized the opportunity to clear away his last obstacle to the paramount position. Tawanlongo was not loved. . . . It would be great fun to see the old chief himself take the ordeal *nkasa* and reel and fall, and then to throw him on the fire. No witch doctor was necessary for such a straightforward case ; had not the woman seen the chief in her dream ? What could be clearer ? Tawanlongo was a wizard." The missionaries interposed, and obtained a promise that the ordeal should not take place, but " the natives did not keep the letter of their promise, for they did make the chief drink the *nkasa* ; but they made such a weak infusion that the chief vomited, and his innocence was established. The chief sent me a very grateful message, declaring that to me alone he owed his life. . . . Many others remarked to the same effect. Nevertheless, he came empty-handed to me a few days afterwards, and told me he expected me to show my pleasure at his escape from the peril, by ' dressing ' him. I gave him a fathom of cloth, a knife, a cap, and a few small sundries, though I felt that there was no such necessity for me to give him anything. Instead of thanking me for this further kindness, he began to abuse me for not giving him a much larger present. He said that I was shamelessly mean, and went away quite disgusted with me." [1] It is the same in Gaboon. " You save a person's life, and you must expect to receive a visit from him before long ; you are now under an obligation to him, and you will not get rid of him except by giving him presents." [2]

With respect to other services rendered to them, natives make the same demands, especially in the case of the care and instruction bestowed upon their children. " We educate their children, we give them food, clothing, a home, and all the mental and moral care possible. Well ! for all

[1] Rev. W. H. Bentley : *Pioneering on the Congo*, i. p. 475–6.
[2] Rev. Fr. Bulléon : *Sous le ciel d'Afrique*, p. 61 (1888).

that, they have taken it into their heads that we ought to make a payment to each child and to its parents." [1] On his side, Fr. Bulléon says : " The children are living entirely at the expense of the Mission. We feed, clothe, educate, and teach them a trade without payment of any sort. We consider ourselves lucky if their parents do not come and ask for presents, and make us pay for the satisfaction of keeping their children ! Note, too, that we only take the children of free subjects, and that most of our pupils are the sons of kings or village chiefs." [2] Among the Bechuanas " the parents no longer encourage the children to come to school, doubtless preferring to send them into the fields to gather in the corn or tend the cattle. When we have asked why they had stopped sending us their children, they say that we do not pay them, or that we are paying them too little." [3] In the island of Tahiti, also, " some of our pupils seemed to think they were doing the missionaries a favour by coming to be taught, and that they ought to be paid for doing so." [4]

One last fact which is very significant. Captain Lyon tells the story of an old Esquimau woman whom he had found abandoned, half frozen, and in a dying state. " I shall never forget," he writes, " the piteous state and squalid looks of this deserted woman ; but I cannot describe my astonishment when, on producing blankets and skins to wrap her in, for the purpose of carrying her on board to be recovered, she turned to me and demanded that I should pay her for her trouble ! " [5]

All these facts imply the same lack of mutual comprehension as that noted and analysed above. The white man considers the demand made by the native unreasonable, absurd, and inexplicable. That he should claim indemnity for having had his life saved, or his children educated ! On his side, the native is shocked by the pettiness, meanness, and barefaced greed of the white man who

---

[1] *Missions catholiques*, xv. p. 39 (1883). (Lettre du P. Angouard.)
[2] Rev. Fr. Bulléon: ibid., p. 110.
[3] *Missions évangéliques*, xii. p. 40 (1837). (Arbousset.)
[4] Rev. W. Ellis : *History of the London Missionary Society*, p. 190 (1844).
[5] *The Private Journal of Capt. G. F. Lyon, of H.M.S. " Hecla,"* p. 385 (1824).

is so rich, and yet is not ashamed to cheat poor folks out of their just due! Perhaps the reason for this mutual misunderstanding will reveal itself if here again, instead of taking for granted that the natives explain and regard such occurrences just as the Europeans do, we try to see things from their point of view, and judge the matter as they do.

Crudgington the missionary has saved the life of a Congolese about to drown. He expects thanks from him, even to receive some token of his gratitude; he attributes to the native the sentiments he would experience under the same circumstances, and these appear the natural thing. As a matter of fact, the black man is strongly convinced that, by saving his life, Mr. Crudgington is under an obligation to *him*. At first we do not see how this can be. From the European's point of view, the matter is quite simple. The Congolese owes his life to Crudgington, who owes *him* nothing. If there is any obligation in the matter, then it is the Congo native who is the party obliged; that needs no telling. The black does not deny the actual fact, but his mind is so orientated that, whatever happens, the mystic elements are much more important in his eyes than the actual events. There is no chance; what we call accident is a revelation, a manifestation of the unseen powers. What made the canoe upset in the whirlpool? Was it the deed of a wizard, who had " doomed " him and his two luckless companions, or due to the anger of some neglected and outraged ancestor? Since he was the sole survivor, will he not be henceforth " suspect "? Will they not accuse him of having " delivered them over "? It seems inevitable that it should be so. And why should the white man's canoe have been ready, just at that moment, to come to his rescue? By what right did the white folks intervene? By doing so they have assumed a responsibility the consequences of which he is sure to feel, both by the action of the unseen powers and in his own social group. The least they can do is to indemnify him for it.

Captain Lyon cannot believe his ears when the old woman, dying of cold and hunger, whom he receives on his ship to look after, asks him how much she is to be paid

for coming. From the white man's point of view, this
woman owes her life to the captain, who owes *her* nothing ;
there can be no question about that.   But, in the woman's
eyes, it is a very serious thing to be wrapped up in the furs
and blankets of these strangers, who have nothing in common
with her social group, to allow herself to be carried on board
their ship, to partake of their food, and touch things
belonging to them.   The European sees but the material
circumstance ;   she will be warm, comfortable, and well
fed ; her life will be safe.   On the other hand she at once
asks herself what magic spells all these unknown objects
may exercise upon her.   What may be the mystic consequences to her of the sojourn on this ship, what dangers
may she be exposing herself to, dangers so much the more
to be dreaded because she cannot even imagine them !
At least, if she is to suffer all this, let her be paid for giving
her consent !

Possibly the difficulty is not yet entirely solved.   There
still remains the fact that on the one hand, whatever the
mystic dangers of the white man's intervention may be,
the native nevertheless owes him his life, that he recognizes
this, and that that seems indeed to constitute an obligation ;   and on the other, that we have to account for the
vexation, sometimes even rage and fury, shown by natives
whose lives have been saved, or who have had some service
rendered them, when they find that they are refused what
they claim in return.   The man whose hand was amputated,
who was tended for two months on board a fishing-boat,
demands a gun, does not get it, and in revenge sets fire to
the captain's drying-houses. The black man saved by
Crudgington, not receiving what he demands, becomes
abusive, and has to be imprisoned.   In most examples of
this kind the whites remark that the native not merely
shows no gratitude, but, if his " unreasonable " demands
are refused, he becomes insolent, and even threatening.
What irresistible inner influence impels him thus to defy
the European ? We shall never understand it unless we
penetrate to the very depths of his group-ideas and sentiments, at the risk of being likely to distort them by expressing them in set terms, seeing that he himself feels and

translates them into acts without ever having defined them in his thoughts or expressed them in words.

As we know, primitive mentality does not represent life or death or the personality of the individual as we do. To any given individual, to be alive means to be actually forming part of a complicated system of mystic " participations " in common with other members, both living and dead, of his social group, with the animal and vegetable groups belonging to the same soil, with the very earth itself, with the occult powers who protect these groups and the other more personal ones to which he specially pertains. At the moment when he is about to die of hunger, cold, disease, or drowning, it may happen that the intervention of the white man saves his life, in the European and entirely objective sense of the word, and that is all we perceive in it. The fact that escapes our notice is that at the same time this intervention endangers his life in the native and mystic sense of the word. Who knows whether it may not, first of all, anger the occult powers who arranged the " accident," and above all, whether it may not alienate those whose continual protection safeguards him from the dangers menacing him on every side, and from an unlimited number of malevolent spirits ? The white people are mighty wizards, and from them and everything belonging to them there emanate mystic influences of irresistible power. The native who is subjected to them finds himself by this very fact separated from the powers without which he cannot live. It is to be feared that henceforth, therefore, the participations which are necessary to his existence may be weakened, and possibly ruptured.

What, then, will be the condition of such a native if, on the one hand, after he has undergone medical treatment at the hands of the white man, after staying with one of them, or in a hospital, or on one of their ships, or after having been " saved " from some accident by them, he has forfeited the goodwill of the unseen powers without which he cannot exist, and if, on the other hand, the white man who is the cause of this estrangement ceases to take an interest in him ? He is threatened with an isolation which is unbearable and, in his eyes, worse than death. It is as if the white man, after having compromised him hopelessly, after having endangered what we might call his individual mystic status, were to abandon him. By looking after him, giving him a home, feeding him, sending him to hospital, and saving him, the white man has taken charge of him. He has assumed a responsibility, and become involved. He doubtless knew what he was doing. " You are now my own white man," said the man whom Mackenzie had cured of a horrible wound in the face, " and I shall always come to beg of you." That means : " Henceforward you are my refuge and my support, and I have the right to reckon on you to compensate me for what your intervention has cost me with the mystic powers upon whom my social group depends, and upon whom I myself have depended · till now." As Elsdon Best has aptly remarked, the native, deprived of that mystic atmosphere which is necessary to him, tries to find its equivalent among the Europeans.[1] He who, on his own initiative, has so effectually intervened in his life, is bound to give him all he asks ; in the future, too, his generosity *must* be inexhaustible. If he avoids his duty and refuses to give, there is more than greed behind it. It is, as it were, a refusal to honour a sacred pledge ; it is treachery, almost crime. The native who believes himself thus victimized will proceed to the direst extremes, if he is bold enough.

If this be so, the native, in such circumstances, does not consider himself to have been obliged by the white man in any way ; on the contrary, he has an acute sense of the responsibility of the latter as regards himself. He is, therefore, neither " ungrateful " nor " unreasonable," as he is bound to appear in the eyes of anyone who has cared for and saved him, and who is conscious of having rendered him signal service, often from purely disinterested and humane motives. It is to be hoped that this humanity may not confine itself to dressing his ulcers, but that it may strive towards sympathetic penetration of the obscure recesses of a consciousness which cannot express itself.

[1] Cf. *Les Fonctions Mentales dans les Sociétés Inférieures*, p. 312.

CHAPTER XIV

CONCLUSION

I

An analysis of the preceding facts—facts which can easily be confirmed by many others, leads yet again to the conclusion that the primitive's mentality is essentially mystic. This fundamental characteristic permeates his whole method of thinking, feeling, and acting, and from this circumstance arises the extreme difficulty of comprehending and following its course. Starting from sense-impressions, which are alike in primitives and ourselves, it makes an abrupt turn, and enters on paths which are unknown to us, and we soon find ourselves astray. If we try to guess why primitives do, or refrain from doing, certain things, what prejudices they obey in given cases, the reasons which compel them with regard to any special course, we are most likely to be mistaken. We may find an " explanation " which is more or less probable, but nine times out of ten it will be the wrong one.

The African " ordeals " furnish an instance of this. To interpret them as if their end were the discovery of a guilty person and see in them a kind of judicial proceeding, like the Divine judgments of mediæval times, or even the ordeals of Ancient Greece (which, however, are not so far removed from them), is to condemn oneself to non-comprehension, and to be, as the missionaries of West and South Africa were ages ago, overcome with astonishment at the unfathomable folly of the poor negroes. But if we enter into the natives' way of thinking and feeling, if we trace their actions back to the group-ideas and sentiments upon which these depend, we find that their behaviour is by no means foolish ; it is, on the contrary, the legitimate consequence of these. To them the ordeal is a kind of " acid test," the only possible way of discovering an evil force which must have become incarnate in one or more members of the social group. This test alone has the mystic power which is necessary to destroy such a force, or at any rate to put its noxious influence out of action. Unless they wish to see misfortunes and deaths increase in number indefinitely, the natives cannot renounce the ordeal under any consideration, and the objurgations which it calls forth from the white man seem as unreasonable to them as their methods do to Europeans, until the latter have discovered their *raison d'être*.

Less tragic, but no less characteristic, is the misunderstanding we have been examining as existing between primitives and Europeans with regard to the medical attention which the latter bestow upon the natives. In order to dissipate it we must have obtained a clear idea of the natives' conception of disease and its cure, of the remedies and regimen which the " white doctors " prescribe for them, and the consequences to which they are exposed in submitting to them, etc. Moreover, we must have recognized, at the basis of representations so different from our own, that thoroughly mystic conception of participation and causality which is the very foundation of primitive mentality.

If misunderstandings of this kind, which have occurred so frequently, had been carefully noted by the white men who were the first to live in close association with natives, we should have lighted upon valuable data for the study which we have essayed here. But this has not been done, and the opportunities for it have gone by for ever. The Europeans who first entered into continuous relations with primitive peoples had other cares than to notice how the latter thought and felt, and to report precisely what they noted, and even if they had undertaken a task at once so lengthy, delicate, and complicated, few of them would have been able to succeed in it. For such a matter, an exact knowledge of the natives' language is necessary to ensure success. It is not sufficient to have acquired enough of it to be able to make oneself understood in ordinary transactions, to communicate one's wishes or one's orders to them, or to receive from them useful information regarding their everyday life. Something quite different from this is necessary. These primitive languages often possess a grammatical complexity and a richness of vocabulary which are perfectly surprising, and they are of a very different type from the Indo-European or the Semitic, to both of which we are accustomed. To be able to perceive the shades of meaning in the primitives' ideas which often prove so puzzling to us, to grasp how these are bound up with one another in their myths, legends, rites, it would be absolutely indispensable to master the genius and the intricacies of their language. In how many cases would this condition be even approximately fulfilled ?

." The longer anyone stays in the country," says an English administrator, speaking of the New Guinea Papuans who had never yet seen Europeans, " the more one realizes that the great difficulty, above all others, in dealing with natives is the difficulty of making them understand the exact meaning of words said to them, and in understanding the exact meaning of what is said by them." [1] The two mentalities which encounter each other here are so foreign to one another, their customs so widely divergent, their methods of expressing themselves so different ! Almost unconsciously, the European makes use of abstract thought, and his language has made simple logical processes so easy to him that they entail no effort. With primitives both thought and language are almost exclusively concrete by nature. " The method of reasoning of the Esquimaux," says a careful observer, " gives us the impression of being very superficial, because they are not accustomed to retain what we call a definite line of reasoning or a single, isolated subject for any length of time ; their thoughts, namely, do not rise to abstractions or logical formulas, but keep to pictures of observation or situations which change according to laws we find it difficult to follow." [2] In short, our mentality is above all " conceptual," and theirs hardly at all so. It is therefore extremely difficult, if not impossible,

---

[1] "Papua," *Annual Report*, p. 128 (1911).
[2] H. P. Steensby : "Contributions to the Ethnology and Anthropology of the Polar Eskimo," *Meddelelser om Groenland*, xxxiv. pp. 374-5 (1910).

for a European, even if he tries, and even if he knows the natives' language, to *think* as they do, although he may seem to *speak* as they do.

When investigators noted the institutions, manners, and beliefs before them, they made use—how could they do otherwise ?—of the concepts which seemed to them to correspond with the reality they had to express. But, precisely because they were concepts, encompassed by the logical atmosphere proper to European mentality, the expression of them distorted what they were trying to render. Translation had the effect of betrayal. Examples of this kind are very numerous. To express the invisible being, or rather beings, which, together with his bodily presence, make up the primitive's individuality, nearly all investigators have made use of the term " soul." We know how much confusion and error has been engendered by this use of a concept unknown to primitives. An entire theoretical system, once in great favour, and still counting a large number of adherents, is founded upon the implied postulate that a concept of " soul " or " spirit," similar to our own, exists among primitives. It is the same with such expressions as " family," " marriage," " property," etc. Investigators have had to make use of them in describing institutions which presented analogies (striking ones, as it seemed) with our own. Nevertheless, here again careful study shows that the group-presentations of primitives cannot be bound by the framework of our concepts without being warped.

Let us take a simple instance which does not demand a lengthy analysis. Observers constantly apply the term " money " to the shells which the natives use in their barter in certain districts, in Melanesia among other places. Richard Thurnwald has recently shown that this " Muschelgeld " (shell specie) does not exactly correspond with what we call " money." To us, it is a question of a medium (whether of metal or paper, is immaterial) which makes it possible to exchange something, whatever it may be, for something else. It is a universal medium of exchange. But the Melanesians do not view the matter in this general kind of way. Their ideas are more concrete. The natives of the Solomon Isles, like their neighbours, use shells for their purchases, but always with a very definite specification. "This money," says Thurnwald, "serves two chief ends: firstly, it will purchase a wife; secondly, it will obtain allies in warfare, and pay the compensation due for the dead, whether these have been simply murdered or killed in fight.

"Hence we understand that 'money' is not used, properly speaking, for economic purposes, but is designed to accomplish certain social functions. The ends attributed to it above show us why, before everything else, it is the business of the chief to collect and keep treasure in the form of shell specie. He keeps his 'funds' in special huts . . . and they are used for loans which he grants his people when they wish to buy a wife, for instance. Shell money, of fine cowries, is also used 'for personal adornment.' Besides this money, bangles play an important part in Buin as a measure of value. They send to Choiseul for them. . . . Another standard of value is the pig, which is used for various payments, especially for the many festive repasts which are *de rigueur* in certain circumstances."

As for commercial transactions, properly so called, it does not seem as if any money, not even the shell specie, is used. They are carried on by means of barter, but the exchanges made are specialized, and even regulated. Thurnwald says: "In the system of barter, in particular, certain things can only be exchanged for certain other things, a spear for a bangle, for instance, fruit for tobacco, pigs for knives. They willingly exchange things which can be made use of in the same sort of way; thus, taro or coco-nuts may be bartered for tobacco, for example, or weapons for ornaments (spears for bangles or glass beads), etc." [1]

We need not pursue further the interesting description given by Thurnwald of the economic existence of the natives of the Solomon Isles. What we have quoted suffices to show that our concept of "money" but very imperfectly corresponds with the "shell specie" used by the natives. If, therefore, we persist in saying that they possess such

[1] R. Thurnwald: *Forschungen auf den Bismarck-Archipel und den Salomo Inseln*, iii. pp. 38–40.

" money," we can have only a vague and incorrect idea of the matter. But a careful and exhaustive study of the special ends which the shell specie serves leads to a more thorough knowledge of certain institutions and at the same time helps to a better understanding of the mentality of these natives, who do not proceed by general abstract ideas, but who, lacking what *we* call money, organize a regular exchange of certain objects for certain other definite objects.

A similar critical analysis might be applied to other abstract terms which those who have observed primitive races have employed to express their collective representations and describe their institutions.

Thus, through a kind of necessity inherent in the nature of things, i.e. in the profound difference in mentality and in language, the greater number of documents at the command of science for the study of primitive mentality can only be made use of with many precautions and after being subjected to severe criticism. In all sincerity the earlier observers, whether clergy or laity, nearly always distort and pervert the institutions and beliefs they report, from the mere fact that they unhesitatingly express them in terms with which they themselves are familiar. Those who follow them proceed in the same way, with the added circumstance that the institutions and beliefs of primitives have already been contaminated by association with the whites, and that their mentality as well as their language is threatened with more or less rapid decay. On the other hand, where are we to find the necessary data for the study of this mentality, if not in the writings of those who have observed primitives at close range, who have lived with and among them, who have been present at their life's daily round, as well as the ceremonies relating to their religion, if they have an organized one ? Science has at its disposal no documents but these, and their inevitable imperfection, the too much or too little that they communicate, is almost enough to account for its slow progress and the oft-times uncertain nature of the results hitherto obtained.

This difficulty, however, is not irremediable. It is found

to a greater or lesser degree in all sciences, the materials of which consist of evidence, and the well-established rules of criticism, both external and internal, can be applied to ethnographical documents just as efficiently as to any thing else. Moreover, as the analysis of primitive mentality makes proportionate progress and arrives at results which may be considered definitely established, the investigator has at command criteria, both more numerous and more stable, from which to judge the value of evidence, remote or recent ; he is better able to decide what must be rejected and what can be retained in each case. Finally, a satisfactory knowledge of the essential characteristics of the mentality of primitives leads to a more profound and searching study of their institutions. The first stage, once traversed, makes all the succeeding ones easier, or at any rate, more approachable.

II

The primitive mind, like our own, is anxious to find the reasons for what happens, but it does not seek these in the same direction as we do. It moves in a world where innumerable occult powers are everywhere present, and always in action or ready to act. As we have seen in the earlier chapters of this book, any circumstance, however slightly unusual it may be, is at once regarded as the manifestation of one or another of them. If the rain occurs at a time when the fields are badly needing water, it is because the ancestors and spirits of the neighbourhood are content, and are thus manifesting their goodwill. If a persistent drought parches the corn and causes the cattle to perish, some *tabu* must have been violated, or possibly an ancestor considers himself injured, and his wrath must be appeased. In the same way, no enterprise will succeed unless the unseen powers give it their support. No one will start out hunting or fishing, nor begin a campaign ; he will not attempt to cultivate a field or build a house, unless the auguries are favourable, and the mysterious guardians of the social group have explicitly promised their aid ; it is necessary that the very animals needed should have given their consent, and the tools required have been consecrated and invested with magic qualities, and so forth. In short, the visible world and the unseen world are but one, and the events occurring in the visible world depend at all times upon forces which are not seen. Hence the place held in the life of primitives by dreams, omens, divination in its various forms, sacrifices, incantations, ritual ceremonies and magic. A man succumbs to some organic disease, or to snake-bite; he is crushed to death by the fall of a tree, or devoured by a tiger or crocodile: to the primitive mind, his death is due neither to disease nor to snake-venom; it is not the tree or the wild beast or reptile that has killed him. If he has perished, it is undoubtedly because a wizard had " doomed " and " delivered him over." Both tree and animal are but instruments, and in default of the one, the other would have carried out the sentence. They were, as one might say, interchangeable, at the will of the unseen power employing them.

To minds thus orientated there is no circumstance which is purely physical. No question relating to natural phenomena presents itself to primitives as it does to us. When we want to explain any such we look for the conditions which would be necessary and sufficient to bring it about, in the series of similar phenomena. If we succeed in determining them, we ask no more; knowing the general law, we are satisfied. The primitive's attitude is entirely different. He may have remarked the unvarying antecedents of the phenomenon which interests him, and in acting he relies a good deal on what he has observed. But he will always seek the true cause in the world of unseen powers, above and beyond what we call Nature, in the " metaphysical " realm, using the word in its literal sense. In short, our problems are not his, and his are foreign to us. That is why we find ourselves in a blind alley, when we ask how he would treat one of ours, and imagine it and try to draw from it inferences which would explain such-and-such a primitive institution.

Thus, Sir James Frazer thought to apply the theory of totemism to the ignorance shown by primitives to the physiological process of conception. Long discussions were carried on regarding the way in which the lowest types of primitives are accustomed to represent the reproductive function in man, and the ideas they form of pregnancy. But possibly it might not have been altogether unprofitable to examine first of all the preliminary question—Can the problem of conception be brought before the primitive mind in terms which allow such discussions to have any determining value ?

Orientated as such a mind is, we may unhesitatingly affirm that if its attention is directed to the phenomenon of conception, it is not the physiological conditions thereof which will arrest it. Whether it is aware of them, or knows little or nothing about them, does not matter much, since in any case it sets them aside and seeks the cause elsewhere, in the world of unseen powers. Otherwise, among all the phenomena that Nature presents to him this alone would have to be considered from a point of view differing from all the rest. In such a case, the problem being absolutely unique, his mind would occupy an unusual position with regard to it, and he would suddenly be engaged in the search for secondary causes, but nothing allows us to imagine this. If death is never " natural," to primitives it is self-evident that birth cannot be either, and for the same reasons.

In fact, even before any intercourse with white people had taken place, primitives—the aborigines of Australia, for instance—had indeed noticed some of the physiological conditions of conception, and of the sexual act in particular. But here, as in the other cases, what we call the secondary cause, the antecedents which according to our point of view are necessary and sufficient, remain quite subordinate as far as they are concerned ; the true cause is mystic in its nature. Even when they have noticed that a child does not come into the world unless impregnation has taken place, they do not draw the conclusion which appears quite natural to us. They persist in thinking that if a woman is pregnant, it is because a " spirit " (usually that of an ancestor awaiting reincarnation and among those ready to be born), has entered into her, which of course implies that she belongs to the clan, sub-clan and totem proper to that spirit. Among the Arunta, women who are afraid of pregnancy, if they find themselves obliged to pass the place where these spirits waiting to enter upon a terrestrial life are to be found, hurry by, and take all the precautions they possibly can to prevent one or other of them from entering their bodies.[1] But Spencer and Gillen do not say that they abstain from all sexual relations. These would not be followed by conception, however, unless the " spirit " entered into the woman.

With regard to San Cristoval in the Solomon Islands, Fox asks : " Is the physical fact of fatherhood acknowledged ? At the present day probably it is. If the reason be asked for the custom of burying alive the first-born child, . . . almost universally the reply is that this is because the child is not likely to be the man's true child, but born of the woman by some other man. But there are certainly a number of facts on the other side ; and the embryo is said to be put into the womb of the woman by an *adaro* named Hau-di-Ewavi, which lives on a mountain in Marau Sound in Guadalcanar (Marau Sound is the place where the spirits of the dead go after death), or by Kauraha, a snake spirit." [2] The two theories are not mutually exclusive. The inhabitants of San Cristoval may have learnt from the white men, or themselves observed, the close relation between the sexual act and conception ; but they none the less consider that the real cause can only be a mystic one, the action of a spirit which decides to enter a certain woman.

With many primitive peoples, and the Bantus in particular, the wife's barrenness is a real misfortune, and it is sufficient reason for a breach of the marriage contract. By virtue of a well-recognized " participation," which we have already noted, the plantation of a man with a barren wife is also threatened with sterility, and he must therefore divorce her. Barrenness is always considered to be the wife's fault, yet these natives are not ignorant of the physiological rôle played by the sexual act. But since they do not really imagine pregnancy to depend upon it, they do not think that a failure to conceive offspring may arise on

---

[1] Spencer and Gillen : *The Native Tribes of Central Australia*, p. 125.
[2] C. E. Fox : "Social Organization in San Cristoval," *J.A.I.*, xlix. p. 119 (1919).

the man's side during copulation. It assuredly proceeds from a mystic cause, i.e. it is due to the fact that no spirit-child consents to become once more incarnate by entering into his wife. She, in despair at her barrenness, thinks she can only be cured by supplicating the ancestors and unseen powers to be favourable to her desires, and she redoubles her offerings and sacrifices.

This attitude of mind of the primitive makes it difficult to find out what a given tribe does really imagine with regard to what we call the physiological conditions of conception. Since the primitive does not fix his attention on this point, because he does not consider it of any importance he can have no clear idea of it, and he does not rightly know what he himself thinks about it. Certain social groups may have traditions regarding it, which are rather more definite than their neighbours', but we cannot infer anything from this. The testimonies afforded by different investigators may not agree, and yet they may be veracious. For the same reason, a mind like this which, as we know, is indifferent to the law of contradiction, will admit both that the sexual act is the ordinary condition of conception, and at the same time declare that conception may occur without it. The *Lucina sine concubitu* may be exceptional, but in itself it is nothing extraordinary. If a spirit enters into a woman during a dream, for instance, she will have conceived, and her child will be born. The primitive's stories, legends, and myths are full of tales of this sort, nor do they occasion him any surprise. We must not, however, infer that he does not know the part played by coition, but that, even when he knows it, or has more or less vague ideas [1] concerning it, he yet does not believe that conception really depends upon it.

[1] Of the Azanda of the Upper Congo, Harold Reynolds says : " Their ideas about conception are—at any rate to a European—very strange. . . . They believe that the foundations of the fœtus are not laid in one impregnation, but in several successive fertilizations of the ovary, extending through a number of days."—H. Reynolds : " Notes on the Azanda Tribe of the Congo," *Journal of the African Society*, xi. p. 239 (1904). The same idea is found in the Papuans studied by Landtman. " If a child is contemplated, the husband must cohabit with her regularly, till the making of the child is completed."—" The Folk-tales of the Kiwai Papuans," *Acta societatis scientiarum fennicæ*, xlvii. p. 460 (note).

III

When faced by natural phenomena, then, the primitive mind does not propound the same problems to itself as ours does, it often does not bring forward any at all. " These uncivilized tribes," says an explorer when speaking of the Sakais of Sumatra, " have but very slight need of causality. . . . They react only to impressions which are very powerful and very direct. . . ." [1] " Need of causality " here means " interest aroused " by the phenomena they see around them. This semblance of apathy and mental torpor has often been remarked upon in the most primitive communities, and especially in certain South American tribes. It soon leads to incorrect conclusions about primitive mentality in general. If we wish to avoid error, we must not try to find among these peoples, either the very lowest or those who are somewhat more civilized, a " need of causality " of the same type as our own. As we have seen from the facts and institutions studied in this volume, they have their own causality and it is the one suited to their needs, though it readily escapes the notice of investigators who are too hasty, or else prejudiced. Their mentality, essentially mystic and prelogical as it is, proceeds to other objects, and pursues other paths, than our minds do. The importance which divination and magic have assumed in their eyes is enough to show this. To follow primitive mentality in its course, to unravel its theories, we must, as it were, do violence to our own mental habits, and adapt ourselves to theirs. It is an effort which it is almost impossible to sustain, and yet without it their minds are likely to remain unintelligible to us.

Besides the almost irrepressible tendency which leads us, in spite of ourselves, to conceive of their minds as like our own, another fact contributes towards concealing their true characteristics from us. In actual practice primitives, in order to live, must pursue ends which we can readily comprehend, and we see that in doing so, they set to work much as we should do in their place. From the fact that in these circumstances they act like us, we are tempted

[1] Moszkowski : *Auf neuen Wegen durch Sumatra*, p. 90.

to conclude at once, without being more fully informed, that their mental operations in general resemble ours. A more careful observation and analysis alone enable us to perceive the difference.

Les Fonctions Mentales dans les Sociétés Inférieures tried to show how primitive mentality, often absolutely indifferent to the law of contradiction, is nevertheless quite capable of avoiding it, when the necessity for action demands it.[1] In the same way, primitives who betray no apparent interest in the most obvious causal relations are quite able to utilize them to procure what is necessary to them, their food, for example, or some special tool. As a matter of fact, there is no type of community however inferior, in which some invention, some process of industry or art, some manufacture may not be found to wonder at—canoes, pots, baskets, cloth, ornaments, etc. The very men who, devoid of almost everything, seem to be quite at the bottom of the ladder, in the production of a special thing will obtain results which are surprising in their delicacy and accuracy. The Australian aborigine makes the boomerang ; both the Bushman and the Papuan reveal themselves artistic in their designs ; the Melanesian is very skilful in the arrangement of his snares for fish, and so on.

A course of reports on the technicology of primitives will undoubtedly be of great help in determining the stages of their mental development. Up to the present time, since inventive processes, not very well known when our minds are in question, are still more unknown in their case, we can but make a general remark. The exceptional value attaching to certain manufactures or certain processes of primitives, contrasting so forcibly as these do with the rough and elementary character of the rest of their civilization, is not the result of reflection or of reasoning either. If it were so, there would not be so much disparity shown, and a faculty that was universal would have been of use to them on more than one occasion. Rather is it that their hand has acquired its skill by a sort of intuition which is itself directed by acute observation of objects possessing peculiar interest for them. Such intuition would carry them far.

[1] *Les Fonctions Mentales dans les Sociétés Inférieures*, p. 79.

The intricate arrangement of a combination of methods appropriate to the end pursued does not necessarily imply deliberate activity of the understanding, nor the possession of knowledge capable of being analysed, generalized, and adapted to unforeseen cases. It may be merely practical skill, formed and developed by use, and thus maintained—a skill comparable with that of a good billiard player who, without knowing anything either of geometry or mechanics, has acquired a ready and accurate intuition of the movement required in a given position, without needing to reflect upon his stroke.

In the same way we can account for the subtlety and sagacity shown by many primitives in varied circumstances. According to Martius' report, for instance, Indians of the lowest Brazilian tribes can differentiate all the species and even all the varieties of palms, and they have a name for each one. Australians recognize the individual footprints of each member of their social group, etc. We often hear of the natural eloquence shown in ethical matters by natives in a number of uncivilized communities, the wealth of argument displayed in their palavers, and their readiness of attack and defence in their disputes. Their legends and their proverbs often betray a delicate and roguish power of observation and their myths, a ready and oft-times poetical imagination. All these things have been noted many times over by observers who were by no means prejudiced in favour of " savages."

When, therefore, we see them—physiognomists, moralists, psychologists (in the practical sense of the words)—like ourselves, sometimes better than ourselves, it is hard for us to believe that, frcm other points of view, they should be almost inexplicable enigmas, and that a world of difference lies between their mentality and our own. Let us note, however, that the points of resemblance always refer to mental processes in which primitives proceed, as we do, by direct intuition, immediate apprehension, rapid and almost instantaneous interpretation of what has been perceived ; when, for instance, it is a case of reading, from a man's facial expression, thoughts which he perhaps does not admit even to himself ; of finding words which cause the vibration of the hidden chords one desires to touch ; of seeing the ridiculous side of an action or situation, and so on. In such cases primitives are guided by a kind of special sense, or by tact. Experience develops and refines this, and it may become infallible, without having anything in common with intellectual processes, properly so called. Directly the latter come into play, the differences between the two kinds of mentality shine out so clearly that we are inclined in turn to exaggerate them, and the disconcerted observer who but yesterday was estimating the intelligence of the primitive as virtually equal to that of any other man, to-day accuses him of incredible stupidity, when he finds him incapable of even the simplest form of reasoning.

The solution of the engima is to be found in the mystical and prelogical character of primitive mentality. Confronted by the collective representations in which it expresses itself, the pre-connections which link them together, the institutions they objectify, our conceptual and logical thought moves with difficulty, as in the presence of some mental entity which is foreign and even hostile to it. As a matter of fact, the world in which primitive mentality operates only partially coincides with our own. The network of second causes which to our way of thinking is infinite in extent, rests unperceived and in the background in theirs, whilst occult powers, mystic influences, participations of all kinds, are mingled with the data directly afforded by perception, and make up a whole in which the actual world and the world beyond are blended. In this sense their world is more complex than our universe, but on the other hand it is complete, and it is closed. According to the ideas of most primitives, the vault of heaven rests like a dome upon the flat surface of the earth or of the ocean. Thus the world ends on the circle of the horizon. In it space is felt rather than imagined ; its directions are weighted with qualities, and each of its regions, as we have already seen,[1] participates in all that is usually found there. The primitives' idea of time, which is above all qualitative, remains vague ; and nearly all primitive languages are as deficient in methods of rendering the relations of time as they are copious in

[1] Vide supra, chap. vii. p. 208–15.

expressing spatial relations. Frequently a future event, if considered certain to happen, and if provocative of great emotion, is felt to be already present.

In this closed world, whose space, causation, time, are all somewhat different from our own, communities feel themselves solidary with the other beings, or groups of beings, whether seen or unseen, which inhabit it with them. Each social group, according to whether it is nomadic or stationary, occupies a more or less extensive territory, the limits of which are as a rule definitely fixed for it and for its neighbours. The group is not only the master of it, possessing the exclusive right, for example, of hunting there or of garnering its fruits. The soil " belongs " to it, in the mystic sense of the word : a mystic relation binds its living and its dead with the occult powers of all kinds which people this region, which permit the group to live there, and which undoubtedly would not tolerate the presence of any other. In the same way, by reason of an intimate relation, whatever has been in direct and constant contact with a man—his clothing or ornaments, his weapons, his cattle—actually *is* the man himself, and that is why, when he dies, they often cannot belong to anyone else, but must accompany him to his new state ; in the same way the piece of land upon which a group of human beings lives *is* the group itself : it could not exist elsewhere, and any other group which might try to seize it and establish itself there would be exposed to the very gravest dangers. Therefore, between neighbouring tribes we may find conflicts and warfare on account of incursions, raids, violation of territory, but not conquests, properly so called. An enemy group may be destroyed, but its territory will not be annexed. What would be the good, since one would have to encounter the dread enmity of the " spirits " of all kinds and species, both of animal and plant life, which own it, and which would certainly avenge the conquered ? The conquerors could not live there, and they would be very certain to die there. Possibly in these bonds of participation in essence and locality between one human group or sub-group and a certain living species, we see one of the root-principles of what is called totemistic kinship.

In the midst of this confusion of mystic participations and exclusions, the impressions which the individual has of himself whether living or dead, and of the group to which he " belongs," have only a far-off resemblance to ideas or concepts. They are felt and lived, rather than thought. Neither their content nor their connections are strictly submitted to the law of contradiction. Consequently neither the personal ego, nor the social group, nor the surrounding world, both seen and unseen, appears to be yet " definite " in the collective representations, as they seem to be as soon as our conceptual thought tries to grasp them. In spite of the most careful effort, our thought cannot assimilate them with what it knows as its " ordinary " objects. It therefore despoils them of what there is in them that is elementally concrete, emotional and vital. This it is which renders so difficult, and so frequently uncertain, the comprehension of institutions wherein is expressed the mentality, mystic rather than logical, of primitive peoples.

INDEX

moloki, 55, 56
MONDAIN, 157
monstrosities, 156, 157, 158
MONTEIRO, 49, 50–1, 380, 397
MOONEY (*J*.), 355
moquisies, 42
MORICE (*A. G.*), 337
MORTLOCK ISL., 354
MOSCHI, 149
MOSSI, 27, 80, 81, 278
MOSUTO (*v.* BASUTO), 110, 320, 373, 401
MOSZKOWSKI, 442
MOTU, 67
muavi, *mvai*, 220–1
muimu, 84–5, 257, 258
MULLER (*Ægidius*), 208, 392, 395
mulogi (*v. balogi*), 55
MURRAY (*A. W.*), 291, 297, 361, 362
muru, 289, 304
MURRAY (*T. H. P.*), 54–5
MUSIL (*A.*), 350, 351
muzimu, 86
MYERS (*F. H.*), 216
mystic hold, 206
mystic mentality, 59, 124, 337, 445–7
mystic powers (*v.* forces), 36–43, 48–50, ch. ii. esp., 89–90, 159, 232, 315–20, 404, 429–30
mystic preconceptions, 37
mystic remedies, 257, 295, 336, 379
myths, 353, 384, 441, 444

NAMALAND, 208
NAMAQUAS, 27, 78
names, 204–7
nampok, 166
NANSEN (*F.*), 281
NARRINYERI, 74, 102, 171, 381
NASSAU (*R. H.*), 36, 46, 69, 223, 236
native acuteness, 273, 444
natural laws, 35, 48, 268
negroes, 27, 94
nekedzaltara, 66
NEKES, 181
NEUHAUSS (*R.*), 41, 62–3, 74–6, 81, 104, 176, 195–6, 308–10, 332.
NEW (*Ch.*), 350, 399
NEW BRITAIN, 171
NEW CALEDONIA, 317, 358, 374

NEW FRANCE, 67, 102, 112–3, 125, 137, 160, 168, 223, 308, 324, 345
NEW GUINEA, 41, 45, 54, 62–3, 70, 74–6, 77, 81, 104, 134, 176, 180, 194–6, 202, 204–5, 213, 308–13, 330, 382, 386–7, 390–1, 405, 406, 413, 419, 420, 433
NEW HEBRIDES, 290, 361, 389
NEW MECKLENBURG, 175
NEW POMERANIA, 313, 334, 390
NEW SOUTH WALES, 381
NEW ZEALAND, 37, 100, 103, 146, 214, 290, 298, 389
NEWTON (*H.*), 30, 213, 390, 413
NIAS, 50, 300, 376, 391, 402, 406
NICHOLAS (*J. L.*), 298
NIEUWENHUIS (*A. W.*), 127–9, 133, 135–6, 141, 145, 187, 274–5, 313, 374
◡NIGER, 49, 56, 71, 80, 94, 156, 222, 233, 343
NIUÉ, 361
NORDENSKIÖLD, 420
notu, 243
NUUHIVA, 353
nyarong, 176
NYASSA, 51, 153, 221, 226

objective data, 62, 447
offering, sacrificial, 88, 183
OLDFIELD (*A.*), 174, 210–11, 344
omens, 122–58
ORANGE RIVER, 41, 151, 369, 412, 416
ordeals, 219–60
orenda, 57
OREGON, 346
ORINCCO, 292, 318
OUTAGAMIS, 324
Ovambo, 47, 316, 418

PALAOS ISL., 354
PANGWE, 241
PAPUANS, 29, 45, 54–5, 179, 194, 197, 206, 312–5, 366–7, 377, 386–7, 390–1, 405, 413, 419–21, 433, 441, 443
PARAGUAY, 396
PARIWARA ISL., 382
PARKINSON (*R.*), 29, 335
parnaga, 309
participations, mystic, 35, 55, 79, 119, 129–131, 198, 210, 214, 218, 318, 432, 445, 446